BLACK BRITISH WHITE BRITISH

DILIP HIRO

BLACK BRITISH WHITE BRITISH

A History of Race Relations in Britain

GRAFTON BOOKS
A Division of the Collins Publishing Group

LONDON GLASGOW
TORONTO SYDNEY AUCKLAND

Grafton Books
A Division of the Collins Publishing Group
8 Grafton Street, London W1X 3LA

First published by Eyre & Spottiswoode 1971
Revised edition published in Pelican Books 1973
This edition published by Grafton Books 1991

British Library Cataloguing in Publication Data

Hiro, Dilip
  Black British white British.
  1. Great Britain. Race relations, history
  I. Title
  305.800941

ISBN 0-246-13618-9

Phototypeset by Computape (Pickering) Ltd, North Yorkshire
Printed in Great Britain by
William Collins Sons & Co. Ltd, Glasgow

Contents

Preface   vii

Introduction: A Historical View   1

PART I: WEST INDIANS

1 The New Jerusalem   13
2 Children of Slavery: The Anglicized Afro-Caribbeans   19
3 Everywhere the Cold Shoulder   26
4 Blacks Look West   37
5 White Rejection, Black Withdrawal   50
6 Black Consciousness: An Afro Identity   59
7 Rise of Rastafarianism   67
8 Urban Violence   81
9 Step-Citizens of Britain   97

PART II: ASIANS

1 The Coolies of the Empire – and Britain   107
2 Money is All: The Rise of Asian Enterprise   116
3 No Faces Like Sikh Faces   127
4 Equal before Allah   133
5 Communal Leadership   138
6 Culture of the Indian Subcontinent   145
7 Asian Youth: Conflict and Synthesis   153
8 Asians in Transition   164
9 Political Integration, Cultural Co-existence   174
10 The Rushdie Affair: Dialogue of the Deaf   182

PART III: WHITE BRITONS

1 The 'Open Door' Closes   197
2 Coloured Immigration and Race Relations:
  A Composite Policy   209
3 Inter-racial Harmony and Integration   233
4 White Powell, White Power   246
5 Room at the Bottom   261
6 Contemporary White Attitudes and Practices   279
7 The Future: Assimilation or Social Pluralism?   303

Notes 314

Appendix I: General Election Results, and Race and
  Immigration Laws, since 1945 330
Appendix II: Figures of Immigration from Colonies and
  New Commonwealth: 1948–88 331
Appendix III: Estimated Ethnic Minority Populations
  of Great Britain 333
Appendix IV: Correlation between Ethnicity and
  Educational Performance 334

Select Bibliography 335

Photo Credits 339

Index 341

Preface

A perusal of the 1973 Penguin edition of *Black British, White British* fifteen years later led me to two major conclusions.

One, were I to update the work it would require no change of tone at all. When viewed in the context of the general theme of my book, the events that unfolded during the seventies and eighties seemed almost predestined. I simply had more material to substantiate my basic thesis that racism is deeply embedded in white British society and eradicating it would take generations. In retrospect, the sixties can be seen as a seminal period for race relations and Commonwealth Immigration control. The first Commonwealth Immigrants Act went into effect in 1962, and the first Race Relations Act in 1965; and the intertwining of the two issues, too, occurred during this period. Since then this link has remained intact; and the comparative tightening or relaxing of the provisions of these Acts or their successors has left the basic situation virtually unchanged. The fact that I researched my original book in the late 1960s has, in retrospect, stood me in good stead.

Two, my idea of social pluralism has become accepted wisdom. When first articulated in my work at some length, it was misconstrued as another term for 'separate development' by some reviewers, including Nigel Lawson, then a columnist in *The Times*, who was to become the Chancellor of the Exchequer in the mid-1980s.[1]

This version of the book, like its predecessors, is in three parts, written from a West Indian, Asian and white British viewpoint respectively. In the last case I have attempted to subdue my emotional antipathy towards the illiberal British perspective to meet the demand of objectivity. The result may appear ambivalent to some readers, particularly those who identify themselves totally with the illiberal or liberal camp, and those who are specialists. But my book is not addressed to experts or policy-makers but to the general reader.

A feature of race relations which has not changed is the debate on describing racial minorities. Are they to be defined in terms of colour or their regional or continental origins? As it happens, the two categories are not mutually exclusive.

Yet something has changed. The term 'coloured' has practically disappeared from everyday usage here in the same way as 'negro' has in America. For over a quarter of a century after the Second World War the

British generally called anybody who was not white and caucasoid 'coloured'. But, as the civil rights movement began to gather momentum in America in the 1960s and the terms 'black' and 'Afro-American' came into vogue, the West Indians, especially the young, increasingly described themselves as 'black' instead of 'coloured'. Others followed.

This creates something of a dilemma for social historians. Writing in the 1990s, how are they to overcome the fact that for nearly three decades after the Second World War the terms 'coloured' and 'coloured immigrants' were foremost in the vocabulary of race relations in Britain? By striking a compromise. I have done so by reducing the frequency with which I used these terms in my original work.

Next, the term 'West Indian'. It is true that West Indian society is multiracial: it has Africans (negroids), East Indians (brown caucasoids), Chinese (mongoloids), Europeans (white caucasoids) and various combinations of these. But most of the West Indian settlers in Britain are from Jamaica and Barbados where the population is overwhelmingly of African stock. Hence, in this context 'West Indian' is to be regarded as synonymous with 'Afro-Caribbean'.

By the same token 'Asian' should be taken to mean Indian/Pakistani/ Bangladeshi from the Indian subcontinent or East Africa. It does *not* include the Chinese, whether from Hong Kong, Singapore or Malaysia.

While the title of the book, chosen in the early 1970s, makes plain my preference for 'black' over 'coloured', the chief unresolved question remains. Does, or should, 'black' include Asians? The answer needs to take into account linguistic, political and racial aspects. There is no popular term for 'coloured' in Urdu, Punjabi, Bengali or Gujarati, the major languages of the South Asian immigrants. (At one stage the official and quasi-official agencies in Britain took to using *rangdar*, meaning coloured in Urdu and Punjabi.) The terms in common use among South Asian immigrants are *kala* (black) and *gora, chita, shadha* or *dhorha* (white). Secondly, if black is to be defined as the colour of the oppressed and disadvantaged, then Asians are 'politically' black. But then, so are gypsies. Finally, in strictly racial terms, South Asians are more brown than black. All in all, therefore, including Asians among blacks is not wholly satisfactory.

A collection of the various terms used singly or aggregately for the two major racial minorities amounts to a small treasury: African-Caribbean, Afro-Asian-Caribbean people, Afro-Caribbean, Asian, black, brown, coloured, ethnic group, ethnic minority, minority, minority group, New Commonwealth (versus Old Commonwealth – Australia, Canada and New Zealand) immigrants, non-white, racial minority, South Asian, visible minority, West Indian; and such combinations as 'Asians and

West Indians', 'blacks and Asians', 'blacks and browns', 'black immigrants', 'black settlers', 'coloured immigrants' and 'coloured settlers'. To relieve the tedium that inevitably results from using the same term time and again, I have opted for a variety.

Of the above phrases, 'blacks and Asians' is probably the most satisfactory. Since white prejudice against Afro-Caribbeans and Africans stems primarily from racial/colour differences, the term 'black' seems most appropriate – particularly when it has the advantage of covering people from different regions of the world: the West Indies and Africa. Prejudice against Asians, however, stems as much from colour considerations as cultural. This makes the term 'brown' inadequate. So the group needs to be identified by its regional background: Asian or South Asian.

I am aware that an increasing number of young people of West Indian background are now describing themselves as African rather than Afro-Caribbean. But since there is a brief reference to West Africans in my text I have stuck to the original idea of using the terms Afro-Caribbean and West Indian.

Since the first edition of the book, the proportion of the ethnic minorities in the national population has risen from about 2 per cent to 4.8 per cent. This translates into an increase from less than a million to 2.65 million. There has been change, too, in the relative sizes of the West Indian and Asian communities. In the early 1970s they were about equal. Now Asians are two-and-a-half times as numerous as West Indians.[2]

Even though racial minorities are a tiny percentage of the overall population, the subject of race and inter-racial relations remains emotive and highly newsworthy. Its emotional nature, and the lack of natural affinity between different races, make it very susceptible to controversy, tension and conflict.

The history of race relations in post-Second World War Britain shows amply that the subject can rise abruptly in popular consciousness and dominate British politics. It has done so several times. During the decade 1965–74 the national debate on this issue rivalled the one on Britain joining the European Community. And, more than once, it has had a direct impact on the result of parliamentary elections.

Indeed, the root of the unbroken Conservative rule of the 1980s and later can be traced to the stance that Margaret Thatcher, then leader of the Conservative opposition, took on race and immigration in January 1978. 'People are really afraid that this country might be rather swamped by people with a different culture,' she said in a television interview. 'You know, the British character has done so much for democracy, for law, and done so much throughout the world, that if there is any fear that it might be swamped, people are going to react and be rather hostile to those coming in.'[3] This statement caused an immediate spurt in Conservative support in the opinion polls. From then on the party never lost its edge over Labour, which came to lose the general election of June 1979.

Ironically, ten years later these words came to haunt Thatcher. The occasion was her government's proposed Hong Kong Bill as a prelude to returning the colony to China in 1997, at the end of a 99-year lease. The bill's provision to admit to Britain some 50,000 Hong Kong Chinese civil servants, along with their 175,000 dependants, was vociferously opposed by right-wing Conservatives. Leading the attack, Norman Tebbit, an eminent Conservative MP and former party chairman, wrote: 'To use the Prime Minister's own word, the fear is that they [the British] will be swamped by a different culture, history and religion and, even if it costs them something in economic terms, they would rather not have another vast wave of immigration.'[4]

Conceding that immigration was one of the issues which drove traditional Labour voters to support Margaret Thatcher (in 1979 and later), Tebbit warned that they were vital to a fourth general election victory for the Conservatives. 'The Government is now driving those voters back into the welcoming arms of the Labour Party,' he stated.[5]

The prospect of seeming 'soft' on non-white immigration deeply worries such Conservative figures as Tebbit, who are aware that being tough on race and immigration has enabled their party to subvert, repeatedly, the traditional loyalty to Labour of a section of white working-class voters.

The political dividend that the Conservatives or others can derive from such a strategy is inversely proportional to a rational, historical understanding that the electorate has of these subjects.

If this work succeeds in creating such a perception of the issues, on whatever scale, then it would have amply served its purpose.

DILIP HIRO
London, 15 July 1990

Introduction:
A Historical View

*I think that the past is all that makes the present coherent, and further,
that the past will remain horrible for exactly as long as we refuse to assess it
honestly.*

JAMES BALDWIN[1]

*Slavery was not born of racism: rather, racism was the consequence of
slavery.*

ERIC WILLIAMS[2]

*In order to justify the exploitation of Africans as slaves and Asians as
virtual slaves, it was necessary to believe that these races were biologically
inferior to white Europeans. This belief underpinned the economic structure
of the Empire, and in South Africa it still does so today.*

ANGELA LAMBERT, a British journalist[3]

The first major contact of the (Anglo-Saxon) English with coloured
people occurred during AD 193–211 when Septimius Severus, a north
African, ruled England as the Roman emperor. He once remarked that
the English made 'bad slaves'. The English later came into contact with
coloured people in the Middle East during the Second Crusade
(1189–91) and the Ninth Crusade (1271–2), which failed to release the
Holy City of Jerusalem from the hands of the 'infidel' Muslims.

Later still, contact developed through trade, by sea, with West Africa
and Asia. In 1554, John Locke, an English trader, brought slaves from
West Africa to England, and sold them as household servants. By then
Spain and Portugal had established extensive colonies in the New World,
and were developing them as producers of cotton, sugar-cane and
tobacco for export to Europe as fast as the supply of labour – consisting
of native Indian tribes, poor whites and African slaves – would allow. As
the supply of American Indians and poor whites began to dwindle, the
Iberians began to lean more heavily on the expediency of securing slave
labour from Africa.[4]

It was the lucrative prospect of supplying the Iberian colonies with
African labour that tempted Sir John Hawkins to engage in the slave
trade. He transported the first 'cargo' of 500 slaves from West Africa to

the New World in 1562. Later, during the early 1600s, as England established its own plantation colonies on the north American mainland and Barbados, its economic and political interests in the slave trade and slavery increased. In 1655, Oliver Cromwell gave a further boost to this development by seizing Jamaica from Spain.

Under the treaty of Utrecht in 1713, Britain acquired from France the contract to supply African slaves to the Spanish colonies from its Caribbean territories. The result was that within fifty years Britain became the leading slave-trading nation in the world, the foremost slave carrier for other European nations, and the centre of the Triangular Trade. Its ships ferried manufactured goods to West Africa, transported slaves to the New World, and brought back sugar, tobacco and cotton to Britain. In 1757, in the month of July alone, 175 ships with cargo worth £2 million (equivalent to £210 million today) docked in British ports.[5]

As British involvement in, and the profits from, slavery and the slave trade increased, the concept of the African slave as a commodity or, at best, a workhorse began to emerge. Aboard ship the African was considered an item of cargo. This seemed to be the legal position, as was illustrated by the case of the slave-ship *Zong* in 1749. During a rough crossing of the Atlantic by this ship, 130 slaves were thrown overboard. When the case went to the court, the issue was not the deliberate drowning of 130 human beings, but whether throwing slaves overboard was 'an act of jettison', for which the insurance company was obliged to pay, or 'an act of fraud', which released the insurance company of its obligation.[6] On plantations, African slaves were catalogued along with livestock and treated as work-animals, to be worked to the maximum at the minimum cost of maintenance.

A similar view of slaves as property was taken by the courts in England where, by the mid-eighteenth century, thousands of households of English aristocrats and retired planters[7] used African slaves, often wearing padlocked copper or silver collars around their necks,[8] as serving-boys and menservants. Some Englishmen, who deplored this inhuman treatment of Africans, challenged the system of slavery in English courts by providing legal aid to runaway slaves. But they lost their cases. Twice, in 1720 and 1749, courts ruled that a runaway slave in England could be recovered. Until 1771, Lord Mansfield, the Lord Chief Justice, was unwilling to face the consequences of the masters losing 'their property by bringing slaves to England'. He hoped the proposition would never be finally discussed.[9]

However, a year later, Lord Chief Justice Mansfield was obliged to give judgement in the case of James Somersett, an escaped slave who had been recaptured and put aboard a ship sailing for Jamaica. The point under dispute was the master's right to remove his slave from England to the sphere of colonial law. Lord Mansfield concluded his verdict with the statement: 'The state of slavery is … so odious that nothing can support it but positive law … I cannot say that this case is allowed or approved by the law of England and therefore the Black must be discharged.'[10]

This judgement is popularly construed to mean that thereafter the slaves in England were set free, and that slavery became illegal. Nothing of the sort happened. '[Lord Mansfield's] decision freed no slaves,' writes Professor Michael Banton; 'it declared that, until Parliament enacted legislation explicitly covering the question, the power in dispute [regarding shipping a slave from England to the colonies] could not legally be exercised.'[11] Indeed, by then, there was a strong vested interest in England, committed to the continuance of slavery and the slave trade, which had learned to rationalize these practices.

To counter the criticism from liberal, humane quarters, the slave masters and merchants argued that the African slaves were 'an equivocal race, between man and monkey', and that they were only 'half human'.[12] In other words, in order essentially to justify their economic greed, while simultaneously exorcizing themselves of any guilt they might have felt, the slave masters and merchants argued that the slave was sub-human and received the treatment he (naturally) deserved. Was it 'inhuman', for instance, to whip a recalcitrant horse or donkey? The fact that the slave was of a different race, and black, led the British masters and traders to apply their beliefs to the whole race.[13] They ceased to call the slave African and, instead, referred to him by his racial label – negro. Generalizations about negroes proliferated, and became part of the popular beliefs and myths in Britain.

At the intellectual level, religious and cultural justifications were often advanced to establish the inherent inferiority of negroes as a race. It was argued that they were the descendants of Ham, the black son of Noah. As such they were *natural* slaves, condemned for ever to remain 'hewers of wood and drawers of water'. Besides, they were not only physically black, the colour of Satan, but also morally black. They were, in short, savage creatures, who jumped from tree to tree in the steamy jungles of Africa, and ate one another with relish. To transport these sub-human, biologically inferior, mentally retarded creatures from the hell of African jungles to the tranquillity and order of the plantations of the New World, where they were assured of protected existence, was almost an act of Christian charity.

David Hume, the historian and philosopher, arrived at the conclusion of inherent negro inferiority from another, wider perspective. In his essay, 'Of National Characters', published in 1753, he stated: 'I am apt to suspect the Negroes to be naturally inferior to the Whites. There scarcely ever was a civilized nation of that complexion, nor ever any individual, eminent either in action or speculation. No ingenious manufacturers among them, no arts, no sciences. On the other hand, the most rude and barbarous of the Whites such as the Germans, the present Tartars, still have some thing eminent about them in their valour, form of government or some particular. Such a uniform and constant difference could not happen in so many countries and ages, if Nature had not made an original distribution between these breeds of men.'[14]

Since this 'original distribution' of intelligence and ingenuity by nature was everlasting and unalterable, any negro manifesting mental agility could only be considered a freak or a hoax. Referring to one negro – Francis Williams, in Jamaica – reported to be a 'man of learning', David Hume wrote that 'it is likely that he is admired for his slender accomplishments, like a parrot who speaks a few words plainly'. A similar argument was advanced by another British historian, Edward Long. In his *History of Jamaica*, published in 1774, he wrote: 'We cannot pronounce them unsusceptible of civilization since even apes have been taught to eat, drink, repose and dress like men. But of all the human species hitherto discovered, their natural baseness of mind seems to afford least hope of their being (except by miraculous interposition of Divine Providence) so refined as to think as well as act like men. I do not think an orang-outang husband would be any dishonour to an Hottentot female.'[15]

By the late nineteenth century this type of racism had become so ingrained in social thinking at all levels of society that the abolition of the slave trade in 1807, and of slavery in 1834, seemed to leave the basic attitudes essentially unaltered. Now the efforts of the freed negroes to 'civilize' themselves became a subject of mockery. Following his visit to Jamaica in 1859, Anthony Trollope wrote of the negro: 'He burns to be regarded as a scholar, puzzles himself with fine words, addicts himself to religion for the sake of appearance, and delights in aping the little graces of civilization … If you want to win his heart for an hour, call him a gentleman; but if you want to reduce him to despairing obedience, tell him that he is a filthy nigger, assure him that his father and mother had tails like monkeys, and forbid him to think that he can have a soul like a white man.'[16]

It was in the British plantation colonies in the western hemisphere that race relations emerged in their clearest form: the whites, as masters, were the superior race; and the blacks, as slaves, were the inferior race. A basically similar model of race relations also emerged in the eastern hemisphere once the British had consolidated their hold over the Indian subcontinent. This was ironic, because the British, like the pioneering Portuguese, had ventured into India as a result of the reports of India's riches, originating in Marco Polo's descriptions in 1298 of the countries of the East, which had excited the imagination of many European traders and rulers.

Of the king and three brothers of Maabar (Malabar), a part of the Greater India, 'being the noblest and richest country in the world', Marco Polo wrote, 'they import as many as five thousand [horses] at a time and for each pay five hundred saggi of gold which is equal to one hundred marks of silver [about $1000].'[17] He described Zailan (Ceylon) as the island which 'produces more beautiful and valuable rubies than are found in other parts of the world and likewise sapphires, topazes, ameythysts, garnets and many other precious stones'.[18]

The *sole* purpose of the Latin European exploration of the high seas which began in earnest in the mid-fifteenth century was to find a sea route to India, since the land route continued to be blocked by the generally hostile Muslim rulers in the Middle East. It was this exploration which brought the Portuguese to the deltas of the Niger and Senegal rivers on the West African coast and led, in due course, to the trading of African slaves.

Christopher Columbus in 1492 thought he had discovered 'The Indies', and hence he called the islands' inhabitants Indians. It was seven years later that Vasco da Gama, a Portuguese sailor, finally succeeded in reaching the real India via what was later to be called the Cape of 'Good Hope'. He was captivated by the country and by its inhabitants. British ambassadors and traders who followed the Portuguese, and other Europeans too, evinced great interest in, and fascination for, Indian people and their religions, philosophy and languages.

But as British trading interests became allied to territorial ambitions, and as the British, by virtue of their successive military victories over the rulers of the fragmented parts of the subcontinent, began to acquire self-confidence, they grew less and less interested in the Indian people and culture. With the loss of the American colonies in 1783, the centre of the Empire shifted to India; and, with it, the distance of the ruling British from the subjugated Indians grew further. 'As the occupation of India proceeded,' writes V. G. Kiernan, a British historian, 'English masters were no longer in a humour to admire anything Indian.'[19]

By 1792, Charles Grant, a British historian, was calling the Indian people 'a race of men lamentably degenerate and base, retaining but a feeble sense of moral obligation ... governed by a malevolent and licentious passion ...' And this 'race of men' was by then commonly referred to by the British as 'blacks'. In his autobiography William

Makepeace Thackeray mentioned travelling to England from India (in 1817) as a child in care of a 'black servant' from Calcutta. 'Englishmen were already prone to this racialism as a result of long involvement with African slavery,' writes V. G. Kiernan, 'and there was some coming and going between the East and West Indies.'[20] Another term which had its origins in African slavery – nigger – was also freely applied to Indians. By the 1850s, Indians had been described as 'the wild barbarians, indifferent to human life ... yet free, simple as children, brave, faithful to their masters' by the historian Herbert Edwardes. This could well have been a general description of African slaves by their white masters.[21]

'Europeans lord it over the conquered natives [in India] with a high hand,' observed Edward J. Trelawney in 1831. 'Every outrage may be committed almost with impunity.'[22] And yet the British reacted to the mutiny by Indian soldiers in 1857 with an unprecedented savagery. 'History shudders at the recollection of the terrible "Spanish fury" which desolated Antwerp in the days of William the Silent,' wrote George O. Trevelyan, 'but the "English fury" was more terrible still.'[23] The degree of the 'English fury' was described, in a single line, in a letter to a London newspaper by an Englishman in India: 'Every nigger we meet [we] either string up or shoot.' While the British reacted to the Indian Mutiny in openly racist terms, the basic reason for the uprising lay in their racist attitudes. Discussing the major cause that led to the Mutiny, a correspondent to *The Times* wrote, 'The most scrubby mean little representative of *la race blanche* ... regards himself as infinitely superior to the Rajpoot with a genealogy of a thousand years.'[24]

Following the Mutiny, India was formally annexed to Britain. With that began the century of imperialism proper.[25] The British in India evolved an elaborate code of behaviour for dealing with the natives resting on 'the cherished conviction of every Englishman in India, from the highest to the lowest ... that he belongs to a race whom God has destined to govern and subdue' (as Seton Kerr, once Foreign Secretary of the Government, put it).[26] This policy of racial apartheid was effective in uniting the upper and lower echelons of the British society in India: they all considered themselves as belonging to an inherently superior race. 'As a white man,' writes V. G. Kiernan, 'he [the indispensable Tommy Atkins] had the privilege ... of seeing all Indians from His Highness to sweeper officially regarded as inferior.'[27] The situation was almost identical with that then prevalent in the southern states of America. On the eve of the Civil War in 1861, Jefferson Davis, the Southern leader who later became president of the Confederacy, said: 'One of the reconciling features of the existence [of negro slavery] is the fact that it raises white men to the same general level, that it dignifies and exalts every white man by the presence of a lower race.'[28]

Charles Darwin's theories of evolution and the 'survival of the fittest', enunciated in his *Origin of Species*, first published in 1859, led most white people to believe that they were in a dominant position throughout the world because of their inherent superiority. 'It is this consciousness of the inherent superiority of the Europeans which has won for us India,' declared Lord Kitchener, Commander-in-Chief in India from 1902 to 1909. He then illustrated the doctrine of 'inherent inequality' thus: 'However well-educated and clever a native may be, and however brave he may have proved himself, I believe that no rank we can bestow on him would cause him to be considered an equal of the British officer.'[29]

However, once the doctrine of superiority and its evidence – power of arms and efficient organization – had been established, the imperial father-figure could well afford to show a paternalistic concern for the 'native' child-figure without, in any way, undermining his own dominant position. It was this attitude of superiority blended with a paternalistic concern that underlay the actions of those who administered the Empire. Rudyard Kipling's celebrated poem 'The White Man's Burden', published in 1899, captured these feelings aptly:

Take up the White Man's burden –
Send forth the best you breed –
Go bind your sons to exile
To serve your captives' need;
To wait in heavy harness,
On fluttered folk and wild –
Your new-caught, sullen peoples,
Half-devil and half-child.[30]

In practice, the policy of sending forth 'the best you breed' by the British was complemented by receiving, in Britain, the best among the black natives to educate them in British theology, law, literature and medicine. Hence, from about 1875 onwards, students from the coloured colonies began arriving in Britain to study at the universities. But the British public could not be expected to make an exception of these selected few among the 'fluttered folk and wild'. In *The Anglo-Fanti*, Kobina Sekyi noted that 'Coloured students studying social welfare or methods of teaching in the poorer quarters of London and other cities still complain fairly frequently of attitudes of "superiority" as well as curiosity towards them on the part of the down-at-heel and decrepit inhabitants of the districts concerned.'[31]

Even British university and college students often showed prejudice and antipathy towards black and brown fellow-students. 'In England it appears as if the negro students were left to live their lives apart, even from the student class, and some, it seems, sought companionships and consolation in less desirable directions,' wrote K. L. Little, a British academic. 'In some universities – Cambridge is cited as a case – prejudice against them was shown; although in this respect Indians were apparently even less popular. In London they were regarded with tolerance, but also with apathy.'[32] The situation was so unsatisfactory that a special meeting of those interested in the welfare of colonial students was called in 1913.

Then came the First World War. It created an unprecedented shortage of manpower and materials. The government requisitioned ships trading with Africa and Asia for troop transport and, with the ships, their black crews. Labour gangs were drafted in many ports of the Empire in Asia, Africa and the Caribbean, and brought to England. Black colonials were employed in ordnance factories. Others were recruited as merchant seamen to replace the white seamen transferred to the Royal Navy. Several thousands of coloured workers were involved.[33]

But once the war was over, almost all of them were dispatched to 'where they belonged': they had served the interests of the metropolitan country and were of no more use to it. The few thousands who did not return to their countries of origin took to seafaring, the only avenue of employment open to them in peacetime, and settled in the dockside areas of London, Liverpool, Bristol, Manchester, Glasgow, Swansea, Cardiff and South Shields.

Racist feeling in Britain was so strong then that even this insignificant number proved too much for the British public to bear. The result was a series of race riots in many of the port towns of Britain, when black settlers became targets of violence. The general attitude of the British public was summed up by an editorial in a Cardiff newspaper which said, 'The government ought to declare it to be part of the national policy that this country is not to be regarded as an emigration field, that no more immigrants (as distinguished from visitors) can be admitted – and that immigrants must return to whence they came from.' That this demand had to do with racist considerations rather than immigrants *per se* became evident when the newspaper added, 'This must apply to black men from the British West Indies as well as from the United States.'[34]

In 1920 there was a series of articles in the *Spectator* which established, beyond doubt, that a colour bar existed in Britain. This was also the conclusion of R. T. Lapière, a French sociologist, who after long research during the post-war period, published his results in America in

1928. For example, of the twenty hotels in England he visited, only four were open to non-white guests.[35]

'It was usually found at the hotels and boarding houses where they [coloured people] were refused accommodation,' wrote an Indian correspondent to the *Spectator* in March 1931, 'that the "objectors" were white lodgers who had been in the East and "had seen the native in his den".'[36] It was particularly galling for the Briton who had enjoyed the 'white man boss' position[37] in the coloured colonies to treat the dark 'natives' as equals in the metropolitan country. He found it hard to reconcile with the practice of racial equality for all those resident in Britain.[38] He considered it subversive to cast Paul Robeson, a black American, as Othello to play opposite Peggy Ashcroft as Desdemona, as happened in the West End in the 1930s, and joined the chorus of protest that arose. 'How then is it possible to maintain the stern creed in the policy of the Empire, the eternal supremacy of the white over the black?' asked one protester in his letter to a London newspaper.[39]

A quarter of a century later, in her field research in south London, Sheila Patterson found that, 'The only people, apart from a pathologically prejudiced handful, who displayed uncompromising verbal hostility towards the coloured newcomers seemed to be those who had had … first-hand contacts with people overseas during the war. This "wog complex" … was reasonably widespread, and of course tended to influence the views of others to some extent.'[40]

To be fair, racist views were not the monopoly of the British public: they were reflected in some of the actions of post-war British governments. For instance, the Labour administration of Clement Attlee forbade Seretse Khama, a member of the ruling family of Basutoland, from returning to his country in 1948 after he had married a white woman in London. In Roi Ottley's view the reasons for this action by the government were rooted in 'race-sex-colonial policies'.[41] As a resident American journalist in Britain, Ottley came into contact with government authorities and discovered that stereotypes regarding Africans existed in the highest circles. 'I asked the Secretary of State for the Colonies if he envisioned eventual self-government for the African people,' he wrote. 'He was frankly shocked by the question. "You must remember," he countered, "the Africans are savages, still eating each other in places like Nigeria." '[42]

That was in 1950 when three major Asian colonies – India, Burma (later Myanmar) and Ceylon (later Sri Lanka) – had been freed from British domination. Apparently liquidating the coloured Empire did not mean discarding the notions and beliefs that had grown during the centuries of imperial experience. But nor did the abolition of slavery dispel the belief in the inherent inferiority of the black African. Had the freed slaves in the Caribbean then migrated to Britain, instead of to the Central American republics and islands in the Caribbean, as they did, they would have realized this – as would have most British people. But they did not. In the 1950s, however, the situation developed differently and ironically: the liquidation of the 'dusky' Empire was accompanied by the growing presence of black and brown colonials in Britain.

This development brought into relief the dichotomy between the British practice of racial apartheid in the non-white colonies, and the general British regard for human dignity and a belief in the equality of all British subjects. This conflict had always existed, but because the coloured colonies were overseas, in far-flung parts of the world, most Britons had still been able to consider themselves racially liberal and fair-minded, censorious of the white American and South African mistreatment of the blacks. But as the presence of blacks in Britain itself became more and more noticeable the situation changed: the contradiction between the moral attitudes of most Britons and their socio-historical attitudes became apparent. The constant interplay between these contradictory attitudes keeps race relations in Britain (as well as in America) in a dynamic state.

Part I

WEST INDIANS

1 The New Jerusalem

---

*I remember a Christmas pantomime in Barbados where everyone departed
for England. That was the happy ending of the plot.*

CLIFFORD CHASE, a West Indian settler
in Birmingham.

The people of the West Indies are where they are now because their
forebears were transported in large numbers from Africa and Asia,
involuntarily or voluntarily, as part of the colonial policies of European
powers. Between 1680 and 1786, for instance, more than two million
slaves were carried across the Atlantic,[1] a third of them for the specific
purpose of developing Jamaica, then a British colony, into a lucrative
sugar-cane island.

This was done because the major source of labour supply initiated by
Charles II after his restoration in 1660 – banishment of English felons,
criminals, rioters and indentured servants to the Caribbean – proved
inadequate and unsuitable to meet the ever-expanding demand of the
planters. Population statistics illustrate this change-over to the policy of
an almost total reliance on African labour. In 1673 the black and white
populations in Jamaica were nearly equal: almost 10,000 each. Fifty years
later, slaves outnumbered whites by ten to one: 74,000 blacks to 7500
whites. Jamaica was fast becoming the leading sugar producer in the
world, a position it occupied for more than a century, and which brought
unprecedented prosperity to British planters. In contrast, irreparable
damage was done to the economic interests of Jamaica itself.

By inundating Jamaica with a population out of all proportion to its
inherent resources, the seed of an insoluble problem was implanted. This
fact, and this alone, is the root cause of the economic troubles that have
plagued the island since then, and which became uncomfortably apparent
as soon as sugar-cane ceased to be a prized crop and slavery was
abolished. Following the Emancipation in 1834, Africans left plantations
en masse, eager to explore the environment on their own, as free men and
women.

What did they discover? Between the 40 per cent mountainous
non-arable land and the English plantations, there was very little fertile
land left for them to develop. So they cleared the mountains here and

there, and eked out a hazardous living. One of the few means of relieving their poverty was to leave the island altogether – to migrate.

By the 1860s migration had become a part of the island's life. Jamaicans went to Panama to build railways and then to assist in survey work and construction of the Canal. At one time or another 68,000 Jamaicans participated in these projects. Jamaican labour was engaged to boost sugar-cane production in Cuba after the United States had dislodged Spain as the imperial power in 1898. Later, Jamaicans were recruited to develop coffee and banana plantations in Honduras and Costa Rica, and Venezuela tapped this source of labour for its oil exploration. But despite these temporary and permanent migrations, and a severe epidemic of cholera, the Jamaica population leapt from 320,000 in 1830 to 832,000 in 1910. The pressure to migrate kept rising.

Latterly, migration and seasonal work in the United States became popular. Before 1920 it was an open country, a haven for immigrants. It was also English-speaking. Migration to the United States grew. Before America introduced literacy tests and visas for immigrants in 1924, more than 200,000 British West Indians had settled there.[2] But the immigration restrictions and the economic depression in the United States reduced the West Indian intake dramatically. In turn, this led to economic and political unrest in the British West Indies. A rash of strikes and serious rioting broke out in Jamaica, Trinidad and St Kitts during the late 1930s.

The situation would have grown worse had not the Second World War broken out. The war provided opportunities for employment *and* adventure to the unemployed and the young. Thousands of West Indians joined the British (and, later, American) armed forces and war industries.[3] Others joined as 'Overseas Volunteer Workers' to man British ordnance factories.

There was little, if any, overt racial discrimination in the highly structured military. Outside the barracks, too, the British people, in the midst of war, noticed more the uniform than the colour of the wearer. Indeed some black servicemen, on being demobbed, decided to settle down in Britain, especially when they had married English women.

The vast majority, however, returned home, but were soon disillusioned. The economic prospect was bleak. They also had considerable psychological difficulty in readjusting to civilian life in the West Indies: it was twice removed from wartime conditions in Britain. This was particularly true of those West Indians who had joined the military straight from school.

Roy Terrelonge was one such person. Born in Jamaica, he joined the Royal Air Force after he left school and served for six years. When demobbed he returned to Jamaica, but found 'not enough jobs, bad pay, tough conditions'. So he left for England, in June 1948, aboard the SS *Empire Windrush*. So did 491 other Jamaicans with similar backgrounds; and at least half of them had jobs or friends waiting for them in England.

Much to the British authorities' relief, this shipload of West Indians did not prove to be the first wave of 'an unarmed invasion'. Despite the widely known labour shortage in Britain, no more than a thousand West Indians arrived each year – until 1952. Why? Because the West Indian migrant vastly preferred America to Britain. It was nearer; it was richer; it already had a large, established West Indian community. And, once the West Indian passed the literacy and medical tests, it was easy to gain entry. The American law-makers had included the British West Indies in their immigration quota for Britain – a generous (and never fully subscribed) 65,000 a year. But after the war, as West Indian migration to the United States rose, the American legislators, out of racist consider-ations, modified the law.

The resulting McCarran–Walter Act of 1952 detached the British West Indies from Britain, and allocated a separate, meagre quota of 800 to the area: 100 to Jamaica, 100 to Trinidad, and so on. This amounted to a virtual ban on West Indian migration to the US and caused much resentment among the islanders and the authorities.

Finding themselves deprived of the American outlet, West Indians vigorously explored other avenues of migration. And imperial Britain with its 'open-door' policy seemed a natural choice. Consequently, there was a sudden upsurge in West Indian migration to Britain. Nearly 11,000 West Indians came to Britain in 1954. The following year the figure more than doubled. After that, the number stabilized at about 17,000 a year until rumours of impending restrictions on Common-wealth immigrants created the 'beat the ban' rush. The peak was reached in the first half of 1962 when more than 34,000 West Indians arrived in Britain as immigrants. The rate in the late 1960s stabilized around 7000 a year, consisting mainly of dependants of the immigrants already here. In contrast – thanks to the introduction of an equitable immigration system in America in 1964 – the number of Jamaicans leaving for the United States surpassed 15,000 in 1968.

Clearly the McCarran–Walter Act boosted West Indian migration to Britain. Before the Act, for every West Indian migrating to Britain, at least nine went to the US. After the Act, the ratio was reversed. West Indians were obliged to look at Britain as their country of settlement, a prospect they had not seriously considered before. In any case, the idea of permanent migration is never contemplated lightly. As long as the native island offers some prospect of reasonable life, the chances are that the islanders will stay rather than leave. The wide variance in the migration rates for different islands in the Caribbean proved this.

Trinidad, the richest of the islands, was a net importer of labour, drawing people from the smaller and poorer neighbouring islands. The comparatively poorer and the more populous island, Jamaica, drove out its native sons and daughters in thousands.[4] With over two million people, Jamaica accounted for more than half the population of the British West Indies. Its population density was three times that of its neighbour, Cuba. Its birthrate of 4.3 per cent was one of the highest in the world; and so was unemployment, which fluctuated between 20 and 35 per cent.

The most densely inhabited island in the Caribbean, however, was Barbados. A quarter of a million people managed to survive in an area of twenty miles by eight. (At that density Great Britain would have a population of 135 million.) No wonder then that the Barbadian government was the first (and the only) authority in the Caribbean to inaugurate an official emigration scheme. That happened in 1950. They sent twenty orderlies to British hospitals. Within a decade, nearly 4000 Barbadians had been processed and sent to work for London Transport, British Railways, hotels and hospitals. And for every government-sponsored Barbadian emigrant there were three who left on their own initiative.

Elsewhere migration was unprocessed and, given the funds, simple to undertake: inter-island passports were valid for travel to the British Isles. Though the legal and financial aspects of migration to Britain did not change between 1948 and 1962, the profile of the typical West Indian migrant did. During the earlier phase – from 1948 to 1955 – the migrant was generally skilled or semi-skilled, and was often motivated (subconsciously) by a desire to acquire the social graces of the West Indian middle class by travelling to England, which was considered the historico-cultural navel of the West Indian society. During the second phase – from 1955 to 1962 – the typical migrant was unskilled or semi-skilled, with a rural or semi-rural background of poverty.

Two categories of West Indians pioneered the trail to the British Isles. Firstly, there were those already familiar with Britain, having served during the Second World War, and their relatives and friends. Secondly, there were those professionals and skilled workers who, being well-informed about the manpower needs of post-war Britain, were willing to migrate in order to earn more money and find a social niche in a society which had moulded their thinking and attitudes. Above all, they were the only ones who could afford the fare. Subsequently, however, their enthusiasm began to ebb. Positive and negative forces came into play to bring about this change.

On the negative side were the reports of difficulties encountered in securing suitable jobs in Britain, the general prejudice against black people, and the high cost of living. On the positive side was the growth of manufacturing, service and tourist industries during the 1950s in the West Indies. The number of tourists to Jamaica, for instance, increased from 74 in 1950 to 226,000 in 1960. During the period 1954–60, the overall contribution made by industry towards the gross national product of Jamaica rose by 75 per cent.[5] The bauxite industry opened up opportunities for skilled and professional people, offering wages almost equal to those in Britain. The prosperity of the oil industry in Trinidad did the same for the islanders. However, the comparative decline in the rate of migration of skilled West Indians was more than offset by a rise in the migration of unskilled workers, which became substantial during the latter period (from 1955 to 1962).

Previously, the rural, unskilled labourer had been deterred from migration by lack of information and, more importantly, funds, since it cost six months' wages to undertake the journey to Britain. In time, both these hurdles were lowered. Friends and relatives already in Britain provided information as well as money. An extraneous element also entered the picture: travel agents, many of whom painted a glowing portrait of Britain, and in some cases even arranged loans for travel. Nearly two-thirds of the West Indian male migrants to Britain in 1960–61 were found to have received monetary help from one or other source to come to Britain.[6]

Throughout, the island governments maintained a posture of benevolent neutrality: they neither encouraged nor discouraged the prospective emigrant. Their reasons were economic. Emigration relieved, albeit partially, the increase in population and the consistently high unemployment.[7] The moneys remitted by the expatriates were beneficial to the West Indian economy. Between 1955 and 1960, Jamaicans in Britain sent home £16,500,000.[8] It was also believed that the West Indians were performing a useful function within the British economy by taking up jobs that were least popular with the indigenous population.

In the final analysis, the pull of the British labour market was what mattered. The rest was peripheral. As Hugh Gaitskell, the Labour Party leader, pointed out in 1961, there was 'an almost precise correlation between the movement in the numbers of unfilled vacancies [in Britain] … and the immigration figures.'[9] This correlation held until late 1960, when it was distorted by political controversy on immigration control, which led travel agents in the West Indies to fill all available space on ships and aeroplanes to help prospective migrants to 'beat the ban'.

But whatever reasons prompted West Indians to leave home –

economic necessity, joining relatives, a spirit of adventure, academic or professional ambition – most of them visualized their migration as an interlude during which they intended to earn a lot of money and/or acquire skills to ensure a better future in their home countries. This was borne out by the composition of the immigrant inflow. Initially the newcomers were predominantly male and young and even when, by the early 1960s, the male/female ratio had nearly balanced, most of the children were left behind.[10] This was an unmistakable indication that most immigrants had no definite plans for permanent settlement. As late as 1961 the *Economist* Intelligence Unit survey of Commonwealth immigrants showed that, of those in London, only a third intended to stay permanently.

Indeed, a few years earlier, some West Indian leaders from the Midlands suggested to the Colonial Office that West Indians be allowed to enter Britain on a contractual basis, for a limited number of years. This suggestion was rejected by the Colonial Office because it argued that, 'The people living in the British colonies are British subjects; and there can be no restrictions whatsoever on their movement into or out of Britain.'

The British authorities were apparently taking a legalistic stand which was applicable to *all* British colonies. Nevertheless, there was a special factor about the West Indian colonies: apart from their experience of European colonialism, the modern West Indian had no history. The original inhabitants, the Indian tribes, with their own history and culture, had become extinct as a result of bloody conflicts with, and subsequent servitude and overwork under, European colonizers. The territories had then been populated with slaves from Africa (and, later, indentured labour from India) at the express wish of the British planters. Having been forcibly denied the practise of their own languages and religions, African slaves grew up under the cultural shadow of their British masters, a development which the British authorities, in the post-Emancipation era, had actively encouraged. Thus there had developed a correlation between the length of British rule over a territory and the extent of anglicization of its (imported) inhabitants.

2 Children of Slavery: The Anglicized Afro-Caribbeans

Twenty million Africans made the middle passage, and scarcely an African name remains in the New World.

V. S. NAIPAUL[1]

I remember, in my school in Jamaica, our teacher would ask: 'What's your mother country?' And we children would shout, 'England!'

PATRICIA FULLWOOD, a West Indian housewife in
Wolverhampton.

Barbados, the oldest British possession in the Caribbean, showed the strongest symptom of anglophilia, and is considered one of the most anglicized parts of the world outside England. So too was Jamaica. (These two islands accounted for nearly three-quarters of the total West Indian immigration to Britain.) The three counties in Jamaica are called Cornwall, Middlesex and Surrey. Trafalgar Square and the Nelson's column in Bridgetown, Barbados, are much older than London's. Lord Nelson is closely associated with the island of Antigua. Not surprisingly, therefore, to most West Indians the names of places and people in Britain often conveyed images of places and people in the Caribbean.

However, anglicization did not stop with names: it went further, deeper. It was induced by the authorities, religious and secular, through the church and school. It began early – with nursery rhymes:

Mary had a little lamb,
Its fleece was white as snow ...

Old King Cole was a merry old soul,
And a merry old soul was he ...

It did not matter that there were no lambs or snow on the island, or whether King Cole had any historical significance to the islanders. Simply because these were English nursery rhymes they were going to be sung in the West Indies as well.

Children saluted the Union Jack before starting their classes in school. Textbooks written before the Second World War were still in use in the mid-1950s. They extolled the 'crusading' William Wilberforce and benign British parliament which outlawed the slave trade, a clever distinction having thus been made between the 'baddie' white planters and the 'goodie' British statesmen. On the whole the emphasis was on British history and life in Britain, the West Indies being treated as a rather insignificant freak.[2]

In the West Indies the impact of this traditional indoctrination could still be felt. For instance, when asked in 1960 to name 'People most important in West Indian history', senior school students in Jamaica chose Wilberforce, Queen Victoria and Captain Henry Morgan (who was once a pirate) – in that order. Ralph Abercrombie and Sir Walter Raleigh topped the list in Trinidad.[3] There was no mention whatsoever of Christopher Columbus, an Italian, who discovered the islands during the period 1492–8, or of Deacon Paul Bogle who led the Morant Bay rebellion in Jamaica and was executed in 1865, or Marcus Garvey, the father of the 'Black is beautiful' movement. No wonder then that these same children in the cinema yelled for Tarzan to beat the hell out of the tribal Africans. They had after all grown up memorizing Kipling's 'White Man's Burden'.

Eulogizing Queen Victoria as the 'good' queen who set the slaves free had left a deep imprint on the West Indian psyche. Even Marcus Garvey, the Jamaican leader denounced by the authorities as an extremist, could not refrain, in his speech in London in 1928, from referring to 'a woman by the name of Victoria the Good'.[4] In the West Indies the Queen's birthday and Empire Day were the most celebrated events of the year – days of rejoicing, flag waving and parades. During the last war, particularly, the air would ring with

We'll never let the old flag fall,
For we love it best of all.
We don't want fight just to show our might,
But when we start we will fight, fight, fight.
In peace or war you'll hear us sing
God save Britannia, God save the King.

Identification with Britain and its monarchy could not have been more total. The sinking of HMS *Hood* during the Second World War brought tears to many West Indian eyes. Generally speaking, conscious and subconscious attachment to English values was more prevalent among the middle class, the educated. The rest tended to take their cue from this minority.

Formal education in the West Indies meant a thorough grounding in the concept of Britain as the mother country, the land of hope and glory;

and the imbibing of Victorian social values – church marriage, marital fidelity, dressing for dinner, chivalry to the 'ladies', social snobbery and formality in conduct. West Indian teachers, the recipients and propagators of these Victorian middle-class values, were especially notable for their educational role. They and other middle-class West Indians took pride in naming their children after British statesmen and soldiers: Vernon Lancelot Barron Hammond, Ivanhoe Constantine Gladstone Hemmings, Raeburn Hume Hogarth Miles *et al*. The pinnacle of educational achievement for such children was to win a British university scholarship. For others, being able one day to play cricket at Lord's was their most cherished dream.

The education system in the Caribbean stressed standard English and encouraged the West Indian to disown the commonly spoken creole English. This is not a dialect or 'broken English' (as many non-West Indians seem to think) but a fully-fledged language with its own vocabulary, syntax, grammar, imagery and folklore.[5]

The evolution of the creole language was related directly to the mechanics of slavery. African slaves from different tribes were systematically banded together in work gangs to prevent communication among them. Teaching English to slaves was strictly forbidden. Work had nevertheless to be done on the plantation, and some communication was therefore essential, so the slaves were instructed to imitate the lip movements of their masters and their (white) assistants. Thus they were able to accumulate a limited vocabulary of distorted and mispronounced English words. On this foundation, in time, a whole language was built.

The emergence of a new, common language created just the situation that the master had dreaded. The slaves could now communicate with one another without the master understanding what they were saying. Often the slaves used this language in their speech and song – spirituals, as they were then, and are even now, called – to deride the master, to express their dissatisfaction, and to forge plans for rebellion. However, it remained the slave's language – inferior – a fact so deeply instilled among its users that even today many West Indians would not speak it in a white person's presence, and would sometimes deny that they know it. (This was one of the reasons why it took a long time for many British teachers to discover the existence of creole English in West Indian homes in Britain.)

The intermixing of tribes had another deleterious effect on the slaves. It dramatically ruptured the continuity of their social order, and destroyed their communal way of life. It also tended to encourage a 'go-it-alone' attitude among the slaves, though the cruelty of the system periodically brought them together to revolt. Extreme individualism remains one of the noteworthy characteristics of the modern Afro-Caribbean. The absence of any tradition of following a recognized leader – tribal, communal or caste – which is found in the settled societies of Africa or Asia, makes it difficult to organize such positive collective activities as, say, establishing community centres. However, when faced with a common threat of violence against them, the West Indians close ranks – temporarily.

Indeed, every important facet of the contemporary Afro-Caribbean way of life – family relationships, sexual morality, social class, music and literature – as well as personality traits and behaviour, is rooted in the historical experience of slavery. A slave existence for centuries, for instance, undermined the African's self-confidence and destroyed his spirit of adventure and enterprise. The result is that in the West Indies, as well as in black America, business concerns are mostly in the hands of non-Africans. In Britain, too, compared with Asians and Cypriots, the number of West Indians running their own business is insignificant.

The cruelty of slavery bred into the slaves hatred and distrust of the white man. But since open expression of dislike or disobedience was summarily and barbarously punished, the slaves devised subtle means of expressing their feelings. They lied; they played dumb; they deliberately, yet undefiantly, slowed their movements and thus reduced their work output. They perfected circumlocution as a fine art. In short, they developed repression of their real feelings and 'playing it cool' as defence mechanisms against the system.[6] Unable to fathom the slave's real feelings, the white masters dubbed them 'devious, shifty and habitual liars', the traits which are still today, to a certain extent, associated with blacks by whites.

The slave also learned to release his frustration and misery into humour and laughter – often at himself, sometimes at his fellow-slaves. For him, laughter became a safety valve. Post-Emancipation literature in the West Indies is full of self-derisive humour. But sometimes the slave's defence mechanism and diversionary tactics would collapse. Suddenly, unable to bear the misery of life any longer, he would go wild. Here then was the historico-cultural origin of the mercurial change of mood of many West Indians – from being sulky and withdrawn to being emotional and outspoken – to which frequent reference is made by many white British employers, social workers and teachers.

A system which by virtue of its instant rewards and punishments bred informers and lackeys among the enslaved made the slave conduct his life with a certain wariness. To drop suspicion was to become vulnerable. A general distrust of all, except a few chosen friends, was essential for his personal safety and survival. Distrust of all 'outsiders', particularly the whites, by many West Indians has continued. This is coupled with a general reluctance to express themselves, fully and truly, in front of whites. It is salutary to discover the gap that lies between what a black tells the white man and what he really thinks, particularly concerning white people.[7] The memories of all persecuted people, unlike those of their persecutors, are long. And blacks in the Western world, being the most and longest persecuted of all, nurse in their subconscious the deepest memories of the past.[8]

They survived three centuries of servitude by undergoing a psychological transformation which enabled them to hold themselves together. It was essential for them to accept their station in life with resignation, which came as they concurred, however subconsciously, with the masters that they were inherently inferior to whites. Racial and colour differences provided the visual foundation on which they were made to base their belief. Unable to release themselves from their blackness and negroid features they gradually began to despise themselves. Proverbs such as 'Every Jim Crow think him pickney white, and every jackass think him cubby race horse' ('Every black man thinks of himself as a child of a white man just as every jackass thinks of himself as an offspring of a race horse') grew among the slaves. Legal emancipation from slavery did not bring about pyschological liberation of the Afro-Caribbean. Despite generations of 'free' existence he continued to suffer from self-contempt. This affected his behaviour towards the white man. He tended either to evade him or to be aggressive and truculent towards him. Both stemmed from an inner feeling of inferiority and were symptomatic of the neurosis regarding colour, a legacy of the slavery which gave rise to the colour-caste system based on varying degrees of pigmentation: white, fusty, musty, dusty, tea, coffee, cocoa, light-black, black and dark-black.

This happened as a consequence of the sexual exploitation of subject women by white masters which led to the birth of mulatto children. As a rule, white masters were partial towards their mulatto progeny. They made them house slaves, promoted them as overseers, or even set them free. The mulattos (also called coloured) reciprocated by proving themselves loyal supporters of the system, often acting as lackeys and informers faithfully reporting to the 'massa' what they had seen or heard in the fields.[9] Many freed mulattos became slave masters: on the eve of Emancipation, mulattos in Jamaica owned 50,000 slaves. They hated the 'niggers' even more than the whites did, and bitterly opposed the abolition of slavery. The attitude underlying this colour-caste system is aptly summed up by the rhyme:

If you're white, you're right;
If you're brown, hang around;
If you're black, get back.

This rhyme could be heard throughout the black districts of the Western world – be it Kingston, Jamaica, or Harlem, America, or Brixton, England – well into the 1970s. One of the bitter disappointments of early West Indian migrants was the discovery that the British made no distinction between different pigmentation hues. To them, you were either white or 'coloured' (black).

'Commercial photographers [in Jamaica] know that the secret of success is to make portraits look several shades lighter,' reported Colin McGlashan. '"God, man, why you make me so *black*?" exclaimed a government minister furiously when he saw his official photograph.'[10] Air Jamaica advertisements for stewardesses stipulated 'good complexion, good hair'. The word 'good' implied 'fair' or 'straight'. 'In a Birmingham school only two West Indian mothers ordered school photographs,' wrote a correspondent of *The Times*. 'When asked [why], they said that the children's faces were "too dark". The mothers' idea of a good picture is one in which their child is shown to be almost white. They prefer obvious deception to reality.'[11]

Nothing illustrates the impact of the past on the present better than the contemporary family structure and sexual mores among Afro-Caribbeans and Afro-Americans. Under slavery, marriage was meaningless because the 'husband' could not protect his 'wife' from the sexual demands of other men. Any attempt to protect his 'wife' from being ravished by the white master meant stiff punishment. By law the slave had no rights; nor could a free man plead for him. Subject women were the exclusive 'property' of the master for whom they performed three major functions: labour, satisfying his sexual needs, and breeding slaves.

There was a popular notion among the masters that a slave woman would breed more and better if she was mated with different men. The male slave's sexual function, therefore, began and ended with being an inseminator. As the slave children, too, were the master's property and could be separated from their mothers at whim, there was no such thing as a 'slave family'. The end result was the total destruction of the conventional family system.

After Emancipation the slaves tried to emulate their former masters' model of the stable, patriarchal family, but were only partially successful. The previous anarchy of family life was replaced by the custom of a man and a woman cohabiting without necessarily going through the formal, legalistic ritual of a 'wedding'. This practice continued. The census for Jamaica in 1953, for instance, showed that only a third of the mothers were legally married.

Under the circumstances there is a more frequent change of sexual partners among them than is the case with societies where legal marriage is the norm. It is customary for the mother to assume the exclusive responsibility of bringing up the children, a function in which she is aided by her own mother and aunts. The man has remained in some ways dispensable to the family. His impermanence, and the frequent presence of children born from unions with different men in a given family, have inhibited him from exercising his traditional role of disciplining the children. Instead, the disciplinarian role has generally been assumed by the mother. The main reason for the evolution of this pattern among the Afro-Caribbeans was that the woman, as a productive slave in her own right, was never economically dependent on the man. Over the generations, like her Afro-American 'soul sister', the Afro-Caribbean woman has emerged as an energetic, hard-working and resourceful person, combining within herself the dual role of mother and father.[12] She has become the central arch of the Afro-Caribbean family.

In the Caribbean the matriarchal family nucleus exists within an extended family system which developed in the post-Emancipation period and which, seen in a historical context, is a variant of the communal way of life that many African tribes lead. The extended family system, wherein young children are brought up by older female members, thus releasing young mothers to go out to work, proved especially suitable as more and more West Indian males were compelled to migrate in search of work. The migrant male worked abroad for a few years and then returned to cohabit with his previous woman or established a new liaison; or he settled in the new country and then sent for his spouse first, and later their children.

We get the job the white man does not want, the room the white man does not want to live in, the woman he throws out.

JONATHAN CLARKE, a West Indian settler
in Birmingham.

Brotherly love was always at a premium, and the more obvious the differences between brothers, the less the loving.

E. R. BRAITHWAITE[1]

The primary reason for the West Indian leaving his native land was economic.[2] It seemed logical therefore that, once in Britain, he should give top priority to securing a job. He tried to get one on his own initiative or, if that failed or proved cumbersome, through the British Caribbean Welfare Service.[3]

In the beginning, while both his enthusiasm and his hopes were high, the newcomer attempted to find work he considered commensurate with his skills and experience. But as application after application ended in failure, he became desperately anxious and willing to take whatever was offered. A study of West Indians by Ruth Glass in 1958–9 showed that 55 per cent of them had undergone job downgrading due to migration. The professional and clerical West Indian male suffered most. His chance of finding a similar job was one in four.[4]

'It didn't take me long to realize that I couldn't get a job in that trade,' said a West Indian welder, recalling his early days in London. 'So I start' to ask for anything which take me off the dole … When I start' riding the buses looking for a job, I would jump off wherever I saw a chimney … At last I went to Lyons, and get a job there as a porter.'[5]

A police sergeant from Barbados became a bus conductor in London. Not that it was always easy, in the early 1950s, for a black immigrant to find work on the buses. Until 1954 jobs on the Birmingham buses, for instance, were the exclusive domain of white people, native or immigrant.

For the black immigrant a job was the first economic necessity; but shelter was the prime physical necessity. Having a place to live was a *sine qua non* of his search for work. He could hardly afford to live in a hotel, even if he could find one that would take him in, and go job-hunting from there. He discovered a frustrating situation prevalent in Britain: jobs were available precisely in those conurbations where the housing shortage was most acute. No doubt all newcomers to these areas faced problems in finding suitable accommodation, but the West Indian immigrant faced something extra – because of his colour. Discrimination by private landlords against him was widely practised.

John Darragh, a white British journalist, found through a private poll in 1956 that only 15 out of 1000 white Brummies were willing to rent accommodation to coloured people.[6] The situation in the preceding years had been no better.

When, in 1953, Stanley Bryan arrived in Wolverhampton from Jamaica he could find no place to live, not even a room for the night. Finally he arrived at a West Indian's house which was 'like a satchel filled with human beings: there were men sleeping under the stairs'. But at least this was better than the fate of a pioneering West Indian group which arrived in High Wycombe in 1953 on a summer evening, and had to pass the night talking and napping at a bus shelter, because no hotel or lodging house would accommodate them. Friendless new arrivals in London from the West Indies were often forced to pass the night in trains, under bridges, in telephone kiosks, and sometimes in public lavatories.

'A twenty-year-old Jamaican girl who went to Birmingham had to share a room with four [West Indian] men,' noted Donald Hinds, a West Indian writer. 'The young lady said that the men were very "gallant" about it. They would give her time to put up her screen and get into bed before they came in … Another West Indian lived in a large room converted from the hall of an old people's centre. There were fifteen beds in it.'[7]

No wonder then that trail-blazing was not popular. Instead, the preference was for following the footsteps of those already here, to arrive in England with a few addresses of early settlers. Besides, personal contacts were crucial in securing jobs and were used extensively for this purpose. R. B. Davison discovered that 80 per cent of the West Indians had found employment through friends or chance application.[8]

Accident and tradition had placed the pioneering West Indians where they were to be found in the early 1950s. The contingent from the SS *Empire Windrush* was sent to Clapham simply because an empty air-raid shelter was available there. Later, the Brixton Labour Employment Exchange assisted them in finding jobs. So they tried, and gradually managed, to find accommodation in Brixton. Some West Indian ex-servicemen settled in Nottingham because during the Second World War they had been posted at one of the three Royal Air Force stations in the vicinity, and had thus become familiar with the city. It was the same with Birmingham and Wolverhampton. Since Greater London and the West Midlands also had jobs to offer, latter-day West Indian migrants generally headed for these areas.[9]

Tradition played its role. Newcomers to London tend to settle in the first stage near a railway terminus, such as Euston or Paddington. Black immigrants followed the same patterns, but with one difference; they had much less choice. As only one in six white landlords was willing to let rooms to blacks, they were restricted to smaller districts within these areas. They also had to pay premiums on rent.[10] As a rule, newcomers to London put up with a bed-sitter as a stopgap arrangement. But with many black settlers a single room with shared facilities for cooking, washing and personal hygiene became the norm.

A study of black immigrants in Notting Hill in 1963 by Pearl Jephcott showed that nearly three-fifths of households had the sole use of one room only.[11] Describing a 'typical [black] family' of 'a couple with three little girls', she wrote: 'The father is a factory worker in his early thirties. The mother came to this country in 1956. They have lived at five different addresses since 1960, all local. The present one, a single room with a minute stairhead for the gas-oven and sink (at £3 10s. a week) is tidy, clean and grossly inadequate, especially since this mother, tied to the house by her own children, acts as a minder to other children too.'[12]

Earlier, the situation in Brixton had been summed up by the authors of *Immigrants in London* thus: 'Most West Indians in Brixton have evolved their own short-term solution to the housing shortage by living in single-room units, usually in one of the several hundred houses now owned by West Indian landlords.'[13]

The several hundred landlords among an estimated 11,000 West Indians then in Brixton had not emerged overnight. It had taken fourteen years for this to happen. In the provinces, however, this period was greatly reduced, because rented accommodation was more or less barred to black immigrants. This happened against their will and inclination. They were generally undecided whether to settle permanently or return home after a few years' stint. Also, they could not afford to buy houses. But they had no other choice.

Since one man's savings were seldom enough, joint pools had to be organized. Thus 'pardner' groups emerged. Five to fifteen 'pardners' – immigrants from the same parish or island – would pool their weekly savings and quickly build up a substantial fund.

However, at this point other obstacles appeared. Very few estate agents were prepared to do business with West Indians; and fewer still white vendors. But a blockage could not be maintained *ad infinitum*. Demand from among blacks was rising, and supply was bound, however niggardly and reluctantly, to follow. Some small, fledgeling estate agents, wishing to establish themselves in business, were tempted to help the eager blacks with money on hand 'on certain terms'. These were: extra commission for the agent in cash under the table, sometimes called 'an initial fee';[14] and 50 per cent or more cash to be paid for a house obtainable at a certain premium to overcome the white vendor's resistance. To the seller such an offer was doubly attractive: higher price and more hard cash, and quick sale of old property in slum areas which was least in demand among white buyers.

How much premium was paid by black buyers? According to the *Birmingham Post*, 'A house costs £300–£400 more [to coloured people] than the market price of £1,000–£1,200'.[15] It could therefore be claimed that by paying premiums black immigrants subsidized Britain's housing development plans. A building firm manager in Wolverhampton told Elizabeth Burney, a British researcher, that immigrants had 'indirectly done the business a good turn by helping to boost demand for new houses from white people fleeing from the older areas.'[16]

Formation of partner groups compelled black buyers to purchase large houses, preferably with vacant possession, so that three or more families sharing common facilities could be accommodated. That was why in Wolverhampton, for example, large boarding-houses on Waterloo and Newhampton Roads came into West Indian possession in the mid-1950s.

However, these houses were soon overcrowded. The reasons were economic and psychological. There was a steady stream of black new-comers. Families were reunited. Relatives and friends came. Children were born. But there was no corresponding growth in the overall accommodation available to black people. Consequently there was con-tinual pressure to make intensive use of space already available to the black immigrants, and to buy more property even if it was dilapidated and costly.

By the late 1950s various factors were simultaneously at work to keep the black newcomers together in concentrated knots. Racial discrimina-tion in housing was widespread, and was known to and accepted by blacks. This made them rely solely on mutual help and support.

The tendency to 'stick together' is common to immigrants throughout the world, and is the result of the unfamiliarity and insecurity that they feel on arrival in a new country. West Indians proved no exception to this pattern. In their case the general unfamiliarity was compounded by the racial alienation that they felt from white society. In addition, there was a contrast between their temperament and that of the English. They were exuberant, gregarious, expressive and full of zest – quite antithetical to most of the English. All these elements tended to hold the West Indians together – and apart from British society.

Above all, there were practical advantages in staying together in the same household or street. Socialization and friendship with fellow-islanders were guaranteed. Child-minding under the same roof or in the same street by fellow West Indians was easy to arrange, thus enabling mothers to work. In times of unemployment, ill-health or personal calamity, help and human warmth were close at hand.

A close examination of West Indian settlements proved the seminal importance of these considerations. Since the contingent from the SS *Empire Windrush* was Jamaican, their place of settlement, Brixton, attracted their relatives and friends from Jamaica. The result was that 80 per cent of the West Indians in Brixton were Jamaicans. In Notting Hill and Paddington, on the other hand, the majority of the West Indians were from the smaller islands. 'Relations and people from the same island tend to live in the same house,' wrote Pearl Jephcott, describing the black community in Notting Hill. 'A case in point is a house with seven sets of tenants (19 persons) all of whom are related and come from one of the smaller West Indian islands.'[17]

Because the first migrants from St Vincent were directed to High Wycombe by the Colonial Office's Welfare Office in 1953, St Vincent-ians came to comprise 85 per cent of all West Indians settled there. Similarly, most of the West Indians in Leeds were from St Kitts; and Slough had a large colony of Anguillans.

In time, as his savings grew and the urge to reunite with the family mounted, the single West Indian tenant began to consider buying a house. It seemed natural for him to want to purchase one in a familiar neighbourhood where, somehow, houses seemed to be available for sale more frequently than before. A slow but definite exodus by whites had begun, and the neighbourhood was becoming increasingly black. Unknown to him, his road had been nicknamed 'Banana Row' by the town's native residents and considered undesirable. At this point, in Wolverhampton, for example, more and more of the smaller houses in side streets between Waterloo Road and Newhampton Road were being sold to blacks. Geneva and Somerleyton Roads in Brixton were commonly known as 'Little Jamaica'.

Rejection, or at best avoidance, of black immigrants was not limited to housing: it included other spheres such as pubs, clubs and dance-halls. Even the churches generally failed them. This was the most galling discovery for the West Indian who, after Emancipation, had adopted Christianity with the zeal of a new convert.

During slavery knowledge of Christianity was systematically withheld from the slaves, although one of the earliest justifications for embarking upon the slave trade and slavery given by Europeans in general, and Sir John Hawkins in particular, was to 'Christianize the Africans'. (The first ship that Hawkins used as a slave-carrier was named the *Jesus*.) But with the development of plantation economy in the West Indies, the planters considered it imperative to deprive the slaves of any knowledge that might lead to their 'enlightenment', and possible disobedience. That included knowledge of the Christian doctrine.[18] Furthermore, by intermingling slaves from different tribes to form work gangs, and banning the practise of their respective language and religious rituals, the masters ensured the decline of African religions. The slaves were thus made to lead a barren life, in a religious sense. But gradually the situation changed.

Over generations a class of 'house slaves' developed: they worked in the master's mansion, and were allowed to stand in at the rear of the church on Sundays. Through them, and through periodic, distant observation of the white masters at church, a garbled version of Christian ritual and doctrine percolated down to the field slaves. The result was an amalgam of orthodox Christianity and African beliefs in witchcraft, spirits and the supernatural. The masters in Jamaica considered this development disturbing, and attempted to formalize it by importing, in 1745, Moravian missionaries from America to instruct the slaves properly. Later they let in Baptist ministers from America and England to preach the gospel. By the time Emancipation came in 1834, almost all slaves in Jamaica had been exposed to Christian doctrine in one form or another. After Emancipation, the freed slaves embraced Christianity with the fervour of people long deprived.

The biblical story of Moses leading the 'herd' back to Israel aroused strong emotion among slaves who had been dragged from Africa. The cry 'Jesus Saves' had an irresistible appeal to the African, caught inextricably in the wrench of life-long slavery. The present was unbearable as well as unchangeable. Only the future, promising the miracle of a messiah, held out hope. Deliverance would come, but only from above. Thus the African belief in the supernatural was blended with the Christian concept of Jesus the Saviour, producing an irresistible compound. Out of the marriage of Baptist fundamentalist gospel and African belief grew the 'native Baptist', or Pentecostal school of Christian doctrine which, in the post-Emancipation period, attracted thousands of ex-slaves, and which today claims the allegiance of about 20 to 25 per cent of the Jamaican population.

The participatory approach to service at a Pentecostal church – consisting of congregate singing, richly interspersed with responses of 'True!', 'Amen!', 'Praise the Lord!', 'Thank you, Jesus!' and 'Hallelujah!', and incorporating the spiritualist practices of trances, spirit possession and 'speaking in tongues' – proved particularly popular with the rural and/or poor Jamaicans. Consequently the influence of this church on its members was high, and did not diminish with their migration to Britain. Among the rest of the island community, conventional churches such as Anglican, Baptist and Methodist were popular. More than half of the Jamaican population was Anglican or Baptist;[19] and the membership of the Anglican church in Barbados, the most anglicized island, was high.

On the other hand, in Trinidad, St Vincent and St Lucia, initial colonization by the Spanish and French left a deep Roman Catholic mark, which remained entrenched despite the later British takeover of the islands. The Roman Catholic Church, for instance, had, and still has, a grip over schools; and Catholicism in a wider sense remains an important part of Afro-Caribbean life there.

Similar trends manifested themselves in Jamaica and Barbados, the islands held longest by the British. That is, religion and religious service acquired profound meaning. Much potential leadership has been channelled into religious institutions, a development that preceded Emancipation. Church became an open, warm and lively place, an integral part of the community, where people gathered every Sunday, dressed in their best, to sing and engage in a participatory ritual. Church attendance on Sundays in the West Indies remained high: almost 70 per cent of the total population were regular churchgoers.[20] Even the smallest parish provided religious instruction to children. Larger, richer churches often maintained schools.

It is against this backcloth that we need to examine the arrival of West Indian migrants in the Britain of the mid-1950s. To their utter bewilderment and disappointment, they found the British, the very people who brought Christianity to the West Indies, mostly indifferent to religion. Ralph Barry, a young West Indian in north London, for instance, was appalled to count only nineteen people in his Anglican church 'during Christmas season'.

But by far the most disturbing aspect was the reception accorded to the individual West Indian by the congregation. It was frosty. Nobody said 'Hello!' Nobody smiled. Even worse, English people would often sit apart from the West Indian, or would walk away from the pew where he took his seat. This behaviour, although deplorable, should not have been unexpected because, as the authors of *Colour and Citizenship* point out, 'Research, both here and in the United States, has shown that regular churchgoers are no less inclined than the population at large to display rejecting attitudes towards coloured peoples.'[21]

An open demonstration of white hostility against coloured people (in a religious context) occurred in Liverpool in July 1969. When a sculpture of Christ was unveiled at the Methodist church in Liverpool's Princes Park, many white Liverpudlians were incensed. The minister-in-charge was threatened with murder and the burning down of his church. This violent reaction was due to the colour used for Christ's body – a blend of brown, orange, pink and white to represent the skin colours of West Indians, Latin Americans, American Indians and Europeans.

The generally monolithic Roman Catholic Church seems to have fared no better. Most Catholic Trinidadians felt no nearer to the British or Irish Catholics than did the Anglican Barbadians to their English counterparts. 'It's surprising to see how the same doctrine has one meaning for some people and another meaning for others,' said Rose Lipton, a Trinidadian nurse living in Paddington, London. 'As a Roman Catholic I don't feel any nearer to white Roman Catholics, nor they to me. You're white or black first, and a Roman Catholic afterwards.'[22] Apparently colour, the divider, had proved weightier than Catholicism, the unifier. 'In Sparkbrook, Birmingham,' wrote Robert Hughes, 'there is evidence that West Indian Roman Catholics felt themselves squeezed out of the church to which they belong because of the Irish influence there.'[23]

Rose Lipton called herself a Catholic, but attending Mass every Sunday seemed to belong to a 'very distant past'. In this she was typical of the vast majority of the West Indian settlers. According to the researches of the Revd Clifford S. Hill, an English minister and a student of race relations, only 4 per cent of the West Indians in London regularly attended church on Sundays.[24]

It was not only conventional British churches that were written off by the West Indians as 'cold, dreary, unreceptive places' but also the (white) Pentecostal churches. Of the six Pentecostal churches in Wolverhampton and the surrounding district, for example, only one managed to retain a substantial number of West Indians. Having been disillusioned with the established churches they decided, after much soul-searching, to strike out on their own.

As early as 1954, the West Indians in Wolverhampton started meeting in their homes for Pentecostal services on Sundays. Out of this evolved a Church of God of Prophecy, a New Testament Church of God, and a Church of God in Christ, with the first two acquiring their own buildings by the late 1960s. Of the estimated 1000 regular churchgoing West

Indians in Wolverhampton, some 700 to 800 attended these Pentecostal churches and the Seventh Day Adventist church. By the late 1950s eight halls were being hired in London every Sunday for Pentecostal services. Within a decade as many churches had acquired their own buildings. The number of Pentecostal congregations nationally was estimated in 1962 at 77.[25]

During the next decade this number rose further, and most of these congregations became part of the three major national Pentecostal churches. One such national body alone had 35 ministers and owned 22 buildings throughout the country. Each Sunday these churches overflowed with black worshippers, who actively participated in the mid-week activities as well. Indeed, the Pentecostal Church was the only purely West Indian institution in Britain that had its own identity, and was functional.

The only other church which showed some warmth towards black settlers – the Seventh Day Adventists – proved so popular with them that by 1963 they constituted a third of its national membership. In areas of black settlement the West Indian proportion became overwhelming – 83 per cent in Luton, 75 per cent in Huddersfield, 70 per cent in London and 60 per cent in Birmingham.[26] However, one of the reasons for this imbalance was the white members' propensity to leave as West Indians joined in numbers.[27] In Brixton, for instance, within a few years a Seventh Day Adventist church changed from being all-white to being almost exclusively West Indian.

Summing up the overall situation in the country, Clifford S. Hill wrote in *Race: A Christian Symposium* that, in 1967, 'it was estimated that at least 50 per cent of the West Indian immigrants who were regular churchgoers attended churches run by and attended mainly or exclusively by coloured people'.

But, in any case, church was (and still is) of marginal importance to life in Britain. No more than 7–12 per cent of Britons aged fifteen or over in the large conurbations attended church regularly.[28] So, even if the West Indian had been accepted as a 'Brother in Christ', it would have made little difference to the general acceptance which he, as an anglophile, was anxiously seeking.

Positive acceptance and friendliness were expected to flow from contact in a social context; and no place in Britain is better suited for that than the pub. Knowing this, the West Indian hoped to make English friends in the pub – provided of course he was allowed in and served, which was not always the case. One refusal to serve, one statement, 'We don't serve the coloureds here', was enough to make the West Indian feel generally unwelcome and rejected and, more importantly, to implant in his mind the seed of doubt, making him wonder every time he went to a new pub whether or not he would be served – hardly a state of mind conducive to striking up friendships with the English.

To be fair, not all pubs erected a colour barrier, but there were enough, especially in the incipient black settlements, for the newcomer to be exposed by his peers to the idea that a colour bar existed in the country and that it was based, as many publicans claimed, 'on their [white] customers' objections'.[29] The West Indian had no legal or even moral redress since the publican had the right, by law, to refuse service to whomsoever he pleased.

Managements of clubs and dance-halls had a similar right, and often used it against coloured customers. As private and formal institutions, many clubs kept out West Indians without any difficulty or fuss. There was little that the black settlers could do, except set up their own clubs. Which they did. At one time there were fifty basement clubs in south London managed and/or owned by West Indians. However, they could not establish public dance-halls of their own.

As a predominantly single, male group, black immigrants had all the greater need for female companionship. Hence, to be barred from local dance-halls was all the more galling to them. When this happened, the West Indians complained. Sometimes their protest was echoed in the national press. In 1954, for instance, it became known that a Sheffield dance-hall had imposed a colour bar. Liberal circles were enraged. Questions were asked in Parliament where an MP from Sheffield openly defended the dance-hall management in the name of 'freedom of choice'. There the matter rested. The black settlers, locally and nationally, accepted the situation with the same degree of resignation they had shown with regard to verbal and physical violence perpetrated against them in pubs and dance-halls which allowed them entry.

The earlier phase of West Indian immigration – from the late 1940s to the end of the mid-1950s – was littered with violent incidents which, as a rule, went unreported or were at most accorded small headlines in local papers. Instances of rejection and refusals at hotels, pubs, restaurants and barber-shops were too numerous, and were generally considered too trivial by the mass media, to warrant reporting. Robert Hamilton, a West Indian cleaner in Birmingham, summed up the life of most West Indian immigrants in the mid-1950s thus: 'Bad accommodation, lack of social amenities and hurtful taunts.'

None of this, however, changed the economic facts of life. The pressure on the West Indian to emigrate – or languish in the West Indies – was high. The British economy, on the other hand, surging ahead, needed as much labour as it could get. While unemployment in the West

Indian islands varied between 15 and 30 per cent, Birmingham alone had 48,000 job vacancies in 1955. West Indians were willing to fill these even if it meant travelling 5000 miles and accepting social restrictions imposed by whites.

But many Britons took a totally different view. They considered West Indians as indolent blacks, draining the National Assistance funds while simultaneously living off the immoral earnings of white women. By 1958 this image of the West Indian was past the stage of grapevine, pub talk, occasional newspaper headline or readers' letters. It was echoed at the highest level of government. Commenting that the newcomers were a 'headache', a junior minister at the Home Office in 1958 said, 'They come in by air and at once begin to draw National Assistance.'[30] There was little or no evidence to support such statements.

The image of the 'lazy black man' was as old as the slave trade; and, being a part of the British subconscious, was easy to revive, notwithstanding the contrary evidence that the prime reason for the West Indian's presence was his search for *work*. When this image was compounded with the fear of sexual relationships between black men and white women, a very old taboo, the result was bound to disgust and infuriate many whites. Here again the facts were to the contrary. The incidence of pimping and soliciting in Birmingham, for instance, was low. In 1954 there were only 212 cases of prostitutes being charged in Birmingham, a city with a population of over one million, of whom 11,000 were black and single.[31] Hardly a cause for concern.

Nevertheless, the stereotype of the black pimp, ostentatiously dressed and driving a flashy car, was becoming a fixture of popular mythology. This development happened to coincide with the emergence of Teddy boys, white youths dressed in Edwardian style. They were often aggressive and, in the social milieu, they found in the black man their perfect target. He was highly visible; he was in a hopeless minority; and he aroused antipathy among the white majority. Attacks on black people, especially when alone, became frequent.

4 Blocks Look West

This is a white man's country, and I want it to remain so.

SIR CYRIL OSBORNE, a Conservative MP.[1]

The Notting Hill riots taught us one bitter lesson: we were black first and British last.

A West Indian leader in Wolverhampton.

My trip to America (in 1963) made me realize that we in Britain too needed a radical approach to achieve racial and social equality.

PAUL STEPHENSON, a leader of West Indians
in Bristol.

It has often been argued in Britain that white people's hostility towards blacks is related to the size of their community. It is not the dislike of black people as such, but the psychological threat of their 'flooding the country' that creates anxiety and can lead to aggression. But the racial history of the country provides no evidence to support this argument.

The first race riot in Britain took place in 1919 in Liverpool, and was soon followed by similar disturbances in almost all the dock areas where coloured people lived – Cardiff, Manchester, Glasgow, Hull and London. There could not have been more than 30,000 racial minority settlers in Britain then. The rioting consisted chiefly of whites attacking the person and property of blacks, and the terrified victims trying to defend themselves as best they could.

During the week of 4–10 June 1919 white rioters attacked black Liverpudlians in the streets and in their homes and hostels, and looted and burned their houses. An assault on a coloured seamen's hostel rendered some 400 occupants homeless. The police were compelled to remove about 700 blacks – out of a total of 5000 – to a jail for their own safety. In the words of a local magistrate, the white hooligans were making 'the name of Liverpool an abomination and disgrace to the rest of the country'.[2]

A scuffle between a few white and black men on the evening of 10 June 1919 in Bute Town, Cardiff, led to a riot when a mob of white men, about 2500 strong, went on a rampage, assaulting blacks and destroying a lodging house where coloured seamen lived. Pistol shots were fired; and one seaman was killed.

A more elaborate 'nigger-hunting' occurred the following evening. At one point, a house with black occupants was attacked by a white mob led by two uniformed soldiers firing pistols. The scene was later described by a local paper as 'reminiscent of the French Revolution'. As a result of this, the black residents of Bute Town were too scared to leave their barred and boarded houses for the next few days.

It was in Liverpool again, nearly thirty years later, that violence against non-whites erupted. A fight outside an Indian restaurant led to a race riot that lasted two nights and resulted in scores of arrests. The racial violence against blacks in 1919 could be rationalized as attributable to unemployment among seamen. But how was one to explain the Liverpool riot in 1948 when jobs were going begging and there were no more than 8000 blacks and Asians in the city?

During the summer of 1949 there was a series of fights between blacks and whites in Deptford, London, which culminated in a siege of a black men's hostel by a white mob. Frustrated by the police cordon around the place, the mob finally attacked the policemen. The number of blacks in Deptford was insignificant, as was also the case in 1954 in Camden Town, London. There, in assaulting the blacks, whites used bottles and axes – and finally a petrol bomb, which burned out a building inhabited by blacks.

But these proved to be minor incidents compared to what followed four years later, first in Nottingham and then in Notting Hill, London. The extent of violence; the type of slogans used – 'We'll get the blacks', 'Down with niggers', 'We'll kill the blacks' – and the number of arrests (177 in London and 25 in Nottingham of whom 149 were white and 53 black) underlined the seriousness of the rioting.

The citizens of Nottingham became familiar with black faces during the early 1940s when many West Indian servicemen posted at the nearby Royal Air Force stations used the city's YMCA for 'rest and recreation'. On demobilization, some of the West Indians and West Africans, married to local women, settled there. From that base, gradually, the number of West Indians and Africans grew to 2500 by 1958 – and that of Asians to 600. Together the Afro-Asian-Caribbean community formed a mere one per cent of the total population.

Yet many Nottingham citizens seemed too willing to believe the worst of blacks. They were thought to be 'slow in their movements [at work]' and were liable 'to fall asleep on the job'.[3] Those out of work were widely believed to be living off white prostitutes, wearing expensive suits, sporting flashy cars and holding parties where scores of people sang and danced through the night. Also they were thought to be carrying knives and jumping queues at the Labour Exchange.

The blacks' experiences were altogether different. They were often turned down for jobs which continued to be advertised. The local Labour Exchange had started treating blacks and whites separately. This had exacerbated mutual antagonism, already high. When the whites saw a black leave the counter with a card they presumed he had been offered a job whereas, in fact, the card was merely for an interview.

At work, blacks were often objects of racist abuse. The young among them retaliated in kind. The resultant ill-feeling was carried over outside the factory gates. It poisoned the atmosphere of St Ann's, a slum where most blacks lived. During the few weeks before the final flare-up in August 1958, at least a dozen black men were beaten up and robbed by Teddy boys, with the police showing scant interest in catching the culprits.

A minor incident triggered off an eruption of the bottled-up feelings. During an argument in a pub on 22 August a West Indian hit his white woman friend. That led to a scuffle: the few blacks present in the pub were badly beaten by the many whites. Next evening, a Saturday, a group of West Indians returned to the pub bearing knives and razors. At closing time they attacked, injuring six whites. The word spread quickly. A mob of 1500 whites launched a counter-attack with razors, knives, palings and bottles. Eight people, including policemen, were hospitalized.

This flare-up made national radio and newspaper headlines, and had an immediate effect on the Notting Hill area of London, where trouble had been brewing for several weeks. Some right-wing organizations, with headquarters in the district, had been active, distributing leaflets, scrawling slogans, holding indoor meetings – generally inciting the white people to 'Act Now' to 'Keep Britain White'. Within hours of the news of the Nottingham riot, a gang of Teddy boys went 'nigger-hunting' with iron pipes, table legs and knives, and left at least five blacks unconscious on the pavement.

The following Saturday, 30 August, more violence erupted in Nottingham and Notting Hill. A crowd of 3000 to 4000 whites gathered at the junction of St Ann's Well Road, Pease Hill Road and Pym Street in Nottingham. No blacks were to be seen in the streets: they were following their leaders' advice to stay indoors from Friday evening to Monday morning. Frustrated, the mob attacked the police for 'having protected the blacks on the previous Saturday'.

In Notting Hill widespread and vicious violence against black people and property broke out. Shortly before midnight a crowd of 200 whites attacked blacks' houses near Bramley Road. One property was set alight.

The next day, Sunday, a mob of 500 to 700, shouting 'We'll get the blacks' and 'Lynch the blacks', and using knives, bottles, crowbars and dustbins, assaulted blacks in their houses. There were also attacks and fights in Latimer Road, Harrow Road and Kensal Rise. Violent activity, albeit in a low key, went on for another fortnight.

Once the blacks in Notting Hill had overcome their initial alarm, shock and despondency, they tried to help themselves. They provided elaborately arranged escorts for those black London Transport employees who had to work late-night or early-morning shifts, and formed vigilante groups which patrolled the area in cars.

This self-defence, coupled with the stiff sentences passed against nine assailants in west London by Judge Salmon in mid-September, had a salutary effect. By the end of September the situation returned to near-normal; but not quite. It could not.

'The Age of Innocence' had come to a dramatic end, at least as far as the West Indians were concerned. They were made to realize that they were not 'overseas British' now in Britain, but were black men and women living in a white society. This opened a new chapter in the racial history of Britain.

Significantly enough, politically conscious West Indians had realized the need for an organization of their own some time earlier. In 1957 a number of them, concerned with 'unemployment, housing problem and colour bar' had talked to some 2000 West Indians in their homes, pubs and Labour Exchanges, and concluded that 'West Indians want an organization to represent their interests ... and welcomed efforts to unite [them], and to further British–West Indian unity'.[4]

From this evolved in March 1958 the *West Indian Gazette*, a monthly publication, under the editorship of Claudia Jones, a Trinidadian by birth. In its inaugural issue the magazine pointed out that 'West Indians in Britain form a community with its own special wants and problems which our own paper alone would allow us to meet'.

In reality, however, the West Indian community in Britain was composed of many sub-communities, each one loyal to its own island of origin; and forging a single West Indian identity was not easy. Long distances between islands in the Caribbean – stretching across a crescent whose two ends are as far apart as south-east England and Morocco – had fostered individual identities among islanders as well as inter-island rivalries. The British hegemony had further strengthened these tendencies by encouraging liaison between each island and the metropolitan country, and discouraging inter-island contacts. For instance, it took ten weeks for a letter to travel directly from Jamaica to Trinidad but only a month if routed via Britain.

But residence in Britain, the common experience of racial discrimination, and contacts with people from other Caribbean islands had begun to erode inter-island rivalries. Gradually a West Indian identity was emerging and, sometimes, assuming a formal existence in the form of local bodies.

The events of the summer of 1958 were viewed with much alarm by the authorities in the West Indies. Norman Manley, the Chief Minister of Jamaica, had flown to London with the specific objective of reassuring the West Indian migrants by touring the areas of racial disturbances, and by meeting them informally. Later, in December, when the West Indies Federation was formally inaugurated, it took over the British Caribbean Welfare Service, expanded it, renamed it the Migrant Services Division, and appointed two community development officers to help organize the West Indian settlers in general, and to set up a co-ordinating body for them in the London area.

They brought a dozen West Indian organizations in Greater London together under one umbrella called the West Indian Standing Conference (WISC). The West Indians in Wolverhampton and the surrounding district formed the West Midlands Caribbean Association in 1959. And a year later the West Indian Standing Conference was inaugurated in Birmingham. By mid-1961, WISC in London had secured the affiliation of eighteen organizations, some of which were multiracial. This was reflected in the composition of the executive committee where, in 1962, four of the nine members were white. But a year later, responding to a new climate, they resigned, leaving the executive committee all black.

In short, West Indians began building and consolidating local and national organizations of their own. This proved to be an irreversible step, and marked the next phase in Britain's racial history. From then on, much of the West Indian political energy was channelled into these organizations, and not into the major British political parties.[5]

In any case, British politics as such did not seem to impinge on the daily life of the West Indians. It was racial prejudice and discrimination that mattered; and these seemed to transcend conventional political loyalties. Before and after the violence of 1958, racist statements were issued by many local leaders of both the major parties. This made the West Indians even more apathetic to British politics in general as well as to the autumn 1959 national election campaign in particular.

The Conservatives were returned to parliament with a large majority. The restrictionist lobby, which wanted coloured immigration to be banned or stringently controlled, became active. Its activities, widely reported in the mass media, made the black settlers fear that immigration control was imminent. They therefore decided to send for their families, relatives and friends before the gates finally closed.

By encouraging more West Indians to come faster to Britain, black immigrants inadvertently provided ammunition to the restrictionist lobby. All that these lobbyists had to do was to quote statistics to show that an 'unarmed invasion' of Britain by black people had begun in earnest: the number of West Indian immigrants had tripled in a year – from 16,400 in 1959 to 49,650 in 1960.

At the Conservative Party's annual conference in October 1961 a motion demanding control of Commonwealth immigration was passed by a huge majority: an event to which the Jamaican *Daily Gleaner*, a solidly middle-class newspaper, reacted thus: 'That this great free centre of the world, the United Kingdom, mother of all modern parliamentary freedoms, should this day fear the entry of coloured people – the core of the problem is colour – and give up the unique basis upon which its own undoubted claims to greatness have grown and flourished. The Britain of the Magna Carta, of *habeas corpus*, of freedom, has had to bow to fear of race.'[6]

Along with the hyperbolic extolling of Britain as the 'great free centre of the world' went the moral rage at her racism: '*the core of the problem is colour*'. If further proof of the racist bias of the proposed legislation was needed it came with the government's decision to exempt the Irish Republic from its application. With this the last nail was driven into the coffin of the concept of Black British. But the death of one concept often leads to the birth of another.

Just as the 1958 race riots helped to forge a West Indian identity, the 1961 Commonwealth Immigrants Bill made the West Indian and Asian organizations coalesce to oppose it. For the first time in Birmingham's history 450 West Indians, Asians and white Britons marched under the aegis of the Co-ordinating Committee Against Racial Discrimination (CCARD), an umbrella body of Indian, Pakistani, West Indian and sympathetic British organizations. At a conference in London the Committee of Afro-Asian-Caribbean Organizations (CAACO) was formed. It sought the support of the non-white Commonwealth High Commissions, and received it.

This was a highly significant development. For the first time, black and brown immigrants, faced with a threat to their rights, decided to enter the arena of British politics and apply direct pressure to safeguard their interests. CAACO actively co-operated with other bodies committed to the defeat of the Bill.

However, contrary to CAACO's expectations, the Labour Party watered down its opposition to immigration legislation during the parliamentary debate in early 1962. With this, the battle against the bill was lost. the traditional 'open-door' principle was abandoned in order to come to terms with the widespread prejudice against racial minorities.

The only consolation, perverse though it was, that could be drawn was that the long, emotional controversy that preceded and followed the publication of the 1961 bill, and which filled column after column in serious newspapers, made many black settlers politically conscious and interested in struggling to redress the inequities resulting from racial discrimination.

Now black activists, supported by white sympathizers, turned their attention to promoting legislation against racial discrimination. The Birmingham-based CCARD was the first to act. During the summer of 1962 it organized a petition for legislation against racial discrimination and incitement. Later, armed with 10,000 signatures, it lobbied MPs.

But this was not enough. It seemed to many black settlers that 'other means' might have to be adopted to right the racial wrongs. By then they had, through television and newspapers, become familiar with the non-violent direct action – sit-ins at lunch counters and bars, 'freedom rides' on inter-state buses, pickets and demonstrations – that black Americans were using, with some success, to gain racial equality. Due to common bonds of slavery and race, the Afro-Caribbeans identified with Afro-Americans, and began to consider whether similar tactics might not be employed in Britain. But when? In what circumstances?

An opportunity presented itself in, of all places, Bristol – associated in black people's minds with slavery. In April 1963, the Bristol Omnibus Company said to a West Indian applicant, 'Sorry, no coloureds'. This incensed black citizens, many of them settled in Bristol for three generations. Among them was Paul Stephenson, a young man born in the city of West Indian parentage. He had just returned from a three-month tour of America where he had closely studied the Civil Rights organizations. As an official of Bristol's West Indian Development Council, he called for a boycott of buses to force the management to rescind its policy of colour bar. This call was followed by a demonstration against the bus company. The controversy acquired national importance, causing much embarrassment to the management, and dragged on for weeks. Finally the management capitulated, oddly enough, on 28 August: the day of a massive Civil Rights march in Washington, DC, which was addressed by the charismatic black leader Martin Luther King. The Bristol episode, although minor in scale, was significant, since it broke new ground in the struggle of black people in Britain to achieve racial equality.

In general, the pressure of national and international events was making more and more Afro-Asian-Caribbean people politically conscious.

Probably the most important event yet in British politics, for black settlers, occurred in October 1964 when in the parliamentary general election Peter Griffiths, the Conservative candidate at Smethwick, a Birmingham suburb, defeated Patrick Gordon-Walker, an important member of the Labour shadow cabinet. The main thrust of the winner's campaign was summed up by the frequently aired rhyme:

> If you want a nigger neighbour,
> Vote Liberal or Labour.

Peter Griffiths told the Midlands correspondent of *The Times*: 'I would not condemn anyone who said that [rhyme]. I regard it as a manifestation of popular feeling.'[7] Contrary to the national swing of 3.5 per cent against the Conservatives, Griffiths improved his position by 7.2 per cent over his predecessor and it was reckoned that at least four other Labour candidates lost to the Conservatives on the issue of race and immigration. Given a slender majority in Parliament, this meant a lot politically to the Labour Government.

For the first time in Britain, racism was openly injected into politics at the national level, and was seen to pay electoral dividends. The general alienation of black immigrants grew as race and immigration were dragged from the fringe of British politics to its centre. A formal recognition of this came when *The Times* published a series of eleven articles on the subject the following January under the ominous heading of 'The Dark Million'.

In December 1964, during a stop-over in London (on his way to Oslo to receive the Nobel Peace Prize), Martin Luther King helped to bring together the leaders of the three federal organizations of West Indian and Asian immigrants: the West Indian Standing Conference (WISC), the Indian Workers' Association–Great Britain (IWA–GB), and the National Federation of Pakistani Associations (NFPA). The result was the Campaign Against Racial Discrimination (CARD), an umbrella body, formally inaugurated in February 1965 under the chairmanship of Dr David Pitt, a Trinidadian physician.

At its first conference in July 1965, CARD defined its aims and objectives as 'the elimination of all racial discrimination against coloured people; opposition to all forms of discrimination on the entry of Commonwealth citizens into the UK'; and 'co-ordination of the work of organizations already in the field ... for the fight against racial discrimination'.

CARD sought the affiliation of the IWA–GB, the NFPA and WISC. The IWA–GB spurned the offer as it was already the main force behind the Birmingham-based Co-ordinating Committee Against Racial Discrimination with its similar aims. After some hesitation the NFPA and WISC joined.

By then the Racial Adjustment Action Society (RAAS) had emerged as a rival to CARD. Its aims and objectives were to guarantee 'the human rights of coloured people', to re-examine 'the whole question of Black Identity' and to strengthen 'links with Afro-Asian-Caribbean peoples in a common fight for the freedom and dignity of man'. Unlike CARD, it was open only to coloured people. The contrasting attitudes of CARD and RAAS paralleled the differences that existed between King and Malcolm X, an Afro-American radical and an electric personality.

In the summer of 1965 a plum fell into the lap of black militants: the White Paper on Commonwealth Immigrants issued by the Labour Government. As against the current yearly intake of 20,000 work-voucher holders, the White Paper imposed a ceiling of 8500. There were further restrictions on dependants' rights of entry. It made the task of RAAS leaders and other militants easier. They could argue, convincingly, that the Labour Party was as racist as the Conservatives. Hence, instead of following CARD's strategy of attempting to generate goodwill in the white community, black and brown settlers should concentrate on strengthening 'coloured only' organizations, such as RAAS.

A series of threatening letters in July and August allegedly written by the Deputy Wizard of the north London branch of the Ku Klux Klan (KKK), a US-based white supremacist body, to the Indian secretary of CARD received wide publicity. At a meeting in Birmingham in mid-August a resolution was passed calling on all West Indians to mobilize themselves for self-defence against the threats of the KKK, since the authorities had shown reluctance to do so. Plans were made to organize vigilante groups for self-defence in Birmingham and London.

Unlike in 1958, the black settlers showed themselves capable of taking care of themselves if threatened with violence. Whatever the moral and political issues involved, the British authorities could not have viewed this development with a benign eye. It was obvious that relations between races were rapidly worsening.

One of the reasons for this deterioration was a lack of national policy regarding black and Asian immigrants. As a prisoner of its dogma of equality of all British subjects, the Conservative Government – during whose tenure the bulk of coloured immigration had occurred – had refused to acknowledge that some British Commonwealth citizens were racially different from the others. According to this view, once Commonwealth citizens or overseas British subjects entered Britain they became indistinguishable from the native-born, so the question of relations between the two, or lack of them, simply did not arise. However, the 1964 Labour Government showed some realism when its 1965 White Paper recommended integration of those already here, thus indirectly recognizing the difference between these two categories of British citizens.

From this stemmed the National Committee for Commonwealth Immigrants (NCCI), an independent body financed by the government. It was charged with the task of 'generally promoting and co-ordinating efforts of liaison' between Commonwealth (that is, coloured) immigrants and the 'host' society.

It began functioning in early 1966, and sought the co-operation of most black and white leaders active in the field of race relations. The net effect was to disrupt the incipient protest movement. The decision by two CARD leaders, Dr David Pitt and Hamza Alvi, to join the NCCI caused a split in the organization. WISC disaffiliated from CARD; and so did the NFPA. This damaged CARD's standing at a time when the 1965 Race Relations Bill was being discussed in Parliament.

CARD's conclusion – as a result of a survey in Manchester, Leeds and Southall in the summer of 1966 – that racial discrimination was rampant failed to draw public attention. It was the publication of a survey undertaken by a non-partisan body – Political and Economic Planning Ltd (PEP) – in April 1967 which succeeded in having an impact on the press, politicians and people. The report concluded unequivocally that there was widespread discrimination against coloured citizens in employment, housing and personal services.

Until then the blacks' complaints of racial discrimination had never been taken seriously by most whites, who had either dismissed them as allegations made by people with 'chips on their shoulders' or viewed them as 'difficulties' experienced by all newcomers, irrespective of colour or race, and which were expected to disappear 'with time'. Now the PEP report concluded that more discrimination existed than the racial minorities themselves had claimed.

A new life was infused into black militancy which, after its first flourish, had begun to subside, partly due to the assassination of Malcolm X, who had first kindled the light here, and partly due to the subsiding of restrictionist demands regarding coloured immigration following the 1965 White Paper and the 1966 general election, which returned a Labour Government.

In America, too, the racial scene was changing rapidly. The influence of Martin Luther King was on the decline. And the demand for Black

Power – first heard in Greenwood, Mississippi, in the summer of 1966 – was gaining ground. By the spring of 1967 faint echoes of the Black Power slogan could be heard in Britain. By confirming black militants' view of British society as racist, the PEP report acted as a catalyst in bringing together the Black Power supporters to form, in June 1967, the Universal Coloured People's Association (UCPA). They viewed white racism in Britain not in isolation but as part of a world-wide phenomenon, and conceived the fight against racism in international, rather than national, terms.

The arrival in London, in July, of Stokely Carmichael, the originator of the Black Power slogan, boosted the morale of black militants in Britain. In his paper to the International Congress of Dialectics of Liberation, Carmichael expounded a thesis which could be summarized thus: 'White Western [i.e. West European and North American] societies enjoy the fruits of international racism through the exploitation of the Third World, i.e., Afro-Asian-Latin American countries. In recent times these white societies have ruled the rest of the world where they have successfully indoctrinated the people, especially intellectuals, into accepting their own [basically racist] view of history. The notion that the West is "civilized" is a Western idea. But, most important, it is the white West which defines what civilization and progress are. Whosoever defines the terms, and makes them stick, is the master. Only when the slave refuses to accept the master's definition can he feel psychologically free, not before.

'History shows that Western "civilization", since the times of ancient Greece, has thrived only on the exploitation of others. Furthermore, the Western world has a most barbarous history of violence practised within itself, and on non-Western people. White societies have often mouthed the ideals of freedom and democracy while committing atrocious violence against non-whites. For example, the white colonies in America were demanding freedom from England on one hand while decimating the (American) Indian population on the other. Where white societies could not decimate the non-white people (as in Asia and Africa), or had reason not to (as with the African slaves in the Western hemisphere), they tried to destroy their sense of dignity and their indigenous cultures.

'But blood is thicker than water. Present-day Afro-Americans feel emotionally and economically part of the Third World, even though they are trapped in the bowels of America, the leader of the white West. To counteract the growing imperialistic and racist tendencies of white America manifested in Vietnam and a chain of counter-insurgency coups, engineered with the aid of the Central Intelligence Agency, the Afro-Americans realize the need to attack the white racist, imperialist system from both inside and outside of America.

'To be most effective the Afro-Americans must co-ordinate their strategy with progressive forces everywhere. That is where organizations such as the UCPA came in.'

Being a negro by race, a Trinidadian by birth, and an American by nationality, Stokely Carmichael was instantly able to establish rapport with his Afro-Asian-Caribbean audiences. The hysterical reaction of the British media and his (threatened) expulsion from Britain by the government testified that the authorities were apprehensive of his ideology and, above all, his appeal to the racial minorities.

The coining of the term 'Black Power' was a pragmatic act.[8] Carmichael used it simply as an antithesis to the term 'white power structure' that was then current in the American Civil Rights vocabulary, and to popularize the idea that blacks should hold offices in black areas. But within a year the term had acquired a wider and more profound meaning. In July 1967, Carmichael defined it as 'the coming together of black people for their liberation – by any means necessary'.

The term 'liberation' – freeing oneself – was applied in socio-psychological and political contexts. An examination of the historical background of the Afro-American and Afro-Caribbean underlined the need for liberation. Having been deprived of the use of their languages and religions, and having imbibed self-contempt, the African slaves in the Caribbean and North America grew up imitating their 'massa' (i.e. master), wishing to be Europeans in cultural, and even physical, terms. Abolition of slavery did not free them from this subtle, self-imposed cultural subjugation. They continued to spend countless hours and cash on thinning their lips and noses, straightening their hair, and bleaching their skins. It was to free them from these self-debasing shackles that Carmichael declared: 'Black is beautiful' and 'We're black and beautiful'.

Actually, Carmichael had picked up something articulated fifty years earlier by Marcus Garvey, a charismatic West Indian leader. 'The Anglo-Saxons see beauty in themselves to the exclusion of all others,' Garvey had said. 'The people of Mongolia, the Chinese, the Japanese ... [do the same.] I shall teach the black man to see beauty to the exclusion of all others.'

No matter where the African found himself in the Western world, and in what state of racial purity, he was exhorted by Black Power militants to discard the stigma attached to kinky hair, flared nose and thick lips which the European, through centuries of domination, had impressed on his psyche. The point about being proud of what one *is*, is so fundamental to normal human existence that it allowed no compromise.

What allowed variation was the second plank of the Black Power ideology: the attainment of economic and political muscle. The forms it took and the tactics to be employed varied from country to country, and situation to situation.

America was a country of black islands scattered in the rural counties in the South and the urban centres elsewhere. Given this, the achievement of political power was both feasible and desirable. In Britain there was a concentration of blacks in some factories and services at the local level. Two-thirds of the bus crews in Wolverhampton in the late 1960s were black or Asian. The majority of junior doctors in many hospitals were black or brown, as were the nurses. Many textile mills in West Yorkshire were 50 to 80 per cent coloured. So were paper mills in High Wycombe as well as foundries, bakeries, and rubber and plastic works in the Midlands. The black workers, therefore, found themselves the possessors of industrial power. This gave them a certain leverage in the overall (industrial and political) power relationship.

Then there was the rapidly growing concentration of West Indians and Asians in the inner perimeters of cities and towns. Such a situation was pregnant with a promise of Black Power on the American model. The racial composition of infant and primary schools in these areas was a clear indicator of the future. In 1968, in fourteen out of thirty-three London boroughs, 'immigrant' children constituted 13 to 31 per cent of the total primary school population.[9] Since coloured settlers were not evenly distributed throughout the boroughs, but were concentrated in smaller areas, it meant that coloured enclaves had already formed in Britain.

Such a situation had not developed overnight, nor was it of black settlers' making. It was thrust on them. It was, in the final analysis, the cumulative result of thousands of refusals by white Britons, over a generation, to let accommodation, or sell houses, to blacks.

5 White Rejection, Black Withdrawal

The ghetto is the geographical expression of complete social rejection.

CERI PEACH[1]

Nobody believes that thousands of coloured Britons in Birmingham schools have an equal chance of life ahead of them.

The Midlands correspondent of *The Times*.

Of all the [black] youngsters I talked to, the sudden break with white friends at thirteen or fourteen had left scars and hardened attitudes.

COLIN McGLASHAN, a British journalist.[2]

Before the 1968 Race Relations Act, which outlawed discriminatory advertisements, 'No Coloured' and 'Europeans Only' signs for rooms and flats to let were so common that they hardly evoked comment from racial minorities. Yet these signs were merely the tip of an iceberg. In her 1959 study of the West Indians in North Kensington, London, Ruth Glass, a sociologist, found that only one-sixth of the 'Accommodation Available' advertisements in the local paper specified 'No Coloured'. But when she followed up the 'neutral' advertisements by telephoning 'on behalf of a West Indian friend', only one out of six white landlords was prepared to consider the application.[3] In other words, white landlords not attaching the 'No Coloured' restriction to their advertisements were not colour-blind: they were merely practising the art of English reticence.

The 1967 PEP survey revealed that three out of four accommodation agencies practised racial discrimination. Yet the PEP investigators found half of their coloured respondents living in rented premises.[4] This was not paradoxical since, almost always, their landlords too were coloured.

Avoidance of blacks was what – according to the PEP report – two out of three estates agents were found to be practising. Their stock responses to the black enquirers were: 'No property available' and 'Mortgages will be difficult to get'. If a coloured settler approached an agent with a particular property carrying a 'For Sale' sign in mind, he was frequently told that the house in question was 'under offer'.

Those agents who did business with racial minority members usually did so under special conditions, which were spelled out by such respondents in the PEP survey. Some of them had bought houses by paying cash; others had bribed building society officials, through the agent, to obtain mortgages. Still others had been forced to raise short-term loans from banks and/or friends at high interest rates.

What the buyers got in return were mainly sub-standard or condemned houses in those areas of towns and cities which had been, over the decades, losing population. As had happened earlier in the labour market, black immigrants were offered leavings from the table. And just as certain job categories had over a period of time become 'black', a similar development took place in housing.

The West Indian who succeeded in buying a house almost invariably treated his property as a symbol of his material well-being. He painted and wallpapered it; he often installed a bathroom. The result was a general upgrading of the street. Apart from enjoying better amenities inside his property, the new owner was keen to recover his investment in case he decided to move to another district or town.

Such behaviour ran contrary to the belief prevalent among many white residents that the arrival of black or Asian families in a street lowered property values. Nevertheless, the fear of falling property values, and the popular association of colour with low social status, undesirable social behaviour, and a general downgrading of the area accelerated the rate of exodus of the indigenous population from the twilight zones which had begun long before coloured immigration became substantial. On the other side of the colour line there were, as explained in Chapter Three, practical advantages accruing to newcomers from clustering together. The end result of this two-headed process was an emergence of ethnic enclaves in practically every town and city where coloured immigrants found jobs. And this had happened fairly rapidly. For example, in 1962 only three houses out of fifty-one in Ranelagh Road, Willesden, London, were coloured; in 1969 the number was thirty-four. King Edward Road in Chalvey, Slough, became 90 per cent black in less than six years.

This change was reflected in the racial composition of schools. The Grove Lane Infants' School in Handsworth, Birmingham, for instance, altered from being all-white in 1957 to 80 per cent coloured in 1965. Two years earlier the Conservative Minister of Education had responded to the situation by recommending to the local authorities to disperse 'immigrant children' so that they would not form more than 30 per cent of the rolls of any school.

Later, in June 1965, the Labour administration gave official sanction to the policy of dispersal of 'immigrant children' in the form of a circular by the Department of Education and Science, entitled 'Education of Immigrants'. An 'immigrant child' was later defined as 'a child born overseas, or in the United Kingdom, of immigrant parents who came to the United Kingdom on or after first January ten years previously', although children born in Eire, or of Irish parents, were excepted.[5] It was patently ludicrous to include a child born in the UK in the definition of 'an immigrant child'.

It would have made some sense if the government action had applied to non-English-speaking children. As it was, wherever local authorities followed a dispersal policy it applied to all immigrant children; and this in practice meant coloured children. Paul Stephenson, the local liaison officer in Coventry, asked a class of twelve-year-olds, 'Who is an immigrant?' and received a reply, 'Someone like you.' He was born in Bristol of West Indian parents. When he pointed out that Prince Philip, the Duke of Edinburgh, was an immigrant (having been born abroad), his statement was received with incredulous gasps. In common parlance, the terms 'immigrant' and 'coloured' had become interchangeable.

In the popular mind 'coloured' meant anybody who is not white and caucasian. Hence most Britons made no distinction between West Indians and Asians. This was a continuing symptom of the general incuriosity and indifference with which the British, in their days of the Empire, viewed the 'natives'.

It often took years of day-to-day contact with coloured pupils before British teachers realized that there were basic cultural and socio-psychological dissimilarities between West Indian and Asian children. Outside school these differences were noted by researchers and others in such negative terms as indiscipline and unsatisfactory academic perform-ance among West Indian students.

Describing 'the difficulties affecting the educational attainment of the West Indian immigrants', David Beetham, a researcher, wrote:

> Any generalization must be tentative, though the unanimity of
> opinion on the subject expressed by teachers and Heads is impressive.
> To begin with, there is the problem of language. Though the West
> Indian has English as his native tongue, it differs considerably from
> standard English, not only in vocabulary but in structure and syntax as
> well … When it comes to work which requires sustained effort the
> West Indian seems to lack concentration and staying power. Teachers
> who have experience of both compare the West Indian unfavourably
> with the Asians in this respect. By nature the West Indian is emotional
> and exuberant, and this leads to behaviour problems in school. Some
> attribute these largely to the difference between the educational
> methods employed in the West Indies and here; used to more

Victorian methods of teaching, the immigrant finds it difficult to adapt to the freer discipline of an English school. Others see emotional disturbances as the inevitable reaction to the sudden change from rural surroundings to the urban environment ... Though teachers, therefore, may differ about the precise cause, they nevertheless agree in regarding the West Indians as presenting particular behaviour problems. One teacher ... writes succinctly: 'By nature and upbringing quick, energetic, emotional and noisy, the West Indian disturbs the life of an English school.'[6]

Many teachers attributed West Indian exuberance to the tropical climate in the Caribbean. Yet Asian children, who share with the West Indians all these background elements – Victorian methods of teaching, rural environment and tropical/subtropical climate – did not present behavioural and emotional problems in school. On the contrary they tended to be shy and withdrawn, and did not 'misuse' the new freedom of the British school. Apparently this set of cause-and-effect was superficial. In order to understand correctly the characteristics and personality traits of contemporary Afro-Caribbeans, adults as well as children, one had to study the impact that centuries of slavery had left on them (see Chapter Two).

Beetham's reference to 'the sudden change from rural surroundings to an urban environment' pertained to the practice among the Afro-Caribbean parents settled in Britain of letting their children be raised by elderly female relatives in the Caribbean, and then have them brought over just before they were fifteen. The parents did so partly to comply with the immigration rules and partly to ensure that the child acquired British scholastic qualifications, thus improving his chance of getting better jobs than they themselves had. In this they were to be disappointed. British employers' resistance to placing black school-leavers in jobs other than manual and semi-skilled remained as high as with their elders. Despite the higher number of West Indian school-leavers in the market in the mid-1960s, the 1966 census showed that job distribution among West Indian immigrants in Greater London had not altered since the 1960 census.[7]

In other words, no matter what the educational achievement of a black school-leaver, he was denied the opportunity of a white-collar job. Keith T., a nineteen-year-old Trinidadian, educated entirely in Britain and with three General Certificate of Education 'O' levels, applied for the following jobs in the summer of 1966: 'cleaning offices, selling encyclopaedias, canvassing for laundry orders, doorman at a cinema, bookmaker's assistant, junior clerk and shop assistant'. He was turned down for each one of them, whereas the white youth he was with was offered, or kept in mind for, every one of them.[8]

During the period in question, London had an almost insatiable appetite for office staff. Each year three-fifths of the female and one-fifth of the male school-leavers in the metropolitan area found work in offices. This was certainly not the case with black youths. Their employment in offices was still rare. Those few who were hired as shop assistants or usherettes in local cinemas were often to be found only in the areas of coloured settlement.

Outside the capital the picture was bleak. In the summer of 1968 the vast city centre of Wolverhampton, for instance, did not have a single black or brown shop assistant. The explanations given by large stores as well as small shops were: 'There just weren't any vacancies', and 'The coloured community, in any case, can't speak English well enough'.[9]

In short, the skilled and 'face-to-face' jobs that had been more or less out of the reach of the adult black immigrants continued to elude their children. Like their parents the black youths ultimately found work; but the time and effort spent by the Youth Employment Officers was quite staggering.

During the period 1966–8 in London, where there were three jobs for every two school-leavers, the Youth Employment Officers described their experiences thus: 'It takes three times as much effort to place a coloured school-leaver as the white'; 'Placing a coloured youth is as difficult as placing a physically handicapped white youth'; and 'They [coloured youths] are in the same position as women used to be'.

It was not uncommon in the late 1960s to meet black youths in London who had been jobless for many months after leaving school. More than half of the 143 unemployed youths at the Brixton Youth Employment Office in December 1968 were coloured,[10] though they constituted only one-seventh of the total secondary school population in the area. According to a survey published in June 1970, the unemployment of young West Indian males in some areas of London was at least four times the national average for all races and age groups.[11]

This situation needs to be viewed against a changing background, physical, psychological and economic. First, the old stock explanations of white employers – 'They don't know English'; 'They speak English with a peculiar accent'; 'They don't have British qualifications'; 'They don't know our way of life' – were becoming outdated as more and more black youths left British schools, speaking English with local accents, and having undergone longer and longer periods of schooling in Britain. Unlike their parents, black youths made comparisons with their white classmates. 'Why do they [the employers] say "No job" when my white classmate after me gets one?' asked a puzzled and angry West Indian youth from Handsworth.

Second, the absolute and relative numbers of racial minority school-leavers were rising sharply. Simultaneously, the nature of demand in the labour market was changing. There was less and less need for blue-collar jobs, and more and more for white-collar.[12]

Third, black youths disliked the idea of accepting unskilled and manual semi-skilled jobs even more than their parents. They knew from their parents' experience that 'If you start with a broom you'll end up with a broom.' So they found means of breaking the vicious circle by trying hard and long for suitable jobs, or by staying at school longer and/or going to university or college. All along they were persuaded by school authorities to lower their sights – that is, take the typecast jobs their parents had.

Fourth, working in jobs they disliked engendered dissatisfaction and a general grievance against white society. The author's informal interviews with black youths in 1968 made him conclude that only one in five considered his work satisfactory.[13] A study by Peter Figueroa in north London showed that of those West Indian school-leavers who had failed to get the job of their choice, more than half expressed dissatisfaction (compared with only one in eleven English boys), and that far more West Indians wanted to leave their present job than whites.[14]

Fifth, most black teenagers did not share their parents' awe of whites, or their obsequious dependence on them. The differences went beyond the normal generation gap. For, unlike their parents – born in the Caribbean and reared by their ancestors and the education system on stories of Britain as the land of hope and glory and of 'Queen Victoria the Good' – the youngsters born and brought up in the United Kingdom had no such illusions. Also, growing up in this country meant that the vision of the youngsters was not distorted by the physical distance between the West Indies and Britain which, in their parents' case, gave British society a certain glitter. Young West Indians grew up sharing classrooms with white British children, an experience that provided them with a yardstick against which to measure their own progress and behaviour patterns. All this made them less likely to accept meekly inequitable treatment by whites.

However, if experience at school familiarized black children with whites, it also made them aware of their racial difference, often through ridicule. Early black arrivals at school suffered most. 'Before I came to this country [thirteen years ago] I had no idea of whites,' recalled Sydney Harris, a nineteen-year-old West Indian in north London. 'But when you go to school here, you're made to realize the difference. The white kids pick on you and pick on you. First you try to bribe them – sweets, ices, the lot. But then one day you can't stand it any more. You get vicious, real vicious; and you lick them.' Such experiences were at odds with the view, widely held in governmental circles then, that the smaller the size of the black community the better the chance of its 'integration'.

This perspective was often linked with another: racial integration in schools would grow and spread to the rest of society. Despite its popularity in official and semi-official circles, this view too could not be sustained by what actually happened.

At the end of a long enquiry in 1963 the Midlands correspondent of *The Times* concluded that integration at school had few lasting effects and that white and black boys were to be seen leaving school separately. Whatever black–white friendships developed were not continued outside the school; or, if they were, they were seldom maintained beyond the years of puberty. Almost invariably it was the whites who rejected the blacks. 'From four until fourteen I grew up with white friends,' said Louis, a West Indian youth in London. 'Then they started acting cold. I couldn't join their conversations. I was always left out when they went anywhere. Their mothers looked at me like I was a leper. Now I don't see any of them.'15

However disappointing these rebuffs might have been to black adolescents, their parents were not surprised. After all, many of them had undergone similar experiences. During their early years of arrival most West Indians had invited their white workmates to parties as well as christening and wedding ceremonies. Very few whites had accepted, and fewer still had turned up. In any case, West Indians were seldom, if ever, invited by whites in return. So they got the message, and stopped their friendly gestures.

It so happened that the continual rejection of black schoolmates by whites was accompanied by a steady growth in the number of black students – a situation which released blacks from the pressure to mix with whites during school breaks and in the playground, and simultaneously enabled them to create a self-contained social life. Besides that, larger numbers helped them to counter the fear engendered by the overwhelming presence of whites both inside and outside school.

As children grow older their awareness of and contact with the adult world increases, as does the importance and frequency of their out-of-school activities. In the 1960s black children saw no evidence of social integration between races in the adult world: they did not, for example, notice racially mixed groups of adults walking in the streets, or entering or leaving pubs or restaurants together. At home their families neither visited white friends socially nor were they visited by whites. The only whites calling at their homes were those who had to do so in the course of their jobs – meter-readers, postmen, child welfare officers, social workers and policemen.

In his social circle the black adolescent seldom, if ever, met West Indians with authority or social status. The relatives, friends and neighbours he knew were nearly always factory workers, transport employees or nurses. Persons with power – teachers, youth employment officers, policemen, magistrates, driving-test examiners, Labour Exchange officials – were almost always white. The only institution where he saw black people in authority was the Pentecostal Church, but then the congregation there too was all black. His social life remained limited to contacts with fellow West Indians. The only place outside school where he could mix with whites was the youth club, if there was one in his district.

By the late 1960s the youth clubs had proved to be the prototypes of factories. That is, they either remained all-white, barring blacks, or became predominantly black; or, if they managed to stay multiracial, they became places where voluntary segregation was practised and accepted. 'It is virtually impossible to find an integrated youth club in the area,' said Bill Harte, a senior white youth officer in Brixton, in 1969. 'Sometimes you'll find one which has about one-quarter West Indian membership, but when you go there you'll see them standing by themselves in a corner.'

One of the main reasons given by West Indians for preferring black youth clubs was 'the bad behaviour of English youths'; the other being, 'Black people speak the same language as me'.

In this regard the national situation was summed up by the House of Commons Select Committee on Race Relations and Immigration in 1969 thus: 'There was an apparently successful multi-racial club in Ealing [London]. Mainly coloured clubs in Wolverhampton and Huddersfield, and all-coloured clubs in Liverpool and Hackney [London], also appeared to be active. But all such clubs rapidly change their membership and activity. In particular the success of a multi-racial club, as such, may be short-lived. They tend, all too soon, to become all-coloured or all-white.'[16] Apparently, youth clubs were already reflecting the values and attitudes of the adult world. Temperamental differences and racial antipathy were proving to be insurmountable barriers against creating inter-racial understanding and friendship.

In April 1968 Enoch Powell, a senior Conservative politician, was widely criticized for devoting a whole speech to the subjects of race and immigration, and for using highly charged language. (The speech is discussed in Part III, Chapter Four.) Long before his speech, voluntary separation of races among youths as well as adults had become an accepted norm. None the less, many whites and blacks were jolted out of their complacency by Powell's words. In the case of West Indians, after their initial anger and apprehension had subsided, the event accelerated their search for identity.

In the Caribbean, this process had begun a decade earlier as the hold of British imperialism loosened and as the politics of new African states, particularly the Congo (renamed Zaïre), acquired international importance. Describing a procession in Port of Spain, Trinidad, some weeks after the assassination in 1960 of the Congolese Prime Minister and militant nationalist Patrice Lumumba, V. S. Naipaul, a Trinidadian by birth, wrote:

> It was an orderly procession made up wholly of negroes. They were singing hymns, [carrying] banners and placards [which] were anti-white, anti-clerical and pro-African in an ill-defined, inclusive way. I had never before seen anything like it in Trinidad … I thought then that it was a purely local eruption, created by the pressure of local politics. But soon, on the journey I was now getting ready to make, I came to see that such eruptions were widespread, and represented feelings coming to the surface in negro communities throughout the Caribbean.[17]

6 Black Consciousness: An Afro Identity

It is simplicity itself ... to link West Indians in Britain with those in the Caribbean and the Americas, and with their African brothers and sisters everywhere.

NEVILLE MAXWELL[1]

My ancestors were Africans taken to the New World to do a job, so obviously I'm not detached. And I cannot see myself or any other black person being detached from his African heritage.

LANCE DUNKLEY, a West Indian leader in
Wolverhampton, 1969.

Events in the Congo/Zaïre in 1960–61 caused many people in the Caribbean to identify themselves openly with Africa, whereas the Afro-Caribbean minority in Britain needed the stimuli of two immigration laws, four race riots and the emotive speeches of Enoch Powell to consider the issue of their origin. The explanation for this delayed reaction by the black settlers lay partly in their status as immigrants – wherein they seemed primarily concerned with their personal and economic problems of survival, with little interest or energy left over to ponder the abstract question of self-identity – and partly in their historico-cultural background.

Though emancipated from bonded slavery the freed men and women remained psychologically locked in their past, servile to the values embedded in their psyche. 'The West Indian negro knows nothing of Africa except that it is a term of reproach,' wrote Anthony Trollope in 1860. 'If African immigrants are put to work on the same estate with him, he will not work beside them, or drink with them, or walk with them.'[2] This attitude was coupled with constant insistence by the post-Emancipation, educated West Indians that they belonged, exclusively, to Western civilization. 'It is necessary to see ourselves in perspective as far as we can to recognize that ours is ... a part of that great branch of civilization that is called Western civilization,' wrote Dr Hugh Springer in the *Caribbean Quarterly* a century after the publication of Trollope's journal. 'Our culture is rooted in Western culture and our values, in the main, are the values of the Christian-Hellenic tradition ...

the Greek ideals of virtue and knowledge and the Christian faith.'[3] This statement illustrated as well as any other the persistent refusal by many Afro-Caribbeans, especially those of the middle class, to come to grips with their past.

For many West Indians, migration to Britain was a continuation of the same self-denial, a part of the psychological flight undertaken in the belief that residence in Britain would bestow upon them the inheritance of a Christian-Hellenic civilization, and release them, for ever, from the chains of their African heritage. But discriminatory experiences in Britain led many to examine their past. 'We had heard about slavery in Jamaica but we didn't sort of put it together and put ourselves within it,' said Dorothy Pearson, a West Indian nurse in Slough. 'We didn't think it happened to the people we descended from. We thought it was some-body else or some other people we didn't know about. But, coming to this country, you get to realize that we're part of slavery.'

Life in Britain also caused the West Indians to conclude, with much pain and sorrow, that Western civilization was the prerogative of white people, and that colour differences counted far more than cultural affinity. The result was that most West Indians ceased trying to be accepted in white Western society and limited themselves to socializing with fellow West Indians, while still nursing a sneaking hope that at least their descendants, born and bred in Britain, would be considered and treated as inheritors of British civilization. 'No matter how white people hurt you, you're still not inclined to be really divorced from them,' said Patricia Fullwood, a West Indian housewife in Wolverhampton. 'There's something between us, this love–hate. There shouldn't be, but there is.' In this hope they were to be disappointed. 'They [black children] learn English history, but when they want to join English society they're shut out and there's nowhere [else] they can go,' said a West Indian social worker in London in 1967.[4] A year later he heard Enoch Powell declaring that a West Indian or Asian did not, by being born in England, become an Englishman.

The cumulative effect on the young West Indians of the general behaviour of the white British, the speeches of Powell and the continual discussion of race and immigration in the media, especially from 1968 onwards, came to undermine their belief that they were British.

To some, this development might have seemed undesirable, even cruel; but it had its merits, the principal one being that it signified a halt to the traditional West Indian flight from the past, and his unwillingness to face his problem of identity and origin. 'Each day I'm getting more aware of the fact that I'm black because of the situations that one comes up against,' said a West Indian nurse in Wolverhampton. 'Sometimes you feel, oh, the white person and myself are equal, but there's always something there to tell you that you're not the same, even though you speak the same language, eat the same food, and have the same customs. Therefore you try to find out your background, and the customs of your ancestors.'

Part of the credit for this development went to Enoch Powell. Black militants were openly thankful to him for helping them achieve in a year what might otherwise have taken them a decade. Mainly due to his speeches, the socio-political awareness of the West Indians in Britain increased.

In the Caribbean, however, they did not need the stimulus of an Enoch Powell to spur them to examine their past. Political independence since the early 1960s meant that each island had to write its own history, and erect a pantheon of national heroes, to help the inhabitants feel a sense of national identity. As a result, previously ignored leaders of slave revolts, and leaders of movements which emphasized self-pride and African heritage, were resurrected and accorded the status of national heroes. For instance, the late Marcus Garvey, much maligned and ridiculed during his lifetime by the Jamaican power élite, was declared a national hero by the government of independent Jamaica. Garvey had died penniless in London in 1940: in 1964 his body was flown home to be reburied in the Jamaican capital of Kingston with full state honours.

At universities and colleges much intellectual energy was channelled into examining those elements of creole life which were of African origin and which had hitherto been ignored or altogether denied by the European-oriented élite in the Caribbean. It had by then been established that popular culture and folklore in the West Indies had much in common with African traditions. The rhythm of creole speech was noticed to parallel that of West African speech. The 'nonsense' words in the creole language were recognized as derivatives of African words. Many Caribbean dishes, such as callalou, cachop and cou-cou, and the method of preparing soup were shown to have African origins.

The natural rhythm and grace with which most blacks in the Caribbean and America danced were related to their ancestors in Africa, where dancing was more a form of self- and communal expression than a means of entertainment. Describing the various body movements in '[African] war dances, victory dances, stage dances, remedial dances etc.', Dunduzu Chisiza wrote: 'We nod our heads, rock our necks, tilt our heads and pause. We shake our shoulders, throw them back and forth, bounce breasts and halt … We rhythmically shake our hefty rear ends, our tummies duck and peer, our legs quick march, slow march, tap dripple, quiver and tremble while our feet perform feats. "Dance!" [5] Afro-Caribbeans danced with the same ecstatic abandon as Africans.

Neville Maxwell, a West Indian leader, pointed out that African customs and beliefs had been retained, in essence, in the Shango dance in Trinidad, Grenada and Jamaica as well as in the voodoo and obeah cults throughout the Caribbean. The Trinidadian calypso, too, was African in origin, 'a very important aspect of the "oral", as against the "written", tradition of the African'.[6]

In religion, African beliefs and practices had been amalgamated with conventional Christian practices; and the result was the Pentecostal Church (see Chapter Three). Many of these churches in the Caribbean had their headquarters in America; and thus West Indian Christians maintained contact with their 'soul brothers and sisters' in the United States. In addition to these formal, religious contacts, there was increasing communication between Caribbean intellectuals, writers and politicians and their counterparts in black America and Britain. A three-way dialogue between the black people in the West Indies, the US and Britain developed rapidly. The elements that brought blacks in the Western world together were: race and common history, search for identity, and growing interest in Africa and Black Power.

Already the term Black Power had proved so popular with the masses in the Caribbean that many conventional, old-style politicians could not resist publicly supporting the idea. 'I say Jamaica must restore to her sense of independence and nationhood a basic pride and hope – respect of dignity and self-confidence – which are expressed in that great phrase which ... I salute: "Black Power"!' said Norman Manley, former Prime Minister of Jamaica, in the autumn of 1968. Some time later the Jamaican Prime Minister, Hugh Shearer, made a similar statement – as did Vere C. Bird of Antigua.[7] However, this was by common consent the 'moderate' version of Black Power, which emphasized only racial pride and neglected the economic dimension. It was considered inadequate by many radical Caribbean intellectuals, industrial workers, young urban lumpenproletariat and some segments of the armed forces. These radical elements wished to engineer a social revolution to free the West Indies from its subjugation to 'the white economic power structure' consisting of multinational corporations based in America, Britain and Canada. They seemed to have substantial support.

It was indeed to pacify this force in Trinidadian politics, manifesting itself in March 1970 in the form of massive demonstrations, that Prime Minister Eric Williams said: 'The fundamental feature of the demonstrations was the insistence on Black dignity, the manifestation of Black consciousness and the demand for Black economic power ... If this is Black Power, then I am for Black Power.'[8] However, Williams followed up this statement with the arrest of prominent Black Power leaders, thus precipitating a rebellion by a considerable section of the military, which he quickly crushed.

Radical Black Power parties existed in almost all the West Indian islands, bearing such varied names as the Black Panthers and the Young Power (in Trinidad), the Progressive Labour Party (in Bermuda), or the Educational Forum for the People (in St Vincent). They maintained informal contacts with Black Power movements in America and Britain. Roosevelt Brown, a PLP leader in Bermuda, was elected a member of the Black Power Conference in Philadelphia, USA, in August 1968. As a result the first Caribbean Black Power Conference was held in Bermuda in July 1969. It was attended by 200 delegates from the Caribbean, America and Africa, an unprecedented event which emphasized identity of colour.

Along with this went actions. In October 1968 when Walter Rodney, a Guyanese lecturer and a radical Black Power advocate, was banned from returning to the University of the West Indies at Mona, Jamaica, the students rebelled in protest. Troops had to be called in to restore order. To show their disapproval, many Jamaican nationals in London staged a sit-in at their High Commission. At the time of the Commonwealth Prime Ministers' Conference in London in January 1969, black citizens demonstrated in support of black Rhodesians against the white minority government in Rhodesia (later Zimbabwe). When a Nigerian diplomat in Brixton, London, was manacled by the police for a motoring offence, many West Indians in the area protested and obstructed the police, for which some of them were arrested and charged.

During the summers of 1969 and 1970, militant black groups staged at least six demonstrations in London and Manchester to protest against police harassment and maltreatment of blacks. Meanwhile, many black organizations in Britain, moderate as well as radical, undertook projects of self-help and education. The militant Universal Coloured People's Association and the Black Panthers pursued their aim of spreading 'black consciousness' by holding periodic meetings in London and Manchester where Black poetry was recited, Black music played and Black films shown. The moderate West Indian League set up its own youth club in London, and so did the Willesden West Indian Association. Volunteers from the West Indian Student Centre at Earl's Court, London, travelled to London's black districts to coach children in school subjects as well as

Black history. A Free University for Africans, Asians and West Indian studies was launched in London in September 1969 by the British Black Power Party.

It was obvious that more West Indians were joining more organizations and attending more meetings than ever before. In the wake of Enoch Powell's April 1968 speech, old, defunct organizations were revived, and new ones founded.

As for the militants, they already had an active national body: the Black People's Alliance. Representatives of more than fifty organizations affiliated to it met periodically in the Midlands. The number of Black Power militants in 1969 was estimated, by the Home Office's Special Branch, at 2000.[9]

Numbers aside, it is more meaningful to judge the undramatic, socio-psychological change that the black community underwent by examining the proportion of West Indian girls who stopped straightening their hair, the extent to which West Indians ceased to consider the word 'black' pejorative, and the attitude they held towards Africa in general, and African settlers in Britain in particular. In all these areas signs of change were unmistakable. In Leeds, for instance, nearly a third of West Indian girls had 'gone natural' in their hair-style. When asked to tick off the appropriate term to describe their race – coloured, black, negro – two-thirds of the young West Indian males in a random survey conducted by the author in London (in 1968) chose 'black'.

Most significantly, change was to be noticed in the attitude of the young as well as old Afro-Caribbeans towards West African settlers in Britain. Until recently, locked in their historic conditioning, the Afro-Caribbeans and West Africans eyed one another warily from a distance. The Afro-Caribbeans thought Africans 'savage' and 'uncivilized'; whereas most Africans considered Afro-Caribbeans as 'descendants of slaves'. This changed. Africans were now warmly welcomed in Afro-Caribbean circles as 'brothers and sisters'. Together they blamed the white man for warping their minds and creating the gulf that had existed between them for so long.

The young Afro-Caribbeans were even more interested in Africa and Africans. The scene of Tarzan knocking down six Africans with one swipe no longer amused them. It offended. 'Films and television about Africa always showed the bad things about black races, never the achievements,' said Barry, an Afro-Caribbean youth in London, reflecting a widely held view.[10]

Nor were the images and descriptions of Africans swinging from trees, and eating one another, accepted as true because, as many Afro-Caribbeans argued, all the books had been written by whites. 'But even if these stories are true, it was the way people lived there,' said Kate McNish, a West Indian teacher in Wolverhampton. 'It was their way of life.' Most Afro-Caribbeans, it seemed, ceased to feel ashamed or apologetic about their African ancestry. Consequently when they saw West Africans with their tribal marks or in native dress they no longer sneered but, instead, respected this as a manifestation of a way of life which was different from white people's. The West Africans in Britain practising their native customs provided living evidence to the Afro-Caribbeans that they had not always been black duplicates of a white culture.

Though black, and negroid by race, the West African could be distinguished from the Afro-Caribbean by his accent, dress, hair-style and mannerisms. At the less obvious, psychological level, too, his attitudes and behaviour towards whites were different from those of the Afro-Caribbean, because of the differences in their historical experiences with the whites. Unlike the Afro-Caribbean, the West African did not undergo a traumatic uprooting nor did he suffer the indignity of slavery. Hence he had not developed the feeling of 'intimate enmity' towards the British that the Afro-Caribbean had.[11] He did not suffer from the anxiety and neurosis about his colour that was part of the Afro-Caribbean sub-conscious. He did not wish to be white, nor was he a product of a 'white-biased' society. Indeed, in his culture white was the colour of death. He did not suffer from self-contempt, nor did he wish to run away from his past. Quite the contrary. West Africans were rooted in their past and their own socio-cultural tradition. Though they were governed by the British for about a century, the foreign rulers did not interfere with their tribal system and social structure. Hence their sense of cultural being was not impaired.

Later, migration to Britain did not disrupt their social continuity, or undermine their loyalty to their tribe, religion or language. They remained Yorubas, Ibos, Hausas or Fantis, especially when these tribal origins were recognized and accepted by the West African community in Britain, and also because their close friendships and immediate social life tended to revolve around members of the same tribe. Many African women retained ethnic dress. As a rule West Africans maintained a much greater interest in their country of origin and did not seek to submerge themselves into British society. Like the Asians in Britain, they never fully gave up the idea of ultimately returning to their home country.

Furthermore, the West African retained a strong sense of the family, with its well-defined structure of rights and obligations. As a father he took a keen interest in the future of his children, who in return offered him respect. He encouraged them to be studious and ambitious; and he expected them to look after him in his old age.

In his dealings with white people the West African was likely to be more natural and self-assured than the Afro-Caribbean. He was also more likely to take his exploitative landlord to the rent tribunal, and more inclined to enter private business. He believed in himself and was very much a man on his own.

The main reason why cultural and social differences between the West Africans and Afro-Caribbeans did not attract popular, or even academic, interest was the imbalance between the size of the two communities. Compared with the Afro-Caribbeans, the number of West Africans was small. Furthermore, they were not concentrated in a particular district of the British conurbations, but were scattered throughout the areas of coloured settlement. Hence no single district with a special flavour of West African life has emerged. If it had, it would most likely have been a cross between the Afro-Caribbean and Asian settlements.

7 Rise of Rastafarianism

British-born Jamaicans cannot look forward to return home, because they are home. Neither Jamaican nor fully English, they often look to their blackness as a basis for identification.

NANCY FONER[1]

For whites there's always been Teds, Skins, Mods, Rockers, Punks; but for blacks there's never been anything they could really identify with that was really culturally theirs, until Rastas came along.

A West Indian male.[2]

In the 1970s many young West Indians came to identify with Africa as the continent of their origin, in particular with the Ethiopia of Haile Selassie. This was the result of an amalgam of social, educational, psychological and economic factors.

The seventies witnessed a rapid increase in the number of British-educated Afro-Caribbeans. They grew up in families which continued to suffer racial discrimination. The 1971 census revealed that while only a third of the national labour force worked in manufacturing, about a half of coloured immigrants did so.[3] In service industry black and Asian settlers were to be found mainly in catering, public transport and the National Health Service. The disproportion could be gauged from the fact that while West Indian and Asian immigrants formed less than 3 per cent of the national population in the mid-1970s, they supplied a quarter of the workforce in restaurants and cafés. They furnished about a third of hospital staff, a little over one-fifth of student nurses and midwives, and about one-sixth of general practitioners in the National Health Service of England and Wales.[4]

A more detailed profile of the disadvantage endured by the racial minorities was provided by the surveys conducted between 1973 and 1975 by Political and Economic Planning Ltd. These involved a representative sample of 3300 West Indians and Asians as well as a comparative sample of whites; 300 factories; and ten local authorities.

An enquiry conducted at the manufacturing plants, consisting of interviews and case studies, revealed discrimination prevalent at more than half. In unskilled jobs West Indian and Asian applicants encountered discrimination in 46 per cent of the cases. When it came to white-collar work, 30 per cent of them faced discrimination at the initial stage of a written application whereas the figure for Italian applicants was 10 per cent. (The Italian subjects were used in order to differentiate between the disadvantage stemming from foreignness and that from colour.) Typically, an employer informed a West Indian applicant that due to the oil crisis (of 1974) the company management had decided against increasing the sales staff, while the same day he offered an interview to a white job-seeker.[5]

The class profile of the West Indian community outlined by the PEP surveys differed sharply from that of the white British. At 32 per cent, the proportion of the West Indians engaged in unskilled and semi-skilled manual work was nearly twice the percentage for whites. At the other end of the spectrum, at 8 per cent, the West Indian males engaged in non-manual pursuits were about one-fifth the figure for white men.[6]

These PEP surveys revealed that whereas four-fifths of whites with academic degrees were in professional or managerial positions, only about a third of West Indians and Asians with similar degrees were so placed, with another quarter of them engaged in manual work. Similar results were obtained from an enquiry into the hiring practices of the Civil Service in 1976. A study of the recruitment of clerks by the Department of Health and Social Security showed that the 18 per cent success rate of the racial minority applicants was one-third of the whites'. Of the 100 clerks already employed, 30 were over-qualified, with 23 of those being Afro-Caribbean or Asian. This confirmed a prevalent belief that many non-whites accepted jobs below their qualification level.[7]

Summarizing the overall situation, David J. Smith stated in 1974:

> The minority groups ... are concentrated within the lower job
> levels in a way that cannot be explained by lower academic or job
> qualifications; within broad categories of jobs they have lower
> earnings than whites, particularly at the higher end of the job scale;
> they tend to shiftwork, which is generally thought to be undesirable,
> but shiftwork premiums do not raise their earnings above those of
> whites, because the jobs are intrinsically badly paid; they are
> concentrated within certain plants, and they have to make about twice
> as many applications as whites before finding a job.

This was so primarily because, as Smith explained elsewhere, 'Few employers have taken steps to ensure that members of minority groups have equal opportunity in recruitment, in promotion or in access to training.'[8]

The quadrupling of oil prices in late 1973 fuelled inflation, and this in turn damaged the British economy. The number of unemployed rose steadily. Racial minorities suffered more than the white majority. When the supply of labour exceeded demand, employers gave added preference to white applicants over black or brown. Between 1974 and 1980 the jobless total rose by 130 per cent, whereas the figure for the Afro-Caribbeans and Asians increased by 290 per cent.[9] A survey of 500 white and black school-leavers in the London borough of Lewisham published by the Commission for Racial Equality in 1978 showed that the unemployment rate among blacks was three times that of whites. Black as well as white jobless were actively seeking employment, with two-thirds of the blacks believing that employers were discriminating against them. Overall, however, the educational achievement of the black sample was lower than that of the white.[10]

Apparently, under-achievement at school was a major contributory factor in creating high unemployment among young Afro-Caribbeans. Indeed the two were mutually reinforcing. By the early 1970s it had become clear that black schoolchildren were three times more likely than whites to be categorized as educationally subnormal (ESN), and that comparatively fewer of them continued their studies beyond the secondary level. It had become clear too that the selective systems in use at school worked against them. 'All three biases against the West Indian child – cultural, middle class and emotional-disturbance – apply as much to the *actual questions asked on the IQ [Intelligence Quotient] test* administered to the children, and the very nature of *"the test situation"*,' noted Bernard Coard, a West Indian teacher at an ESN school in London. 'The vocabulary and style of all these IQ tests is white middle class ... The black working class child, who had different life experiences, finds great difficulty in answering many of the questions, even if he is very intelligent. The very fact of being "tested" is a foreign experience to many black children.'[11]

While black teachers such as Bernard Coard blamed the inadequacy of schools' resources and procedures for the under-achievement of black pupils, others explained their poor performance, implicitly or explicitly, in terms of their hereditary deficiencies.

As for the black child, he faced still another major perplexing and depressing element: lack of a viable alternative to the British culture in his domestic environment. 'No one told me about Marcus Garvey, Paul Bogle, [and other] national heroes of Jamaica,' said a young Afro-Caribbean in High Wycombe. 'There are a lot of black people who have contributed to history but have never been mentioned. So, at school you have no feeling of worth as a black people. All you're doing is learning about another man's culture.'[12] In short, by failing to provide the Afro-Caribbean pupil with positive information about and back-up on the black people's achievements, teachers and parents allowed a negative self-image to take root in the child's mind. It was against this background that the West Indian pupil faced selective tests which were biased against the working class in general, white or black. His poor performance in these tests reinforced a feeling of deficiency and failure. His relegation to a disciplinary or remedial class made the situation worse by providing white teachers with evidence of the inherent intellectual inferiority of Afro-Caribbeans and strengthening their stereotypes of black children. Referring to a study by the National Foundation for Educational Research concerning the responses of white teachers to certain questions about children from 'different backgrounds', Professor Alan Little of London University stated: 'The teachers as a group saw West Indian children as being "stupid" and being "trouble makers" – very clear negative stereotypes.'[13]

Afro-Caribbeans responded to this situation in different, yet complementary, ways. Socially aware black parents combined their protest against the placing of their progeny into educationally subnormal classes with demands that the school should provide multi-ethnic education and Black Studies courses to all children, and supplementary coaching for their children. As for the bulk of the Afro-Caribbean under-achievers, they increasingly turned to a doctrine which encouraged them to find self-esteem in their blackness and African roots. It was called Rastafarianism, or merely 'Rasta'.

> Black activists highlighted the racism built into the school curriculum.
> In this they were assisted by white anti-racists who had by the early
> 1970s established Teachers Against Racism and the National
> Association for Multi-Racial Education. Together they advocated
> incorporating Black Studies courses into the school curriculum so that
> all pupils, white or otherwise, would be exposed to them.

They pointed out that history texts routinely glorified Abraham Lincoln and William Wilberforce as the leading abolitionists who brought about the emancipation of African slaves, but ignored the slaves' own efforts, organized and spontaneous, in their long struggle for liberation. For instance, slaves in the British West Indies revolted 73 times during the eighteenth century. Geography lessons described the Third World states as poor entities dependent on financial and other aid from the West without stressing the dependence of the Western nations on their crops and raw materials, and the mechanisms by which they manipulated the prices of these commodities to their own benefit. Much needed to be done to balance the view long held by whites, that they had altruistically undertaken a 'God-given' duty to improve the fate of the African heathen, with the historical facts: that the Europeans avariciously exploited the human and natural resources of Africa, totally oblivious to the damage they inflicted on indigenous cultures and societies. By so doing, argued the anti-racist lobbyists, the educational system would make black pupils feel that they were as much participants in learning as passive recipients of it.

Though this argument had much intellectual weight, its proponents faltered in their attempts to have it accepted and implemented by the authorities. A pioneering self-help organization called the Afro-Caribbean Educational Resource Project, founded in 1976, failed to secure funds, and folded the next year. It was only after the Commission for Racial Equality, an official body, decided in 1981 to concentrate on changes in the schools' curriculum to reflect the multicultural aspect of contemporary British society that some progress was made. By 1983 a quarter of the country's 115 education authorities had adopted multicultural policies. This had not happened a day too soon; for by then the proportion of Afro-Caribbean and Asian pupils in the schools in the Inner London Education Authority area, for instance, had gone beyond 20 per cent.

Outside school, young Afro-Caribbeans had found their remedy for the myopic attitudes of white society and its power wielders. Many of them had taken to Rastafarianism in varying degrees.

Originating in Jamaica, Rastafarianism focused on Ras Tafari, son of Ras Makonnen of Harar, who in 1930 was crowned Emperor of Ethiopia – as Haile Selassie, King of Kings and Lord of Lords, Conquering Lion of Judah. This event was hailed by, among others, Marcus Garvey, who was aware of the defeat that independent Abyssinia/Ethiopia had inflicted on the invading Italians in 1896. As the only truly independent black country in Africa, with its own Orthodox Church, Ethiopia had a special place in the heart and mind of Garvey. 'We have great hopes of Ethiopia in the East – the country that has kept her tradition even back to the days of Solomon,' he wrote in *The Blackman* of 30 October 1930. 'They are part of the great African race that is to rise from the handicaps, environments and difficulties to repossess the Imperial authority that is promised by God himself in the inspiration that Princes shall come out of Egypt and Ethiopia stretching forth her hands.'[14] Taking their cue from Revelation 19:11 and 16, the strict followers of the Bible among them concluded that Haile Selassie was King of Kings. Acceptance of Haile Selassie as a messiah implied instituting a link between Christianity and blackness in place of the hitherto unchallenged tie between Christianity and whiteness – a psychological revolution.

From the inception of the movement in Jamaica in the early 1930s, the followers of Ras Tafari – called Rastafarians (or Rastas) – took to wearing long hair and beards. During the next decade, when pictures of Ethiopian fighters became available in Jamaica, the Rastas copied the Ethiopian hair-style by twisting their long hair into coils, called dreadlocks. The general idea was to challenge the prevalent white-dominated Jamaican view of beauty by looking as African and fearsome as possible. By the early 1940s, Ethiopia had been occupied by fascist Italy, Haile Selassie had established the Ethiopian World Federation Incorporated to spawn racial solidarity, and the Rastafarians in Jamaica had formed the United Afro-West Indian Brotherhood.

Rastafarianism is a millenarian movement which perceives the world as composed of good/Zion and evil/Babylon. Its followers consider themselves as the reincarnation of the ancient tribes of Israel, who had been taken into exile by their slave-masters working for Babylon – the kingdom whose ruler Nebuchadnezzar (604–562 BC) had enslaved the Jews in their homeland and dragged them to his realm. To them Haile Selassie was a messiah, Jah: a fact which, they claimed, deliberate mistranslations of the Bible had withheld from the faithful. He was capable of destroying the contemporary Babylon/Jamaica, and leading his followers back to Zion/Africa, where they would live as free and dignified human beings. Indeed, Rastafarians believed that repatriation to Zion/Africa was inevitable as it was foretold by biblical prophecy. In short, Rastafarianism emerged as an amalgam of African redemption and negritude, pride in being black African. So deep was the belief of Rastafarians in the divinity of Haile Selassie that his death in jail on 27 August 1975 (after his overthrow by leftist military leaders a year earlier) left them claiming that he had acquired 'another form' and gone into hiding.

In the Britain of the early 1970s the soil was ripe for the Rastafarian seed to germinate. The rise of the Black Power movement in the late 1960s had engendered a general consciousness of how colour was the prime determinant of the lowly status of blacks in a white society. At the same time the rapid popularity of this radical doctrine had alarmed the British government and led its agencies to prosecute its leaders, often for inciting racial hatred, and disrupt its meetings. By 1971 the largest formal organization advocating Black Power, the Universal Coloured People's Association, had disintegrated.

It was against this background that two Jamaican settlers, Immanuel Fox and Gabriel Adams, set up a local branch of the Ethiopian World

Federation Incorporated in London after a visit to Kingston, Jamaica, in 1971. The slums of Kingston were then throbbing with reggae music, developed by deprived youths, many of them Rastas, driven to make a living through music and dance. They developed music for dancing in open-air yards, based on the traditional African drumming, praising the virtues of Africa in general and Ethiopia in particular. Out of this arose political and socio-religious songs – like 'Man to man is so unjust', 'Why men must suffer', 'Africa must be free, Blackman must be free, Rastafari', and 'By the rivers of Babylon' – sung to the tunes of rock and reggae music, with the dancers waving the red, black and green flag of Ethiopia. (During his state visit to Jamaica in 1966, Haile Selassie had received a rapturous welcome by the people.) By the late 1960s reggae music had become a popular vehicle to examine the injustices of society and uphold the Rastafarian concepts of African redemption and negritude. The speciality of reggae lay in its 'dread tunes' – involving African drumming, improvisation and rhythmic syncopation – which conveyed an odd mixture of menace and calm. Reggae thus evolved as an integral part of the radical politics of Kingston's shanty-towns. In 1973 this music began arriving in Britain from Jamaica. A year later when Bob Marley, a member of the Jamaican band called Twelve Tribes of Israel, emerged as a cult figure among young Jamaicans, reggae became hugely popular among Afro-Caribbean youngsters in Britain.

Reggae proved to be the principal agent through which Rastafarianism won converts in this country. The version of the doctrine which prevailed here was somewhat different from that popular in Jamaica, the parental version being strong on religion and the Bible. The outward modes, however, were the same: the dreadlocks covered with a green, red and yellow hat, representing Ethiopia's national colours. In Britain such a gesture had a political connotation, implying rejection of white society and values.

Rastafarianism satisfied a deeply felt need among young blacks who were plagued with uncertainty and confusion, far more so than white youths. The typical problem of identity, a hallmark of adolescence and youth, was compounded in the case of the Afro-Caribbean, who wondered what he, as a West Indies-born black, was doing in Britain. More generally, he tried to comprehend why almost everywhere in the world blacks were a subordinate race.

The Rastafarian ideology provided him with a clear view of his identity, explained to him the salient features of the world at large with special reference to the role and status of blacks, and was a platform for racial solidarity. In his song 'African', Peter Tosh, an eminent Rasta singer, summed up the message about identity thus: 'Don't care where you come from / As long as you're a black man / You're an African.' Bob Marley crystallized the prevalent feeling among Afro-Caribbean young-sters that they had long been deprived of opportunities to know well African cultures thus: 'It's not all that glitters is gold / Half the story has never been told.' In other words, imperialist Europe had banished the abundant cultural heritage of Africans underneath centuries of slavery and slave trade and colonialism. These oppressive, dehumanizing layers needed to be removed if black people were ever to liberate themselves. However, this liberation could only be achieved by undermining the evil and exploitative system, called Babylon, which had enslaved blacks physically and mentally. So their real enemy was the social system rather than white people, who were in fact themselves caught into it. This analysis was akin to the secular, anti-imperialist view which held that European imperialism had colonized not only the lands of non-Europeans but also their minds.

The other major theme of Rastafarianism was its derision of the idea of accepting suffering now in the hope of a better after-life. In his 1973 track 'Get up, stand up', Bob Marley summed up the Rastafarian view as follows:

> We're sick and tired of your easing kissing game
> to die and go to heaven in Jesus' name.
> We know and understand
> Almighty God is a living man.

In other words, instead of contemplating final salvation in the after-life and considering their present existence as something moulded by Almighty God, the exploited blacks should take a grip on their existence. The Rastafarian term 'I and I' implied that the divine spirit could exist within human beings. As such, protests against the present state of affairs and efforts at improvement could be seen as actions worthy of divine sanction.

Overall, therefore, young Afro-Caribbeans found Rastafarianism attractive for three major reasons: (a) it offered a clear statement about their own identity; (b) it provided a satisfactory explanation of how things were, nationally and globally, and why; and (c) it presented a platform upon which black solidarity could be forged. In the words of Ernest Cashmore, a British race relations specialist, Rastafarianism pro-vided to young blacks 'new modes of comprehending ... not only their current positions but also their history and future, for explaining ways to escape their present circumstances and aspire to higher goals, and for identifying who they were.'[15]

Bob Marley's successful tour of Britain in the summer of 1975 had an electrifying impact on young Afro-Caribbeans. His dreadlocks, slurred Jamaican patois and routine use of the colours of the Ethiopian flag became the items for emulation by his black admirers. His music fell on highly receptive ears and minds. In addition to responding instinctively to the reggae rhythms, young Afro-Caribbeans were able to associate Babylon intuitively with four centuries of slavery as well as with the inequities of the contemporary selection procedures in British schools. As Cashmore put it, 'Depressions in living conditions, lack of a solid matrix of existing institutions and values, and systematic exclusion from mainstream institutional activities led blacks to retreat into a sub-cultural existence where the need to develop a distinct identity went largely unsatisfied until presented with a persuasive set of guidelines as formulated in the music of Marley.'[16]

In the Britain of the mid-1970s, when many adult West Indians aspired to having straight hair and a light skin, and employed a battery of appliances to achieve them, the deliberate growing of thick and matted manes by young Afro-Caribbeans signalled a deliberate rejection of white values, and an attempt to project a distinctive identity of their own. It was a highly visible instrument used by them to uplift their self-image, and set themselves apart from not only white people and their values but also those West Indians who accepted non-African values. The other visible feature was the wearing of clothes and accessories in the national colours of Ethiopia.

However, not all those who accepted, or sympathized with, Rastafarianism took to adopting its outward forms. Since it was more a movement than a party, its followers could best be classified as active or passive. Around a nucleus of activists there was a very large body of sympathizers. A study by Ernest Cashmore in the late 1970s revealed that the Rastafarians were mostly young (modal age 18), male, working class, Jamaican. Poorly educated in general, they were either unemployed (50%) or in unskilled or semi-skilled jobs (45%): packers, warehousemen, factory workers, painters and carpenters.[17]

Interestingly, the Rastas had grown up in families where the (working-class) parents were practising Christians. Even though the Rastas were studious readers of the Bible, particularly the Old Testament with its apocalyptic ideas, none of their parents joined the movement. This was an illuminating measure of the gap that existed between the two generations. It could be argued that the immigrant parents had been too preoccupied with waging an economic battle of survival to bother about their ancestral roots, whereas their children, growing up in a white society, could not circumvent their crisis of identity.

The specific point of contention between the two generations was the smoking of marijuana, *ganja*, by Rastafarians. They referred to it as the 'herb', and found sanction for its use in the Book of Genesis where, they claimed, it had been described as the 'sacred weed'. They argued that it was a source of health and vitality – as well as wisdom, which in turn led them to 'unity with God'. In short, they treated smoking marijuana as part of their religious belief and practice.

If nothing else Rastafarianism had an aura of spirituality, something the secular Black Power ideology had lacked. It was true that unlike their parents, British-born or raised Afro-Caribbeans did not turn to religion to seek relief or solution to their existence as virtual outcasts in a white society. But Rastafarianism was not wrapped up in any formal religious ritual. Its general spirituality, coupled with fashionable music, made it attractive to young blacks.

Their radical, secular elder brothers or fathers, who had founded the Racial Adjustment Action Society and the Universal Coloured People's Association in the mid- to late 1960s, had now regrouped under smaller organizations: the Black Panther Movement and the Black Unity and Freedom Party. By and large these groups believed in an independent black struggle for liberation, and shunned joint activities with white organizations. Then there was the confederal body called the West Indian Standing Conference (WISC) based separately in London and Birmingham. WISC's constituents co-operated with all state agencies including the police. In between lay such groups as the Race Today Collective in London, the publishers of the monthly magazine of the same name, and the Bradford Black Collective. They oscillated between the extremes of nonco-operation and co-operation with the establishment.

Overall, West Indians had three options of political organization. These could be labelled as ethnic, black unity and class unity. Black unity implied organizations encompassing both West Indians and Asians. There was little evidence of that emerging during the 1970s. Ethnic associations of Afro-Caribbeans could be seen as either permanent or transient entities. If the latter, then their primary function was to ease the passage of their members into the mainstream institutions. Since most Afro-Caribbeans were working class, it meant their ethnic organizations encouraging them to become active members of their trade unions, and thus strive, consciously or subconsciously, for working-class unity against bourgeois forces. Time, a high rate of union membership among West Indians, and the growing familiarity of black faces in factories and public services, seemed to favour the process of the racial identity of Afro-Caribbeans being overlaid with class identity. The countervailing factor was the continuing racism on the shop floor.

However, during the early 1970s noticeable changes occurred in the political colouring of the Labour Party, mainly due to the party being in opposition to a Conservative Government. There was a movement to the left in the party constituencies and its National Executive Committee, as well as in the trade union hierarchy. Labour leaders were shamed by the Tory administration's acceptance of 27,000 Asian refugees from Uganda in 1972, which contrasted with their own shabby treatment of the British passport-holding Asians from Kenya in 1968 (see Part II, Chapter Two). Furthermore, rising agitation by the right-wing, anti-black National Front called for a resolute response from the leading force of the left and its trade union allies. Finally, on the eve of the 1979 parliamentary election, it dawned on Labour leaders that ethnic minorities held the balance in 41 marginal constituencies. This had happened due to the movement of the white working-class population out of the inner-city districts – the traditional bastions of Labour support – and the settlement of racial minorities in these areas. Also, the upward social mobility of the white working class had caused a shrinkage in Labour's popular base. The party was therefore obliged to forge a new coalition of votes consisting of white and black working class, and women. Thus, willy-nilly, Labour began evolving as a major vehicle of anti-racist action. The formation of the Race Action Group within the Labour Party signalled as much.

These developments made Labour more attractive to West Indians, who had traditionally backed it at the polls. An indication of the increased participation of Afro-Caribbeans and Asians in the local politics of Labour came in the May 1974 elections to Greater London's 33 boroughs (including the City of London Corporation). The number of Labour councillors from racial minorities rose from nil to ten – with the Conservatives trailing behind at two. The next year a Trinidadian, Dr David (later Lord) Pitt, who had been a member of the Greater London Council from North Hackney and Stoke Newington for many years, became the first black chairman of the GLC. In the subsequent London borough elections in 1978 the number of ethnic minority councillors jumped to 35, with Labour claiming all but six seats. While an improvement on the past, the 2 per cent representation of the racial minorities in Greater London was woefully short of their proportion in the population.

A much worse situation prevailed at the national level. After the poor performance of David Pitt as Labour candidate for Hampstead, London, in 1959, no major party nominated a black or brown member for a parliamentary constituency in the general elections of 1964 and 1966. In 1970 the Liberal Party fielded three racial minority candidates, and Labour one: David Pitt. Despite the fact that this time he contested the safe seat of Clapham, London, he lost. In the February and October 1974 parliamentary polls, one coloured candidate ran on the Liberal ticket and one on Labour. Neither won. A survey conducted in that year showed that if a major party's white candidate were replaced by an Afro-Caribbean or Asian, Labour's support would decline from 80% to 59%, Conservative from 81% to 49%, and Liberal from 77% to 57%.[18]

Three more years were to pass before the British political system began responding, at the national level, to the racial changes that the urban conurbations had undergone since the Second World War. The occasion was the August 1977 by-election in Ladywood, Birmingham, where 40 per cent of the voters were Asian or West Indian. Block voting by racial minority electors enabled the Labour candidate to win. Had they gone to the other side he would have lost.

This led the Conservative Party to take more interest in minority groups. It had made a start a year earlier by establishing a Community Affairs Department at its Central Office. Its task was to develop ties with representative minority organizations, produce literature aimed at racial minorities, and inform the party's parliamentary and local council candidates on minority issues. In September 1978 the Conservatives mounted an advertising campaign to improve their standing among ethnic voters. In the general election of May 1979 their party nominated two racial minority candidates, something it had not done since 1895, when it adopted Mancherjee Bhownaggree, a rich Indian Parsee (i.e. Zoroastrian), as its candidate for Bethnal Green North-East, London – a decision which ended in victory. This time, however, while one of the ethnic candidates improved the Tory performance in Greenwich, London, by 6.5 per cent, he failed to win the seat.

On the eve of the 1979 poll, the ethnic minority councillors formed the Standing Conference of Afro-Caribbean and Asian Councillors and issued a Black People's Manifesto. It included several demands for the welfare of black and Asian people. This showed a growing political awareness among the New Commonwealth settlers and indicated their steady integration into the political system.

A Harris opinion poll on the eve of this election revealed that backing for Labour at 42% among the non-manual A, B and C1 classes in the West Indian and Asian communities was twice as much as among their white counterparts; and at 50% among the manual C2, D and E classes of West Indians and Asians was well above the 36% among whites. Overall, the Conservatives received the support of about 13% among West Indians and 25% among Asians versus 46% among white Britons.[19] Labour's immense popularity with black voters stemmed from the predominantly working-class composition of the Afro-Caribbean community, the Conservative Party's imperialist past and its association with anti-immigrant Powellite sentiments, and the Labour Government's passing of a fairly stiff Race Relations Act in the spring of 1976 followed by the party conference's call in September for a strong campaign against racism and the extreme right.

This poll also revealed that a relatively high proportion of West Indians abstained, and that 23% under-registration among them was three times the figure for whites.[20] No age breakdown was available. But it was a safe guess that the proportion of unregistered voters among young Afro-Caribbeans was higher than among the middle-aged and old.

With jobs growing more scarce black youngsters became increasingly uninterested in trying to get on in society. Instead, they became drifters, lacking motivation for a normal life with steady work. Their relations with their parents became strained as they took to mixing with unsavoury characters in the black community, keeping late hours and having brushes with the police. The parents were doubly disappointed. As immigrants they had endured years of hard life and insults in the hope that their progeny would fare better. In reality, it seemed, they were actually doing far worse, not managing even to get a job and hold it. So when they displayed deviance or misbehaviour, their parents and older West Indians tended to reject them. This led to homelessness. And lacking any parental control or guidance, the rejected young blacks drifted into petty crime – mainly robbery and selling drugs – which ultimately led to encounters with the police.

Often a local black café would become the haunt of those retailing drugs or running brothels. By the late 1970s virtually all areas of West Indian settlement had spawned groups of hustlers who made an ostentatiously good living out of pimping and/or dealing in drugs, mainly marijuana and cannabis. The fact that Rastafarians smoked marijuana as part of their religious ritual made them a part of that section of the black community which was kept under watch by the local police.

As it was, Afro-Caribbean cafés and clubs had become targets of police raids since the early 1970s. The law officers would arrive either to put a stop to the alleged sale of drugs or unlicensed drinks, or to arrest a wanted offender. There were numerous such instances, with the Mangrove Restaurant in Notting Hill, London, being a repeated target of police raids from 1969. Another Afro-Caribbean establishment in Notting Hill, the Metro Club, received similar treatment in May 1971. The following year, in August, 100 policemen raided a black club in north London. The October 1974 police raid of the Carib Club in Cricklewood, London, resulted in violent resistance by Afro-Caribbean youths. Summarizing the view prevalent among Afro-Caribbeans, Derek

Humphrey, a white British journalist, wrote: 'To many blacks in our inner cities, police harassment has become a way of life. The police are viewed as the army of the enemy.'[21]

As unemployment among young West Indians grew – and with it the number of social drop-outs as well as Rastafarians – police raids on black cafés and clubs increased, as did police harassment of black youths in the streets.

In its evidence to the Royal Commission on Criminal Procedure in 1979, entitled *Police Against Black People*, the London-based Institute of Race Relations argued that police misconduct towards black citizens had become 'an everyday occurrence, a matter of routine'. It identified seven elements of police misbehaviour: stop and search without reason; unnecessary violence in arrests; particular harassment of juveniles; danger of arrest when suspects asserted their rights; risks to witnesses and bystanders; repeated arrests of individuals; and entering black homes and premises at will.

The 1970s thus ended with relations between the law-enforcing officers and Afro-Caribbean youngsters at their worst ever.

8 Urban Violence

The police are trying to appear unbiased in regard to race relations. But if you asked them you'd find that 90% of the force are against coloured immigrants.

A police constable in Bristol, 1980.[1]

They [the police] act in a way which says, 'That person is a criminal, so I'll treat him like shit.' And that criminal thing means all black people. I've experienced it. I've seen it.

WALLY BROWN, a black academic.[2]

Many of the young, particularly (but not exclusively) the young of ethnic minority, had become indignant and resentful against the police, suspicious of everything they did ... It produced the attitudes and beliefs which underlay the disturbances, providing the tinder ready to blaze into violence on the least provocation, fancied or real, offered by the police.

LORD SCARMAN[3]

It was the riots which forced the police to listen, to hear, for the first time.

PAUL SOMMERFIELD, Liverpool Community
Relations Council officer.[4]

The first half of the 1980s proved to be the most violent in the history of British race relations. However, the violence was not between races, but between groups of mainly young blacks and the police. The tension between the two sides had been building up over the past many years – with young blacks viewing the police as an antagonistic force given to bullying and harassing them, and at the same time embodying the established order, which held out scant prospects for them; and the police in turn treating young blacks as trouble-makers and potential criminals. The hostile relations erupted into violence as the country entered the eighties.

Policing in Britain has a fairly long history, dating back to the 1830s, when the government, having established a force in the capital, gradually extended the service to other areas. Except for the metropolis of London, the police force was accountable to the local government and functioned with the consent and co-operation of the community, with the 'bobbies on the beat' being at the heart of the system. The rise of populous cities with sprawling suburbs, followed by the onset of popular motoring after the Second World War, required modification of the policing methods. These came in the early 1960s, with the officers giving up their foot patrolling for cruising in cars so as to cover large areas and react swiftly to criminal activities. Also, reacting to the large-scale demonstrations in London against the American military involvement in Vietnam in the late 1960s, the police authorities took to training special reserve squads. The resulting alienation of the (invariably white) 'bobby on the beat' coincided with the racial transformation of the inner cities. A new generation of assertive police leaders at the administrative and trade union levels shifted the balance away from the local government to the police hierarchy. The procedure which required the force to investigate public complaints against it within the department ran counter to the principle of democratic accountability. On top of that was the persistent reluctance of most of the judiciary to curb police actions. By and large, therefore, the law-enforcing machinery was inclined both to ignore such specific needs of the black community as protection against racial harassment, and to behave aggressively towards it. 'Blacks experience the repressive side of the state in an unusually harsh manner,' noted Professor Bhikhu Parekh, a British race relations specialist. 'Those who run it [the repressive machine] have little understanding of the blacks, and lack those common bonds of sympathy and mutual appreciation so necessary to humanize the exercise of authority.'[5]

Responding to persistent calls from the public to end the system whereby the police acted as its own judge and jury in the case of complaints against its officers, Home Secretary Roy Jenkins piloted the Police Act 1976 which established the Police Complaints Board. However, the new body had little power and even less influence. The complaints had to go through elaborate channels, with each one investigated by a police superintendent or a higher officer. Therefore even simple complaints took months to be processed. Secondly, the provision of 'double jeopardy' proved controversial. If the Director of Public Prosecutions ruled against prosecuting a police officer alleged to have committed an offence, then his decision made the officer immune from any departmental action against him based on the same facts. In practice the proportion of complaints upheld was very low. In Liverpool, for example, of the 1384 out of 1730 complaints submitted in 1981 and cleared by mid-1982, only 71 – that is, 5 per cent – had been upheld.[6] The figures for London in 1989 were even worse. Only 3 per cent of the complaints resulted in an officer being disciplined, and in the case of alleged racist behaviour the figure fell to 1 per cent.[7] Since criminal prosecutions of police personnel on charges of serious crime (often assault) were even lower, the 'double jeopardy' provision ruled out any sanctions against an officer whose behaviour, though not strictly criminal, was below professional standards. So by the late 1970s the new system of handling complaints against police officers had fallen into disrepute, resulting in further loss of public confidence and support.

With this, the ethnic minorities' grievance against the racist behaviour of the police in general and certain officers in particular intensified. The Police Federation openly acknowledged that since officers were recruited from (white) society at large, and since society had racists within its ranks, some policemen were bound to be racially prejudiced. Indeed, a study by Andrew Colman, a psychology lecturer at Leicester University, published in 1981, revealed that police recruits and probationers were significantly more conservative and authoritarian than the public at large and that the racial attitudes of experienced officers too were markedly illiberal. 'Fifty per cent of the trouble caused today is either by niggers or because of them,' said one probationer to Andrew Colman. 'Most of them are just dirty, smelly people who will never change in a month of Sundays. In my opinion all Rastas should be wiped out of distinction [*sic*].'[8]

Rastafarians were the latest of the stereotypes that most urban whites accepted. As described earlier (see Chapter Four), in the 1950s the unemployed blacks were believed to be living off white prostitutes. Later they were to be associated with selling drugs. In the 1970s, owing to the selective use made of the crime statistics by the police and the media, the image of the black mugger took popular hold. 'Mugging' – a term imported in the late 1960s from America – meant robbery in a public place. As it was, the figures about this crime were disturbing enough. A study by Michael Pratt, a former police official turned sociologist, published in 1980 showed that mugging had registered a tenfold growth since the early 1960s, with the number of robberies doubling every four or five years. Contrary to the popular view, however, the typical victim was a male, not female, adult. The typical assailant was, not unexpectedly, male – acting alone or in a group of two or three; but under twenty-one and 'more often than not black'.[9]

This made young blacks even more of targets for harassment by the police. A Home Office study by Philip Stevens and Carole F. Willis in 1978 concluded that black citizens were most prone to be arrested for offences popularly associated with them. The most prominent among these were snatching of wallets and handbags, and acting in a 'suspicious manner'. In such cases blacks had fourteen to fifteen times more chance of being arrested than whites.[10]

As it happened, the police were equipped with a ready-made tool to harass a group it did not like: section 4 of the Vagrancy Act of 1824, which empowered them to arrest a person on suspicion of 'loitering with intent to commit an arrestable offence'. All that was needed to charge the suspected person was the testimony of two police officers. No victim was required to be produced. Furthermore, since section 4 cases were heard by a magistrate, there was no chance of a trial by jury. The frequency with which police used section 4, commonly known as Sus (short for 'suspicion'), varied enormously from region to region. In 1978, Metropolitan London, Merseyside (covering Liverpool) and Greater Manchester accounted for three-quarters of all those arrested under the Sus charges. The police bias was obvious from the fact that although Afro-Caribbeans were only about 6 per cent of London's population, they accounted for 44 per cent of the total Sus arrests. In the London borough of Lambeth, covering Brixton, this figure rose to 77 per cent.[11]

In the second half of the seventies, as economic recession deepened, hitting particularly manufacturing industry and causing a dramatic rise in Afro-Caribbean unemployment, many areas of black settlement experienced a sharp increase in robbery and violent theft. Brixton was a case in point: 55 per cent of black males under nineteen were registered as unemployed and, overall, black joblessness was three times the figure for whites. Railton Road, a main artery of the district, became the centre of Afro-Caribbean working-class sub-culture: black music, gambling, illicit drinking and drug dealing. 'Young people roaming around in the streets all day, with nothing to do and nowhere to go, get together in groups, and the "successful" criminal has a story to tell,' stated the Railton Road Youth and Community Centre in its evidence to Lord Scarman, appointed to investigate the April 1981 rioting in Brixton. 'So one evil breeds another, and as unemployment has grown in both older and younger generations crime has become more commonplace and more acceptable.'[12] In short, Brixton emerged as an area of high crime rate.

The law-enforcement authorities responded by resorting to saturation policing, which meant deploying extra policemen, often by drafting the Special Patrol Group (SPG). Originally set up in 1965, the SPG was specially trained to quell public disorder. By the late 1970s it had expanded greatly from its original strength of 100, and evolved as an élite, belligerent unit. It was often deployed in Greater London to conduct stop, search and arrest campaigns: an SPG campaign in Hackney, north London, in February 1980 led to 100 arrests.[13]

Between January 1978 and September 1980 the authorities engaged the SPG periodically to carry out stop, search and arrest swoops in Metropolitan Police District L, which covers Brixton. The size of such an operation could be judged by the fact that the SPG's November 1978 exercise around four housing estates with a large body of black residents – involving road blocks, early-morning raids and random street checks – resulted in the arrest of 430 people, 40 per cent of them black. Little wonder that severe rioting broke out in Brixton in April 1981 – a year after a violent disturbance in the St Paul's district of Bristol.

Known since the early 1960s as the 'shanty-town' among local blacks, predominantly Jamaican, St Paul's had long ago acquired an unedifying reputation as a haunt of prostitutes. This continued as the area changed from being overwhelmingly white after the Second World War to being about two-fifths black in the late 1970s. Besides prostitution, the police sub-division covering St Paul's had to cope with drugs, unlicensed sale of alcoholic drinks, and robbery. With joblessness among blacks, particularly youngsters, doubling during 1977–80, the incidence of crime rose.

Lacking proper facilities for relaxation and entertainment in a congenial atmosphere, many blacks from all over the city gravitated towards the Jamaican-owned Black and White Café in Grosvenor Road, St Paul's. It was equipped liberally with dominoes and pin-ball machines, popular with Afro-Caribbeans. Although unlicensed, it sold alcohol to its customers and had therefore become a target of police raids.

On 2 April 1980, Wednesday, at about 3.30 p.m., a party of about 50 policemen searched the Black and White Café, and arrested its owner-manager for serving alcoholic drinks illegally and selling drugs. As they began removing the stored drinks, including 132 cases of beer, a crowd gathered outside the premises. They assaulted the officers, who withdrew inside the café for shelter. Two hours later, when a contingent of 100 police constables started advancing towards the besieged premises, they faced a hailstorm of bottles, stones and other missiles. But they managed to rescue their trapped colleagues – at the cost of injuries to 22 policemen and severe damage to 27 police vehicles. During the most violent phase of the riot they encountered some 2000 mainly black citizens, many of them in their mid-teens. In view of the persistent violent hostility of St Paul's residents, the Chief Constable withdrew his men from the area at 7.30 p.m. Not until 11 p.m., after the local force had been augmented by contingents from neighbouring ones, did the police re-enter the district and restore order. During the intervening hours the rioters, many of them white, took to looting major stores. The resulting loss, along with other material damage to property, amounted to about £500,000.

William Whitelaw, Home Secretary, and his deputy, Timothy Raison, rejected repeated calls for an enquiry on the ground that this would create 'recriminations and rancour'. What bothered the minister was the withdrawal of the police from the area for some hours. He later set up a committee of senior law-enforcement officers to examine police procedures for quelling spontaneous public disturbances. (This led to the formation in July 1981 of the Instant Response Units – later called District Support Units – in the police forces nationally.)

Official sources also maintained that what St Paul's had experienced was not a race riot. But while the clash was not between blacks and whites, its roots were indisputably racial. It emerged out of a conflict between white and black cultural values. By and large Afro-Caribbeans took drinking in unlicensed premises and smoking marijuana or cannabis in their stride – activities which most whites condemned and which the police force was determined to eradicate. The outcome was a bloody confrontation between irate Afro-Caribbeans and white police on a black turf.

White youths participated in rioting and looting, but they were in a minority. Of the 134 people arrested, only about a third were white. Of the 91 charged, mainly with assault, theft, burglary and dealing in stolen objects, twelve were committed to the crown court for 'riotous assembly', meaning that they had committed acts of violence 'towards a common end'. It was noteworthy that all of the accused, except one, were black. On 20 March 1981, at the end of two and a half days' deliberations, the jurors acquitted five of the accused. As for the rest, they failed to reach a decision. The judge intervened and discharged them. The £500,000 that the government spent on the trial would have covered the total cost of the riot damage.

The official responses to the Bristol riot angered the Afro-Caribbean and Asian leaders. About 100 of them, representing 45 ethnic minority organizations – including such national bodies as the Indian Workers' Association and the Standing Conference of Pakistani Organizations – met in London. They urged ethnic minority citizens to stop applying for police jobs, withdraw from any ongoing police–community liaison schemes and refuse to participate in identity parades. The authorities should have acted to redress the grievances being aired. Instead, they tried to discredit the assembly by casting doubts on the representativeness of the community leaders who had participated in it. It was a grave mistake, as the violent eruptions in Brixton and elsewhere in the spring and summer of the following year were to prove.

As it was, Lambeth had a poor experience of police–community liaison. In November 1978, three days after the first meeting of the newly formed liaison committee of the local police and the Lambeth Council for Community Relations (LCCR), the Special Patrol Group carried out a stop-and-search campaign in Brixton. Three months later the police picked up three black race relations workers on suspicion of involvement in a pub brawl. They were innocent. Formal police–community liaison broke down. About two years later the borough council instituted an independent enquiry into policing. The local force refused to testify. The bitter and emotive tone of the report submitted by the enquiry committee was later described by Lord Scarman as reflecting 'attitudes, beliefs and feelings widely prevalent in Lambeth since 1979'.[14]

This report was published in January 1981, a month which witnessed a fire at 439 New Cross Road in Deptford, London, in the course of a party, which led to the deaths of thirteen young Afro-Caribbeans and injuries to thirty more. Blacks believed that the mishap resulted from a fire-bomb lobbed at the building by a white racist. Given a history of arson assaults against ethnic minorities in the area, this seemed plausible. But senior police officers ruled out the possibility of an attack from outside the building. Feelings ran high in the black community. Angered at the lack of urgent attention the incident demanded from the police, blacks formed the Massacre Action Committee. Its call for a demonstration against police complacency drew 10,000 supporters. Despite this, the criminal investigation failed to establish the cause of the fire.

The police failure to track down the perpetrator(s) of the murder of thirteen Afro-Caribbeans angered the black citizens of Greater London. It was against this background that Lambeth's force mounted Operation Swamp 81 in Brixton on 6 April 1981, Monday. Working in pairs, 120 local police constables, some of them in plain clothes, stopped and questioned people in the streets. In four days they stopped 943 persons and arrested 118, more than half black. Anti-police feeling in Brixton, already high, rose further.

On the evening of Friday 10 April, a black Brixtonian, nineteen-year-old Michael Bailey, bleeding from a stab wound, was snatched by a group of young blacks from the police waiting for an ambulance to take him to hospital. The officers chased crowds of rioting youths and ended the violence within a couple of hours. But as a rumour circulated that Bailey had died at the hands of the police, tension mounted.

Despite this, the local police commander, Leonard Adams, decided to continue Operation Swamp 81 by posting an extra force of 96 officers on Brixton streets on Saturday 11 April. In the late afternoon, when two policemen attempted to implicate a minicab driver in drug-dealing outside his company office at the top of Railton Road, a crowd of black people gathered, and turned violent. Rioting erupted in Atlantic Road but was quelled by the police. However, in Leeson Road officers were pelted with petrol bombs, the petrol pouring down their shields and setting fire to their uniforms. In Railton Road the rioters trapped an undermanned contingent of police constables. The disturbances were centred on Atlantic Road, Mayall Road and Railton Road and the surrounding streets. Taking advantage of the chaos that prevailed, black and white people looted the commercial area near the northern end of Atlantic Road. They set fire to pubs, shops and houses in Railton Road. By nightfall it appeared as if all of Brixton was alight, with buildings disintegrating in an all-consuming wall of fire which could be seen from the Houses of Parliament, four miles to the north. The inability of the firemen to reach their destination due to a hailstorm of missiles made matters worse. It was not until 11 p.m. that peace returned to a partially burned-out Brixton.

Violent trouble erupted again next day, in the afternoon, in the form of looting and isolated assaults on police constables. It intensified as the day wore on, with the main activity centred around the Town Hall, and the officers receiving heavy injuries under a barrage of stones, bricks, iron bars and petrol bombs. The next day, Monday, witnessed more violence; but it was comparatively minor. That night the disturbances finally ended.

The violent disorder of 10–11 April 1981 in Brixton – which included the first widespread use of petrol bombs on the British mainland – was the most severe that the country had witnessed in the twentieth century. At its peak about 7000 officers, or a third of the total Metropolitan Police Force, were deployed to restore order in an area of less than a square mile. In the process 450 people, including many policemen, sustained injuries. Also, 145 buildings and 207 vehicles, including police cars, fire engines and ambulances, were damaged. The total damage amounted to £6.5 million, thirteen times the figure for St Paul's in Bristol.

Once the government had got over its immediate shock at the events, on 14 April the Home Secretary appointed Lord Scarman, a Lord Justice of Appeal before his appointment as Chancellor of Warwick University in 1977, to 'inquire urgently into the serious disorder in Brixton on 10–12 April 1981 and to report, with the power to make recommendations'. Scarman got to work immediately, but it was not until 30 October that he submitted his report.

Meanwhile, the root causes which led to the Brixton rioting persisted, and Britain experienced a spate of violent disorders a few months later. The most severe was in Toxteth, Liverpool, which housed most of the 30,000 black Liverpudlians. It was a city with second and third generations of Afro-Caribbeans, culturally indistinguishable from white Liverpudlians. Yet unemployment among blacks was estimated to be 60 per cent. How poorly they fared in the job market could be gauged by the fact that of the 22,000 employees of the local council, only 169 were black. At 7 per cent of the total population of 510,000, black and brown Liverpudlians should have been holding 1540 local authority jobs.

On the night of Friday 3 July, police arrested the son of a well-known Afro-Caribbean (then attempting to sue the local Chief Constable Kenneth Oxford for alleged police harassment), charging him with stealing a motorcycle he was riding. He was snatched from the officers by an assembling crowd of some 40 black youngsters and taken away. Two hours of fighting between the youths and the police ensued. The next day, Saturday, some 150 black and white youths took over Upper Parliament Street, the main thoroughfare of Toxteth in the postal district of Liverpool 8. The violence that erupted at night continued until 7 a.m. on Sunday. The police resorted to a baton charge. At night a large crowd of black and white rioters overwhelmed the 800 officers, whose commander approached neighbouring police forces for reinforcements. Armed with missiles of assorted kinds, and driving a stolen fire engine, a cement mixer and several milk floats, the youths succeeded in breaching the police lines. The officers withdrew to the applause of the local residents, who resorted to looting shops and large stores. Fires broke out. With the blaze threatening the Princes Park Geriatric Hospital, the two sides observed a truce as 96 patients were evacuated. This allowed the local Chief Constable, Kenneth Oxford, to gain access to stores of CS gas cartridges. At 2.15 a.m. he ordered his marksmen to fire 59 CS gas projectiles against hard, flat surfaces or vehicles being driven at the police lines. This was the first time that CS gas was used on the British mainland for riot control. Since gas cartridges are likely to cause serious injury to human beings, they are not to be aimed at them. The main use of this weapon is to force out somebody hiding in a room by releasing CS gas, which penetrates closed doors or windows. Despite the precautions supposedly taken by police marksmen, at least two persons were seriously hurt by CS gas cartridges and underwent operations in hospital. By Monday the police presence had been bolstered to such an extent that the officers were able to contain swiftly any violence that erupted.

The four-day-long disorders resulted in 1070 recorded crimes, 705 arrests, injuries to 781 policemen, and property damage worth nearly £15 million, more than double the figure for Brixton.

Hardly had the situation in Toxteth returned to normal when rioting broke out in Moss Side, Manchester. It started in the early hours of Wednesday 8 July, and was quelled quickly. But in the morning there were more serious outbreaks which caused the closure of the shopping centre. After nightfall a crowd of about 1000 people resorted to stoning shops and assaulting the much-hated Moss Side police station. It was not until 4 a.m. that order was restored. The next day officers went on an offensive, with many police vans cruising around Moss Side while constables shouted such racist slogans as 'Nigger, nigger, nigger – oi, oi, oi!',[15] challenging blacks to fight. On Friday 10 July, a stone-throwing crowd of youths once again assaulted the police station but were beaten back by riot-helmeted officers. Other areas of Greater Manchester, too, experienced sporadic violence.

On that day, Brixton erupted into a seven-hour-long riot following the arrest of a local Rastafarian and businessman, Lloyd Coxsone. Elsewhere in the capital, rioting youths damaged shops and cars, and looted in Balham, Fulham, Lewisham, Stoke Newington and Woolwich. The same happened in Ellesworth Port, Handsworth (Birmingham), Hull, Nottingham, Preston, Reading, Sheffield and Wolverhampton. Over the weekend of 11–12 July rioting spread to the Yorkshire cities of Bradford, Halifax, Huddersfield and Leeds, as well as to Aldershot, Birkenhead, Blackburn, Blackpool, Cirencester, Derby, Fleetwood, Gloucester, High Wycombe, Knaresborough, Keswick, Leicester, Luton, Portsmouth, Slough, Southall and Southampton.

Official estimates put the total cost of damage resulting from the July riots at £45 million. Of these about £17 million pertained to the damage caused to private buildings and their contents – a loss which local authorities were required to recompense under the Riot Damages Act – with Liverpool Town Hall landed with a bill of £11 million.

Of the nearly 4000 people arrested, data was available for 3704. Whites constituted 67% of the total, West Indians and Africans 20%, and Asians 5%, with the rest described as 'other or not recorded'.[16] This showed that once violence erupted it provided a channel of expression for the deprived white youths of the inner cities, themselves victims of disproportionate police attention and poor opportunities for work. However, the racial composition of the defendants varied from place to place. In Brixton and Southall blacks and Asians were two-thirds of the total whereas in Toxteth and Moss Side whites were dominant to the same extent. Of those arrested 70 per cent were under twenty-one; and an overall majority of the defendants were jobless.[17]

The official reaction to this spate of violence was summed up by William Whitelaw, the Home Secretary, thus: 'It is criminal hooliganism from many people who have no motive other than simple greed. The causes of that are just the same as the causes of the crime and there is a good deal of copycat activity.'[18] Within that overall assessment cabinet ministers differentiated between the 'real' riots in Brixton and Toxteth and the violent disturbances elsewhere, treating the latter as a manifestation of large-scale criminality to be put down with a decisive hand. To cool tempers, on 10 July the Home Secretary imposed a month-long ban on marches in London so as to abort two impending processions – one by the National Front and the other by the Anti-Nazi League to commemorate the funeral of an Asian family burnt to death in the East End as a result of an arson attack. On Saturday 11 July, as riots raged in a dozen cities all over the country, Prime Minister Margaret Thatcher spent an eight-hour-long day with the top officials of the Metropolitan Police, making a brief foray into Brixton police station.

The initial official reaction, that the riots were merely a matter of law and order, gave way gradually to the argument that the disorders were a violent manifestation of deteriorating socio-economic conditions in the inner cities. By appointing the Environment Secretary, Michael Heseltine, as the head of a task force to examine the causes of, and possible solutions to, the disturbances in Merseyside, the Thatcher administration gave due weight to the social and economic aspects of the crisis.

By then three schools of analysis had emerged. There were those who attributed the disorders to sheer criminality and the propensity among young hooligans to imitate what they had seen on television screens. There were others who put the primary blame on the dreadful living conditions of the populace in inner cities. And finally there was a school which considered police misconduct towards blacks as the prime cause of the conflagrations.

'Just as the sense of public shock at the riots went far deeper than outrage at the looting and violence, so the causes of the mayhem were rooted far deeper in a grievance against material deprivation,' wrote the *Guardian*. 'It is the alienation that arises from a feeling that these hardships [of deprivation] are being caused by institutions that are remote and uncaring. In other words, there has been a chronic loss of faith in our political institutions which has bred cynicism and lost those institutions the support of the community.'[19]

Surveys conducted by the newspapers produced no evidence to support the theory of mindless criminality. The factors that emerged as dominant in popular opinion were an amalgam of poor social conditions and police misbehaviour. Typical of such enquiries was the poll commissioned by London's evening paper, *New Standard*, a fortnight after the Brixton riots in April.[20] It showed the comparative importance of the various factors thus:

	Black and Asian	*Overall*
Unemployment	49%	40%
Police Behaviour	33%	13%

	Black and Asian	*Overall*
Racialism	18%	17%
Bad Housing	12%	15%
Blacks' Behaviour	11%	22%
Too Many Police	7%	3%

Subsequent polls published by *The Times* and *Guardian* after the April and July disturbances showed similar results.

There were noticeable differences in the perceptions of the racial minorities and the public at large regarding the behaviour of both police and Afro-Caribbeans. About a quarter of the population, predominantly white, held blacks responsible for the troubles. On the other hand a third of the black and Asian respondents (with a much higher proportion among the young) placed the blame on the police.

Their view was upheld by various ethnic or multiracial bodies, and later by a survey conducted by the Policy Studies Institute (PSI), London. In its evidence to Lord Scarman the West Indian Standing Conference put the primary blame for the Brixton riot on 'a deep wedge of fear' between blacks and police. According to the Lambeth Council for Community Relations, racist and provocative policing was the root cause of the troubles. Likewise, the Liverpool 8 Defence Committee pinned blame on 'police abuse and aggression against the black community'.[21] The Moss Side Defence Committee listed 'indiscriminate raids, frame-ups and harassment laced with racist abuse' as the major causes, and described the riots as 'legitimate protest by those who suffer from real, identifiable and desperate injustices'.[22] A 1982 survey in London by the PSI established that between one-third and one-half of West Indians lacked confidence in the police and that two-thirds had at least 'considerable doubts' about their behaviour.[23]

If nothing else, in the case of every major conflagration police conduct acted as the spark. In Bristol it was their raid on a black café in St Paul's; in Brixton it was the sight of a bleeding black youth being held by officers; and in Toxteth it was the arrest of a son of a prominent Afro-Caribbean on a false charge of stealing a motorcycle. Such instances had occurred against the backcloth of a growing feeling among many youths of harassment by the police through thwarting of their social gatherings, street searches and arrests on Sus charges. The repeal of the Sus law and its substitution by the Criminal Attempts Act in January 1981 had little impact on police practices. The force resorted to making use of the many stop-and-search powers it had, including section 66 of the Metropolitan Police Act of 1939.

Policemen could justify their behaviour as necessary to combat the rising crime rate. This in turn was related to the growing deprivation of inner cities: decaying neighbourhoods resulting from the closure or flight of traditional manufacturing plants. Given their concentration in large cities and in manufacturing, the racial minorities suffered greater unemployment than others. Black youths were particularly hard hit, with some London boroughs registering 60 per cent joblessness among them.

The report by Lord Scarman in late October aroused much media attention. 'If they [the police] neglect consultation and cooperation with the local community, unrest is certain and riot becomes probable,' warned the report.[24] Scarman gave a great push to the idea of reviving community policing, the 'bobby on the beat'.

Overall, the vast publicity given to the rioting and its causes and consequences made the general public aware of the grievances of racial minorities. Many local authorities began to take the complaints of blacks and Asians more seriously than before. The violent disorders also raised the political awareness of Afro-Caribbeans and Asians, particularly the younger generation. Many ethnic leaders followed a dual policy of issuing strong condemnatory statements against the police, so as to retain the goodwill of the grassroots, while staying in touch with politicians and government officials and negotiating with the police. They thus became a bridge between the angry, radical members of their communities – who viewed the violent eruptions collectively as constituting an uprising or rebellion – and the establishment. The experience encouraged them to become active within the major political parties, especially Labour, and seek office at local and national levels.

This could be gleaned from the figures pertaining to the local elections of 1982 and the parliamentary poll of the following year. Of the 5992 candidates who contested 1914 council seats in Greater London boroughs, 250 candidates belonged to ethnic minorities. Of these 79 were successful (37 Afro-Caribbeans and 42 Asians), a noticeable improvement on the previous 35. With 69 racial minority councillors to its credit, Labour was far ahead of the Conservative total of seven. Laudable though this was, the 4 per cent share that black and Asian Londoners had won was about a third of their proportion in the population. Outside the metropolis, Afro-Caribbean and Asian councillors were elected in Birmingham, Bradford, Leeds and Leicester; but again their share of the total was negligible.

In the June 1983 general election the four main parties – Conservative, Labour, Liberal and Social Democrat – offered eighteen racial minority candidates, an increase of thirteen over the previous poll. While three of the four Conservatives contested constituencies with a large body of ethnic voters, this was not the case with the six Labour candidates.

However, of all these aspirants only one, Paul Boateng, a lawyer of Ghanaian and English parentage, had a chance of winning West Hertfordshire with a nominal Labour majority of 700. In the event, he came third. Though none of the Conservatives was successful, they performed rather well, winning 7262 to 12,418 votes.

A study of all eighteen seats by Muhammad Anwar, a race relations specialist, showed that in seventeen cases, where comparisons with the notional party position in the previous election was possible, the parties' performance had been unaffected by their adoption of ethnic candidates. This was a reversal of the position prevalent four years back. 'The results suggest that party allegiances are more important in determining the outcome of the result than the race of the candidate,' concluded Anwar. This applied as much to white electors as it did to ethnic ones. In the Ealing–Southall constituency of west London, for instance, the vast bulk of Asians voted for the white Labour candidate, Sydney Bidwell, a sitting MP, rather than a fellow-Asian, Mahmoud Nadeem, a lawyer, contesting on a Social Democratic ticket.[25]

In the wake of the 1981 riots, and the gains made by racial minorities in the 1982 local elections, some Labour ethnic councillors organized themselves around a programme of rectifying the ethnic under-representation in the party hierarchy and combating racism within the organization.

By then the idea of autonomous black organizations seeking affiliation to the Labour Party, in the way trade unions do, had caught the imagination of many black and Asian leaders. They saw in this a way to circumvent both the bureaucratic committee milieu prevalent at ward levels (which alienated most black and Asian members) and the procedural racist practices of the party bureaucrats.[26] The first such group was the left-leaning Asian Labour Party Alliance (ALPA) in Brent, London, led by Manibhai Patel. In 1980–81 more than 1000 Asians joined the Labour Party, and several of them were elected to the party's decision-making bodies. Given the propensity of blacks and Asians to vote solidly for Labour, the sitting white councillors, assured of being re-elected, were reluctant to step down and let racial minority candidates contest. Therefore within the Labour leadership white resistance to active black participation was highest precisely in the areas of high ethnic concentration. As such, an organization like ALPA allied with the Afro-Caribbean groups and Labour left to oust the right-winger John Lebor as leader of the Labour Group in Brent, the blackest borough in Britain. Of the twenty-one black and Asian Labour candidates for the local elections in May 1982, eleven were successful, a record. Merle Amory, a black councillor, became the deputy leader of the ruling Labour

Group. In that year Sinna Mani, a Sri Lankan immigrant and a Labour Party activist for twenty years, organized the Black People's Alliance in Lewisham, London. And at about the same time Bernie Grant, a councillor of Haringey since 1978, convened a black trade union caucus.

Assisted by the Labour Party Race Action Group, these activists circulated a resolution for adoption by the Labour Party's annual conference in October 1983. A modified version of this resolution urged the party's National Executive Council (NEC) to establish a working committee to consider mandatory inclusion of 'members of dis-advantaged groups (i.e. working class, women and ethnic minority groups) on parliamentary short-lists … recognizing in particular the right of black members of the party to organize together in the same way as Women's Sections and Young Socialist branches'. Supporting the resolution, James Thakroodin, an ethnic trade union official, made his argument dramatically by pointing out the absence of black faces on the platform. 'We must get away from being a white and male dominated, chauvinistic and often racist and sexist Labour party,' he said.[27] The adoption of this resolution – coupled with the conference's decision to set up a working committee on positive discrimination towards racial minorities – was seen by most Labour delegates as a go-ahead for the formation of Black Sections within the party.

However, the chances of establishing these sections dimmed consider-ably when the newly elected Labour leader, Neil Kinnock, opposed the idea. 'The moment we move, for whatever benevolent reasons, to some form of segregated membership in the Labour party, that invites a major regression in our efforts to change attitudes in society, and indeed within the Labour movement,' he said in April 1984.[28] But this did not stop the holding of a national convention of Black Section supporters in Birming-ham in June. It ratified a draft constitution of the Black Sections. Within the next few months twenty constituency Labour parties, mostly in Greater London, informally established Black Sections with their repre-sentatives sitting on the local management committees.

The Labour working committee on positive discrimination chaired by Jo Richardson came out in favour of Black Sections. Its report to the party conference in October 1984 stated that Labour's political commit-ment to racial equality was not borne out by the number and role of black people in the party, and that Black Sections would make the party more accessible to racial minorities, who were often discouraged from active involvement because of the 'unwelcoming, male-dominated, jargonistic meetings' at ward level. But the proposal for Black Sections was defeated heavily, by 5,457,000 votes to 500,000. Not surprisingly, of the nearly 2000 Labour delegates only eight were black or Asian.

But, refusing to be downhearted about events at the national level, local black activists kept up their grassroots activities. In Hackney, London, for instance, having realized that only five of the sixty councillors were Afro-Caribbean or Asian, the black activists launched a campaign to increase ethnic representation to twenty-four to match its proportion in the borough's population.

The tussle between the pro-Black Sections minority and the anti-Black Sections majority in the NEC continued. In its report, *Black People and the Labour Party*, a majority of the NEC's working party favoured Black Sections. It argued that by establishing an official Black Section, the party would draw minorities in a positive fashion and thus broaden its base especially in inner cities. But the NEC turned down the recommendation. Even the two leftist members' compromise idea that ethnic minorities should form their own groups which should then affiliate with the Labour Party (along the lines of Poale Zion, a Jewish group) was rejected. Neil Kinnock maintained his opposition on the basis that the party should be able to express the views of all British people, including ethnic minorities. In reality, he and other moderates visualized the Black Sections as potentially divisive entities, which would be dominated by the left and become an electoral handicap. However, as a sop, the NEC consented to appointing an advisory committee on ethnic minorities just as it had done earlier on women and local government.

Kinnock and his camp must have drawn succour from the results of an opinion poll of 2500 Afro-Caribbeans and 2600 Asians in fifty constituencies with over 10 per cent ethnic votes. It showed that only 18 per cent favoured separate Black Sections while 63 per cent were opposed.[29] Among those who were against the Black Sections were certain ethnic radicals. They predicted that their formation would draw black expertise away from the ghettos where it was most needed.[30] This encouraged the Labour leadership to spawn the founding of the Black and Asian Advisory Committee as a rival to the Black Sections.

Surprisingly, the continuing and much-publicized controversy on the subject had little impact on the voting patterns of blacks and Asians. In fact, it whetted the appetite of ethnic groups for mainstream politics and led to an upsurge of ethnic candidates in a growing number of local and national constituencies, as the subsequent elections were to reveal.

9 Step-Citizens of Britain

Black people are more likely than their white counterparts to be stopped by the police. If stopped, they are more likely to be arrested. If arrested, they are more likely to be charged. If charged, they are more likely to be remanded in custody; and if convicted, more likely to receive a sentence of imprisonment.

STEPHEN SHAW, director, Prison Reform Trust.[1]

Black people make up 20% of the remand population in England and Wales ... compared with 4.4% of the general population.

National Association of Probation Officers.[2]

The re-election of the Conservatives to power with an augmented parliamentary majority of 186 in the June 1983 poll on a platform which gave priority *inter alia* to 'law and order' did not augur well for normal relations between police and young West Indians.

Unemployment continued to grow nationally – more so among Afro-Caribbeans, especially the young – crossing the psychologically significant three million mark in 1984. In that year there were a record 3.5 million 'notifiable crimes', an increase of 8 per cent on the previous year. With jobless Afro-Caribbean youngsters in inner cities inclining to minor offences, and with the police seeking to reduce petty crime, the scene was once again being set for violent confrontations.

These came in the summer and early autumn of 1985 – in Liverpool, Birmingham, Coventry, Wolverhampton and London. Invariably police actions acted as triggers for the violence that followed. For instance in Toxteth, Liverpool, the arrest of four black youngsters on 30 August led to an attack on the police station by a crowd of angry youths.

This proved to be a preamble to two days of large-scale disturbances which erupted in Handsworth, Birmingham, soon after the local festival on 7–8 September had passed off peacefully. The violence occurred against the background of massive unemployment. One out of three employable residents of Handsworth (population 56,300) were out of work. The proportion for under-24s was one in two.

Following an incident in the late afternoon of 9 September, in which a policeman harassed a black driver, tension built up. It came to a head at night and resulted in pitched battles between young blacks and the police in which liberal use was made of bricks, petrol bombs and barricades of burning vehicles. Scores of properties, including a sub-post office, were set alight. Over 650 police officers failed to restore order. It was not until 4 a.m. that the last of the exhausted rioters had retired and the fires had been put out. A search through the wreckage yielded the dead bodies of two Asian brothers – Amir Ali Moledina and Qassim Ali Moledina – who ran the sub-post office. (A young white man was later to be charged with their murder.) In the afternoon there was a recurrence of stoning, burning and looting. By then some 1400 officers had been deployed. They managed to restore order.

The two days of rioting and arson left 83 properties damaged, with 50 gutted by fire. The total damage to vehicles and buildings and their contents amounted to £2.5 million. Besides the two dead, 74 officers and 35 locals were hurt. There were 291 arrests.[3]

Part of the reason for the disorder in Handsworth lay with the change in policing methods. Throughout the 1970s the local police super-intendent, David Webb, had employed community policing, with officers patrolling on foot and keeping in touch with the community. His example was followed by his successor. But following his transfer in April 1985 the new superintendent assigned the community policemen to other tasks and attempted to curb such black youth activities as the smoking of cannabis, something that had been overlooked before.

A similar toughening up by the police in Brixton resulted once more in an outbreak of violence. In the course of their fifty-first armed raid of the year, on 28 September, officers broke open the front door of a house and fired two shots in search of Michael Groce, wanted for possessing a shotgun. One bullet hit Mrs Cherry Groce, the mother. A rumour spread swiftly in the black community that she had died. In the late afternoon a crowd of 300 people besieged the local police station. It was not until midnight that the police authorities were able to end the siege. During that period it was reported that 724 serious crimes, including 90 burglaries, were committed; 230 people were arrested, half of them white; and 53 residents and policemen were injured.

A week later, once again the death (this time real) of a black woman at the hands of the police on the Broadwater Farm estate in Tottenham, north London, triggered off a serious riot. On 5 October police officers harassed Floyd Jarret, a black youth worker at the Broadwater Farm Youth Association, because his car registration disc was out of date. Later in the afternoon they searched the residence of his mother, Cynthia, for stolen goods. During the search Cynthia Jarret collapsed and died. The news of her death spread and brought the festering anti-police feeling to the boil.

On the evening of 6 October a riot erupted and continued until midnight. In the midst of large-scale violence and arson a police helicopter with a powerful searchlight was employed to pinpoint rioters. A policeman was hit by a shotgun pellet, another was seriously hurt by a bullet from a gun, and a third, Keith Blakelock, was hacked to death. The next day the commander of the Metropolitan Police, Sir Kenneth Newman, declared: 'I will not shirk from using plastic bullets if necessary.' The Home Secretary stated that he favoured the use of CS gas or other arms to suppress disorder. 'There can never be any justification for rioting,' Prime Minister Thatcher declared at the Conservative Party Conference. 'We will provide more men and equipment to the police if necessary.'[4]

This was in sharp contrast to the feelings prevalent among blacks. These were articulated well by Bernie Grant, a Guyana-born leader of the local Afro-Caribbean community. He publicly expressed satisfaction that 'the police had got a bloody good hiding'. This remark was seized upon by the tabloid press, which portrayed him as 'barmy Bernie'. However, the vast publicity given to him in the media provided him with a high profile he did not possess before even though he had been active in Labour politics for many years. His close association with black youths on the estate gave him an insight most other leaders lacked.

It was the young blacks who were harassed by the police when, in the aftermath of Blakelock's murder, Scotland Yard pressed hundreds of detectives into a frantic search for the killers of their colleague and for those who had initiated the rioting. The result was scores of arrests, and heavy-handedness by the police, emanating no doubt from a desire for vengeance. During the trials at the Old Bailey that followed, several black community leaders claimed that the confessions of the accused had been obtained through force. While the charge was not taken seriously then by the authorities, subsequent internal enquiries produced enough evidence in its support to warrant a serious disciplinary charge against Graham Melvin, the Detective Chief Superintendent who headed the investigation into the rioting.[5]

Despite repeated calls from various bodies, the government refused to institute an enquiry similar to the one conducted by Lord Scarman in 1981. This led to low-level public investigations into the rioting. The enquiry into the disturbance at the Broadwater Farm estate, conducted by Lord Gifford, a Labour lawyer, put much of the blame for the rioting on insensitive policing and economic deprivation of the estate.

As for Handsworth, the Chief Constable of the West Midlands submitted a report to the Home Secretary which was widely seen as a whitewash, a one-sided account of the events and the causes of the disorders. An investigation by Birmingham City Council chaired by Julius Silverman, a former MP, proved deficient because it failed to obtain the co-operation of the ethnic minorities. It was the enquiry conducted by the Ethnic Relations and Equal Opportunities Section of the West Midlands County Council which succeeded in securing the testimonies of 67 black and Asian organizations. The tone of some of the testimonies could be judged by the statement of an unnamed resident of Handsworth. 'This is where we live, where we have to struggle to survive and where we have to defend our existence,' he said. 'The rebellion provided us with a sense of total freedom while it lasted. Since it ended the shackles have been put on even tighter.'[6] Little wonder that the general conclusion of the West Midlands County Council report, *A Different Reality*, was that the events in Handsworth in early September constituted 'rebellion' by racial minorities. That is, unable to bear the police and other pressures to further marginalize them, many among the deprived minorities had offered violent resistance.

The hard line that the government adopted after the riots persisted. The stress was increasingly on 'law and order', a stance that encouraged the police forces in the country to get even with those who had given them 'a bloody good hiding'. In a move apparently stemming from vindictiveness, on 12 August 1986, nearly a year after the riot, the police raided the Broadwater Farm estate. A police helicopter hovered overhead as officers forced an entry into premises where they expected to find cannabis.[7]

Earlier, on 24 July, Scotland Yard had executed a massive operation in Brixton, codenamed Operation Condor, with military-style secrecy and precision to curb the use and sale of drugs. It involved raiding 29 addresses including a children's nursery. The main focus was on the Afro-Caribbean Club situated next to a railway line. To surprise the club members the police hired a train and several British Road Services vehicles to raid the premises. Operation Condor was carried out by 340 police officers, with a further 1500 men – including the Metropolitan Police's D-11 tactical firearms unit – in reserve. On the same day the police in Birmingham carried out raids on several premises in Handsworth – another area of riots in 1985 – in search of narcotics.[8]

But the biggest and most spectacular operation was yet to come. On 11 September, in the course of Operation Delivery, about 1000 police officers were deployed in a raid on the Black and White Café in the St Paul's area of Bristol (another flashpoint of rioting six years earlier) in search of drugs and unlicensed sale of alcohol. Officers arrived stealthily, in covered lorries. Yet a crowd gathered quickly, and was dispersed by the police wielding riot shields.[9]

In theory it would seem normal for the police to try to curb the use of illegal drugs. In practice the targeting of the raids showed an urge for revenge. The Broadwater Farm estate in north London and the Black and White Café in Bristol were the two sites where the image of the police as an efficient, hard-hitting force had been tarnished. The police seemed to indulge in this vendetta without regard to the expense to the taxpayer and the final outcome. Operation Delivery, for instance, cost £965,000.[10] And the result? A derisory number of people charged with possession of small quantities of cannabis.

Given that each police force in the country is accountable to the local government, there was some way in which the taxpayer could exert pressure. But there is a major exception: the Metropolitan Police, in charge of Greater London, reports directly to the Home Secretary and is not responsible to local borough councils either individually or jointly. This mattered a great deal to the West Indian community since about half of its members lived in Greater London.

They were perturbed to learn in late 1986 that Scotland Yard had taken to classifying housing estates as areas of varying risk – high, medium, low – depending on their susceptibility to public disorder, and was making plans for besieging them in case of trouble. It had prepared a list of twenty estates, including of course Broadwater Farm. The high-risk estates almost invariably included those with a substantial black population.[11] This was one more sign that the government was toughening up its law-and-order enforcement machine to ensure that any future disturbances would be crushed speedily and efficiently.

Whatever the administrative pros or cons of such a police strategy, its immediate impact on the black residents of these estates was negative. As it was, blacks faced a much higher chance of being stopped by police than whites, and a far greater chance of then being arrested and charged. A study of corresponding figures for black and white prisoners by the Prison Reform Trust showed that black British were eight times more likely to be sent to prison than white British.[12]

Meanwhile, the conditions which spawned the alienation of blacks from society and its institutions persisted. Joblessness among them remained high, with the young suffering more than the old. With the government tightening up on unemployment benefits, the situation grew worse and the youngsters' despair deepened.

'When you have no job and no chance of getting one, you're faced with the nagging problem of how to kill time,' said Geraldine Ambrosius, an unemployed black youth in Liverpool. 'You become weighed down with an awful feeling that society has no useful function for you to perform at the ripe age of seventeen or eighteen.'[13]

Among the Afro-Caribbean leaders who had tried to help relieve the situation locally was Bernie Grant. Under his guidance the Broadwater Farm Youth Association, formed in 1981, had initiated several community development projects. As a Labour councillor in Haringey since 1981 he had succeeded in winning the backing of the local Town Hall. Such actions, among others, helped him to re-election as a councillor in 1982. He was elected leader of the ruling Labour group in the council in April 1985.

Later, when Norman Atkinson, the sitting Labour MP for Tottenham (with 45 per cent ethnic population), was deselected by the constituency party, Bernie Grant, then (also) chairman of the local Labour Party Black Section, offered to replace him. He succeeded, and contested the May 1987 general election on a Labour ticket.

This poll saw the four major political parties fielding 29 ethnic candidates: Labour 14; Conservative 6; and Liberal–Social Democratic Party Alliance 9.

On the Labour side, four were in marginal seats (with a majority of less than 10 per cent) and only three were in safe seats (with a majority of more than 10 per cent). Of those in the former category, Keith Vaz, an Indian Catholic born in Aden, South Yemen, became MP for Leicester East. Bernie Grant was in the latter category; the others were Diane Abbot, born of Jamaican parents, and Paul Boateng. All three won with comfortable majorities. Abbot was elected by Hackney North and Stoke Newington, which had a 37 per cent racial minority population, and which had (as a ward of the Greater London Council) in the past elected David Pitt to the GLC. Boateng won the Brent South constituency, with 56 per cent ethnic population, the highest in the country.

In the final analysis, these candidates were the beneficiaries of the politicization that racial minorities underwent as a result of the riots of 1981 and 1985. Given a chance to vote for a black or Asian, in a constituency with a substantial ethnic electorate, they backed him or her solidly. It had taken racial minority citizens of Britain nearly four decades and involvement in numerous agitations in the factories and streets, including unprecedently severe rioting, to shake up the political system sufficiently to let them place a few black and Asian MPs at Westminster.

Actually, in the past, when non-white residents of Britain were a minuscule minority, the political establishment had proved far more prepared to let one or two of them enter the House of Commons. The House received its first ethnic minority MP in 1892. He was Dadabhai Naoroji, an Indian Parsee (i.e. Zoroastrian) born in Bombay, elected by the voters of Finsbury Central, London, on a Liberal Party ticket. He was followed by Mancherjee Bhownaggree, another Indian Parsee, who entered Parliament as the Conservative member for Bethnal Green North-East, London. Later, in 1922, still another Indian Parsee, Shapurji Saklatvala, secured a seat in Parliament as a Labour MP from Battersea North, London. At the next general election, in 1924, he was re-elected to Westminster on a Communist Party ticket.[14]

These facts prevented the arrival of four black and Asian MPs at Westminster from making history so far as the British Parliament was concerned. None the less, for contemporary Britons the event was unprecedented. And the media treated it as such. It was only appropriate that Lord Pitt – who, as David Pitt, had been the first serious parliamentary black candidate in post-war Britain – should receive the black MPs at the Palace of Westminster. But once the initial mood of self-congratulation had subsided among ethnic citizens, and the freshly elected junior black MPs had realized the limitations of their membership of Parliament, a highly traditional and hierarchical institution, certain uncomfortable facts came to the fore.

Principal among these was the inadequacy of the representation of ethnic voters in the House of Commons. Four black and Asian MPs in a house of 650 amounted to 0.6 per cent of the total. In contrast, nearly 2.5 million ethnic minority citizens formed 4.5 per cent of the national population.[15] To reflect this accurately, the House of Commons ought to have at least 29 black and Asian MPs. This was certainly not on the cards – for the next several parliaments. Until and unless black and Asian voters acquire parliamentary representation commensurate with their numbers, they can only be described as step-citizens of Britain.

Second in importance was the inadequacy of the representation of visible minorities in the top leadership of the Labour Party, which had emerged as their principal forum for political activity. Allied to this was the continued refusal of the (all-white) party hierarchy to accommodate Black Sections within the organization.

Since Bernie Grant and Diane Abbot had been active with the party's Black Sections, they felt that their election to Parliament would reinforce the cause of these sections and the case for their incorporation into the party.

They were to be disappointed. This happened despite the admission, on the eve of the Labour conference in October 1988, by the party general secretary, Larry Whitty, that the party's Black and Asian Advisory Committee (established as a rival to the Black Sections) had not been a success. The conference instructed the National Executive Committee (NEC) to offer a proposal by the next assembly which would allow black organizations to affiliate on the same basis as existing socialist societies like the Fabians, Labour Lawyers, the Socialist Health Associations,

Poale Zion and the Labour Zionist Society. These affiliated bodies send delegates to the annual conference as well as to the constituency parties.

At the following conference in October 1989 the NEC offered a resolution to the delegates which would have opened the Black and Asian Socialist Society to party members of 'African, Caribbean or Asian descent, or any other ethnic communities likely to be discriminated against on racial grounds, and Labour Party members who, by becoming members of the Society but not eligible for office or delegation in the Society, wish to use this additional means of expressing their solidarity against racism'. It was rejected by 2,893,000 votes to 1,428,000. But the resolution calling for the formation of Black Sections too was defeated – and heavily, by 1,050,000.[16] So the party was back to square one, and had to start all over again. The demand of the ethnic delegates that at least one of the 29 members of the party's National Executive Committee ought to be black too went unheeded.

On the other hand, this controversy and the media attention paid to it firmly established in the popular mind an awareness that blacks and Asians were now an integral part of mainstream politics, and that their principal vehicle was the Labour Party, an organization well-known for its vigorous and democratic debate on important issues: a healthy development. It is no coincidence that it was the Labour Party which had after the Second World War initiated the process of dismantling the British Empire, which at its peak encompassed a quarter of humanity, thanks primarily to the inclusion of the heavily populated Indian sub-continent into it.

Part II

ASIANS

1 The Coolies of the Empire – and Britain

The [European] manufacturers and traders who were the harbingers of imperialism in the hills and plains of Asia and the forests of Africa went there with certain definite economic objects: they wanted to sell cotton or calico, to obtain tin or iron or rubber or tea or coffee. But to do this under the complicated economic system of Western civilization, it was necessary that the whole economic system of the Asiatic and African should be adjusted to and assimilated with that of Europe.

LEONARD WOOLF[1]

Unlike the modern West Indies, which are the creation of Europe (that is, Britain, Spain, France and Holland), present-day Asia and Africa do not owe their existence to European colonization. The people of the West Indies in the New World are where they are now because their forebears were transplanted from Africa and Asia, involuntarily or voluntarily, as part of the colonial policies of European powers. This is not the case with those non-European parts of the Old World which fell under the imperial rule of Europe. Basically, these lands in Asia and Africa have continued to be populated by the indigenous people with histories that stretch back to the dawn of civilization.

When Britain conquered parts of Asia and Africa, it concerned itself mainly with the economic and political administration of these colonies. Throughout its imperial and pre-imperial history, Britain's overriding concern remained economic – first, trade and then, with rapid industrialization at home, adequate supplies of raw materials for British factories, and guaranteed colonial markets for its manufactured goods. In order to achieve this economic end, Britain in India, for instance, established an administrative machinery charged with the tasks of tax collection and the maintenance of law and order, and buttressed it later with an educational system designed to produce clerks, *babus*, to staff its bureaucracy at a low cost. Britain left the social structure and culture of the Indian masses well alone. In any case, it seemed a Himalayan task to mould Indian society with its distinct history, religions, languages, literature and folklore into a European image. Moreover, there was no profit to be made from it.

On the other hand, the value of India as an economic asset came into sharper focus as a result of the abolition of slavery. On Emancipation in

1834, the freed African slaves left the estates, unwilling to work for their old masters under any circumstances. This led to an almost total collapse of the economic system of the plantation colonies. One of the colonies so affected was Mauritius, an island in the Indian Ocean which France had ceded to Britain in 1815.

Faced with an acute labour shortage, the Mauritian planters considered tapping the vast Indian subcontinent for labour. They secured the East India Company's permission to engage agents in India to recruit labour, and offered their Indian agents lucrative commissions of £3 to £5 per recruit. With this incentive, the agents worked hard to produce 'volunteers'. To their gullible audience of landless labourers in the bazaars of Madras and Calcutta, they painted glamorous pictures of life 'across the waters'. They guaranteed free passage to a 'land of milk and honey' – and back, if the actual situation turned out to be less rosy. And, above all, they promised free land, an irresistible proposition to the land-starved people. With these baits, many young labourers – mostly Hindus of lower castes and Muslims – were lured into the planters' net.

Little did the illiterate peasant realize that, by his thumb impression on a contract, he was committing himself to 'semi-slavery'; because the contract bound him to a planter for five years for a small, fixed wage, with a further five years' contract under the same or any other planter on the island, before allowing him a free passage home *if* he chose to return home. That was the origin of 'indenturing' labour from India, a practice which continued until 1916, when it was outlawed by the Indian authorities.

The first batch of indentured Indian labour arrived in Mauritius in 1834 to work on sugar plantations. The scheme worked remarkably well. Its success led the planters in British Guiana (later Guyana) to initiate a similar scheme four years later. Subsequently it was extended to Trinidad and Jamaica.

From then on, whenever and wherever the plans of British capital were frustrated by the unavailability, or lack of co-operation, of indigenous labour in the colonies, Indian workers were invariably imported. This happened in Ceylon (Sri Lanka), Malaya (Malaysia) and Burma (Myanmar) for the development of coffee, sugar, tea and rubber plantations, and tin mining; and also in South Africa, in 1859, for mining and the development of cotton fields. Later it occurred in East Africa for the construction of railways. Indians became the coolies of the Empire, for ever serving the interests of the British capitalist, who found them hard-working, docile and reliable.

During the early phase of the indentured system the morale of Indian labourers was, however, low. They were overworked, underpaid and badly housed. They suffered sexual deprivation and jealousy due to lack of women. Internecine violence and suicide rates ran high. In time came resignation and acceptance. They also succeeded in tempering the harshness of an alien environment by grouping together on a linguistic and religious basis, thus partially recreating the socio-cultural milieu they had left behind. The later practice of being grouped in culturally homogeneous work gangs gave them a sense of security and comradeship.

At the end of their contracts, some of them, thrifty and enterprising, bought small plots of land with their own savings. With these, they established roots in the new country. They brought their families. Thus a small community of 'free' Indians emerged. It grew. It attracted voluntary immigrants from India – traders, skilled craftsmen, even professionals – to service the agriculturist settlers. In short, the milieu of Indian rural society was recreated in the Caribbean, Mauritius, the Fiji islands and South-east Asia. Unlike the West African slaves there was no rupture of continuity, no annihilation of the past. The Indians carried their past with them and recreated the present in its image as, indeed, did the English settlers in North America, and the Iberians in Central and South America. There was, however, one crucial difference. Indians were not the conquerors or imperial colonizers in whom the ultimate political and economic power rested, but were themselves colonial subjects, mere labourers and petty farmers.

From this brief history of Indian settlements abroad emerge two elements which are relevant to the issues of immigration and race in contemporary Britain. First, Indian settlements overseas are a direct result of the actions taken by British entrepreneurs to further their economic interests. Second, like the British and the Chinese – that is, people with a strong sense of their own identity – the Indians are adept at recreating substantially the environment they have left behind; and they do not totally discard their culture, whatever the direct or indirect pressures.

The voluntary immigrants, who followed the indentured Indian labourers into various British colonies, were mostly from Gujarat and the Punjab, the two areas of the Indian subcontinent with a tradition of migration.

In modern times, the business enterprise of the Ismailis (a Muslim sect) and the merchant castes among Gujarati Hindus has often stimulated travel and migration to other parts of India and abroad. There is also a fifteen-centuries-old tradition of overseas trade from the ports of Gujarat – a coastal state facing the Indian Ocean – with East Africa, Iran and the Arabian Peninsula. Hence, foreign trade and travel among Gujarati businessmen are not new. Also, unlike peasants, merchants do not feel attached to the soil and are willing, for business reasons, to migrate to distant places. Nowadays they are to be found in all parts of the British Commonwealth and the rest of the world.

The fertile plain of the Punjab has been through the centuries a scene of major battles between invading foreigners (from the ancient Aryan tribes to the Moguls) and the indigenous people, and is thus a melting-pot of varied human stocks. As such, it produces people who are generally dynamic, thrusting and energetic. Of the three major religious groups in the Punjab – Hindus, Muslims and Sikhs – Hindus were inhibited from migrating abroad by caste considerations. The higher-caste Hindus, aware that caste taboos could not be maintained in an alien land, or even on board a ship, would not normally contemplate migration. But the casteless Muslims and Sikhs were far less restricted in movement as well as in their choice of occupation.

As people with a martial history, Sikhs joined the police and the British Army in large numbers. In this capacity they were often sent to other British colonies such as Singapore, Malaya and Hong Kong. (Sikh soldiers were used by the British to suppress the Boxer Rebellion in China in 1900.) As their knowledge of the world outside India grew, they became more adventurous. Increasingly, Sikh (as well as Muslim) craftsmen and artisans joined the voluntary outflow into those parts of the Empire where Indian labourers had already settled – South-east Asia, the Caribbean and East Africa. In one instance – that of the Fiji islands – Sikh agriculturists, *jats*, became the pioneering Indian migrants. They developed sugar-cane fields in the islands during the 1880s. From there, they grew familiar with New Zealand and Australia. In the early 1900s a shipload of Sikh immigrants disembarked in Australia; but the next ship was refused disembarkation by the authorities, the Australian immigration law having come into force in 1901. Undeterred by this rebuff, the Sikh migrants crossed the Pacific and disembarked at Vancouver in British Columbia. There they mainly engaged in lumbering and, in time, set up a chain of sawmills. By 1910 – when the Canadian Immigration Act came into operation and barred free entry – more than 5000 Sikhs had settled in British Columbia, enough to create the substantial Sikh community which now exists there.

After the First World War there was a steady, though numerically insignificant, trickle of Sikh immigrants into Britain, since it was the only country in the Empire retaining an 'open-door' policy. They were mainly craftsmen; but only those who were fluent in English managed to find jobs in factories. The large majority had to explore areas of self-employment, and often became pedlars. They sold hosiery, woollens and knitwear from door to door in the working-class areas of London, the Midlands and Glasgow.

Of course, there were, at any given time, hundreds of Indian students and doctors in Britain. But comparatively few took up permanent residence. Instead, they returned to India to capitalize on their British qualifications in law, medicine or engineering. The case of R. B. Jillani was exceptional. In 1935 he secured a degree in civil engineering in London. Then, with the help of his professor, he found an appropriate job. He stayed, and was called up when the Second World War broke out, as were most Indian doctors and graduate students. Thus the number of Indians resident in Britain increased. But, even then, their total was small. It is estimated that in 1949 there were no more than 8000 Indian and Pakistani settlers in Britain, including 1000 doctors. Broadly, the Indian and Pakistani communities could then be divided into Lascars (seamen), mostly from what was then East Pakistan; doctors and students; and pedlars, mostly Sikhs.

Labour shortages after the war created a favourable climate for the Sikh pedlars. The handicap of language no longer seemed to matter. Being able-bodied was enough – especially to the managers of Midlands foundries. The Sikhs vastly preferred indoor, steady work with an assured pay-packet at the end of each week to precarious outdoor peddling. This wage-earning community was later to prove to be the nucleus around which Indian immigration to Britain grew.

The post-war boom in Britain happened to coincide with two major, interrelated upheavals in the Indian subcontinent: the partition of British India into Pakistan and India on the eve of independence in 1947; and the conflict between these newly-formed states regarding the border province of Kashmir. As a result of the partition of the pre-independence Punjab, nearly four million Muslims from the Indian side crossed into the Pakistani Punjab, while a slightly larger number of Sikhs and Hindus moved in the opposite direction. The pressure on land, already high in the less fertile Indian Punjab, increased even further. Some of the displaced Sikhs had relatives and friends in Britain, who through their generous remittances (by Indian standards) to India showed that they were doing rather well. The bewildering situation of partition and displacement induced the youngest male members of a few hundred families, whose labour was not needed on the family farm even in good times, to migrate to Britain, where they were readily absorbed into unskilled factory jobs.

For generations, it has been customary for young Sikhs leaving the farms to join the army[2] or migrate to other parts of India. Sikhs are therefore to be found in all the major cities of India – except in the south – engaged in semi-skilled and skilled jobs. For instance, in Calcutta, a city one thousand miles to the east of the Punjab, Sikhs drive most of the city's taxis.

The pressure to migrate is highest in the most thickly populated districts of the Punjab: Jullundur and Hoshiarpur. These adjoining districts contained 2.5 million people, as many as Jamaica and Guyana together. (The population density of Jullundur is 914 per square mile; that of Britain, 535.) It was from these districts that migration to Fiji and Canada had earlier taken place.

The Indo-Pakistani conflict over Kashmir also led to a considerable uprooting of populations across boundaries. One of the affected areas was Mirpur, a district where the terrain is rocky and the agricultural output low, and where, over the past many generations, young men seeking jobs have often been forced to travel to other regions of the subcontinent – or even overseas, to secure work as seamen and deckhands with British and other shipping lines. The disturbed conditions in Mirpur during 1947–50 gave further impetus to the traditional exodus. Almost concurrently, word was spreading among Pakistani seamen that work was easy to get in Britain, and that they could more than double their earnings by taking up jobs ashore. Consequently, more and more Pakistani seamen began to desert ships in Britain to take up factory jobs.

As with the West Indians, initial contacts in Britain were crucial for Indians and Pakistanis. For instance, Jaswant Singh Nehra came to England to join his brother who, after serving in the Royal Air Force during the war, had settled in Nottingham. Gurbachan Singh Gill came to London in 1952 because his father-in-law's family had been living there since 1936.

In some cases, adventurous Sikhs travelled to the Far East first, and then managed to gain contacts for eventual travel to Britain. Umerao Singh Basi, born near Jullundur, was a case in point. He longed to 'go abroad' as soon as he had finished his secondary school. He joined a relative in the Philippines, worked, saved, secured addresses of distant relatives resident in London, and joined them. For a living he took up peddling.

Overall, however, the rate of migration from India and Pakistan was very low. In 1955, for example, there were only 7350 Indian and Pakistani immigrants, about a quarter of the number from the West Indies, even though the combined populations of the principal areas of migration – the Punjab, Gujarat, Mirpur and Sylhet (in East Pakistan/Bangladesh) – was fourteen times that of the West Indies.[3] The recession of 1958 had a dampening effect on immigration. The number of Indian and Pakistani immigrants dropped to 3800 in 1959. The following year it returned to the 1955 level. The reasons for this low rate of migration to Britain were partly historico-psychological and partly administrative.

Although the British governed India for two hundred years, social contact between the rulers and the ruled was minimal. The vast majority of Indians had at most distant, occasional glimpses of the white District Collectors or Superintendents of Police,[4] men who conducted their personal and social life in an exclusive circle of their own. Such a situation was in direct contrast to the African slaves' experience in the Caribbean. There, the white planter and his assistants, living in a mansion surrounded by slaves, and cut off from other whites, could not completely shut off their everyday life from the view of the house-slaves and field hands. Also, the white masters' frequent submission to their weakness for free sexual gratification with slave women, and the consequent creation of a substantial mulatto population, subverted their (moral) efforts to impose and maintain a racial apartheid. In India, by successfully maintaining their aloofness, the British were able to engender in the Indian mind an awe of the white man and his country of origin.

The feeling of awe among Indians went hand in hand with the view of Britain as an alien land where people had strange customs, dress, religion and dietary habits. This (factually correct) view was so widely prevalent that no efforts could have conditioned the minds of Indians, whether at the popular or élite level, to believe that Britain was their mother country. And, indeed, no such exercise was seriously attempted by the British.

Hence, unlike the West Indians, Pakistanis and Indians never visualized their migration in socio-cultural terms. For them, the economic consideration was the sole motive for migration. However, the idea that Britain offered better economic opportunities occurred to only that tiny fraction of the Indian subcontinent's population whose relatives or close friends had earlier made the long journey. Often, those Indians and Pakistanis, contemplating a similar journey, thought concretely in terms of joining relatives or friends already in Britain rather than going to Britain *per se*, a proposition which, in its abstract form, they found too intimidating.

Furthermore, there were the administrative controls rigorously applied by India. In 1954, the central government deprived the Indian provincial authorities of their right to issue passports. It then introduced stringent educational and financial requirements for successful passport applications.

A similar situation prevailed in Pakistan. Many Pakistanis could come to Britain only through a circuitous route: they would first obtain a passport for travel to the Persian Gulf region, or for pilgrimage to Mecca, in Saudi Arabia. They would undertake the journey and then, at a Pakistani embassy abroad, have the passport endorsed for travel to Britain.

With such strict controls at source, Indian and Pakistani migration to Britain was kept to an absolute minimum – until 1960. In that year the Supreme Court in India ruled it unconstitutional for the Indian government to refuse passports to its nationals, that is, deny them the fundamental freedom to travel. The only device by which the central government could then discourage its nationals from migrating was to deny them foreign exchange, as it still does: during the 1950s and early 1960s each traveller was permitted a 'travelling allowance' of only £3. However, such a restriction was meaningless to those who already had relatives and friends in Britain.

In its importance, the Indian Supreme Court judgement in 1960 equalled the McCarran–Walter Act of 1952 in America, and indirectly it led to a relaxation of rules regarding passport issue in Pakistan. Soon after, rumours of impending restrictions on Commonwealth immigrants began to circulate. Both these factors led to an abrupt rise in Indian and Pakistani arrivals in Britain. Their numbers swelled from 8400 in 1960 to 48,850 in 1961, and an almost equal number arrived during the first half of 1962.

In 1962 the Commonwealth Immigrants Act had another far-reaching effect on Asian settlers. As with the West Indians, it compelled them to discard their original plan of a few years' stay in Britain before returning home with their savings. It even forced some 'mature' students, such as G. S. Bhandari, in London for a course in advertising, to stay permanently. Moreover, it led Indians and Pakistanis already here to advise their male kinsmen to join them, and thereby gain a toehold, before the doors finally closed. The result was an excessive imbalance of the sexes. According to the 1961 census, the male–female ratio among Pakistanis in Bradford was 40:1, and among Indians 3:1.[5]

Those who could not get in before 1 July 1962 queued for work vouchers under the new system. But this did not mean that they left for Britain the moment they received these vouchers. Indeed, during the first year of the 1962 Act's operation, only 22 per cent of such vouchers issued to Indians and Pakistanis were utilized.[6] Why? Because Britain experienced economic recession in 1962–3. In other words, once the political hysteria of 'beat the ban' subsided, the old economic law of demand and supply became operative: economic recession proved a more effective deterrent than the administrative and legislative controls of the 1962 Act.

In retrospect, Indian and Pakistani immigration previous to the 1962 Act can be divided into two phases: before 1960, and after. During the earlier phase, its size was small, being less than a third of the West Indian immigration. It consisted mainly of people with a significant knowledge of the English language and/or Britain: seamen, ex-Indian army personnel, university graduates, teachers, doctors and other professionals; and it was controlled at source by the Indian and Pakistani governments. During the second phase, immigration increased, equalling that from the West Indies; and the profile of the typical immigrant changed. More often than not the South Asian immigrant was now an agriculturist, generally unfamiliar with the language and culture of Britain. But one factor remained constant throughout: the importance of the contact or sponsor in Britain. During the 'beat the ban' rush of 1961–2, the houses of the early settlers virtually became reception centres.

2 Money is All: The Rise of Asian Enterprise

Why am I here? For money ... I miss the freedom of my village in the Punjab. Sometimes I think that England is like a sweet prison.

GURDAS RAM, an Indian worker in Slough.

Our food is a constant reminder to us that we're Indians or Pakistanis or Bangladeshis ... Our language? Well, language is the food of mind.

MUHAMMAD FARUQ, a Pakistani settler
in Bradford.

The English are not the only nation of shopkeepers. We are too. And we're proving it daily – in England.

ABDUL LATEEF, a Pakistani businessman
in Birmingham.

The factors that kept the West Indian immigrants together – discrimination by whites, a sense of racial and temperamental alienation from the host society, lack of funds and the need for the companionship of fellow-countrymen – applied equally to the Asians. Indeed, in their case alienation from British society was further accentuated by cultural differences and unfamiliarity with English. The newcomers had to rely heavily on the assistance and guidance of the early English-speaking immigrants. The latter hardly ever failed to oblige.

What motivated the earlier settler to help the latecomer was not rooted in either monetary or altruistic considerations but in a sense of mutual obligation towards kinsmen and fellow-villagers that is characteristic of rural, agrarian society everywhere, be it in India or Pakistan, Cyprus or Sicily. In such a society much value is attached to blood relationships and friendships; and readiness to help friends and relatives even at the cost of personal convenience and expense is the touchstone of interpersonal relationship. Therefore, the early settler was often generous in rendering moral and material help to his relatives or fellow-villagers in *pardes*, an alien land. He would let an unemployed relative or friend stay with him free of charge until he found work. He would collect lower rents from tenants related to him than from others. If he knew English he would freely help those who did not.

The language barrier had individual and collective consequences for the Asians. For instance, lack of English excluded the average Asian immigrant from employment on public transport. He therefore sought, and found, work in factories where gang work, or menial tasks, were offered; that is, where demands on his English were minimal. Two such industries were heavy engineering (foundries, steel mills) and textiles, located mostly in the Midlands and the North. Demand for unskilled and semi-skilled labour in these industries was high. Consequently Asians had little difficulty in getting jobs. In Bradford, a woollen textile centre, for instance, there were 250 Pakistanis in 1953. Eight years later there were 3500; but they were all employed.[1]

Altogether, these factors tended to keep most of the Asian immigrants out of the Greater London area. In 1966, while three-fifths of all West Indian immigrants in Britain were living in Greater London, the corresponding proportion of Indian and Pakistani immigrants was only half as much.[2] Comparatively fewer Asians than West Indians were employed on trains and buses in London and elsewhere.

Economic considerations also led many Asians to settle in the provinces. Living is after all cheaper in, say, Tipton, Staffordshire, than in Tooting, London: rents are lower, travel costs less, and so do cinema tickets; and the temptations to spend are fewer. In the early 1970s an unmarried Pakistani worker in Bradford could live on £5 a week. All these points were important to the Asian immigrant. His *raison d'être* for being in Britain was economic, much more so than in the case of the West Indian. Summing up a general feeling in the Asian community, Gurnam Singh, an Indian settler in Wolverhampton, said, 'Money is our mother, money is our father; money is all.' That is why many Asians sought jobs offering overtime. An 84-hour week was not uncommon among Pakistani workers in West Yorkshire.

Economic pressures on the typical Asian immigrant were immense. He most probably mortgaged his meagre assets to raise a loan for travel to England and the loan had to be repaid. At the same time his immediate family as well as his parents, living in an Indian/Pakistani/Bangladeshi village, had to be supported. Additionally, the demands of other members of the joint family had to be met. In the rural Punjab or Bangladesh, a male expatriate's social status was measured by the size of his monthly or weekly remittances home. After these obligations were discharged, money had to be saved either to buy a house and pay for the fares of his wife and children to join him or, alternatively, to finance his travel and a long holiday at home. The complex web of social and filial obligations drove the Asian immigrant to work as long and hard, and as submissively, as he could.[3]

Saving 50 per cent of his income was quite common among Pakistani and Bangladeshi workers; the figure for the average Briton was 5 per cent.[4] Taeeb Ali, a Bangladeshi/East Pakistani millworker in Bradford, for instance, saved £14 a week in the late 1960s. He remitted £10 a week home, a sum on which he not only supported his family but also paid for the university education of his two brothers.[5] Taeeb Ali was typical of the Bangladeshi immigrants in Britain, nearly seven-eighths of whom were in the late 1960s living here without their families. Previous to the 1962 Act this was true of Indian and Pakistani immigrants as a whole. That is, before that Act, Asian immigrants were predominantly male and single.

However, being unaccustomed to the Western way of life, most of them did not visit dance-halls or clubs. They did not seem interested in dating white women. Therefore such limitations as a colour bar at a dance-hall or club did not disturb them. At the time of the national controversy over a colour bar operating at a Wolverhampton dance-hall in 1958, Rashmi Desai, an academic researcher, noted that the Indian immigrants to whom he talked 'did not admit any great feeling of corporate indignation ... they considered the privilege of dancing to be of doubtful value. Some welcomed the affair as a deterrent to those immigrants who would otherwise want to go dancing ... There was no collective militancy among the Indians ... As individuals also most of them were indifferent.'[6]

For the Muslims among Asian immigrants there was (and still is) a religious prohibition against drinking – so pubs were generally out of bounds. Whatever drinking a Muslim eventually succumbed to took place in his bed-sitting room in all-male company. For his entertainment the Asian immigrant went to an Indian or Pakistani film, or listened to Indian music in Asian cafés. His sexual gratification came from the odd white prostitute who dropped in to service a household of Pakistani or Indian men. That cost little. Life became literally 'bed to work, work to bed'. And he did not mind.

Outside the economic field, the average Asian had no aspirations or expectations. He had come to Britain knowing full well that white people were culturally alien, quite apart from his own. And he had neither the inclination nor the intention to participate in their social life. It was therefore not surprising for the PEP survey team in 1966 to find that 'a coloured community in a West Riding town' – in fact, Pakistanis in Keighley – complained the least about racial discrimination. This was so because the Pakistanis had only minimally exposed themselves to situations where they might be discriminated against. 'By avoiding notice the Pakistanis hope to avoid trouble,' explained a Pakistani leader in Nottingham.

By creating a self-contained life of their own, and by being genuinely indifferent to British social life, many Asians spared themselves the indignities and rebuffs inflicted on the West Indians.[7] Their expectations from British life, outside employment, were minimal; their attempts to socialize with white people almost non-existent. Consequently, racial tension in cities such as Bradford, where Asians formed the bulk of the coloured settlers, was much less than in, say, Brixton, London, where West Indians were the predominant group.[8]

Most of the bitterness expressed in the Asian community came from English-speaking and educationally qualified persons. And that too was mainly in the sphere of employment. They almost invariably found it a waste of time to follow up job advertisements in newspapers and professional journals. Either no interview calls came or, when they did, British employers often treated their university degrees and professional experience as worthless. A typical experience was that of an Indian teacher in London who made nearly 300 applications but did not obtain a single interview.[9] Not surprisingly, therefore, many qualified, experienced teachers became bus conductors.[10] A holder of MA and LL B degrees from the Punjab became a moulder in a Southall rubber factory; a police superintendent from Delhi, a machine operator. A survey by the Campaign Against Racial Discrimination in Southall in 1966 revealed that there were nearly 1000 Indian and Pakistani university graduates, 84 per cent of whom were engaged in semi-skilled, manual jobs.

Nor did the subsequent system of B vouchers, issued to people with special skills (teachers, doctors, engineers and scientists) improve the situation. Before leaving his country a qualified Indian/Pakistani teacher or scientist felt, with some justification, that possession of a work voucher would ensure him an equivalent job. But most British employers treated work vouchers as another meaningless piece of paper. Although there was an acute shortage of doctors, many qualified Asians had to apply forty or fifty times before securing a job. Of the 3500 Indian and Pakistani teachers who were issued B work vouchers between 1965 and 1967 only a few hundred managed to find teaching posts.[11]

This situation prevailed not only among those with Indian or Pakistani university degrees, but also for those with a British education. The case of Zulfikar Ghose, a poet and writer, is illustrative. Born in Pakistan, he finished his schooling in London. Later he obtained a degree in English and Philosophy at Keele University. 'I wrote to some daily papers ... two put me on their availability lists,' he stated in his autobiography. 'To this day, I have heard nothing from them ... I wrote off to some advertising agencies. Some interviewed me and felt that my background of journalism and poetry was an excellent one for being a copywriter ... I have heard nothing more ... I wrote to several headmasters who advertised for teachers. Not one replied.'[12]

Employment was one area in which Asian immigrants were totally dependent on British society. They could not all become grocers and restaurateurs.[13] Ambition and enthusiasm were not enough. Capital was needed. And capital, during the early period of settlement, was better used for buying a house than starting a business, particularly when, like West Indians, Asians concluded that the only way they could solve their housing problem was by purchase.[14]

In some cases, business-minded Asians soon realized that buying a house could also prove a worthwhile capital investment, and acted accordingly. For instance, ten Indians in Handsworth, Birmingham, formed a mortgage club. Each member paid £10 a week into the pool. Thus in ten weeks they accumulated £1000. With this sum, they bought outright – in the name of one member – a short-lease property, where there was very little competition from white Brummies. They then rented out the house. Shortly, with the rent money and their own savings, they purchased another house in the same street in the name of the next member on the list. And so on until, in less than eighteen months, each of them had a house of his own plus income from rent.

The elements of self-help and enterprise apparent in that project were soon to be applied to other areas, particularly in meeting needs arising out of the distinctive linguistic and religious identity of the Asians and their special sartorial and culinary habits. The earliest examples of this were the Indian grocery shops.

The gradual expansion of the Asian community and the corresponding growth in the demand for Indian spices, pickles, vegetables and chapati flour led some enterprising Asian settlers, with previous business experience, to become traders. Often such an immigrant began by importing groceries in bulk from India or Pakistan, and engaging his recently arrived family in packaging goods in small quantities. To build a clientele, he delivered groceries by van to Asian households. At first, while he held his factory job, he limited deliveries to weekends; but as his clientele grew, and with it his business confidence, he gave up his job and became a full-time retailer.

When he had saved sufficient capital he bought a shop and stocked British as well as Indian items. He added Indian sweets, snacks and vegetables, and West Indian items – yams, tinned okra, brown rice, green bananas, etc. – to his stock. His apparent success aroused envy. Other ambitious Asians, anxious to relieve themselves of the drudgery of factory work, followed his example. More Indian groceries opened.

By the late 1960s, however, there was an over-abundance of Asian grocers. An Asian community of 15,000 in and around Southall, for example, was then served by over thirty grocers and butchers. In Bradford, the number of Pakistani grocers and butchers rose from two in 1959 to fifty-one in 1967.[15] A whole network of retailers and wholesalers dealing in Indian groceries and vegetables had emerged.

Asian enterprise also went into clothing. Aware that Indian and Pakistani women like to buy cloth and make their own dresses, Asians opened draperies. Trained Indian and Pakistani tailors started working – at home or in business premises. Others opened goldsmiths' shops, since Asian women prefer gold ornaments individually made. And so it continued.

The result was that by 1965 in Bradford there were 105 immigrant-owned commercial and business premises. These included grocers, butchers, cafés, restaurants, travel agencies, photographic dealers, booksellers, car-hire firms, drapery shops, sweet shops, electrical goods stores, estate agencies, banks, dry cleaners, coal merchants, furniture dealers, tailors, car driving schools and barbers.[16]

Obviously, such dynamism and business acumen could not for ever remain circumscribed within the immigrant market. It had to break out; and it did. Asians in Nottingham, for example, bought taxis as soon as they had saved enough from working overtime on the local corporation buses. Others put their money into off-licence shops. Asian publicans appeared in the Midlands and the North.

But, more significantly, Asians entered the garment and mattress manufacturing industry in London's East End and elsewhere. In Birmingham they created a clothing industry where none existed before. Each week a score of Asian entrepreneurs turned out thousands of anoraks and quilted car-coats at highly competitive prices. Some of them cut the cloth in one place, then distributed it to 'outworkers' – that is, Asian housewives – thus slashing overhead costs while concurrently tapping the unused skills of Asian women in their own homes. Others employed their family and near relatives to keep costs down. It was a hard life for all, but financially rewarding and psychologically satisfying.

Kareemi Fashions Ltd was a case in point. Its owner, Abdul Kareem, a trained men's tailor, worked with the Indian Army and the Pakistani Railways, cutting uniforms. He came to Birmingham in 1960, and gained a City & Guilds diploma in ladies' tailoring. However, he failed to secure a suitable job. So he worked in a post office, saving as much as he could. In 1966 he brought his family over from Pakistan. Two years later, goaded by the idea that he must have something of his own to pass on to his children, he set up a clothing firm. 'At first it was hard going,' he recalled. 'I went from store to store to get the buyers to look at my samples.' With long-term supply orders from a few large stores in Birmingham, he did not have to worry overmuch, except that he considered it unbusinesslike to be tied to one line – anoraks.

This was precisely the view of Gurbachan Singh Gill in 1957 when, with the aid of his family, he began manufacturing shirts (with such brand names as 'Soho' and 'Superlene') in the East End of London. In spite of the lack of credit facilities from his British bank, he expanded and diversified his company which made 'everything that fits the human body'. His clientele was 80 per cent British.

Such a preponderance of white customers held true in another context: Indian, Pakistani and Bangladeshi restaurants in Britain. A large majority of these were owned and staffed by Bangladeshis. Pioneers in this field were the seamen from what was then East Pakistan who worked as cooks in British ships plying between Britain and Pakistan/India. When they settled in Britain they first established cafés in dock areas and then graduated to running restaurants in better districts.

Managing a restaurant is by its very nature a small business, and not highly profitable. Yet it was attractive to many Asians because it offered a congenial atmosphere, comradeship, plenty of food and a slower pace of work than was expected in factories.

Travel was another business which attracted ambitious Asians, aware of the fact that British travel agencies were unpopular with most Asians due to the language barrier. Initially, money was to be made out of transporting Indians and Pakistanis to Britain. Successive immigration control regulations curtailed this traffic, but with settlement and comparative prosperity, Asian immigrants developed a pattern of periodic visits home for holidays. Asian travel agencies stepped in to arrange charter flights. Besides that, they went to great lengths to find routes and airlines that offered the cheapest flights to India, Pakistan and Bangladesh, somtimes at rates as low as half the scheduled fares. Even English-speaking Asians found it in their economic interest to approach Asian, not British, travel agencies.

The settlement of thousands of South Asians brought another avenue of business within the enterprising Asian's range: estate agencies. Starting in the late 1950s, and especially in the early 1960s, there was a fairly rapid build-up of Asian families and, consequently, of Asian house-owners. During the period 1959–63 the number of Asian house-owners in Southall, for instance, quadrupled.[17] By the mid-1960s there were enough houses under racial minority ownership and a sufficiently large turnover of property within the ethnic communities to make it feasible for some Asians to establish estate agencies. They did. And they prospered. As new entrants to business, they tried hard to please their clients.

They showed none of the superciliousness with which many well-established white estate agents treated their racial minority enquirers. On their part, most ethnic clients placed their trust and confidence in Asian agents to a degree they could never do in the case of white agents. Thus Asian estate agencies thrived and multiplied.

From there on, it seemed logical to establish mortgage companies, followed by private loan companies and finance brokers. The arrival in Britain, from 1965 onwards, of many Asian entrepreneurs from East Africa along with their capital gave a further fillip to the financial and business activity of the Asian community. In some cases they acquired financial control of British companies which continued to be managed and staffed by white Britons.

Concurrently, Indian, Pakistani and Bangladeshi banks expanded and opened branches throughout the country. In Bradford, for instance, there were six Pakistani banks by 1971. They proved popular with non-English-speaking Asian settlers who generally felt intimidated by the very businesslike ambience of a British bank, and found it cumbersome to fill in forms and answer questions in English. At the Asian banks, on the other hand, they found the atmosphere congenial. Urdu- and Bengali-speaking staff were always co-operative and willing to help, aware that remittances to India or Pakistan or Bangladesh were beneficial to their respective country's economy and balance of payments.

In short, a complex infrastructure of Asian business establishments, estate agencies, mortgage companies, banks and financial brokerage firms grew. In some areas it was almost independent of the larger economic structure; in others, not so.

All this led to another development: the establishment of an Asian press in Britain. The major stumbling block to the successful launching of an Indian-language journal in Britain hitherto had been the lack of a distribution channel, since British distributors had refused to co-operate. Mahmood Hashemi, an experienced Pakistani journalist and broadcaster, settled in Birmingham in the late 1950s. Working as a teacher, he visualized the potential of Asian shops as sales outlets for an Urdu journal he wished to publish. That was in 1960. By then, the need for such a publication had been felt by thousands of Asian settlers.

Because of the language barrier many Asians felt cut off from the primary sources of information and entertainment: English-language radio, television and newspapers. Even the English-speaking Asians missed detailed news about their home countries. Subscribing to an Indian/Pakistani newspaper by air was costly, and listening to short-wave broadcasts by All India Radio or Air Pak inconvenient. An Indian-language journal published in Britain was the only solution.

By conveying this point and appealing to their communal sense, Hashemi was able to secure the co-operation of most Asian grocers and butchers regarding distributing his Urdu weekly news magazine, *Mashriq* (*East*). His beginning in 1961 was modest: a 12-page publication at 2s. 6d. (12.5 pence). Later he tripled the size and halved the price.

As in other fields, Hashemi's successful lead was followed by others. By the late 1960s there were nine Indian-language weeklies – four in Urdu, two in Punjabi, one each in Gujarati, Bengali and Hindi; and one monthly in Urdu. In addition there was one English-language periodical, *India Weekly*. The combined circulation of the Indian-language weeklies was over 70,000, a third of which was accounted for by the pioneering *Mashriq*.

For thousands of Indians and Pakistanis these weeklies were the only windows to the outside world. Aware of this, the editor of *Mashriq* crammed his magazine with news of the Indian subcontinent; reports from its correspondents in Britain; important British and international news; correspondence columns; reviews and comments on Asian films; and special columns for women and the immigration laws.

The healthy state of these publications was due to the advertisers, predominantly Asian, who bought a third to a half of the total space, an indication of the strength of the internal economy of the Asian community. A very substantial share of the advertisement revenue came from Asian film distributors and exhibitors – another Asian industry which emerged to meet a keenly felt need of the community.

The pioneer in this field was a non-profit organization, the India League, which was the spearhead of the Indian independence lobby. After 1947 it redefined its major aim as creating better understanding between the Indian and British peoples. One of the means to achieve this objective was to show Indian films, suitably subtitled in English, to predominantly English audiences in London.

However, as the Indian community in Britain grew, some enterprising Indians discerned a business potential in catering for Indian audiences alone. By the 1950s Indian films were being sporadically shown, for profit, at weekends in hired cinema halls. Later every town with a substantial Asian community came to offer weekend Indian films.

Gradually, as films in general declined in popularity with British audiences and an increasing number of cinemas fell into disuse, Asian entrepreneurs bought them outright. All told, every weekend some 200 cinemas from Maidenhead to Middlesbrough and from Glasgow to Gravesend showed Indian films to an estimated audience of 100,000. By the late 1960s it was a £1.5 million-a-year business.

With a steady inflow of Asians from East Africa from the late 1960s onwards, culminating in 1972 – when half of the 50,000 Asians expelled by Uganda arrived in Britain – the size of this community grew. By early 1973 it was estimated that there were at least 200,000 Asians from East and Central Africa resident in Britain. Since a substantial minority of them were engaged in trade and industry in Africa, they possessed both capital and business acumen.

The enterprising spirit of East African Asians could be judged from the fact that of the 21,800 Uganda refugees housed by the British government in sixteen camps, only about a third agreed to take up the local authority housing offered to them,[18] with the rest managing to find their way into the private sector. This enabled the government to wind up the Uganda Resettlement Board in January 1974, within less than a year and a half of its creation.

Even though the authorities made no particular effort to channel these immigrants into commercial activity here, a majority of them seemed to end up in retail trade. This, and their general familiarity with the English language in East Africa, meant that unlike their counterparts from the Indian subcontinent, most of them could be classified as lower-middle or middle-middle class in social terms as well as economic. With this, the Asian community became more sharply stratified, socially, than the West Indian, with a larger middle class than the other major racial minority.

Earlier, another difference between these two groups had emerged. This had to do with a demand by a Campaign Against Racial Discrimination meeting in early 1965 that the British Broadcasting Corporation ought to make programmes for immigrants which would help them 'feel at home'. Soon after, the BBC called a meeting of prominent West Indian and Asian spokespersons. The (English-speaking) West Indians were not keen on a separate programme, but the Asians were. The result was the BBC's Immigrant Programme, with the twin-headed objective of education and entertainment. The first programme was broadcast in October 1965.

By the late sixties the BBC's programmes in Hindustani on radio and television were proving immensely popular. It was estimated that nearly 80 per cent of Asian households listened to or watched these programmes each Sunday in spite of the fact that they were broadcast fairly early in the morning.

Initially the stress was on education and instruction. These programmes were generally well received. The course of English lessons by direct method teaching appealed to the viewers, especially to Asian housewives. A sale of more than 30,000 booklets, to be used in conjunction with this programme, indicated its popularity. Later the magazine-type programme consisted of interviews, discussions and entertainment.

Besides these specific aids, the general process of acculturation was at work, particularly among Asian men, who had to leave home daily to work. Thus their familiarity with the English language and culture grew. An overwhelming majority among them came to understand English. A survey of Asian immigrants in Keighley in 1968 revealed that only one in seven had 'no knowledge' at all of English.[19] However, four out of five Pakistani and Bangladeshi women did not know English. The reason was obvious. An Asian housewife was not compelled by economic necessity or tradition to participate in the (English-speaking) outside world. Her place was in the home. Outside it, as long as she could manage shopping and the laundromat, she could survive. After all, human beings adjust themselves only to the degree their immediate environment demands. That was why very few, if any, British memsahibs in India, for instance, managed to wade through the Hindustani–English primer.

The acculturation and socialization processes were of course more pronounced in the case of Asian children who attended British schools. Most were bilingual, and enriched the English language – undetected and unacknowledged though it might have been – with their idiom, imagery and original turns of phrase. No one knew for sure whether their children would be bilingual or unilingual. But whatever might happen to their mother tongue, it seemed their religious identity would remain unaltered, as had been the case with the descendants of Jewish immigrants in Britain.

Under the pressure of mass education, designed to serve an industrial society based on mass production, the minority languages such as Welsh and Gaelic tend to fall into disuse.[20] But this does not apply to minority religions since these are not in any way involved in the complex mechanisms of production in an industrial society. Jews, scattered throughout the world, speak different languages, but are nevertheless Jews. The Indians in the Caribbean are another case in point. Even when they lost touch with their language, most of them remained Hindu, Muslim or Sikh, and had names that identified them as such.

3 No Faces Like Sikh Faces

I constantly tell my sons that there are no faces like Sikh faces in the entire world. They must never forget that.

GURNAM SINGH, a Sikh settler in Wolverhampton.

No religious identity is as sharp and dramatic as a male Sikh's. This is as true in the Western world as it is in Africa or the Far East, or even India, where Sikhs form only 2 per cent of its overall population.

Sikhism is a comparatively young religion. Its founder, Guru Nanak, was born near Lahore, now in Pakistan, in 1469. However, it was the last, tenth guru, Gobind Singh, who two centuries later gave male Sikhs the distinctive look they now have. He prescribed the five symbols of Sikhism – *kess*, long hair; *kanga*, comb; *kachha*, long underpants; *kara*, steel bangle; and *kirpan*, dagger – and moulded the Sikh sect into a militant brotherhood, the *Khalsa Panth* (Pure Brotherhood). He called his male followers *singhs* (lions).

The physical and sartorial prescriptions were indeed designed to make the *Khalsa* (Pure) Sikhs distinctive from the surrounding Hindus and Muslims – a people apart – and give them a lasting identity. Both purposes were well served. Long hair and beards gave the Sikhs instant unity, and also put to rest the nagging fear of the founders that Sikh converts would gradually be reclaimed by their original religion, Hinduism, noteworthy for its inclusive tendencies. These prescriptions, therefore, became the cornerstone of Sikhism; and to question them was tantamount to questioning its very foundations.

Wearing a dagger at all times in fact proved too cumbersome for ordinary Sikhs, and fell into disuse. But the Sikh's right to wear it was never questioned or disallowed in the Indian subcontinent. Of course, Sikhs migrating to Britain did not arrive carrying daggers. They did not even keep one at home, which, by custom and tradition, they should. This is just one example of how Sikhs have adapted to the British environment. On the other hand, the steel bangle, which is easy to wear, was almost invariably retained by the Sikhs in Britain.

The main dilemma male Sikhs in Britain faced was how to conform to their religious prohibition against cutting hair which, in practice, meant having to sport a beard and wear a turban to cover long hair. They noted, dejectedly, that time after time they were turned down for jobs for which other Indians and Pakistanis were freely hired. The almost universal objection of British employers, in both private industry and public services, seemed to them unjust and depressing. In spite of his war service, and three years spent as a Japanese prisoner-of-war, the bearded Gurbachan Singh Gill was jobless for three months when he arrived in London in 1952. By chance he approached a personnel officer who, as an ex-Indian Army officer, had a certain regard for bearded Sikhs, and secured a job. He was lucky. Thousands of other Sikhs were not. They were faced with a bitter choice: to cut their hair or return home.

When faced with this situation, Trilok Singh Dhami, a newcomer to Wolverhampton, booked a passage home. But relatives and friends prevailed upon him to reconsider. He went through an agonizing reappraisal of his religious identity. Reluctantly he cut his hair. 'Afterwards I felt less than a man,' he later recalled. 'I didn't want to go out in the street: I didn't want to be seen by people. It was like I had got a scarred face overnight.' As with Dhami so with thousands of other Sikhs. Caught in the conflict between religious identity and economic interest, they submitted to the material need, but only at the cost of suffering a sense of spiritual degradation.

Cutting their hair, however, did not signify a diminution in the Sikhs' devotion to their religion. Quite the contrary. Having compromised with the outward form, they felt impelled to reiterate their attachment to Sikhism in other, more significant ways. They attended, more often than before, religious services on Sundays, held in homes or rented halls, and contributed generously towards gurdwara (lit., the Guru's house) funds. As a result of regular and generous contributions from Sikhs, various gurdwara committees in the country were able to buy properties and establish proper gurdwaras. As early as 1957 the Sikh community in Birmingham, for instance, bought an old church in Smethwick and converted it into a gurdwara, inadvertently contrasting their religious ardour with British Christians' lack of it. By the late 1960s there were at least forty gurdwaras in the country.

In an alien land, a gurdwara became more than a place of worship: it was simultaneously a social welfare centre, a hub of communal activity. It also acquired a socio-psychological significance, became an important link with the past. It helped to maintain religio-cultural continuity. The familiarity of congregating on the carpeted floor, the gaudy pictures of the ten Gurus, the smell of incense, the hymns and loud reading of the *Ad Granth*, the Sikhs' holy book, reassured the worshipper that though his environment had changed the essence of being a Sikh had not. The long, leisurely service on Sunday mornings provided a relief from the rigid demands of an industrial society. And the presence of fellow-Sikhs all gathered in one place, on the same floor, generated anew a feeling of 'belonging'.

The function of the gurdwara did not cease after the Sunday service. It remained open to all Sikhs at all times of the day and night. A hungry Sikh could walk in and cook a meal for himself in the refectory, if one was not already prepared. A homeless Sikh could sleep there during the night and stay during the day. The gurdwara committee in Southall owned a house to which homeless Sikhs were transferred after a fortnight at the gurdwara.

Like other immigrant groups in Britain the Sikhs maintained an interest in politics at home. For a long time their specific point of interest was the agitation for a Punjabi-speaking state, with a Sikh majority, in India, which had been brewing since 1956 and which reached a climax in 1966. The leader of this movement was Sant Fateh Singh, a revered religious leader of Sikhs, who visited Britain in the spring of 1966.

Sikhs from all over the country turned up in their thousands at London's Heathrow Airport to give Sant Fateh Singh a tumultuous reception. During his short visit he became the undisputed spokesman of the Sikh community in Britain. He led deputations to British authorities at local and national levels, urging the removal of the ban on beards and turbans on Sikh employees in public transport. He reminded politicians of the services that Sikhs had rendered to the British in India and abroad: 36,000 Sikhs in beards and turbans had died for Britain in the Second World War. More pertinently, he argued that if Sikhs in beards and turbans could operate a tank they could certainly drive a bus or ring a bell without endangering the safety of passengers or causing offence. The Sikh leaders in Manchester had been repeating these points, and more, to the local councillors since 1959, but in vain. Now Sant Fateh Singh was able to convince the local transport committee that religious edicts were involved. As a result, Sikh employees on the buses were granted a special dispensation, provided the colour of their turban matched that of their uniform. The Sikhs' sense of righteousness was further strengthened when, in November 1966, their demand for a Punjabi-speaking state was conceded by the central government in India.

By January 1967, the tricentenary of Guru Gobind Singh,[1] however, Manchester's lead had been followed by only a few other local councils. That many councils were adamant on the issue became clear in August. In Wolverhampton, Tarsem Singh Sandhu, a bus conductor, returned to work after a long illness, wearing a turban and a beard. He was told to remove them if he wanted to continue working. He refused. He was summarily suspended. The incident highlighted once again the illiberal policy of many local authorities on the subject.

As a result, thousands of clean-shaven Sikhs, who had learned to live with their shorn hair with a certain resignation, were jolted into re-thinking the whole issue. It did not matter whether, given the freedom to wear beards and turbans, they would all return to them, but to regain that freedom, in principle, became to them a very important issue. To show their solidarity with a fellow-Sikh, who had been victimized for following his religious edicts, they gathered from all over the country in Wolver-hampton in February 1968 to march silently, with dignity, in a mile-long procession from their gurdwara to the Town Hall. But the local council was unmoved.

The Shromani Akali Dal (SAD) – a national body interested exclu-sively in the religious affairs of Sikhs – formed in the wake of the February 1968 march,[2] kept up pressure on the Wolverhampton council. But nothing happened. The councillors, aware that the issue had been transformed into a battle of will and nerves, remained obdurate. Finally, in sheer desperation, Sohan Singh Jolly, SAD's president, warned the council that if its decision was not reversed by 13 April 1969 (the beginning of the Sikh New Year), he would immolate himself. The councillors were unmoved, and let it be known publicly.

By late March this controversy had aroused deep interest among Sikhs in Britain and in India. In Wolverhampton a chain of Sikhs pledged to burn themselves – one every fifteen days – until the ban was lifted.[3] Outside Wolverhampton fourteen Sikhs vowed to follow the example of Jolly. On 6 April thousands of Sikhs, wearing black arm-bands, marched towards the British High Commission in New Delhi. The event was widely reported in the British media, although the underlying point was not stressed. The message was: if Jolly were to burn himself in Wolverhampton the repercussions would not remain limited to Britain but would involve India as well, very likely jeopardizing the lives and property of British nationals resident there.[4]

The British High Commission in Delhi and the government in London seemed to have grasped the grave implications of the case. On 8 April, Ernest Fernyhough, a junior government minister, was des-patched to Wolverhampton to meet the local transport committee.

On 9 April, after a two-and-a-half-hour meeting, the Transport Com-mittee decided to lift the ban. Announcing the reversal Alderman Ronald Gough, the committee chairman, maintained that their decision 'in the first place' had been 'right and proper'. He conceded the national and international aspects of the case when he added: 'We feel we have been pressured; but we had to take into account the wider implications ... Mr Fernyhough put to us what might happen if he [Mr Jolly] did take his life.'5 He went on to mention 'the anxiety by and on behalf of the High Commissioner for India' as one of the factors taken into account.

Whatever the reasons and explanations, the Sikhs finally won their case. 'This is not a victory for myself,' said Jolly, 'but a victory for the whole Sikh community.'

The national controversy about Sikh bus workers had overshadowed the more widespread, and continuing, injustice against Sikhs in industry. There, the ban on employing bearded and turbaned Sikhs was almost total. Even 'liberal' employers generally failed to recruit Sikhs wearing beards and turbans.

If Sikhs were, for various reasons, assertive of their religious identity, Hindus were exceptionally unobtrusive. In spite of their substantial population in Britain they had, by the late 1960s, established only a handful of temples – and one Hindu centre in London, which was more a community centre than an exclusive place of worship.

It is somehow in the nature of Hinduism and its followers to be amorphous and vague rather than crystallized and dramatic. For instance, unlike Sikhs, Christians, Jews or Muslims, Hindus do not have a single book which to them is the repository of the absolute truth. Instead, there is a voluminous religious literature and scripture.

Then there are the social implications of Hinduism, such as the caste system, which are an integral part of life in (Hindu) India. The twin principles of specialization and division of labour which originally led to the evolution of the caste system and which, incidentally, underlie modern industry, seem, on the face of it, quite sound and rational. It was the hereditary nature of the caste system which made it unjust and un-democratic. However, the rapid urbanization of modern India is under-mining the hold of the traditional system: an urban environment is ill-suited to the maintenance of caste taboos.

Hindu Indians migrating to an urbanized, Western country such as Britain were aware of the practical difficulties of maintaining caste differences and taboos among themselves, and with regard to the British. They were thus psychologically prepared to compromise their caste standing in Britain. In this they were further helped when they dis-covered that the British tended to distinguish people solely on the visual characteristics of colour and race.

That does not imply that caste differences among Hindus in Britain disappeared altogether. Between Brahmins, the highest caste, and Untouchables, the outcastes, a distinction remained. Yet there were no practical or *public* manifestations of this difference, simply because those who differentiated held no levers of power – economic, legal or moral. It remained a matter of 'internal' relationship, meaningful only to the Hindu community. At most, such considerations were sometimes emphasized during election campaigns for the prestigious positions in the local Indian Association or the Indian Workers' Association.

About the only Hindu taboo which manifested itself in a wider context was the abstinence from beef. Many Hindu employees, for instance, avoided beef at works canteens. Hindu (as well as Sikh) children were instructed by their parents to avoid beef at school lunches.

Among Indian immigrants almost all Gujaratis were Hindu, as were a small proportion of the Punjabis. Though these groups spoke different languages, they shared their first names because of the common religion. As in the Western world, first names in the Indian subcontinent show religious influence. Hindu names are often Sanskrit in origin, the language in which the Hindu scripture is written: Shiv, Kanti, Ashwin, Pushpa, Chitra, Ashok, Om Prakash, Praful, etc. Accordingly, most Muslim names are Arabic in origin since the Quran is written in that language: Haroon, Zeenat, Kareem, Muhammad, Mansur, Rashid, Razaq and so on. Sikh names are identical for both boys and girls – Gurjeet, Amolak, Man Mohan, Charan, Sukhdev, Gurdayal, etc. – because these are chosen at random from the holy book, *Ad Granth*. The sexual distinction is made later in life when the suffix Singh is added for men and Kaur for women.

Whatever else may be the influence of the British environment on the Indian, Pakistani or Bangladeshi immigrants and their children, their names have not altered radically. In the case of children going to predominantly white schools some adaptation may ensue – Jagjit may become Jock or Sundri become Sandra, for ease of speech – but the essence will remain. This is likely to happen in the whole socio-cultural make-up of the Asian community.

Since surnames among Hindus indicate caste or sub-caste, the founder of Sikhism (a Hindu by birth), rebelling against the caste system, advised his followers to drop them. He himself was called simply Guru Nanak – and his followers Sikhs, that is, pupils. The equality of all Sikhs is regularly reiterated through a *langar*, communal meal, shared by fellow-Sikhs sitting at the same (floor) level, often after the weekly service. Earlier, the propagators of Islam, a religion which made substantial impact on the Hindu population of India, had also stressed its caste-lessness and the equality of all Muslims before God.

4 Equal before Allah

A Bulgarian Muslim is likely to conduct his family affairs (e.g. marriage, death, inheritance, etc.) much more like an Indonesian Muslim rather than like a Christian Orthodox or a Communist next door.

FARRUKH HASHMI[1]

For Muslims, cultural and political identity is indissolubly tied to religion so that to attack the latter is to undermine the former. In this tight bonding of religion and identity, Muslims are more like Jews.

RANA KABBANI[2]

Though physically less obtrusive than Sikhism, Islam lays down stricter and more thorough-going edicts for its followers. One edict requires the Muslim to offer prayers, facing Mecca, five times a day. This is possible in a rural, agrarian society, but rather inconvenient in an urban, industrial environment. The 9 a.m. to 5 p.m. syndrome or shift work, whether in Pakistan or Britain, forces a paring of the ritual. The final burden, therefore, falls on the afternoon prayer on Friday, which corresponds with the Christian Sunday.

It was the absence of a large meeting-place for the Friday prayer that led the Pakistani Muslims in Birmingham, for instance, to form the Pakistani Welfare Association (PWA) in 1957. Funds were collected, and soon the PWA bought a house to be used for the Friday prayer as well as other religious and social functions.

Historically, Muslims were the first non-Judaeo-Christian community in Britain to establish a place of worship of their own. The Shah Jahan mosque in Woking, financed by the Muslim ruler of Bhopal, then an Indian princely state, was built in 1900. Arab seamen (from South Yemen), settled in South Shields, built their own mosque during the inter-war period. During the Second World War, in order to meet the religious needs of Muslim seamen and servicemen, a mosque was opened in London's East End.

However, the majority of the eighty mosques that existed in the late 1960s had been established during the previous decade and, almost always, by Pakistani settlers. The Pakistani community in a town would organize a mosque committee to raise funds, buy property, and appoint an imam (religious leader) to lead prayers on Fridays and religious days, perform marriage and burial ceremonies, and impart Islamic instruction to Muslim children.

In the British context mosques, first and foremost places of worship, tended to become part of the Pakistani community's social welfare system. Of course much depended on the vigour and devotion of the imam. Haji Taslim Ali, the resident imam of the East London mosque, provided a welfare service to the Muslim community of 7000, most of them (East) Pakistanis. He and his wife taught Muslim children Arabic and the Quran, collected and distributed old clothes within the community, and looked after children if their mothers were in hospital and could not make satisfactory alternative arrangements. Besides, as an interpreter, he was on call to translate at coroners' inquests, in courts and for the police.

Plans were constantly being made to upgrade existing mosques by purchasing better properties and building traditional mosques with a dome and four minarets. Part of the contribution for such projects as building a mosque inside London's Regent's Park came from the embassies of various Muslim countries in the capital. In addition, such Urdu weeklies as the *Mashriq* and *Asia* provided channels through which appeals were addressed to the national body of Pakistani Muslims, estimated to be a quarter of a million strong in the late 1960s.

These ambitious, multinational, co-operative projects continually reminded Muslims in Britain that Islam was a unifying force which often transcended nationality and race. The response of the Muslims in Britain to the arson attack, in July 1969, on Islam's third holiest shrine,[3] Al Aqsa mosque in the Israeli-occupied Arab sector of Jerusalem, was dramatic evidence of this fact – as well as of the hold that religious leaders and institutions had over Muslims. In response to a world-wide call to Muslims by the Saudi king, Faisal ibn Abdul Aziz, to protest against the attack on Al Aqsa mosque, marches and meetings were organized in London and major provincial cities. Thousands of Muslims participated. In Bradford, for instance, responding to a call from the imams and leaders of the Markazi Kameet Tabligh-e Islam (Central Committee for the Propagation of Islam), 8000 Muslims, principally Pakistanis, gathered for a protest march and meeting. Commenting on the event, Stuart Bentley, a British researcher, wrote in *Race Today* of 'the persistence of religious institutions transported to a new and alien society and their efficacy in mobilizing support', and compared it with the 'considerably less support' given by local Muslims to the anti-Powell demonstrations.[4]

This event was the main drive to found a confederation of Muslim associations in Britain. It materialized in July 1970 in the form of the

Union of Muslim Organizations in the United Kingdom and Eire (UMO), and had the blessing of the Saudi regime. The main functions of this confederate body were to safeguard the interests of Muslims and submit their demands to the government. With the economic boom in oil-rich Saudi Arabia that followed the quadrupling of petroleum prices in 1973–4, Saudi interest in the welfare of Muslims in Britain grew, and manifested itself in cash grants to the burgeoning Muslim organizations either directly by the embassy or through such Saudi-sponsored bodies as the Muslim World League established in Geneva in 1962 (and later transferred to Mecca).

The UMO won the affiliation not only of the mosque committees and Islamic centres but also the welfare and cultural organizations. But it decided to keep the educational field apart. It did so formally in 1979 by sponsoring the National Muslim Educational Council, which became the umbrella body for numerous local and regional Muslim educational organizations, including the Saudi-funded Muslim Educational Services.

This happened against a background where many mosque committees worked in conjunction with the local Islamic Cultural Centre (often run by the Muslim Education Board) to ensure that the religious identity of Muslim children was not blurred as a result of growing up in Christian Britain. They often objected to local education authorities about the Christian instruction given to Muslim children in schools. Once their protest was registered, they co-operated with the authorities by providing volunteers to instruct Muslim pupils in Islam. As a result, more and more Muslim children received Islamic instruction at school. In any case, the circumcision of male children leaves an ineradicable religious identity mark. This edict is invariably followed by Muslim parents.

Another edict that a devout Muslim should follow is fasting during the holy month of Ramadan. In a country such as Pakistan, where religious fervour runs high, the entire social milieu is changed during Ramadan. Life is rearranged to fit the pattern of fasting between sunrise and sunset. This socio-religious custom was transferred intact to Britain. Indeed, in the new Christian environment, this practice signified something more: it reiterated religious identity and kept alive communal feelings.

Middle-class, Westernized Pakistanis, employed in white-collar jobs in a city, could disregard the custom and go unnoticed and unreproached by their community. But for the bulk of Pakistani settlers, living in the ethnic quarters of Birmingham, Bradford or London, deviation could create a scandal. Unnoticed by others, Pakistani enclaves in Britain underwent an internal transformation during Ramadan: the sale of dates (used traditionally to break a fast) and yoghurt (considered alleviative for an empty stomach) rose; and the takings of Pakistani cafés declined. The only Britons who noticed the change were those employing large contingents of Pakistanis. In the factories where Pakistanis staffed entire sections, work-breaks were often adjusted to fit the fasting pattern.

Thus, through Friday prayers and fasting during Ramadan, Muslims in Britain preserved and reaffirmed their religious identity. In addition, there were Islamic taboos on food and drink – with alcohol and pig's meat forbidden to the faithful. The taboo on alcohol in Britain, where drinking beer is as much part of daily life as sipping tea, was difficult to maintain. Even so, drinking in pubs, likely to be noticed by fellow-Muslims, remained minimal. In any event, compared to a British pub, an Asian café or 'social club' – offering sweet, strong tea and the latest Indian and Pakistani film songs on juke boxes, reminiscent of tea-shops in Mirpur, Lahore or Campbellpur – was any day a better bet.

Abstinence from pig's meat is observed as strictly by Muslims as it is by Jews. Knowing this, during their early days of settlement many Pakistani immigrants patronized a Jewish butcher. Also, kosher meat sold there was the nearest to the Muslim halal (i.e. legitimate) meat. In both cases, a bird or animal is killed by cutting its jugular vein and letting the blood drain; the only difference is in the prayer that is said during the ritual.

Like Jews, Muslims do not regard Jesus as the son of God but as only one of the prophets in the line of Abraham, Isaac, Jacob, Moses and David. Muhammad, the founder of Islam in the first quarter of the seventh century, himself made no claims to be the son of God – only the last of the prophets. Nevertheless, Islam shares with Judaism and Christianity a common ground: monotheism. The Quran may be read as the last of the holy volumes beginning with the Old Testament. Aware of this, many British clergy in the areas of Pakistani settlement tried to woo Muslims into the fold of Christianity by distributing literature in Urdu. But their attempts proved unsuccessful.

Theological sophistries aside, Pakistani Muslims knew only too well, from direct observation and experience, that the gospel of Christian brotherhood and love was seldom practised by most white Britons towards West Indians, who were fellow-Christians. They also knew of the general lack of interest of white Christians in their own religion. So they remained contemptuously indifferent to the proselytizing overtures of the British clergy.

In any case, religion does not exist as a separate entity but is part of the general culture of a society. And as far as British and Indo-Pakistani cultures in their indigenous forms are concerned, they stand apart. The languages, culinary and sartorial habits, social customs and the very loci of thinking of the two peoples are different. Along with these socio-cultural differences there existed a general feeling on both sides of

self-sufficiency. Cultural pride, tradition and socio-psychological confidence enabled the Indo-Pakistani immigrants to preserve their languages, cuisine and dress; to recreate their religious institutions; and to
establish in Britain thousands of business enterprises which catered for
the special needs of their community (as well as the general needs of
others).

One of the remarkable features of many self-made Asian entrepreneurs
was that they pursued their business objectives while simultaneously
maintaining an interest in the well-being of their community. Indeed, in
some cases, success in business was accompanied by growing interest in
communal problems. It was a Pakistani businessman in Birmingham who
founded the first Pakistani social organization in 1956. Balbir Singh
Sandhu, a prosperous Indian grocer in Wolverhampton, was the first
president of the local Sikh gurdwara committee. An Indian estate agent
in Southall was well known for his social work in his community. The
increasing demands of his expanding and diversified business did not
deter Gurbachan Singh Gill from active participation in the affairs of
Southall's Sikh community. It seems that the economic prosperity of the
Asian entrepreneur and the confidence with which he conducted himself
in the white world inspired admiration from the community which, by
virtue of circumstances, relied heavily on its English-speaking members
for guidance and leadership.

5 Communal Leadership

I spend most of my time in Handsworth filling in all kinds of forms, writing letters, advising my fellow-countrymen on their problems. It's tedious work; but that's the only way to win my countrymen's respect, and keep it.

An Indian leader in Birmingham.

Very early in the history of Indo-Pakistani immigration, a person conversant with English became a valuable asset to his group. During every step of their settlement non-English speaking immigrants called on him for help. It began with the Labour Exchange (Job Centre), and National Insurance and National Health Service forms, and continued with post office savings account, bank, income tax form and electoral registration papers. In between were letters to and from the High Commission in London concerning foreign exchange and passports, and from local authorities regarding, say, rates and overcrowding. Consequently, the English-speaking kinsman or fellow-villager felt overtaxed.

The case of Manmohan Singh Basra in Wolverhampton is illustrative. He arrived there in 1953 from Singapore, where he had settled after leaving the Indian Army three years earlier. In Wolverhampton he found himself filling in forms and writing letters for fellow-Indians to the extent that he hardly had a moment to relax. As a result, he and other socially active Indians decided to establish a formal organization dedicated primarily to providing voluntary service to the community. Supported by a membership of 150, they founded the Indian Workers' Association, South Staffordshire, in 1956. The reason for assigning this name to their organization was historical.

In 1938 three Indian workers – Udham Singh, an active member of his electrical workers' union and a delegate to the local Trades Council; Ujjagar Singh; and Akbar Ali Khan – had formed the first Indian Workers' Association (IWA) in Coventry. They chose this title to distinguish their group from the middle-class India League (formed in 1929 and concerned exclusively with achieving Indian independence) and the Birmingham Indian Association, consisting of students and doctors. In time, the IWA in Coventry became dormant, and was largely forgotten. But Udham Singh survived as an Indian martyr; for in 1940 he assassinated in London Sir Michael O'Dwyer who in 1919, as

Lieutenant-Governor of the Punjab, had approved the action of Brigadier-General R. E. H. Dyer[1] in massacring hundreds of Indians in Amritsar, Punjab. Udham Singh was subsequently hanged. It was to honour his memory that the Indian settlers in Coventry named their newly formed organization in 1953 the Indian Workers' Association. In the subsequent years their lead was followed by the Indian communities elsewhere in the country.

By 1957 there were enough local IWAs in Britain to elicit advice from the visiting Indian Prime Minister, Jawaharlal Nehru, to form a central body. He also urged India High Commission officials to help bring this about. The 1958 race riots – when a group of Sikhs was assaulted by white hooligans in Notting Hill, London – provided further impetus for creating a national body; and the race riot in Nottingham that year led to the formation of the first Asian organization there, the Indian Association.

At its first conference in September 1958, the Indian Workers' Association of Great Britain (IWA–GB) adopted a constitution and spelled out its aims and objectives, which were to organize Indians to: safeguard their conditions of life and work; promote co-operation and unity with the trade union and labour movement in Great Britain; fight against all forms of discrimination based on race, colour, creed or sex; co-operate with other organizations, national and international, striving for friendship, peace and freedom; and undertake social welfare and cultural activities to further those aims and objectives.

From the beginning the leadership of the local IWA consisted of two major groups: moderate entrepreneurs and political radicals. The moderates stressed social welfare work whereas the radicals advocated trade union and political activities. The aims of the national body, which emerged in September 1958, were broadly enough based to contain both groups.

The leftist element continued to exhort IWA members to participate in trade union activities, and even to set up unions where they did not already exist. In this they were quite successful. Many local IWAs could justly claim that their members, in spite of victimization and the threats of employers, managed to found unions. Also, without exception, IWA members supported whatever militant action was taken by established unions in factories and public transport, because they believed that the economic lot of Indian workers was intimately intertwined with that of British workers.

Due to their diligent interest in trade unionism some Indian workers became shop stewards and even union officials. Local IWAs gained enough standing and acceptance to be invited by employers, particularly in the Midlands, to help resolve problems, social as well as industrial, arising out of hiring Indian workers.

The IWAs also showed much vigour and initiative in combating racial discrimination and opposing racist immigration policies. The Birmingham IWA, for instance, was the first in Britain to foster in 1960 an anti-discrimination umbrella body of various coloured and British organizations – the Co-ordinating Committee Against Racial Discrimination (CCARD) – and the first to lead a demonstration of black and white citizens against the 1961 Immigration Bill.

The IWA–GB, with a national membership of 20,000, actively participated in the formation of the Committee of Afro-Asian-Caribbean Organizations which lobbied against the immigration legislation. Later, in 1963, it supported the struggle of black Americans for Civil Rights.

Simultaneously, the IWAs were active at the local level. When in April 1963, Peter Griffiths, then the leader of Smethwick Conservative councillors, suggested to the Home Secretary (of a Conservative Government) that all immigrants who had been unemployed for six months be deported,[2] the Birmingham CCARD wrote to the joint chairman of the Conservative Party that the local Conservatives were pursuing policies 'which will ultimately result in a second Notting Hill'.[3] When the joint chairman replied that local Conservative Associations were autonomous bodies, the Smethwick IWA decided to campaign actively for Labour candidates at the local elections in May 1963. This had an important bearing on Labour's political fortunes.

During the 1964 general election the Smethwick IWA once again worked hard for the Labour candidate, Patrick Gordon-Walker; but he lost. Likewise the IWA in Southall, west London, actively canvassed for the Labour candidate. He won, though by a reduced majority of 1800 votes, a clear indication that but for the IWA's support of nearly 2500 votes he would have lost.[4]

The Southall IWA had a membership of 120 at the time of its formation in 1957. In the late 1960s it had some 12,500 members. Its assets included freehold property that housed its office and reading room, and a partly-purchased cinema hall which showed Hindi and Punjabi films throughout the week. It was probably the first Indian or Pakistani organization in Britain to elect its officials by secret ballot. That was in 1963. The April 1968 IWA poll aroused more passion and controversy in the Indian community than did the local council election which followed a fortnight later.

A full-time welfare officer gave guidance to Indians and Pakistanis (who could join as associate members) regarding obtaining house mortgages or applying for council housing; supplied information on all aspects of immigration and (British) nationality; provided help in finding accommodation for those members who had failed to do so on their own; and filled in all kinds of forms as well as drafting letters to various authorities. The organization also sponsored cultural evenings of Indian dance, song and music. It engaged in political lobbying at local and national levels. Thus the Southall IWA came nearest to the ideal of an active community organization which blended social welfare work and cultural activity with political lobbying.

Almost concurrent with the formation of the IWAs was the emergence of local Pakistani organizations, and for similar reasons: language difficulties and cultural identity. But it was not until 1963 that a successful attempt was made to form a national body. Twenty-three local organizations joined together to form the National Federation of Pakistani Associations in Great Britain (NFPA). Its annual conference in March 1970 was attended by 300 delegates; of its six elected officials three were from West Pakistan and three from East Pakistan. On the eve of the transformation of East Pakistan into the sovereign state of Bangladesh in December 1971, the NFPA claimed the affiliation of 35 locally-based Pakistani organizations.

At the grassroots level Pakistani organizations were concerned almost exclusively with social welfare services, providing Pakistanis with an interpreter service, advising them on police and legal matters (such as how and where to lodge a complaint with the police, which solicitor to contact, etc.), or guiding the male immigrant who wished to bring his family to Britain – a complex exercise involving the Pakistan High Commission (or embassy) and the Home Office in London, and the British High Commission (or embassy) in Pakistan.[5] The local leadership came mainly from among the Pakistani restaurateurs, estate agents or teachers, who were considered by the community to be well-equipped to deal with the Town Hall, Chamber of Commerce, building societies or police. They were often politically moderate.

At the national level, however, the radical element, mainly from East Pakistan, managed to remain in the forefront from the NFPA's inception in 1963. The worsening racial situation in Britain strengthened the hands of this group. The NFPA, when asked to affiliate with CCARD, did so, but this relationship did not last long (see Part I, Chapter Four).

The NFPA diligently tried to redress the Pakistani settlers' problems and grievances, and did not shirk even from criticizing the Pakistani mission in London, if and when necessary. At first its leaders protested, verbally and in writing, against the bureaucratic sloth shown by the High Commission's staff in their dealings with Pakistani nationals. But when this tactic failed, in early 1968 NFPA officials organized a protest march and demonstration against the High Commission in London. The event received much publicity, embarrassed High Commission officials, and jolted the staff out of their complacency.

But by far the most disturbing and demoralizing experience for Pakistani and Indian settlers was the 1968 Immigration Bill designed primarily to bar Kenyan Asians with British passports from entering Britain. One of the prominent and vocal critics of this bill was the IWA–GB. It brought coachloads of its members from the Midlands and North to London to join a demonstration against the Bill on 25 February. But in vain. The bill was passed; and the Act became effective on 1 March as originally planned. One of its results was to arrest the trend among Indian and Pakistani settlers towards acquiring British nationality.

It seemed to many Indian and Pakistani leaders that racism was on the rise, and that a broad front of ethnic organizations was needed to combat it. As in the past, the IWA–GB took the initiative. Its general secretary, Jagmohan Joshi, sounded out various racial minority leaders and found the response encouraging. It was decided to hold a national convention of such representatives. Then, on 4 April 1968, came the news of Martin Luther King's assassination in America. Interest in the project mounted.

In spite of this the IWA–GB stuck to its original plan of inviting to the convention only those black organizations which had in the past taken an uncompromising stand against racism. Prominent among the twenty such bodies were the West Indian Standing Conferences in Birmingham and London, and the NFPA. The convention was scheduled for 29 April in Leamington Spa, West Midlands.

In between came Enoch Powell's speech on 20 April (see Part III, Chapter Four). The dramatic, and at times hysterical, support he received from many whites further fuelled the interest of black and Asian organizations in the forthcoming convention. On the appointed day fifty representatives of various Afro-Asian-Caribbean organizations arrived in Leamington Spa. At the end of six hours' deliberations they announced the formation of the Black People's Alliance (BPA), 'a militant front for Black Consciousness and against racialism'. Summing up the general feeling among the participants, Jagmohan Joshi, the convenor, said: 'Powell's speech and its aftermath ... is just one step in a continuous campaign which was started at the end of the 1950s by the political parties to whip up racial antagonism to make political gains ... There has been no distinction between Conservative and Labour parties.'

Accordingly, the BPA pledged 'to fight racialism from all quarters: Labour Government, Tories, employers, unions, police, press, etc.; to expose the Labour Government and its racialist policies over immigration, and the phoney protection accorded through marginal laws like the present Race Relations Bill, etc.: and to seek allies from the majority community while exposing false allies such as the "do-gooders" who have been using black organizations to further their own vested interests and political ambitions.'

From a historical viewpoint, the emergence of the BPA confirmed a certain pattern in racial politics: 'white' action leading to 'black' reaction, generally of withdrawal and self-help. The 1958 race riots led to the establishment of the West Indian Standing Conferences in London and Birmingham, and the Indian Workers' Association–Great Britain. The 1961 Immigration Bill created a temporary alliance of West Indian and Asian organizations. Now the 1968 Immigration Act and Enoch Powell's speech led to the formation of a permanent front of Afro-Asian-Caribbean groups: the Black People's Alliance.

From the original twenty the number of black organizations affiliated to the BPA grew to fifty. Each constituent maintained its independent existence and functioned at the local level. The general stress was on the quiet, undramatic work of education, organization and recruitment. However, when offered an appropriate occasion, the BPA decided to show its strength in the streets.

During the January 1969 Commonwealth Prime Ministers' Conference in London, the BPA led a march of 5000 black – and 2000 white – supporters to Downing Street demanding that the 1962 and 1968 Immigration Acts be repealed and that an effective Race Relations Act with 'the backing of strong punitive sanctions' be passed.

Pressure of events, inter-organizational rivalries and the persistent insensitivity of many British leaders and institutions at local and national levels gradually led many moderate and non-political organizations and leaders to take stands which were anything but 'non-political'.

Meanwhile the community's socio-cultural life was not neglected by the ethnic bodies. Many Pakistani organizations presented *mushayaras* – poetry readings – in Urdu, thus preserving a long-established tradition among Urdu-speaking people. To encourage continued use of Urdu in writing, the *Mashriq* ran a column for young readers to help them find pen-friends. As for the formal teaching of Indian languages, this role was steadily taken over by religious institutions. Mosques and Islamic cultural centres often taught Arabic and Urdu, languages that shared a common script. Sikh gurdwaras conducted classes to teach the Punjabi script because the Sikh holy book is written in it.

Even if children did not learn to read and write their native language, they grew up speaking it at home and with other Indian and Pakistani children. Though parents wished their progeny to have a British education they did not necessarily want them to forget their mother-tongue or disown their cultural heritage. The vast majority of Indians, Pakistanis and Bangladeshis in Britain did not wish or intend to give up completely their socio-cultural identity. A sense of cultural and racial pride was summed up by an Indian housewife in Wembley, London, thus: 'We have beauty of our own, they [the whites] have their own. In quality we're equal, but we're different from one another.' There was an echo of the 'Black is beautiful' concept in this.

However, though the views expressed were identical, the sources from which they sprang were not. By asserting that 'Black is beautiful' the African in the Western world was attempting to regain his self-esteem, lost through centuries of slavery and cultural imperialism; whereas the Indian or Pakistani settler, having been generally spared the extreme experience of cultural imperialism, was stating something that was an accepted norm in his polyglot nation-state.

Indian and Pakistani societies can best be described as pluralistic, where many linguistic, religious and racial groups co-exist peacefully. (It is as if Western and Eastern Europe existed as two nation-states.) Indians and Pakistanis, therefore, grew up accepting and respecting the religious, linguistic, dietary and sartorial differences of their fellow-nationals. Adherence to the 'different *and* equal' concept, whether applied within their own communities or with respect to the British, was maintained when they migrated to Great Britain. Gujarati Indians, for instance, continued to eat Gujarati food (with its main emphasis on vegetables and lentils), wear saris, Gujarati style, and socialize mainly within the community. So did Punjabis and Bangladeshis. None of this disturbed or agitated the Indian or Pakistani settlers. They did not aspire to a stifling uniformity in culture or language either here or in their home countries. Yet there was unity in diversity among them, just as there was an underlying common set of assumptions and norms, generally labelled 'Western values', that unified such diverse cultures as the French, American, Dutch, British and German. Indians, Pakistanis and Bangladeshis, for example, shared common attitudes towards birth and death, marriage and family, parents and teachers, money and education. Underlying the different superstructures there was a common foundation, vaguely called 'Eastern values'.

6 Culture of the Indian Subcontinent

Instead of calling it Western and Eastern way of life, let's call it an industrial and an agrarian way of life. We're not really that much different from the people in Southern Italy or Sicily or Cyprus.

An Indian teacher in London.

Those who ask us to change our way of life overnight should first answer the question: 'Do English people living in our countries ever adopt our way of life?'

HAIDER KHAN, a Pakistani leader in Bradford.

In order to understand properly the social norms, values and attitudes prevalent in the Indian, Pakistani and Bangladeshi communities in Britain, it is necessary to examine their economic and historico-religious background.

The economy of the Indian subcontinent is basically agrarian; and three-quarters of the population live in villages. Agrarian life revolves around seasons which determine times for sowing seeds and harvesting crops. It is no accident that Holi, the Hindu festival of colours, and Divali, the festival of lights, coincide with harvest times. It is also easy to see why the cow came to be revered: she gave milk, considered a nutritious food and used as a base for many dishes and sweets; and she bred bullocks, used for agricultural production and hauling.

Hinduism, an ancient religion which grew out of Indian soil, remains deeply embedded in the Indian people. So much so that periodic break-away religious sects have not been able to sustain a different outlook and social practices for long. Sikhism is a case in point. Though considered casteless, its followers have succumbed to social distinctions based on occupations which are considered hereditary: *ramgharias*, craftsmen; and *jats*, peasants.

Islam, by contrast, was introduced into India by foreign Muslim invaders whose commanders became rulers of northern India during the eleventh century. Gradually, through force and persuasion, the Muslim rulers won converts from within the indigenous population. On conversion Hindus changed their names and adopted the new religious practices, but they did not, could not, alter their dress, habits, language or method of cooking. Consequently, religious taboos on food, drink and tobacco (forbidden to Sikhs) became crucial marks of distinction. Indeed, animosity between Hindus and Muslims became epitomized in their attitude towards the cow: Muslims were considered 'cow-killers'; Hindus 'cow-worshippers'. Even today this emotional point of religious difference can, and does, lead to violence and rioting in the Indian subcontinent.

Within religious and caste delineations, life is communal and institutionalized through the joint-family system. (It is noteworthy that the joint-family system, a miniature form of tribal life, is not peculiar to the Indian subcontinent but is a hallmark of many agrarian societies elsewhere.) A joint family includes married brothers and their families as well as unmarried brothers and sisters, all living under the tutelage of the eldest male member – usually the father or grandfather. Belongings are shared between the families and, if the family house is large enough, all members live within it, while maintaining separate hearths. All orphans, widows and aged members of the joint family are cared for. The head of the family, the patriarch, has authority over all others, even those who are married and are themselves fathers.

Thus the feeling of belonging to a group larger than one's immediate family is ingrained in the people from rural India or Pakistan or Bangladesh. Individualism, as fostered by Western culture, is almost unknown. Children are not allocated separate rooms in which to live and sleep and do not, therefore, grow up thinking in highly individualistic terms. Moreover, the nature of work – labouring on the family farm – produces a group, rather than individual, identity. On reaching adulthood the male child does not detach himself from the family and start on his own, but remains part of the joint family, loyal and respectful.

In the family, the role and functions of father and mother are well defined. Father is the boss, the provider and disciplinarian, and makes the important decisions. Mother cooks, sews, maintains the house and brings up the children.

The proverbial submissiveness of the Indian woman, however, is deceptive. Beneath the surface docility and self-effacement there lies a hard core. She has subtle ways of pressuring and arm-twisting, and generally gets her way in the areas she regards exclusively her own. She is the central arch of the Asian family. Michael Kraus's description of southern Italian immigrants in America – '[They] had tight knit families, father-orientated but mother-centred'[1] – applies equally to Asian immigrants in contemporary Britain.

Viewed against this socio-economic backdrop, it becomes clear why marriage is considered an alliance of families rather than a union of mates attracted to each other through 'romantic' love. Careful and extensive enquiries regarding the family tree, and the social and material standing of the prospective bride and groom by family elders, precede the 'arrangement of marriage'. (Abdul Kazi, a Pakistani teacher in London, compared the arranged marriage system with 'two countries wishing to sign an important treaty'.) This marriage custom is transferred almost intact when people from the Indian subcontinent emigrate. If no suitable match can be found within the community in its new country of settlement, then marriage alliances are arranged in the towns or villages of the Indian subcontinent. Such a practice persists among, say, Sikh settlers in Canada who have lived there for more than three generations. A study of Sikhs in Vancouver by A. Meyer revealed that 80 per cent of post-war marriages had been arranged in India. These included many Sikhs born in Canada.[2]

Though the practice of arranged marriage exists among all major religious groups – Hindus, Muslims and Sikhs – the religious significance of marriage varies. In the Hindu and Sikh scriptures marriage is regarded as a spiritual union and therefore indissoluble. Although Hindu law, reformed in 1955 by the Indian parliament, allows divorce, the actual divorce rate, particularly among rural Hindus, is negligible. The Quran, on the other hand, considers marriage as a civil contract. Therefore divorce among Muslims, easy to obtain, is much more frequent.

The Muslim practice of polygamy, which often fascinates the Western male and horrifies the Western female, stems from the Quranic verse: 'then you may marry other women who seem good to you: two, three or four of them. But if you feel that you cannot maintain equality among them, marry only one.' (In the Arabia of the Prophet Muhammad's time, when polygamy was common among all tribes, such a condition would have been considered restrictive.)

In fact, Pakistan abolished polygamy in 1961. A government decree stipulated that a second marriage could be contracted only if the first wife consented in writing. Legalistic considerations apart, there was for the average Pakistani peasant the economic problem of supporting two wives. According to a Pakistani leader in London, in the late 1960s only about one in 600 Muslim settlers in Britain had two wives.

But whatever the differences due to religious allegiance, rural society in the Indian subcontinent is marked by a high degree of marital fidelity. Extra-marital sexual liaisons in a village, where all the inhabitants know one another, can be difficult, even dangerous, to initiate and maintain. Besides, there is the notion of 'honour' that the wronged husband is expected to uphold if he is not to lose face in the community. This mode of thinking persisted among Asian settlers in Britain.

Attitudes towards sex and sexual matters tend to be prudish. The subject is seldom discussed openly, or even mentioned. Physical demonstrations of love or affection in public, even between man and wife, are rare. Husband and wife do not participate jointly in socializing within the rural community. They do not visit the village tea-shop together, or play cards together under a peepul tree, or jointly participate in the nocturnal confabulations around a communal hookah (hubble-bubble) in the village square. This pattern continued in Britain. Asian women were rarely to be seen eating in cafés and restaurants, much less sipping tomato juice in pubs.

Places of worship are the exception. Hindu temples and Sikh gurd-waras are visited by both men and women, but on entering they congregate separately. This is the practice in India; and it continued unchanged in Britain. Among Muslims the question of a mixed congre-gation simply did not arise; prayers and religious meetings were con-ducted for men and women in separate rooms or halls. This pattern is followed invariably in the Muslim world.

In general, continuation of old traditions in an alien environment was reassuring to South Asian immigrants in Britain, for it reiterated their distinct religio-cultural identity and created psychological security. Referring to 'the great mass of immigrants from China and India' in South-east Asia, Guy Hunter stated that 'deeply held in their traditional views and beliefs [they] found an emotional shelter and security in a strange land by holding to their own roots'.[3]

Religious practices aside, there are social attitudes commonly shared by South Asian men and women. For example, education is highly re-garded. Since higher education was, and still is, closely associated with ability to read, write and speak English, Asians fluent in English were much respected, as were all those with white-collar jobs, a legacy of the bureaucratic British rule.

Coupled with respect for education goes deference for the teacher, the guru, much fortified by the traditional Hindu philosophical ordering of 'entities'. This concept begins with the 'One Supreme Being' at the top, and comes down through primary, secondary and tertiary gods and goddesses to certain human beings who, in a given context, are to be revered: parents in relation to children, husbands to wives, teachers to pupils, and priests and ascetics to all the rest. This historico-religious conditioning, more than anything else, explained why Indian children in Britain generally showed much respect for their parents and teachers in spite of the contrary tendency often manifested by British children.

Traditional values and attitudes, long preserved in the rural environ-ment of the Indian subcontinent, were undermined by the communi-cations explosion and by growing contacts between the village and the town, to which many villagers migrated out of economic necessity. But as long as the movement of the villagers was to the cities and towns within the same linguistic state, the cultural shock was minimal. It was when, say, a Sikh peasant or craftsman travelled from rural Punjab to distant Calcutta or Bombay that bewilderment set in. To offset it, he sought out fellow-Sikhs, Punjabi restaurants and Sikh gurdwaras. It was as if a kilted Scot from the Highlands moved to Athens where, undoubtedly, he would seek the company of fellow-Scots, preferably in kilts, and look for a pub and a Presbyterian church.

A more pronounced bewilderment struck the rural Indian or Pakistani immigrant when he arrived at London's Heathrow Airport. At the end of his flight he found himself in a country with some 200 years of urbanization, industrialization and secularization.[4] Furthermore, the nature of British society was vastly different from his own. The British value privacy, tidiness, primness, order and quiet; whereas the rural South Asian had grown up in a society where working, sleeping and eating in the open were quite normal. The British put much value on restraint in speech and behaviour, reserve and formality; the Asian was used to informality, openness and loud speech often accompanied by gesticulation. Houses in urban Britain are enclosed and compact, while those in the rural areas of the Indian subcontinent are often open and haphazardly built, where windows are not curtained nor doors tightly fitted to minimize draughts, and where the residents are not in the habit of closing the door every time they enter or leave a room. Early immigrants from the Indian subcontinent demonstrated these differences dramatically as, unaware of British values and practices, they continued to live and act as if they were still in their villages. Unknown to them, the British were offended and scandalized.

However, with longer residence in Britain and guidance from their community leaders, came a realization of British values and taboos. Conscious and subconscious efforts were made by Asian settlers to moderate blatant differences. Some Sikhs, for instance, shaved off their beards and cut their long hair not merely to improve their chance of employment but also to minimize their exotic appearance in a new environment. With time also came familiarization with the English language.

Change in employment, from agriculture to industry, induced a more profound change of attitude. Industrial work made rural Asians time-conscious, altered their rhythm of life from the seasonal cycle of work and leisure to the weekly cycle of labour and relaxation. Simultaneously, it robbed them of the sense of freedom they had in a village society. 'Life here is like a machine,' complained Ajit Singh in Slough, reflecting a widespread feeling in the community. Effects of subservience to the weekly work cycle and a drive for economic betterment were manifested in other spheres of life. If, for example, the birthday of Guru Nanak or Lord Krishna fell on a weekday, it was celebrated on the preceding or following Sunday.

In time religious fervour and intense interest in day-to-day events in the politics of the Indian subcontinent subsided. Revulsion against beef or pork waned. A weekly or fortnightly visit to the gurdwara or mosque, and reading an Urdu or Punjabi journal, published in Britain, sufficed. In contrast, increasingly more time and energy were spent in coping with the problems of buying a house and arranging to bring the rest of the family to Britain.

Once his family arrived, the Asian's life became home-centred. His visits to the pub declined as he spent more of his leisure time on upgrading his house and his savings on buying furniture, household gadgets, car and television. The presence of a large body of settler families from the Indian subcontinent in British towns made an active social life possible. With a car at the door, visiting friends and relatives in or out of town over the weekend or during holidays became feasible. While the material life of the South Asian became almost indistinguishable from his British neighbour's, his social life remained solidly grounded within the self-contained Indian, Pakistani or Bangladeshi community. Their deeply religious wives created, at least partially, a religious aura at home. Small altars of Hindu gods and goddesses were built; the portraits of Sikh gurus decorated the walls.

Yet Asian women did not prove totally immune to environmental influence. Most Pakistani women discarded the veil, while Indian women tightened their *salvars* (baggy trousers), making them more elegant, or limited the use of saris to warm, dry days and formal occasions. When their sons took to wearing tight trousers or pointed shoes, or growing long sideburns, they did not protest or disapprove overmuch.

But a firm line was drawn in the case of teenage daughters. They must dress modestly, must not 'like the cheap English girls' exhibit their anatomy, most Asian parents insisted. They must under all circumstances remain chaste before marriage. They must be told – as they often were by Gurmeet Singh, and Indian settler in Wolverhampton – that 'in our society it's the man who shows his body, not the woman; and that's what makes us different from the whites'.

An overwhelming majority of Asian immigrants considered British society morally decadent. A survey conducted by the author for *New Society* in 1968 revealed that all Asian respondents thought British marriages unstable; and all but one felt that British marriages were adulterous and white women 'over-sexed'. 'Every time you pick up a

ABOVE: Some of the 29,800 immigrants from the West Indies in 1956, at Victoria Station, London

LEFT: SS *Empire Windrush*, used as a troop-carrier during the Second World War, was later to bring 492 West Indians to Britain in June 1948

BELOW: 'No Coloureds' sign in London, before the 1965 Race Relations Act became law

LEFT: Arrival of Kenya Asians holding British passports, February 1968

BELOW: Pro-Powell dockers on their march to the House of Commons on 23 April 1968

FOOT: Enoch Powell outside Parliament, 1974

RIGHT: A demonstration by the
Anti-Nazi League in London,
April 1978

BELOW: Bob Marley displaying a
portrait of Haile Selassie at a
concert in London in 1975

LEFT: Strike by the workers of Grunwick Processing Laboratories, London, June 1977

BELOW LEFT: A demonstration against the arrival of Ugandan Asians in Britain, September 1972

FOOT: A National Front press conference in south London, August 1977, being addressed by its leader, Martin Webster (centre)

Diane Abbot (below), Paul Boateng (below centre), Keith Vaz (foot), and Bernie Grant (right), elected as Labour MPs in June 1987

BELOW: David (later Lord) Pitt canvassing as a Labour candidate in Hampstead in the 1959 parliamentary election

LEFT: The aftermath of the race riot in Brixton, London, April 1981

BELOW: An aerial view of the riot-torn Lozelle Road in Handsworth, Birmingham, on 10 September 1985

OPPOSITE ABOVE: Funeral procession for Parveen Khan and her three children murdered by arson in Walthamstow, London, in July 1981

OPPOSITE BELOW: A British Movement demonstration in London, 1980

A Muslim demonstration in London against Salman Rushdie's
novel *The Satanic Verses*, May 1989

[British] paper you see divorce cases,' said Dilawar Singh Nijjar, an eighteen-year-old engineering apprentice in Southall. 'White men and women go off with one another even when married,' said Amrit Kaur Sondhi, a Sikh female employee in a canteen kitchen at Heathrow Airport.[5]

Apprehensive of the morally corrupting climate, many Pakistani and Bangladeshi males dreaded bringing their wives and daughters to Britain. If they did, they tried to minimize their chance of sexual adventure by restricting them to chores at home, by doing the shopping themselves, and by locking their houses when, say, they had to work night shifts. Undoubtedly, their sense of insecurity was genuine.

Many South Asian husbands disapproved of the idea of their wives attending evening classes in English, not only because that would interfere with their housework but also because of their unexpressed fears that if their wives became familiar with English and mixed with the British, they would end up behaving like white women. They regarded home as the last citadel of emotional security where they could withdraw from a generally unfriendly, alien and competitive milieu, and assert their manhood without challenge or question. No wonder then that they wished to preserve the *status quo*, and prevent their home environment from being transformed into another area of doubt, challenge or competition.

A faithful and obedient spouse and a stable, loyal family provided the Asian with evidence that his culture was morally superior to the white man's. Furthermore, these elements, buttressed by a clear, unambiguous delineation of duties and obligations, furnished him with an environment where his counsel to his children was most likely to be taken seriously. He frequently told his young son that 'Without education you'll be nothing', his adolescent daughter that 'Your destiny lies with your future husband: you must become a good cook and seamstress, and learn to keep a house.' The parents noticed that the more interest they evinced in their children the better response they got from them.

However loving, albeit restrictive, the domestic atmosphere, Asian children, educated in the generally liberal, 'think-for-yourself' environment of British schools found themselves at the centre of a cultural conflict. When very young, they felt confused and culturally ambiguous. But as they grew up they often resolved the problem by adopting some aspects of Western culture and behaviour while retaining many of the traditional values and attitudes.

The main difference between the two generations of Asians is this. The adults, reared and educated in the Indian subcontinent, were not strongly exposed to British values, Christian thought and the history of

Western civilization; their offspring are. Consequently, whatever compromises the adults made in response to the new environment did not detract from the core of their culture. With their children, however, compromises tended to be achieved by shedding parts of their hereditary cultural core.

My parents wanted me to succeed in white society, yet retain my identity as an Indian: and white society was making demands upon me to fully incorporate myself into its culture and only then would I be accepted.

A young British Gujarati male.[1]

I really thought that if I changed my name, dressed differently, made the most of my fair skin, I would be accepted. But my teachers still ignored me. I still got spat at, and one day I thought, this is not worth it ... So now I dress in salvar kameez [baggy trousers and long shirt], and I stay away from them in my social life.

MEENA, a 27-year-old teacher in Walsall.[2]

When you live in a world which makes no attempt to understand you, you begin to chisel off bits of yourself which makes it easier, less offensive to the Western eye or ear. You end up not a lesser person but a distorted person.

ARVIND SHARMA, a college lecturer in Southall.[3]

Some of the rules and practices prevalent in schools, which were taken for granted by British parents, proved causes for concern among many Asian parents. School uniform for girls was an example. As early as 1955, Jaswant Singh, an Indian settler in Gravesend, Kent, objected to his daughter having to wear a skirt, thus 'showing her legs'. His protest, based on cultural grounds, was accepted. His daughter was allowed to wear blue *salvar* in school. *parents forbidding exposure of women/girls*

Many Pakistani parents quoted the Quran to back their opposition to skirts for their daughters. The appropriate verse in the Quran reads: 'And say to the believing women, that they cast down their eyes and guard their private parts ... and let them cast their veils over their bosoms, and not reveal their adornment save to their husbands, or their fathers, or their husbands' fathers, or their sons, or their brothers, or their brothers' sons, or their sisters' sons, or their women ... or children who have not yet attained knowledge of women's private parts.'[4] Some education authorities, such as Leicester, waived the school uniform for Muslim girls; while in other cases, Muslim parents accepted a compromise whereby their daughters wore uniforms only within school premises, but not outside. Objections were also raised, and exemptions won, regarding gym slips and swimming lessons for Asian girls.

School assembly and scripture classes were other examples of conflict between the values of home and school for the Asian pupil. Muslim parents, generally more particular about their faith than Sikhs or Hindus, were prominent in raising the issue; and they often succeeded in getting their children exempted from the Christian assembly and/or scripture classes. Many Asian parents expected school authorities to arrange instruction in Islam or Sikhism wherever there was a large body of Muslim or Sikh children. This did not happen. At most the authorities agreed to allow volunteer instructors if the Muslim or Sikh community provided them. Some local Muslim organizations managed to do so.

Among Sikh and Hindu parents the issue did not cause much concern because of the pervasive feeling that the long-term effect of Christian instruction on the child was minimal, and that children treated religious instruction as one of the 'subjects' to be studied at school. The counter-argument advanced by many was that it would be better if the Sikh or Hindu child regarded Sikhism or Hinduism as one of the 'subjects' and learned about his own religion rather than Christianity.

By and large, though, in the case of Hindus, a relaxed attitude was blended with feelings of inclusiveness and self-confidence. As pantheists, they could easily accommodate the Pope as 'a holy man' or consider Jesus as 'one of the gods' in the massive Hindu pantheon without in any way impairing the essence of Hinduism. They were also quietly confident of their religious survival. If eight centuries of Muslim rule in the Indian subcontinent had not obliterated their faith, they argued, a generation of exposure to Christianity was hardly going to make much difference.

More practically, in contemporary Britain, if a Hindu mother worshipped before the altar of gods at home, fasted regularly on the days of full moon, conducted *puja* (prayers) at home, and read aloud the Hindu epics *Ramayana* and *Mahabharata*, she kept alive the spirit of Hinduism in her children. There were also religious celebrations when Hindus congregated in rented halls and conducted services – periodic reminders of being Hindu in a Christian environment.

Religious identification is much stronger among Muslims. The Muslim child is made aware of his religious faith when he notices that during Ramadan the pattern of eating at home is altered radically, with no food or drink being taken between sunrise and sunset. Then there is always a copy of the Quran at home. If the child was born in Pakistan and could read Urdu, he had no difficulty reading the holy book. If not, he was helped by his parents, or the local mosque or the Islamic Cultural Centre, where facilities for teaching Arabic were available.

'The young Muslims with whom I discussed religion were very clear about the differences between Islam and Christianity,' noted J. H. Taylor, a British researcher in Newcastle upon Tyne, in the mid-1970s. 'The first was, according to Ghulam, "They say Jesus is the son of God, which we don't believe. In our religion we say that he was just a messenger." The second difference mentioned was that Islam, unlike Christianity, had never been changed. The third, in Rasul's words, was "The Muslim religion is very strict and the Christian religion very weak in many ways; it doesn't tend to control the person. But the Muslim religion tells you, 'This is what you've *got* to do.' It is not what you can do, it's what you've *got* to do".'[5] In contrast, Taylor noted, the Hindu and Sikh youths, when asked to compare their religions with Christianity, tended much more to emphasize the similarities.

As for Sikhs, the simmering controversy regarding bearded Sikhs on buses kept the issue of their religious identity alive. The obstinacy of various local authorities goaded many Sikh parents to prescribe long hair and turbans for their sons. For instance, at the time of controversy on this issue in Manchester, 135 clean-shaven Sikhs underwent baptism at the Sikh gurdwara, thus returning to long hair and beards.[6] Following Sohan Singh Jolly's successful battle with the Wolverhampton local council, at one mass baptism ceremony alone 200 Sikhs, many of them young, resolved to wear long hair. In general, the proportion of clean-shaven adult males in the Sikh community – which reached a peak during the mid-1960s – began declining steadily.

All along, the hold of religious taboos on food and drink remained so strong that even those who ate pork (among Muslim boys) or beef (among Hindus or Sikhs) outside the home did not admit it to their parents. 'They would be appalled if they knew,' said Muhammad Akram from Cricklewood, London. 'They don't even buy margarine because someone told them that it had pig's fat in it.'[7]

In short, despite the overwhelming influence of the Christian environment, most Asian children grew up following basically the dietary taboos of their inherited religions. The proportion of habitual beef-eaters among Hindu or Sikh youngsters did not seem higher than among their male parents. The percentage of clean-shaven Sikh youths was by no means larger than among adult Sikhs. And mosques seemed to draw as many young Muslims as old.

As for the children's linguistic identity, it was seldom in doubt at home where Punjabi, Urdu, Gujarati and Bengali thrived as spoken languages. However, both children and parents aspired to become fluent in English as they, very rightly, considered it a prerequisite for economic progress. The child's familiarity with English meant that, unlike his parents, he did

not feel excluded from the British world of information and entertainment. At any given time he had a choice of Hindi as well as English
films. He often went to both and was enriched by the experience.

An attraction of Hindi films was their music and songs. Even the most
anglicized Asian would openly confess his weakness for Indian film
songs, especially the poetic and imaginative lyrics. Admiration for Indian
music and songs, however, did not prevent young Asians from listening
to and appreciating conventional or pop Western music. Almost invariably juke boxes in Asian cafés provided a combination of popular Indian
or Pakistani film songs and a few of the current Top Twenty.

Asian children, following their parents' advice to be studious, showed
little interest in 'frill' activities at school, such as joining clubs. David
Beetham's study of 1966 showed that in Handsworth schools only one in
eight Asians joined school clubs and societies; the proportion of English
students was three times higher. Whereas one out of two English
students joined out-of-school clubs, only one in seven Asians did so.[8] In
the latter case, more often than not, it was likely to be a sports club:
hockey, cricket or football. Club members practised daily or weekly, and
played matches against other Asian clubs – bearing such names as Punjab
Tigers, Pak Players, Indian Giants – or local English teams.

There were also Indian youth clubs, but the number was small. The
youth club, with its indoor games and weekly dances, a by-product of the
urban Western environment, did not appeal to most Asian parents. They
failed to grasp the meaning or usefulness of such an institution; and even
if they let their sons join, they never let their daughters do so. They
wished to keep teenage daughters away from the sexually tempting
company of boys: a decision they viewed within the general context of
their own restraining and disciplining roles. However, without the
goodwill and respect of their children such restrictions would not have
been as effective as they were.

Various factors, historical and contemporary, internal and external,
had combined to create and sustain a harmonious and stable family
system among Asian settlers: traditional cohesiveness of the family with
its clear demarcation of the roles of the father, mother and children; a
substantial concurrence between the social attitudes of parents and
children; hard-working fathers, anxious to provide for their families;
social pressures by the 'in' community on its members to conform to
traditional values; and the general cultural and racial alienation from
British society.

The cohesiveness of the Indian, Pakistani or Bangladeshi family was, as
explained earlier, rooted in the rural, agrarian base in the Indian sub-

continent, and it was invariably weakened when families migrated to towns and cities. However, the fact that South Asian immigrants to Britain were exposed to the influence of competitive and divisive forces of the urban centres in an alien and unfriendly environment simultaneously generated counter-forces of self-protection and communal help – factors which tended to keep the migrant families, individually as well as collectively, cemented together. So long as there was overt identification – such as skin colour – of the settlers, and antipathy towards them from white Britons, the cohesive element would remain strong.

Although at ease with the English language, descendants of Asian settlers felt culturally alien, since the influence of traditional values, epitomized in their parents, remained strong. To a considerable degree they shared their parents' social values. Attitudes towards nakedness and sex was one example. Recalling her schooldays when she had to change for swimming or showers, Mehtab Aslam, a Pakistani woman, said: 'I was surprised at the English girls who simply used to stand there and change. They didn't seem to be embarrassed whereas I used to try and hide everything, and felt conscious of myself.' The reason for this difference of attitude lay in the variation between the home environment of the Asian and English children. Mehtab, for instance, had never seen her mother or father sun-bathing in the back garden. Nor had she ever seen her mother expose her breasts, or even her legs, at home. She had therefore grown up subconsciously feeling that nakedness was undesirable, even immoral.

Attitudes to the child–parent relationship provided another example. Most Asian teenagers felt that British adolescents had too much freedom; that the idea of an independent existence at seventeen or eighteen, away from parents, was too awesome to be considered seriously; and that marriage need not signal a break with parents and/or the setting up of an independent household.

The Asian child's traditional respect for his parents was further enhanced in the present circumstances by his awareness of the unflagging energy with which the mother devoted herself to child-care and housekeeping, and of the father's industry for the family's economic welfare. He often tried to reciprocate by being submissive, so as not to add to the already considerable burdens and worries of his parents.

Although Asian teenagers, particularly girls, aspired to a less restricted existence, very few wanted what they seemed to regard as the 'excessive freedom' that their white counterparts appeared to have and enjoy. When given a choice between freedom and security they often opted for security. They did so partly because they lacked the courage to face the risks and responsibilities that go with an independent existence, and partly because of the confidence and trust they placed in their parents' wisdom and judgement.

When a sample of Asian boys was asked by the author (in the late 1960s): 'If you fell in love with a girl but your parents did not approve, what would you do?', 82 per cent replied that they would yield to their parents' decision. 'I can't put a girl before my parents,' said Harnam Singh, a nineteen-year-old Sikh from Southall. 'I mean, they brought me up. Their blood runs into my veins. But the girl has only my feelings towards her.' Harnam Singh had arrived in Britain when he was only six. He spoke English with a local accent; and, unknown to his parents, he had dated English girls, though not in Southall. There, white animosity was much too strong, as was the grapevine in the Indian community.

The higher the concentration of Asians in an area, the greater was the social pressure on youngsters to stick to traditional behaviour. While British education implanted the seeds of individualism and liberalism in the Asian child's mind, the climate of his home and neighbourhood was not conducive to the seeds sprouting and growing.

If an Asian youngster wished fully to adopt Western values he had no alternative but to sever his connections with the family and disown his religious and cultural heritage. But then how did British society treat him? Did it reward him with social acceptance and equality of opportunity, or did it treat him as it did the West Indian youth? If the latter, which was often the case, then the rebellious youngster was lost to both worlds, voluntarily cut off from one and unaccepted by the other. In that case he had little choice but to return eventually to his original flock.

To be fair, Asian parents were not clinging completely to the traditional ways of the rural Indian subcontinent. They could not even if they wished to. One of the areas of change was the role of women. They gradually assumed a wage-earning role. Two factors caused the shift. One was the need to overcome the boredom which many Asian women experienced on being removed from the gregarious atmosphere of the joint family in their native villages and on being confined, instead, to the four walls of a British home accommodating nothing more than a nuclear family. The other was the constant pressure to increase family income to meet rising needs and aspirations. Consequently, a sizeable minority of Asian women in such places as Southall and Slough began working in factories. Before husbands would allow this, they ensured that their wives would work in a 'hen-house', such as packing departments; that there were other Asian women at the workplace; and that they would not have to wear skirts. But however qualified and guarded, there was nevertheless a fundamental change, and the young Asian could not fail to notice it since it was taking place in his home.

He noticed that his community's marriage custom too was being modified. No longer were the matches arranged 'blindly', as had been the case in his parents' day, without any consultation with the boy or the girl. Instead, a liberal version of the arranged marriage had evolved and become popular. It worked as follows. When a boy or girl reached marriageable age, parents started looking for a suitable match through a network of relatives and friends. When they were satisfied with the boy's background, education and financial standing, and the girl's character, family background and ability to manage a home, the stage was set for the next step: exchange of photographs. *If* mutual interest was shown by the boy and the girl, then a meeting under parental guidance was arranged. The boy and the girl met, talked to each other, perhaps went to the cinema together. If they felt they liked each other, the marriage was on. If not, another round of enquiries, pictures and meetings ensued. In this way the final decision rested with the couple, and not with the parents as used to be the case.

In some instances, a young man who felt sufficiently enamoured of a girl would approach his parents to initiate enquiries which in due course led to marriage. Thus a move spurred by romance culminated in a traditional 'arranged' marriage. With social liberalization proceeding steadily, this pattern of romance-leading-to-arranged marriage is likely to prevail in the Asian community.

Indeed, by the late 1980s a well-defined 'assisted arranged marriage' had evolved in the community. Following successful negotiations between the parties there was a marriage ceremony in the registrar's office, termed 'court marriage' – equivalent to an engagement in the estimation of the ethnic community – followed, up to a year later, by a religious ceremony to sanctify the union, called 'religious marriage'. In between these two ceremonies the couple went out together but abstained from sexual intercourse.[9] Another innovation, which mattered a great deal to young Asians, was the development of *bhangra* dancing – a folk dance of rural Punjabis – as a participatory entertainment which brought the two sexes together. Its growing popularity led to the establishment of *bhangra* discos in the areas of Asian settlement.

These developments need to be viewed against the backcloth of the experiences that the pioneering Asian children underwent in the late 1950s. The case of Manjeet Kaur in Southall is illustrative. As the only Indian in a girls' infant school she was a figure of 'much friendly curiosity'. She picked up English quickly, got on well with her classmates, and had only English friends. 'Up to thirteen I was totally English,' she recalled in 1970. 'At fifteen, I began to realize I was different. The English girls were going out with boys, something I could not do. I found that I had less and less to talk about with my English friends: all they talked about was boy-friends, hair-styles and pop singers. [Being a Sikh] I couldn't cut my hair; and English pop singers bored me to tears. So, at seventeen, I realized that I was Indian. I went to India for a holiday. I loved it.' In a nutshell, this case history illustrates the psychological transformation that Indian, Pakistani or Bangladeshi children growing up in Britain often underwent. As they reached adulthood they became increasingly aware of the gap that existed between the culture of their parents and of society at large.

Identity

And there was still the racial dimension to the Anglo-Asian relationship. Indeed, to most Britons, Asians were merely 'coloured', a racial tag. As for the Asian child, research done in the mid-1960s suggested that he became colour conscious through one or more of the following ways: parents' or close friend's experience; personal experience; and observation of social reactions.

When, for instance, an Asian child found that, in spite of a university degree, his father was working as a moulder in a factory or as a bus conductor, he could not help becoming aware of colour prejudice, particularly when his Urdu- or Punjabi-speaking parents generally referred to white Britons as *gore* or *chite log* (white people) and to Indians, Pakistanis or Bangladeshis as *kale log* (black people).

Jasbir Singh Khatra, an eighteen-year-old youth in Southall, remembered the hoots of 'Not another one!' that greeted him as he entered his class in a Southall secondary school for the first time. (In those days there were very few Asian or West Indian pupils in that school.) He sat next to an English student; and the boy walked away. 'That's how it all started,' recalled Khatra. 'They started to keep to themselves, and we to ourselves.'

In Preetam Sahgal's case, colour consciousness came subtly, through his registering the reactions of white students to a television programme at a boarding school in East Anglia where he was the only Indian student. 'Every Saturday afternoon we watch sports on television, and then one of the Pop shows,' he said. 'There's an Indian boy in the dancing crowd. When the camera pans on him, a cry of disgust goes up from the English boys in the hall. That's when I realize what they *really* think of me. It could be me on television.'[10]

It seems colour prejudice existed in boarding grammar schools as much as it did in secondary modern schools. The only difference lay in its expression. Whereas white middle-class pupils were generally subtle and muted in giving vent to racial prejudice, working-class children were often crude and forthright.

If, however, by chance or design, school proved to be a haven of colour blindness or racial tolerance, there was still the outside world which was not so well-ordered and structured. There was always the chance that an Asian adolescent walking down the street would hear the 'Black bastard!' shout from a passing car or motorcycle. More importantly, there were the stories of assaults on Asian people and property that circulated continually in the community. Mr A's windows were smashed again by white youths. The other day Mr B's grocery was broken into. Mrs C's handbag was snatched by a white youth as she was walking down the street. Mrs D had her sari plastered with eggs thrown from a passing car as she stood at a street corner. Abdul gave up his job as a bus conductor after having been assaulted by white passengers twice in a week during late-night shifts. The other day Mr Singh was assaulted and robbed of his wallet and watch while returning home from work late at night. And so on.[11]

Violence against Asians reached a climax and became national news during the spring of 1970. During March and May the national press reported numerous instances of violence to Asians by skinheads (white youths with shaved heads) in London's East End (where 36 racial attacks were recorded), Southall, Redhill, Aylesbury, Wolverhampton, Coventry, Birmingham, West Bromwich, and Luton (where 25 people were injured in a confrontation between 300 skinheads and 200 Asians). On 3 April skinheads attacked two Asian employees of the London Chest Hospital in Bethnal Green; and the term 'Paki-bashing' came into existence. Four days later Tosir Ali, an East Pakistani, was murdered. In late April gangs of white youths went on a rampage against Asian shops in the East End's Brick Lane. Under the circumstances, Asian youths could hardly remain unaware of racial differences.

Racial discord had been fuelled by the controversy surrounding the 1968 Immigration Bill, apparently designed to bar entry into Britain of British Asians from East Africa, and Enoch Powell's speech in Birmingham. Old fears and suspicions of Asians were revived once again as they felt their economic security, gained over a decade of hard work, suddenly threatened. White antagonism, never far from the surface in Southall or Handsworth, manifested itself openly. A gang of white youths armed with iron bars appeared outside a Southall school. They beat up a few Asian boys at random before the police arrived. Incidents such as this triggered a profound transformation among many young Asians.

'Before Enoch Powell's speech I was accepting English life, going on slowly, moving with the wheels,' said Ranjit Randhawa in Southall. 'But this speech made me stop and take a completely different look at myself and my people.' As a result he became keenly interested in Indian music and culture, and in events in India. His negative attitude towards arranged marriage changed, and he started to see certain merits in the custom. Randhawa was typical of a generation of British-born Asian children growing up in Britain. He spoke Punjabi but could not read or write it. He had had his hair cut. He had even dropped the suffix Singh as he was critical of the beliefs and practices of Sikhism, his parental religion.

Inadvertently, Enoch Powell gave a further impetus to Asians to preserve their culture when he stated in a speech in November 1968 that the West Indian or Asian, by being born in England, did not become an Englishman. As it was, most Asian adults had always drawn a line between economic and educational opportunity, and anglicization. While they had no intention of giving up their basic religious identity, they were determined to make steady progress in the economic sphere. They therefore put much faith and hope in their children's education. They would much rather spend money on their children's education than buy household gadgets or new furniture. No wonder many Asian children, actively encouraged by their parents, stayed at school beyond the statutory age of fifteen (later sixteen).

David Beetham's study of Handsworth schools showed that among fourth-year students 81 per cent of the coloured students wanted to stay beyond the statutory age limit; the corresponding figure for English pupils was 36 per cent. Furthermore, 10 per cent of the coloured pupils, compared with one per cent of the English, proposed to go on to full-time further education.[12]

Most Asians did not consider scholastic achievement as an end in itself, but hoped that their better academic performance would lead to better jobs. And, in the main, this did not imply becoming doctors, accountants, computer scientists or university lecturers. Their aims remained basically realistic – as was shown by David Beetham's study. He found that 75 per cent of Asian school-leavers wished to become motor mechanics, engineers, electricians and radio/TV repairers. (In contrast, only 21 per cent of English school-leavers wished to enter these trades.) But, in practice, only 25 per cent managed to enter 'recognized skilled crafts'.[13]

The reason for this wide gap between the aspirations and achievements of Asian school-leavers lay, principally, in the attitudes and beliefs of Youth Employment Officers and personnel managers. Apparently, many Youth Employment Officers continued, subtly, to persuade Asian youths to lower their aims to even more 'realistic' levels, while most personnel managers continued to associate young Asians with the traits and disadvantages they had previously associated with adult immigrants: they could not speak English fluently and, being unaccustomed to machinery, were slow in their movements and accident-prone. So personnel managers were almost as reluctant to let young Asians into skilled jobs as they were with their parents.

Similarly office jobs continued to elude young Asians almost to the same degree as they did in their parents' case. Once again white managerial attitudes and beliefs were involved. A study of employment opportunities in office jobs in Croydon, south London, in 1966–7 by Julia Gaitskell, a community worker, amply bore this out. 'The belief that coloured workers are not suitably qualified for white-collar work is widely held and self-reinforcing,' she concluded. 'Private employment exchanges reported that even with British qualifications, it was extremely difficult to place coloured applicants in office jobs.'[14]

Nor did the enforcement of the 1968 Race Relations Act make much difference. In the summer of 1969, Roger Jowell and Patricia Prescott-Clarke, two researchers, sent out 256 applications for 128 jobs in sales and marketing, accountancy and office management, electrical engineering and secretarial services in the East Midlands, West Midlands, Greater London and Slough–Reading area – that is, two applications per vacancy. The two letters, matched in terms of personal and professional details, were sent from different parts of the same town; but one was written and signed as if it came from a British-born white and the other from an Australian/Cypriot/West Indian/Asian. All applicants stated that they had received their higher or further education in Britain. The British and Australian applicants were invited for interviews or sent application forms in 78 per cent of the cases; the Asians only in 35 per cent.[15]

These studies and case histories demonstrate the strong reluctance of most British employers to consider black or Asian applicants for jobs other than unskilled or semi-skilled. Rational consideration of academic qualifications, trade skills and experience tended to be overshadowed by unfavourable attitudes and beliefs, and mental reservations.

Such a state of affairs became hard to sustain as the number of Asians born and educated in Britain began to rise sharply in the 1970s, making it a decade of transition.

8 Asians in Transition

Second generation Asians are not suspended in a void ... [But] they have two basic problems: how to sustain self-esteem, and how to negotiate a way between their own and British culture.

BHIKHU PAREKH[1]

For young people from some of the Asian communities, their parents' country of origin is very distant, both physically and culturally, and indeed emotionally, so that there can be no notion of 'return' to a 'homeland'. One consequence of that is that they may be more prepared to defend their position in British society.

ROBERT MILES and ANNIE PHIZACKLEA[2]

The white school kids call me 'Paki' and 'Paki out', and they scrawl on the door of my teaching room.

An Asian teacher in the East End of London.[3]

The seventies proved to be a period of transition for the Asian community. The number and significance of the Asians born and educated in Britain rose sharply; and this gave a fillip to the general confidence of the community. Also, the importance of East Africa Asians, more anglicized and self-assured than the immigrants from the Indian subcontinent, increased. This happened because of the niche that many of them carved out in the retail trade, and because of the much-publicized strikes that those employed in industry undertook. Finally, the violence perpetrated against Asians by white racists, which culminated in two sensational murders of Asians in the second half of the seventies, radicalized the community, particularly its young.

Considerable research was undertaken to define the relationship that the Asian born and/or educated in Britain had established with his family and community, and with white society at large. In the words of Professor John Rex, a leading British sociologist, Asians existed in a situation of 'altruistic solidarity', which required that the individual should subordinate his life and interests to those of his group, which may be as small as a nuclear family or as large as a sub-caste. For boys this amounted to handing over their wages to their fathers and accepting

parentally guided marriages; and for girls it implied considerable curtail-
ment of freedom of movement and arranged marriages. The Western
alternative was the concept of 'egoistic solidarity', whereby an individual
subordinated his interests and desires to an outside (group) ego or
conscience which, though autonomous, was a social creation – that is,
created through social osmosis. In other words, an individual conformed
to the norms of the group out of his free will. Asian students found
themselves subjected to altruistic solidarity at home and egoistic solidarity at school. Most of them attempted to resolve the (personal)
conflict by striving, as individuals, to do well academically in order to
uphold the honour of the group, that is, their immediate family.[4]
However, in a social context, the conflict was hard to resolve because
British values either inclined towards 'eroticism outside the control of the
family' (a working-class model) or towards 'denial of family obligations
and romantic marriage' (a middle-class model).[5]

For all practical purposes, the Asian youngster did not have the option
of breaking with his family. He had grown up as a member of a
tightly-knit home with much greater emotional dependence on his
parents than a white child. This inhibited both the ability to function
outside the supportive network of the family and the growth of individualism, which education and white society encouraged. Moreover, the
Asian parents did not shirk from using violence to control their progeny,
particularly daughters. And, finally, the youngster knew that breaking
away from the family would result in becoming a moral pariah.

None the less, the conflict was real. The socialization process that the
Asian child underwent at school was conceived and executed by whites
who tended to denigrate the culture of his parents. Little wonder that a
minority among young Asians responded by imbibing Western values to
the extent of openly disliking their own. From this arose contempt for
their parents. Some of the outward manifestations of this self-hatred were
pestering their parents to change their names, urging their mothers and
sisters to stop wearing Indian clothes and attempting to turn themselves
white through excessive washing. A large majority of young Asians
responded to white denigration of their culture by being proud of their
own heritage and distinctive identity. Yet there was a difference in the
way they and their parents did so. The youngsters thought and spoke in
general terms of the Indian subcontinent – as a geographical area and a
civilizational entity – whereas their parents defined themselves in specific
regional, religious and caste terms.

Another major difference between young Asians and their parents was
their perception of white British. Most older Asians could not overcome
their awe of the imperial British they had grown up under in the Indian

subcontinent, and the concomitant sense of inferiority and insecurity. In contrast, their progeny gained intimate knowledge of whites through daily contacts, competing with them in education, jobs and sexual partners. Therefore, when encountering unequal treatment, they reacted sharply.

The same could also be said of those Asians who came to Britain from East Africa – but in a different context. In the three most celebrated cases of industrial action by Asians in the 1970s the East African sub-community was in the forefront. The disputes occurred at Mansfield Hosiery Mills, Loughborough; Imperial Typewriters, Leicester; and Grunwick Processing Laboratories, London.

At Mansfield Hosiery Mills the predominantly East African Asian labour was confined to the semi-mechanized part of the plant as semi-skilled workers, while whites operated the mechanized section as skilled employees with better wages and working hours. In December 1972 the Asians went on strike in protest against the management's stubborn refusal to promote them to skilled grades. The strike was opposed by union officials who publicly expressed racist views about Asians. The strikers took their case to the industrial tribunal which found the company and the union guilty of unlawfully discriminating against Asian employees.

The next significant industrial dispute occurred in Leicester at Imperial Typewriters owned by Litton Industries, an America-based multi-national. On 1 May 1974, protesting against poor wages, falsified bonuses, unrelenting pressure for higher productivity, wide differences between the production targets for whites and Asians, and petty restrictions on such routine exercises as washing and tea and lunch breaks, some 400 mainly East Africa Asian employees went on strike. Their trade union, the Transport and General Workers Union (T&GWU), did not back their action. Undeterred, the strikers mounted continuous picketing, organized three major rallies, and won national attention and support. When faced with hostility from the local and district officials of the T&GWU, they appealed, successfully, to the union's national hierarchy to institute an enquiry regarding their complaint of inadequate Asian representation on the shop stewards' committee. On 21 July, after the management had promised not to victimize the strikers and to establish an Equal Opportunity Office, they returned to work.

In the final analysis, what helped sustain the industrial dispute was the company's recruitment policy. Over the years it had hired relatives and friends of its employees, thus creating a close network of Asians from East Africa. Out of this arose solid moral and material support for the strikers and their families: Asian workers used community solidarity as a prime tool in waging an industrial campaign. This had happened many times in the 1960s in those urban centres where the Punjabi-speakers were the predominant group in the local Asian community, and actively involved with the Indian Workers' Association. But this time the phenomenon repeated itself among the largely Gujarati-speaking section of the community – a novel event, which illustrated the proletarization of a group hitherto steeped in petty bourgeois values and aspirations.

A similar event was to occur in Willesden, north-west London, at Grunwick Processing Laboratories two years later. Nearly 80 per cent of the 400 employees at its two processing plants were (Gujarati-speaking) East Africa Asians. On 23 August 1976 nearly half of them walked out demanding the recognition of the union – Association of Professional, Executive and Computer Staff (APEX) – they had recently joined. They were led by Jayaben Desai and her son Sunil, who in turn were assisted by Jack Dormey, an official of the Brent Trades Council. On the other side, the company owner, George Ward, an Anglo-Indian, was backed by right-wing Conservatives and the National Association for Freedom.

The strikers called in the Arbitration, Conciliation and Advisory Service (ACAS) to conduct a survey to determine whether the Grunwick workers wanted to join a union. The survey showed that the Grunwick employees were in favour of having a union, but ACAS could not impose its finding on the employer. When the case was taken to the High Court, it merely confirmed ACAS's conclusion.

It was against this backdrop that Roy Grantham, the APEX leader, advised the cancellation of the day of action on 8 August 1977, when it was planned to close down the works with massive picketing. By then the leading unions of engineers, building workers and miners had taken to despatching hundreds of their members to join the picket line, resulting in violent confrontations with the police which received wide publicity in the media. However, when the postal workers of the area offered to refuse to handle the Grunwick Laboratories' mailbags they were warned by their union officials against it.

Mass picketing resumed in October and November 1977, but the proprietor showed no sign of compromise. Four members of the strike committee went on hunger strike outside the headquarters of the Trades Union Congress in central London. They were suspended by their union, APEX. The final blow came in December when the House of Lords, as the highest judicial authority, overturned the ACAS and High Court rulings favouring trade union recognition.

APEX responded by offering to put in a new bid for recognition, but the company owner, George Ward, remained obdurate. In April 1978 the strike committee issued a call for massive picketing which received a poor response. The following month the strikers appealed to APEX's annual conference to back their plan for a continued strike. In the event, the conference decided to end the industrial action if ACAS failed within five weeks to recommend union recognition once more. In early July, ACAS decided to withdraw from the dispute and APEX officially called off the strike. Thus the year-long industrial dispute, which became a national *cause célèbre*, ended in failure for Asian workers.

But the general impact of the Grunwick strike on industrial and race relations was healthy. The fact that Asian employees had struck against a company owned by someone who was part-Indian showed that class interests overrode the racial factor. This signified integration of Asians into the social class system of Britain, with a large majority in solidarity with the trade union movement, and a substantial minority lining up with the Conservative Party. A long, bitter and frequently televised struggle by Asian employees for improvement of their working conditions helped to bury the widespread belief among white workers that ethnic immigrants were prepared to work for a pittance and thus depress their living standards. As a result there was a decline in prejudice against racial minority workers. At the same time, the Grunwick struggle had the effect of driving a segment of the Asian community into the arms of the Conservative Party. This was to be borne out by a poll before the 1979 general election which showed that the Conservatives had the support of 25 per cent of Asian voters, twice the figure for West Indians.[6]

Unlike the several previous instances – where Asian workers had struck against their immediate union officials as much as against their employers – this time the strikers were actively assisted by the local trade unionists. The enthusiasm with which major trade unions despatched hundreds of their militant members to support the Asian strikers was unprecedented – and so too was their presentation of the dispute as pertaining to the basic trade union rights of all working people, irrespective of colour or race. This show of solidarity with ethnic minority strikers by mainstream unions was a milestone in the history of British race relations, and gave further impetus to the trade union movement to pursue actively anti-racist policies and practices.

In another part of Greater London – the East End of London, encompassing the boroughs of Tower Hamlets and Hackney – trade unionists had joined a struggle against such right-wing, neo-fascist organizations as the National Front (NF) and the British Movement (BM). In the October 1974 general election the National Front contestant received 7.6 per cent of the vote in Bethnal Green and Bow, the second highest figure for any NF candidate in the country. Buoyed by this electoral support, the NF took to projecting a high profile in the area.

In September 1975 it held an 'anti-mugging' march through the East End. As the NF presence and activity expanded, with a sharp increase in NF symbols and racist graffiti on walls, there was a rise in racial assaults mainly in the Brick Lane neighbourhood. Between March and May 1976 the Asians in the area suffered 30 such attacks.

Besides violent incidents there was much harassment, verbal and otherwise, of the Asians. Even those in positions of authority were not spared. 'They write on my blackboard, they write BM [British Movement, which had organized many demonstrations in the area],' said an Asian who had been teaching in the East End for seven years. 'Then they have these Nazi signs under their lapel, and they show it to me. And they ask me to read their [NF/BM] leaflets. They carry them around: the leaflets from these various movements – the New National Front, the National Front, the British Movement. The kids now start saying to me "Oh, you have taken our job" ... So why don't you go back, you Paki, they shout.'[7]

In the western part of Greater London, too, racial tension was on the rise. On 4 June 1976, Gurdip Singh Chaggar, a Sikh youth, was murdered in Southall by a gang of whites. John Kingsley Read, leader of the right-wing British National Party, a breakaway from the National Front, publicly approved the killing. This senseless murder made most members of the local Asian community realize that they were being overly optimistic in thinking that with time racism would subside. In an emotional outburst young Asians mounted demonstrations against the police, and attacked white motorists using a major road through Southall. They organized self-defence patrols. Out of this traumatic experience arose the radical Southall Youth Movement (SYM) as a rival to the older Southall-based National Association of Asian Youth.

The violent incidents in Southall and the East End caught the attention of the national press. In the East End they goaded the local Bangladeshi organizations such as the moderate Bangladeshi Welfare Association and the militant Bengali Housing Action Group (given to organizing squatting in empty public housing) to form the Anti-Racist Committee of Asians in East London (ARC–AEL). They staged a demonstration in June 1976, kept track of racist assaults, and resorted to deploying self-defence patrols. Young Bangladeshis were actively involved in forming vigilante groups. This caused a decline in racial attacks. In November a multiracial conference held in the East End resolved to organize mass demonstrations against the presence of the National Front, especially in Brick Lane, where its members peddled the party paper during the Sunday market hours.

In the May 1977 elections to the Greater London Council the NF contested all but one of the 92 seats, and upstaged the Liberals in about a third of them. Such a performance boosted the morale of the party activists, particularly in the NF strongholds in the East End.

Not surprisingly, racist attacks on Asians revived, with National Front heavies taking up key locations in Bethnal Green on Sundays, and selling the party paper. This in turn led to the formation of the Action Committee Against Racial Attacks (ACARA). Among other things it approached the Bangladeshi High Commission. Nudged by the Commission, the Home Office ordered a report on racist attacks in the area. At the same time ACARA co-operated with other organizations in presenting vocal, but peaceful, anti-racist opinion in the streets. In mid-October an anti-racist procession of 3000 people marched through the National Front strongholds in Bethnal Green and Hoxton on its way to a multicultural festival in east London's Victoria Park. There was comparative calm during the following winter.

But, in line with the past pattern, racial assaults on Asians revived in the spring. On 4 May 1978, Altab Ali, a Bangladeshi garment worker, was killed in Whitechapel, east London. This murder had the same impact on the Bangladeshi community in the East End as Chaggar's had on the Indian community in Southall. A wave of revulsion and anger brought some 7000 Bangladeshis to the streets on 14 May, under the auspices of ACARA, to stage a funeral march from the site of Ali's murder to the Prime Minister's residence at 10 Downing Street. The Bangladeshi community, which until then had been quiescent, was stirred to organize itself.[8]

However, unlike the Indians in Southall, it faced well-entrenched and organized racist forces in its district. This became obvious when, in response to the demonstration in mid-May, some 200 young members of the National Front went on a rampage on Sunday 11 June in the Brick Lane area against Asian establishments and cars. This in turn led to a march on the following Sunday by some 4000 demonstrators under the aegis of the Anti-Nazi League.

The Anti-Nazi League (ANL) had emerged as a national movement in 1977 – on the initiative of militant anti-racists and anti-fascists among leftist and ultra-leftist white Britons – in response to the increased activity of the National Front among school students, community and church groups, trade unionists and pensioners. The ANL established special sections among miners, students and football fans. It also launched Rock Against Racism. It thus combined confrontational politics with a populist appeal so as to neutralize the racist tendencies among sections of working-class youth likely to lead them into the fold of the National Front.

In London's East End the Anti-Nazi League supporters kept up their confrontation with the National Front, especially by occupying the NF's usual places in the streets of Bethnal Green and Whitechapel. In late June 1978 fights broke out between them and NF activists. Police intervention led to the arrests of fifty anti-racists and ten NF supporters.

By now the temperature had risen so high that even the generally sedate Community Relations Councils of Tower Hamlets and Hackney felt a need to intervene. They combined their call for a demonstration on Sunday 16 July with a strike on the following day. The result was a demonstration by some 3000 people, and near-unanimous support for the strike, an unprecedented event in the history of British race relations.

At the same time there was no let-up in the activities of the Anti-Nazi League. Every Sunday in July and August its supporters occupied the public haunts of the National Front members, with their numbers swelling from the initial fifty to a few thousand some weeks later. To keep the peace, Scotland Yard turned the Brick Lane area into the most heavily policed neighbourhood in Britain.

Facing ever-escalating confrontation and overwhelming opposition, the National Front activists retreated by discontinuing the sale of their paper in the district on Sundays. To celebrate this withdrawal, the anti-racists mounted a 5000-strong victory procession on 20 August. Five weeks later, by blocking access to Brick Lane, they managed to frustrate the National Front plan to march through the area to its new headquarters in Great Eastern Street.

In these struggles the role played by the anti-racist whites, belonging either to the mainstream trade unions or fringe leftist groups, was crucial. It was the Bethnal Green and Stepney Trades Council which initially commissioned an enquiry into racist assaults, and which documented more than 100 such cases between 1976 and 1978. The energetic commitment of white anti-racists to confront and defeat the racists in the streets made many Asians, young and old, realize that whites were not uniformly prejudiced.

The street agitation of 1977–8 politicized the hitherto passive Bangladeshi community, particularly the young. The radicalization of young Asians benefited those fringe leftist organizations which were in the forefront of the anti-racist agitation: they gained recruits. Equally, the local town halls and community liaison committees benefited by having a widening pool of socially committed young Asians available.

Once before, too, a large number of young Asians had undergone politicization. This had happened in the aftermath of Enoch Powell's sensational speech in April 1968. The difference between the Asian radicalization then and now was that whereas the previous phenomenon occurred in response to a single event, this time it required repeated confrontations with right-wing, neo-fascist groups in the streets to achieve the same end. The other difference was that while young Asians had failed in the late sixties to transform their newly acquired political consciousness into something concrete, this time around they spawned various organizations of their own.

With this, a chasm developed within the Asian community between the old ethnic organizations such as the Indian Workers' Association (IWA), the Pakistani Welfare Association (PWA) and the Bangladeshi Welfare Association (BWA) and the newly formed ones such as the Bengali Housing Action Group (BHAG) and the Bangladeshi Youth League in the East End, the Southall Youth Movement (SYM), the Asian Youth Movement in Bradford, and other similar bodies elsewhere.

A typical supporter of the newly formed associations was contemptuous of the middle-class, middle-aged leaders of the older organizations for letting white liberals wage their campaigns for them and lacking political savvy and confidence. In contrast to the business or professional background of the older leaders, the younger ones came from working-class or lower-middle-class families. Harbouring neither deeply emotional ties with the country of origin of their parents nor a wish to return to the 'motherland' at some point, the second-generation Asians felt impelled to stand up and fight to safeguard their place in the country of their birth: Britain. The difference between the generations was well illustrated by the reaction to the murder of Chaggar in Southall. While the traditional community leaders approached the police and government for protection, the young leaders openly expressed their distrust of white authority and called on the community to practise self-defence.

As a result of the agitation in the streets, which inevitably invited wide media coverage, the Asian community became more politically conscious. This could be inferred from such indicators as voter registration. In 1970 Asians were under-registered to the tune of 27 per cent. In 1979 the figure was down to 18 per cent (although still much higher than the 7 per cent for whites).[9]

In the 1979 parliamentary election the National Front decided to hold a public meeting in Southall, a decision which incensed the Asian community locally and the Anti-Nazi League nationally. Prominent among the local protesters was the Southall Youth Movement (SYM). Its followers were the first to take to the streets, well ahead of the main anti-NF demonstration, consisting of Indian Workers' Association members and Anti-Nazi League activists. Altogether, there were some 3000 anti-NF demonstrators. To control them the police deployed 2756 officers, including the Special Patrol Group. Both the size of the force and the brutality it used against the demonstrators were remarkable. The police arrested about 700 people, mainly Asians, and charged 342.

There was almost unanimous outrage at the vicious manner in which the police meted out violence to the demonstrators. Among those who were shocked were the reporters of the conservative *Daily Telegraph*. Describing how the police 'cornered' fifty demonstrators, and how 'several dozen crying, screaming demonstrators were dragged ... to the police station and waiting coaches', they stated: 'Nearly every demonstrator we saw had some blood flowing from some injury.'[10] Police violence led to the death of Blair Peach, a white teacher and a member of the Anti-Nazi League.

Peach's death was deplored as much by white anti-racists as by Asians of all political hues. The latter included the supporters of the well-established Indian Workers' Association as well as the newly founded Southall Youth Movement. Together they mounted a sustained campaign to find the culprits among the police responsible for the Peach tragedy. The failure of the authorities to do so only made them more determined.

Meanwhile, the SYM continued to stress self-help and self-defence. Its standpoint was in tune with the rising militancy in the local community which was, unlike the Afro-Caribbeans in Brixton and elsewhere, materially prosperous and socially cohesive. It was thus well-equipped to repel any attack by the racists.

9 Political Integration, Cultural Co-existence

[It] may be asked whether the Asian minorities in Britain face a Jewish future.

JOHN REX[1]

Some of us ... thought we could kill off the bits of us that were not acceptable [to white society] and convert them into museum pieces. The young [Asians] are showing us that you don't have to demolish your immediate environment in order to liberate yourself.

ARVIND SHARMA, a college lecturer in Southall.[2]

On 3 July 1981, the day rioting erupted in Toxteth, Liverpool, some 300 skinheads arrived by bus in Southall from the East End to attend a concert at a local pub, the Hamborough Tavern. A few of them entered an Asian shop on the main road, The Broadway, abused the shopkeeper and broke the window. They went on a rampage, smashing more shop windows as they passed. The word spread rapidly. Soon hundreds of young Asians assembled outside the Hamborough Tavern, now filled with the skinheads. The police cordoned off the pub. This angered the Asians, who threw petrol bombs at the building and set it on fire. Riot police with shields appeared to restore peace. They were pelted with stones by the rioting Asians. Sixty-one police officers and seventy civilians were injured. An uneasy calm returned to Southall the next day.

Although the riot was triggered off by the provocation provided by the skinheads from the East End, the police became as much a target of the angered Asians as the skinheads. This was the common element that the Southall disturbance had with others – in Toxteth, Moss Side and elsewhere. On the other hand, Southall was not an inner city area in decline. Its 30,000 Asian residents formed a fairly cohesive, hard-working community; and the unemployment and crime rates were lower than those of other riot-torn areas.

The short duration of the civil disorder and its specific target – a much-hated pub – also set the Southall event apart. It was more an issue of territorial encroachment, with the militant Southall Youth Movement angered by the vandalism that the skinheads from the East End had perpetrated on their home patch. The involvement of the SYM was openly conceded as its members publicly crowed about burning down a pub they had marked out as a hotbed of racists. What was equally noteworthy was the fact that the traditional middle-aged leaders did not condemn the SYM members for their violent behaviour. The distance between the two generations was narrowing.

In its initial days the SYM was ably led by Harpal Singh Gill. Its street actions in April 1979 (to counter a National Front meeting) and again in July 1981 gave it the aura of a grassroots organization which was capable of retaliating against racist attacks on the Asian community. This in turn opened up possibilities for its funding as a voluntary youth organization by such bodies as the Commission for Racial Equality and the Greater London Council. While adequate cash provided chances for enlargement and efficiency, it also opened up possibilities of political compromise and material corruption.

The SYM was in touch with young militant bodies elsewhere, particularly the Asian Youth Movement (AYM) in Bradford formed in 1977. The AYM had been active in mounting periodic anti-racist campaigns aimed at challenging the local neo-fascist groups politically, ideologically and territorially by supporting anti-National Front marches. In the spring of 1981, after the AYM had accepted state funding and participation in welfare activities, two of its leaders – Tarlochan Gata-Aura and Tariq Mahmood Ali – quit to form the United Black Youth League. They planned to attract both Asian and West Indian youths, and function as a radical, revolutionary organization.

Gata-Aura and Ali played an active role in organizing a counter-demonstration against the National Front march on 11 July 1981. They became involved in a fracas with the police, and were arrested. Based on their interrogation the police arrested ten other young Asians, and charged all of them with conspiring to make 38 petrol bombs. The dozen defendants came to be known as the Bradford Twelve. Their much-publicized case raised two important questions: (a) had the use of petrol bombs become necessary because of the police failure to protect Asians from repeated racialist attacks; and (b) was the making of petrol bombs legal in order to meet the violent threat posed by the neo-fascists against the Asian community?

On 26 April 1982 in Leeds Crown Court, Gata-Aura argued that he had resorted to petrol bombs because he had been told that only 'a wall of flame' would deter the attack that the fascists had planned. The jury of seven whites and five blacks returned a verdict of 'Not Guilty'. This decision was upheld by militant anti-racists locally and nationally in the same way as the 'Not Guilty' verdict was in the case of the accused in the Bristol rioting two years earlier.

However, it did not help resolve the two major problems facing the radical Asian youth organizations: their relationship with official institutions authorized to offer funds to voluntary bodies; and their political ideology. Those who argued for accepting public subsidies claimed that in the final analysis such funds came from taxes, and as tax-paying citizens they should have no qualms about accepting them. Those who opposed the idea asserted that those who paid the piper played the tune, and that it was impossible to maintain a radical ideology while receiving funds from governmental or quasi-governmental bodies.

Then there was the question of ideology. A Southall Youth Movement seminar in 1982 concluded that its political colour was black, the colour of the oppressed, which represented the social position of the Asian and Afro-Caribbean peoples in Britain. But such a statement did not in itself constitute a plan or programme to change the current situation.

When it came to participating in nation-wide action, the issue of acting as a purely black entity or co-operating with white anti-racists came to the fore. This happened when, in the wake of the Brixton riots of April 1981, the SYM became involved in plans to organize a Black Freedom March from Bradford to London during the summer of 1982. Such Marxist bodies as the Indian Workers' Association–Great Britain wanted to include anti-racist white organizations in the march; but they were opposed by the likes of the SYM, which insisted on keeping it as a purely black affair. In the event, nothing came of the idea.

This was a re-run of the unresolved problem of viewing the black struggle as an autonomous movement or as part of a working-class movement which recognized that blacks were under twin oppressions of class and race.

At the same time a process of co-option initiated by the official and quasi-official bodies, which began in the wake of the 1981 riots, affected Asian activists as much as it did West Indians. In the early 1980s opportunities opened up for funding from the Manpower Services Commission and about fifteen local authorities with large ethnic populations. There were paid jobs in community consultation or liaison departments of the town halls; and in multicultural education, youth affairs and ethnic arts. Young Asians with a developed social conscience and some experience of agitational politics were preferred for these posts, since they were thought to be in touch with grassroots feelings and problems.

Along with these non-dramatic changes at the town hall level went dramatic events on the national stage. The most important was the failure of the year-long miners' strike in the spring of 1985 due to the openly hostile attitude taken by the Conservative Government. There was a growing realization in the country that the Prime Minister, Mrs Thatcher, was immune to the pressures of the street, and that she did not care about popular grievances. As such the riots of September–October 1985 in Handsworth and the Broadwater Farm estate in north London proved to be the last symptoms of a vanishing radical phenomenon.

Nevertheless, these disturbances had an impact on electoral politics. By heightening political consciousness they encouraged more and more ethnic minority members to become active in local and national politics. The result was the trebling of the ethnic minority local councillors in Greater London in 1986 – from 60 to 200 – with Asians accounting for half of the total. Once again this reiterated the fact that underneath the continuing inter-racial friction and violence, Asians (as well as West Indians) were being integrated into mainstream British politics.

This had a progressive impact on the local services provided to racial minorities. The participation of a substantial number of West Indian and Asian councillors in the running of the town halls made the system sensitive to the particular needs of ethnic groups. In the London borough of Ealing, for instance, most of the information about local services was made available in four Indian languages as well as Polish and English. There was a marked improvement in opportunities for town hall jobs up to the middle management level for young Asians and West Indians. In education the facilities for teaching Indian languages at school improved, a trend which was also encouraged by the Department of Education and Science.

The 1987 parliamentary poll witnessed the arrival of an Asian, Keith Vaz, in the House of Commons. He was elected from Leicester, a city of 285,000 people, with about a third of Asian or West Indian origins, the largest proportion in any urban centre of Britain. His constituency, Leicester East, contained 30 per cent ethnic minority voters, most of them Asian. A Cambridge-educated solicitor, Vaz was unlike the three new black MPs (see Part I, Chapter Nine), who had graduated to the national assembly through their experience at local government level, having contested, unsuccessfully, the 1983 parliamentary election as the Labour candidate for the affluent constituency of Richmond, Surrey. This time he proved particularly attractive to his local supporters in Leicester East. The Asian electors turned out in large numbers, raising the overall voter turnout by 5.4 per cent. Vaz became the first Asian MP since the 1920s, when Shapurji Saklatvala was elected to Parliament first on a Labour ticket and later on a Communist one. Of course, the social environment that prevailed in the Britain of the twenties was vastly different from the one in the late eighties.

By 1987, for instance, the sight of an Asian grocer and newsagent in almost all English cities had become commonplace. Most of them were East Africa Asians who had arrived mainly during the period 1968–73. Earlier, the immigrants from the Indian subcontinent too had taken to shopkeeping on a substantial scale. This explained why the 1971 census and the 1974 survey by Political and Economic Planning Ltd showed that 8 per cent of working Asian men were self-employed compared to 12 per cent of white men.[3] With the government continuing to issue about 3000 vouchers annually to British passport holders from East Africa, most of them capital-owners, and with Asian students graduating from polytechnics and universities in increasing numbers, the size of the Asian middle class rose noticeably.

As for working-class Asians, a greater number were to be found in public housing in the 1980s than before. Comparing the 1974 and 1982 surveys, Colin Brown of the Policy Studies Institute noted 'a number of changes ... particularly the moves away from the private rented sector and into the council sector, and moves to better-occupied property'. The proportion of sharing households among racial minorities fell from 26 per cent to 5 per cent.[4] This signified a welcome trend towards racial equality in housing.

But the increase in council occupancy by Asians and blacks accentuated the problem of racial harassment. *Living in Terror*, a report on the subject by the Commission for Racial Equality (CRE), published in 1987, established the seriousness of the problem. Racial harassment ranged from verbal abuse and graffiti on the walls to physical assaults and arson. The report showed that 'racial harassment at or near the home was widespread and common, affecting not only areas like the inner cities where there are relatively large black populations but also areas with relatively small black populations'. The latter part of the statement dovetailed with a newspaper report on Leicester published in late 1989. It showed that most racial incidents were occurring on the hitherto all-white estates as Asian and West Indian families tried to move into them. This led to many ethnic minority tenants returning to the inner city and those already living there changing their minds about moving out to better, more spacious accommodation in the housing estates situated in pleasanter surroundings.[5]

A study of six areas – Bristol, Hackney (London), Leeds, Leicester, Lewisham (London) and Reading – by Mohan Luthra and Andrew Tyler for the Department of Environment, published in 1988, established that Asians were twice as likely to be racially harassed or attacked as Afro-Caribbeans. Between 20 and 27 per cent of Asian households had had direct experience. The action of the harasser(s) spread fear among the victims and restricted their basic freedoms, especially for women and children, who felt trapped inside their homes. In Leeds, the life pattern of 45 per cent of the victims had been altered for the worse.[6]

What was true of the Asians living in public housing concerning racial harassment and violence was also true of Asians in general. A breakdown of the 1987 figures supplied by the Metropolitan Police established this clearly. Of the eight areas covered by this force, Area 2 (East) accounted for a third of the 2112 reported racial incidents. Of the five boroughs included in Area 2, Tower Hamlets and Newham – with a high proportion of Asians among its visible minority population – accounted for four-fifths of all racial incidents.[7]

Certainly, not all instances of racial harassment were reported by Asians. Of those reported the proportion that were 'cleared up' was small. In Newham it was 26 per cent, rising to 30 per cent in Tower Hamlets. Even in the gravest cases the proportions were unimpressive, varying between 36 and 40 per cent for serious assault and 17–21 per cent for criminal damage.[8] Little wonder that Asian settlers frequently criticized the cavalier attitude of the police towards their complaints of racial harassment and violence, and their poor record in catching and charging the culprits.

This feeling was quantified by the 1988 Department of Environment study of the ethnic occupiers of public housing. Only 20–40 per cent of the victims of racial harassment or violence expressed satisfaction with police action. Nor was the performance of the local councils, which owned the housing estates, satisfactory. The CRE report established that only a third of local authorities had taken the matter seriously enough to formulate a policy on it. Even when such a policy existed it was improperly executed. About a third of the local councils did not record individual cases of racial harassment on or near their housing estates. More than half of them had not issued any progress report on resolving the problem, and nearly 70 per cent had not re-examined their policies.[9]

However, with 70–72 per cent of Asians being home-owners, those living in publicly-owned housing were a minority. Also, about a half of all Asians lived in south-east England.[10] This meant that a majority of Asians benefited by the steep rise in house prices during the 1980s. Those living in the south-east benefited more as the property boom in the region was all the more buoyant. It was therefore no surprise when a survey by the *Sunday Times* in 1989 revealed that there were 200 Asian millionaires in the country. In absolute terms this looked impressive. But given that there was an official estimate of 18,000 millionaires in Britain, the proportion was not particularly striking.[11]

None the less, the number of Asians active in Conservative politics was much higher than among West Indians. In 1982, for instance, the party's

Anglo-Asian Society had 25 branches and 2000 members, balanced between Asians and whites, ten times the figure for the Anglo-West Indian Society. Both bodies acted as bridges between the respective racial minority and the local Conservative Association. They published regular newsletters, organized meetings and lobbied parliamentarians.

Following claims that the Anglo-Asian Society had been taken over by Sikh extremists, committed to securing the independent state of Khalistan (i.e. Land of the Pure) for Sikhs in the Indian subcontinent by violent means, the Anglo-Asian Society was dissolved by the Central Office of the Conservative Party in December 1986 – with the same fate befalling the Anglo-West Indian Society. (Their place was taken by the 'One Nation Group', stressing the fact that the party leadership had decided to de-emphasize class and ethnic origins.) Here was an example of developments in the Indian subcontinent impinging directly on British politics, or at least on its periphery.

Indeed, the movement for Khalistan had a palpable impact on the Sikh settlers in Britain and their offspring. In India the agitation for Khalistan was led by Sant Jarnail Singh Bhindranwale who, along with thousands of followers, took up residence inside the Sikh holy shrine, the Golden Temple complex, in Amritsar, Punjab. On 1 June 1984 the Indian Prime Minister, Indira Gandhi, ordered a military attack on the holy shrine. Bhindranwale and several hundreds of militants were killed. The incident shocked the Sikh community in Britain; and even moderate community leaders strongly condemned the Indian government's action.

No wonder that the news of the assassination of Indira Gandhi by two Sikhs among her bodyguard on 31 October 1984 was greeted with glee by many Sikhs in Britain. Divisions between moderate and militant Sikhs became acute, with the pro-Khalistanis siding with the International Sikh Youth Federation and the Dam Dami Taskal. In one instance, in Gravesend, Kent, there were running street fights between the moderates and the militants.

With Rajiv Gandhi succeeding his mother as India's Prime Minister, the Khalistan movement intensified and became more violent than before. The influence of moderate Sikh leaders in Britain declined. In February 1986 a pro-Gandhi Sikh businessman, Tarsem Singh Toor, was assassinated in Southall. The killing was carried out by Patrick Tamlin, a white ex-serviceman who had been hired by Gurmail Singh Basra: both were convicted in October 1987. On 11 November 1987 another moderate Sikh leader, Guru Darshan Das, was assassinated, again in Southall. By then, the militant International Sikh Youth Federation and Dam Dami Taskal had expanded their base in the community by gaining control of half of the 144 Sikh temples in the country.[12]

The Khalistan agitation in the Punjab, widely reported in the main-stream and ethnic media, made an impact on young Sikhs in Britain. It engendered much interest among them to know more about Sikhism; and it encouraged them to grow their hair and wear the turban, thus reversing the previous trend. By all accounts young British Sikhs began displaying renewed pride in their culture and religion, in line with a general trend among young Asians towards displaying ethnic identity – chiefly through dress. This was particularly true of females. Whereas, earlier, only those young women with orthodox parents wore *salvar kameez*, with the more fashionable preferring jeans and blouses, the newer generation seemed to take largely to traditional Indian clothing. Even some young men reverted to the clothing of their grandparents in the Indian subcontinent, reversing the trend their fathers had set.

A similar conservatism came to the fore among young Muslims in the wake of the controversy about the novel *The Satanic Verses*, by Salman Rushdie, published in September 1988. However, the Rushdie affair had a far wider impact on race relations because nearly half of Asian settlers were Muslim,[13] and because most whites had a negative perception of Islam, associating it with the bloody upheavals in the Middle East and Iran since the Second World War.

10 The Rushdie Affair: Dialogue of the Deaf

After this affair, Muslims have reason to think the Crusades are not over yet.

SHABBIR AKHTAR, a Muslim leader in Bradford.[1]

What enrages Muslims today is that the slanders and misrepresentation have lived on long after the winding up of Western empires: anti-Islamic references permeate the [Western] culture.

RANA KABBANI[2]

It [the Muslim protest over the Rushdie book] has provided a perspective that on one hand magnifies the British assumption that Muslims are mired in religion, primitivity and regression; and on the other hand reveals a British lack of comprehension and unwillingness to give social space to a faith regarded as too simple, too fundamentalist, too dogmatically unitary for a 'pluralistic' society.

CAL McCRYSTAL, a British journalist.[3]

Events in the Middle East, particularly after the October 1973 Arab–Israeli War which triggered an Arab oil embargo against the West and the trebling of oil prices, reinforced historical prejudices of the British regarding Islam and Muslims as traditional adversaries of the West with a propensity for aggression and blackmail.

The downfall of the pro-Western Shah of Iran, engineered mainly by revolutionary Islamic forces in February 1979, heightened popular British perceptions of Islam as a fanatical, anti-Western ideology. However, this stark view was muddied somewhat when in neighbouring Afghanistan the Islamic partisans took up arms against the Marxist regime in power since April 1978 – later bolstered by the arrival of Soviet troops in December 1979 – and were actively aided by Western powers, particularly America, through Pakistan ruled by General Muhammad Zia al Haq. Having seized power from a civilian government in mid-1977, General Zia al Haq had taken to administering Pakistan according to the Sharia, the Islamic law.

Since Muslims of Pakistani origin were the largest group among their co-religionists in Britain, the impact of these developments on British

Muslims as a whole was substantial. By the late 1970s the Muslim community had passed through the early phase of economic survival and found its feet. With this, its traditional interest in religion revived. The number of mosques grew sharply, with several custom-built mosques, often funded by the oil-rich Gulf states, rising in many British cities. The local Muslim Education Societies increased to such an extent that in 1979 the Union of Muslim Organizations of the United Kingdom and Eire established a separate National Muslim Educational Council.

Throughout the 1980s the events in Afghanistan, as well as those in Iran and the Iranian war with Iraq, impinged on the Muslim psyche in Britain. But since the Iranian leader, Ayatollah Ruhollah Khomeini, belonged to the minority Shia sect – which also claimed the loyalty of most Iranians – British Muslims, belonging largely to the majority Sunni sect, were not too enamoured of Islamic Iran. Khomeini's obduracy in continuing the armed conflict with Iraq, a Muslim country, puzzled and depressed most British Muslims. It was only when Khomeini accepted a United Nations ceasefire plan in July 1988, paving the way for a truce a month later, that his standing among British Muslims improved somewhat.

In late September a London-based publisher, Viking Penguin, published *The Satanic Verses*, a novel by Salman Rushdie, a writer born in India but educated in Britain, who had taken up British nationality.

In the second chapter of the book the author portrayed the Prophet Muhammad – thinly disguised as a fictional character called Mahound (meaning false prophet or devil) – as an unscrupulous, lecherous imposter who hoodwinked his followers. Later Rushdie suggested that Mahound included in the Quran certain verses which turned out to be the work of the devil: the satanic verses. In the fourth chapter of the book Mahound was portrayed as 'spouting rules, rules, rules until the faithful could scarcely bear the prospect of any more revelations'. (This was seen by Muslims as a symbolic attack on the Sharia, Islamic law, consisting of the Quran and Hadiths, Sayings and Doings of the Prophet Muhammad.) Later the writer offered a long fantasy about 'the Curtain', the most popular brothel of Jahilia (i.e. Mecca). Here, in order to attract clientele, the prostitutes assumed the names of the wives of the Prophet.

Soon after the publication of the book, certain Muslim leaders in Britain requested the Prime Minister, Margaret Thatcher, to ban it and prosecute Rushdie for slandering Islam. Mrs Thatcher replied that there were no legal grounds to do either. The content of the book, a literary work, did not contravene British law, which limits freedom of expression only in such areas as national security, personal libel and engendering racial hatred. Secondly, slandering Islam was not an offence in law.

To gain backing in the Islamic world British Muslim leaders mailed photocopies of the objectionable passages in the book to the London embassies of the 45 member states of the Islamic Conference Organization, based in Jiddah, Saudi Arabia. Given that blasphemy against Christianity was a criminal offence according to a law dating back to the 1740s, and that a successful prosecution had occurred in 1979 after the publication, in the London-based magazine *Gay News*, of a poem depicting Jesus Christ as a homosexual, they approached the Home Secretary, Douglas Hurd, to take legal action against Rushdie. In response, Hurd said that prosecution for such cases was the legal duty of the countries where Islam was the main religion, and not a minority faith as in Britain.

Thus frustrated, irate Muslims began demonstrating against the book and its author. The first such event occurred in Bolton, Lancashire, on 2 December 1988. The demonstrators burned a copy of *The Satanic Verses*; but the gesture went unnoticed in the national media. It was not until 14 January 1989, when another copy of the book was burned at a Muslim rally in Bradford city centre, that the media took notice. With this the subject acquired national importance; and Bradford emerged as the epicentre of the Muslim protest. About three-quarters of its ethnic population of 68,000 (amounting to a quarter of the city's inhabitants) were Muslim; and they lived compactly in certain areas. This gave them a sense of cohesion and solidarity which was not to be found in such a conurbation as Greater London. However, to make a mark on the general public it was essential for Muslims to mount a demonstration in the capital. In late January more than 8000 Muslims from all over Britain marched against the book in London and petitioned the publisher to withdraw it.

On 12 February, on the eve of the publication of the American edition of the novel, there was a demonstration in Islamabad, the capital of Pakistan, where the work had been banned. As the demonstrators marched to the American Centre they were fired on by the security forces, resulting in the death of at least six people. Among the countries where this event was broadcast on radio was the Islamic Republic of Iran. Following this, it seems, one or more acolytes of Khomeini approached him to deliver a *fatwa* (religious decree) on the matter.

He did so on 14 February. 'I would like to inform all the fearless Muslims in the world that the author of the book entitled *The Satanic Verses*, which has been compiled, printed and published in opposition to Islam, the Prophet and the Quran, as well as the publishers, who are aware of the contents, have been sentenced to death. I call on all zealous Muslims to execute them quickly, wherever they find them, so that no one will dare to insult Islamic sanctity. Whoever is killed on this path will be regarded as a martyr.'[4] With this the issue became international, involving sovereign states.

Rushdie went into hiding and, being a British national, was given police protection. The Foreign Secretary, Sir Geoffrey Howe, deplored Khomeini's action as 'interference in the internal affairs of another country'.

As the Friday prayer leader of Tehran, President Ali Khamanei welcomed Khomeini's edict in his sermon on Friday 17 February. 'The author may repent and say "I made a blunder", and apologize to Muslims and the Imam [i.e. Khomeini],' he added. 'Then it is possible that the [Muslim] people may pardon him.' The next day Rushdie stated: 'I profoundly regret the distress that the publication [of my book] has occasioned to sincere followers of Islam.' To this Khomeini's office replied: 'Even if Salman Rushdie repents and becomes the most pious man of all time, it is incumbent upon every Muslim to employ his life and belongings to send him to hell.' Earlier, Hojatalislam Hassan Sanai, head of a religious foundation in Iran, had offered a reward of $2.6 million to an Iranian and $1 million to a non-Iranian for the assassination of Rushdie.[5]

Support for Khomeini came not only from Muslim leaders in Western Europe but also from within the Islamic leadership in the Indian subcontinent. Muhammad Ismail Qureshi, the Pakistani president of the World Association of Muslim Jurists, stated that Rushdie's action was 'unpardonable under the Islamic law'. The head preacher at Jama Masjid in Delhi, a leading mosque of India (with a Muslim population of about 100 million), said: 'We are supportive of the death sentence passed by the Ayatollah on the blasphemous dog.' President Hussein Muhammad Ershad of Bangladesh demanded the trial and punishment of Rushdie. Rioting by Muslims in Bombay, Rushdie's birthplace, resulted in twelve deaths from police gunfire.[6]

Khomeini seemed to be on a strong theological ground. He had based his judgement in the Sharia and the Islamic tradition. The most pertinent verse in the Quran reads: 'Those who molest God's Messenger / for them awaits a painful punishment' (9:61). What sort of punishment is to be meted out to those who slander Allah's Messenger or His Word (the Quran) was specified, and practised, by the Prophet Muhammad himself. Shortly after he had captured Mecca in January 630, he had Kaab ibn al Ashraf, a poet, decapitated for mocking the Quran.[7] Since then the Prophet Muhammad's example has been emulated by his followers.

On the other side, Sir Geoffrey Howe's condemnation of Iran received the unqualified backing of the Labour Opposition. The Archbishop of

Canterbury, Dr Robert Runcie, combined his utter condemnation of 'incitement to murder or any other violence from any source whatsoever' with his firm belief that 'offence to the religious beliefs of the followers of Islam or any other faith is quite as wrong as offence to the religious beliefs of Christians'. Abroad, the twelve foreign ministers of the European Community meeting in Brussels decided to recall ambassadors from Tehran and freeze all high-level visits between their countries and Iran. They condemned the 'incitement to murder' as 'an unacceptable violation of the most elementary principles and obligations which govern relations among sovereign states'.[8]

Iran responded by deciding to break off diplomatic relations with Britain and match the action taken by its European Community partners by withdrawing its ambassadors from the European capitals. Its chargé d'affaires, Muhammad Akhundzadeh Basti, left London on 1 March, deploring the fact that the British government had taken the lead 'in making this matter purely political', and stressing that Ayatollah Khomeini had acted primarily as a religious leader.

By now it had become clear to British Muslims that Iran was prepared to take the consequences of its tough stance on the Rushdie affair, however damaging they might be to its diplomatic and economic welfare. This was in direct contrast to the behaviour of the Saudi-funded Islamic Conference Organization (ICO), to which they had turned initially for support and guidance. The ICO had demonstrably failed, because King Fahd of Saudi Arabia, 'The Custodian of the Holy Shrines [of Mecca and Medina]', and his diplomats in London had done nothing more than engage in discreet lobbying against the Rushdie book.

However, following Khomeini's verdict, a seminar organized by the Saudi-funded Muslim World League in Mecca condemned Rushdie as 'a heretic and a renegade' and demanded a trial of him and his publishers by 'relevant courts'. In the wake of Khomeini's *fatwa* other Islamic luminaries and organizations could do no more than either follow his lead or keep silent. Since the issue concerned the Prophet Muhammad, the founder of Islam, there was no question of a Sunni–Shia schism. (This became clear when the Association of Sunni Muslims organized the Day of Muslim Solidarity nationally on Friday 15 December 1989, as part of its drive to get *The Satanic Verses* withdrawn from bookshops.[9]) Khomeini was now seen by most British Muslims simply as the leading Islamic figure on the world stage, upholding the sanctity of the Prophet Muhammad.

Soon Khomeini's pictures became a regular feature of the demonstrations which Muslims mounted in British cities and towns from

Glasgow to Gravesend, culminating in a large procession in London on 28 May 1989, organized by the British Muslim Action Front, which reiterated the communal demands for a ban on the book and an extension of the blasphemy law to cover Islam. A measure of anti-Rushdie feeling was provided by a Harris opinion poll of British Muslims commissioned by BBC Television. It showed that 79% of those questioned favoured action against Rushdie. Of these, 35% endorsed the death sentence, with the proportion rising to 45% among the young respondents (aged sixteen to twenty years).[10] This was a setback for the pro-Saudi Muslim bodies in Britain, often funded through the Muslim World League. They included the Union of Muslim Organizations of the United Kingdom and Eire, the Islamic Cultural Centre based at London's Regent's Park, the Islamic Foundation and the Muslim College. Huge subventions by Saudi Arabia and other Gulf states had made possible the construction of the £1.5 million East London mosque in 1985 and the Central Mosque in Glasgow a year later at a cost of £2.5 million. During his visit to London in 1987, King Fahd publicly donated £12 million for distribution among British mosques. But his failure to provide leadership to British Muslims over the Rushdie affair brought about a decline in King Fahd's standing as well as that of his country.

By providing a rallying forum for the traditional Muslim leaders, committed to maintaining Islamic values in a non-Islamic environment, the Rushdie affair arrested the trend towards secularization among Muslims, particularly those born and brought up in Britain, which had been in train for the past few decades, and which had led to the young questioning the inherited dogma of their elders and marrying outside their religious community. As Nasim Hasnie, chairman of the Huddersfield Community Relations Council, put it: 'Some of us are very liberal and secular but we [Muslims] have been pulled six feet out of the ground to identify with our cultural heritage.'[11] In other words, when the basics of their faith were ridiculed and attacked, secular and liberal Muslims discovered that they had no option but to align with the traditionalists in order to defend their religio-cultural heritage. This gave additional force to the traditionalist school, which deplored the idea of Muslims winning acceptance from white Britons by surrendering themselves to the ways of a permissive society, which included nakedness, immorality, promiscuity and venereal diseases. Those who wished to uphold the Islamic values of modesty, fidelity, sanctity of marriage, strong family ties and teetotalism were particularly keen to save adolescents and young children from the corrupting ways of white society.

Not surprisingly, the Muslim community witnessed the emergence of such militant groups as the Al Mujahed in Bradford, and the Young Muslim Organization and the Hizb-e Tahrir (Party of Liberation) in east London.

Among other things these organizations provided classes on various aspects of Islam. These proved popular with young Muslims who, unlike many of their elders concerned mainly with the ritualistic aspect of Islam, studied Islam as an ideology and a complete social system. This generation of Muslims lacked the easy-going manners of its white counterparts, intent on enjoying their existence. 'Life isn't just about going to discos and smoking ganja,' said nineteen-year-old Kysar Shah Nawaz, attending a class on Islam in Walthamstow, east London. 'There can be no compromise with the divine system that has been revealed to us [Muslims].'[12]

This inner belief in the superiority of Islam over all other religions helped young Muslims to compensate for the blow to their egos delivered by such daily experiences as racial taunts by whites and having to try three times harder than a white Christian to find a job.

Their parents had been agitating, unsuccessfully, for certain changes in the practices in vogue at state schools. The South London Islamic Centre had summarized these thus: (a) withdrawal of Muslim students from religious education (meaning, in practice, Christian) classes; (b) prayer rooms to be provided in schools with a substantial Muslim population; (c) Muslim children to be permitted to attend Friday prayers at the nearest mosque; (d) Muslim pupils to be allowed official holidays on Eid al Fitr and Eid al Adha; (e) halal meat to be provided in school meals; (f) swimming and physical education classes to be sexually segregated; and (g) exemption for Muslim children from singing and dancing (regarded as unIslamic activities).[13]

The incomprehension of the media and the insensitivity of the government, revealed by the *Satanic Verses* issue, added insult to injury. In a sense, the Rushdie affair crystallized a host of Muslim grievances. 'It is about a symbolic controversy in which lots of other Muslim fears and anxieties and aspirations are tied up,' stated Max Madden, Labour MP for Bradford West. 'How they believe that non-Muslims regard them; their feelings that they are unwelcome every day of their lives.'[14]

For twenty years Muslims had been lobbying, in vain, for state aid for their schools. The 1944 Education Act allowed the local and national authorities to finance 85 per cent of the capital costs and all of the running expenses of schools managed by religious bodies. In the late 1980s this provision benefited 2000 primary and 140 secondary Church of England schools as well as 2000 primary and 430 secondary Roman Catholic schools.[15]

The nearly one-million-strong community was now more than twice as large as the Jewish population of 450,000.[16] Yet while the Jews had secured state aid for fifteen primary and five secondary schools, the Muslims had failed to do so even in a single case until 1989. In that year the Islamia primary school in Brent, London, won voluntary-aided status after three years of trying.

But the Zakaria Muslim Girls' High School founded in 1982 in Batley near Dewsbury, West Yorkshire, remained unaided by public funds despite numerous applications by its management. It was financed by the Saudi-funded Muslim Educational Services based in London. The reason for the establishment of this school was the feeling among many Muslim parents that their children were being exposed at school to Western teachings and food as well as subjected to pressures to conform to Western Christian values. In such courses as social studies Muslim parents discerned conflict between the prevalent secular, liberal values and Islamic precepts on several subjects, including feminism, homosexuality and erotic literature.

For a Muslim (or any other religious) school to receive public funds it must first be recognized by the Secretary of State for Education; and the minister does that only on the basis of a report by a Local Education Authority (LEA) stating that the school in question is both educationally and financially sound.

Often a Local Education Authority blocked recognition on the technical basis that the school was too small either physically or in terms of its student body. The Zakaria Muslim Girls' High School, for instance, had 127 pupils. But beyond these tactics lay a more serious point. Most LEAs believed that Muslim schools would discourage social integration of their charges, particularly girl students, into British society, and that funding these institutions would run counter to promoting equal opportunities policies. This stance was in line with the thinking in Whitehall. According to the *Sunday Times*, the Thatcher administration had set its face 'firmly' against the idea. 'Ministers are said to be prepared to use any means at their disposal to block applications for state-funded Muslim schools.'[17] On the other hand the idea of Muslim schools was popular in the community. An opinion poll of Muslims commissioned by BBC Television in September 1989 showed that 48% would like to send their children to an Islamic school while only 35% preferred a 'mixed race' school.[18]

The discriminatory behaviour of the local and national governments angered and depressed Muslim leaders, and provided them with further evidence that the much vaunted multicultural society in Britain was indeed a sham. In some cases Muslims resorted to overt protest. This happened in Dewsbury in February 1989. Following their parents' instructions, some 900 Muslim students boycotted schools for a day and gathered in the town's Islamic Centre to demand public financing for Muslim schools.

However, the situation was not all bleak for Muslims. The Labour Party showed some sensitivity to their feelings. Elaborating on the party's document on multicultural education before a conference on Muslim schools in London in July 1989, Jack Straw, the Labour spokesman on education, called on the LEAs to give private Muslim and Orthodox Jewish schools the same rights as Christian schools to opt out of the state system (under the provisions of the 1988 Education Reform Act) and still be financed by public funds. Simultaneously, they should be free to enter the state system with the same rights and obligations as Anglican and Catholic schools, he proposed.[19]

Jack Straw argued that the controversy on Muslim schools stemmed partly from ill-informed objections to the treatment of women in Islam, that ignorance and stereotyping about women's role in Islam verged on the racist, and that this prevented Muslims from exercising the same choice in education as Christians. He pointed out that while women in Christian Europe acquired rights to property only in the latter part of the nineteenth century they had been given this right in Islam from its inception in the mid-seventh century.

Part of the reason for the understanding shown by Jack Straw lay in the fact that the vast majority of Muslims supported his party. Few Labour MPs who had a substantial Muslim vote in their constituencies could resist for long the pressure they experienced from their Muslim constituents. Some of them came to express genuine sympathy with the viewpoint of their (wronged) electors. Max Madden, representing Bradford West, was a case in point. Another was Keith Vaz, the only Asian MP, who represented a constituency in Leicester. Though a Roman Catholic, he articulated Muslim feelings, and tried to dispel one of the most widely held Western prejudices against Islam. 'I went to a synagogue recently in which women were placed in a different part of the hall from men,' he said in an interview with the *Independent*. 'I saw no demonstration outside urging the Jewish religion to liberate its women.'[20] More importantly, a noticeable change affected the stance of Roy Hattersley, deputy leader of the Labour Party and MP for Sparkbrook, Birmingham, where nearly two-fifths of the 80,000 voters were Muslim. In early March he was one of the signatories to the World Writers' Statement, 'We, the undersigned, in so far as we defend the right to freedom of opinion and expression embodied in the Universal Declaration of Human Rights, declare that we are also involved in the publication [of *The Satanic*

Verses],' it stated. But in mid-May, in an interview with the *Jang*, a London-based Urdu daily, Hattersley appealed to Viking Penguin not to publish a paperback edition of the book as this would increase the offence and hurt caused to the Muslim community. Alastair Darling, Labour's spokesman on home affairs, supported Hattersley. He also reaffirmed the resolution of the party conference in October 1989, which demanded that the blasphemy law should either be extended to apply to non-Christian religions or abrogated altogether.

As for the Muslim leadership, it combined overt, noisy protest with an unflagging drive to pursue the matter in the courts and direct the communal effort towards pressuring the political establishment through lobbying and active participation in the electoral process.

In March 1989, Sir David Hopkins, chief Metropolitan magistrate, refused to grant a summons to Abdul Hussein Choudhary, convenor of the British Muslim Action Front, to prosecute Rushdie and his publishers for the common law offence of 'blasphemous and seditious libel'. The British Muslim Action Front appealed against this ruling and in June, Mr Justice Nolan of the High Court gave permission for a judicial review over whether Rushdie and his publishers should be tried for blasphemy. (Next April the High Court ruled against a trial.)

After a series of meetings of various confederal Muslim bodies, the community leaders produced a Muslim Charter on the eve of Eid al Adha (Festival of the Sacrifice) on 13 July 1989. It could be perceived as a summary of Muslim demands and political strategy in the aftermath of the Rushdie book. It was adopted by most of the nearly 600 mosques in the country. Among other things, the Charter called on Muslims not to vote for any parliamentary candidate who did not support a ban on *The Satanic Verses* and an extension of the blasphemy law to include Islam.

The impact of the Muslim Charter was sharpened by press reports in August that plans were afoot to form a political party to represent Muslims. The new organization was to be led principally by British converts to Islam, including Yusuf Islam (the former pop singer Cat Stevens) and Sahib Mustaqim Bleher, a West German convert of a decade earlier, who was a leading force behind the Dewsbury schools' boycott by Muslim parents demanding state funding for Muslim schools. The Islamic Party of Britain was launched in September.

This made the Labour electoral strategists sit up and take note. They realized that were Muslims to abandon the party, seven sitting Labour MPs would lose their seats and a further five would be under a severe threat.

While the electoral considerations strengthened the argument of those in the Labour Party who wanted to extend a hand of understanding and friendship towards Muslims, no such factor impinged on the Conservative Government. In the absence of any significant backing from Muslim voters, it lacked a Muslim lobby within its ranks. Moreover, philosophically and socially, the Conservative Party was close to the Anglican hierarchy and was more Eurocentric than its rival, the Labour Party.

When faced with demands for action against the Rushdie book, or altering the blasphemy law, or public funding for Muslim schools, both the Home Secretary, Douglas Hurd, and his Minister of State, John Patten, could do no more than strike schoolmasterly postures. They combined their warning to Muslim leaders not to break the law with homilies on the virtues of integration, equating state financing of Muslim schools with a form of educational apartheid.

Underneath this rigid stance lay a calculation that a compromise on the law of blasphemy or on Muslim school funding would whet the appetite of the Muslim leadership. It would then press its demand that Muslim family law – dealing with marriage, divorce, custody of children and inheritance – be incorporated into the British legal system. Indeed, this was done by the delegation of the Union of Muslim Organizations during its meeting with Douglas Hurd and John Patten in late June 1989. The degree of support that the Muslim leaders had from their community on this issue became obvious when the results of the opinion poll commissioned by BBC Television were made public in October. It revealed that in case of conflict between the Islamic law and the British law, 66% of the respondents would follow the Sharia, with the proportion dropping marginally to 61% in the case of young Muslims.[21] Were the adoption of Muslim family law to become as urgent a demand as state-funded Muslim schools, the British liberal tradition would be stretched to breaking point.

This tradition had its followers in both major parties. And any change of government at Westminster was unlikely to resolve the Rushdie problem. Since Ayatollah Khomeini died on 3 June 1989 without revoking his verdict on Rushdie, it was still valid in the eyes of the faithful throughout the world. There was no chance of Khomeini's successor, Ayatollah Ali Khamanei, or any other religious personage in Iran tampering with Khomeini's *fatwa*. To demonstrate that nothing had changed since Khomeini's death, the Association of Sunni Muslims in conjunction with the pro-Iranian Muslim Institute, based in London, celebrated a Day of Muslim Solidarity in mid-December 1989. The prayer leaders in mosques throughout the country were instructed by the sponsoring organizations to deliver a special sermon in favour of a resolution which approvingly referred to the death sentence pronounced on Rushdie by Ayatollah Khomeini. 'The author and publishers should withdraw *The Satanic Verses* unconditionally, admit they made a mistake, apologize to Muslims of the world, and pay adequate compensation to those who have suffered from loss of life, injury or damage to property in the campaign against them,' the resolution concluded.[22] Given this, the British authorities were unlikely to remove the armed guard they had provided Rushdie since mid-February.

Within a year of the publication of *The Satanic Verses*, the term 'British Muslims' had entered the day-to-day lexicon. Yet nobody used the corresponding phrase 'British Sikhs' or 'British Hindus'. The non-Muslim immigrants and their descendants continued to be described merely as 'Asians' or 'British Asians' – that is, without any identification of their religious affiliation. Thanks to the Rushdie affair the racial label of Muslims – Asian – had been submerged into their religious identity within an astonishingly short period of one year.

This phenomenon provided the Muslim community with a confidence it lacked before. Young, articulate Muslims now argued that if the British settling abroad in non-Western societies did not adopt the way of life of the indigenous people, why should they emulate white Christians in Britain? As a female teacher at the Zakaria Girls' High School put it: 'We want the girls here to build up confidence and say to the outside world, "This is me. This is the colour I have. These are the clothes I wear. You have to accept me the way I am." They are ready to integrate on our terms this time, not their [white Christians'] terms.'[23]

It would be hard for the British public or government to accept the idea of overwhelmingly brown Muslims setting their own terms for social integration with white society. This implies a power relationship tilted in favour of the newcomer who is attached to a cultural heritage that has been for many centuries in struggle with Christian Europe. It also undermines the deeply rooted superiority complex of Britons which assumes that allowing non-Western persons to settle in their country, and giving them a chance to adopt their (superior) way of life, is a privilege which the immigrant must be publicly thankful for.

After all, the concept of letting brown and black people into Britain arose out of the institution of the Commonwealth, which arose out of the Empire, which in turn was ideologically justified by the notion of civilizing the heathens in the far corners of the globe.

PART III

WHITE BRITONS

1 The 'Open Door' Closes

The Labour Party is opposed to the restriction of immigration as every Commonwealth citizen has the right as a British subject to enter this country at will. This has been the right of subjects of the Crown for many centuries and the Labour Party has always maintained it should be unconditional.

Secretary to the Parliamentary Labour Party in a letter
to Sir Cyril Osborne, 2 June 1961.[1]

The government are firmly convinced that an effective control is indispensable. That we accept and have always accepted ...

SIR FRANK SOSKICE, (Labour) Home Secretary,
17 November 1964.

The presence of black and brown immigrants in Britain today can only be explained in terms of the Commonwealth. And the Commonwealth evolved out of the Empire. The history of the Empire is tied up with Britain's efforts to emerge as the supreme sea-power, 'the ruler of the waves'. However, the initial impulse was simply to explore the high seas, to follow the example of Christopher Columbus by sailing west. John Cabot did precisely that in 1497. He discovered Newfoundland.

Barbados was another island that fell into English hands as a result of exploration in the New World. That happened in 1605. Two years later came the first permanent English settlement in America. It was called Jamestown, after King James I. The following year Lord Chief Justice Ellesmore spelled out the legal position of the colonizers when he declared that 'King James I is one King over all his subjects in whatsoever of his dominions they were born'. Thus arose the concept of overseas British subjects.

By 1608 a sea-route to India had been found and the East India Company established to trade with the eastern hemisphere. As India was already well populated the question of English/British settlement there never arose even when during the eighteenth century Britain acquired political hegemony over large parts of the subcontinent. After the Indian armed uprising of 1857, Britain's parliament removed the intermediary

East India Company, and placed India under direct rule. Thus tens of millions of Indians became British subjects.

The British authorities, however, showed a contrasting attitude towards the colonies, settled by the people of British stock, and the subject territories inhabited by the 'natives'. For instance, whereas Queen Victoria made Canada a self-governing colony (that is, dominion) in 1867, nine years later she formally acquired the title of Empress of India. The remaining territories colonized by British people – Australia and New Zealand – were granted dominion status in 1907.

The First World War unified the Empire as never before. But the attempt made at the Imperial War Conference in 1917 to organize a central organ of government in London to guide the unified Empire after the First World War failed. Instead, for the first time, the idea of a British Commonwealth of Nations, a family of independent dominions, was aired before a generally receptive gathering of politicians. However, it was not until 1931 that the Statute of Westminster formally established the British Commonwealth of Nations.

On the eve of the Second World War, the British Empire was divided into the Commonwealth, India, and the colonies and protectorates. For all practical purposes the British Commonwealth was 'The White Man's Club'. After the war, India would have become the first non-white dominion had not its nationalist leadership insisted on complete independence. But having won it in 1947, Indian leaders decided to remain within the Commonwealth provided the arrangement did not conflict with their plans to inaugurate at a later date the Republic of India.

The Labour Party then governing Britain was anxious to retain India in the Commonwealth. This necessitated a fundamental change in British law and custom. The result was the British Nationality Act of 1948, which was supported by both major parties. It divided British citizenship (until then assumed to be a common possession of all the British monarch's subjects) into two categories: citizenship of 'the United Kingdom and Colonies'; and citizenship of independent Commonwealth countries, which then meant the white dominions, India and Pakistan. In other words, citizens of a Commonwealth country possessed, as an additional attribute, the *common status* of being British subjects. Thus arose the concept of the New Commonwealth which, for example, allowed Indian nationals to retain their status as British subjects even when India became a republic in 1950 and the British monarch lost the right to appoint a Governor-General of India.

Though the constitutional relationship between Britain and India and Pakistan altered, there seemed little change in British attitudes towards the colonies in Asia, Africa and the Caribbean, past or present. For instance, no effort was made by the government in London to tap the vast manpower resources of India and Pakistan to solve its acute labour shortage problem.

In June 1946, James Callaghan, a young Labour MP, called for 'an addition to our population which only immigration can provide'. The fuel crisis in 1947, stemming directly from labour shortage in the mines, dramatically highlighted the problem. A special Polish Resettlement Act was passed to enable Polish ex-servicemen to settle in Britain. As a result 120,000 Poles did so. The following year the government sponsored the European Voluntary Workers Scheme, and imported some 90,000 workers, mostly from the European Displaced Persons Camps. As a result the number of aliens in Britain rose from 159,000 before the Second World War (excluding 80,000 European refugees) to 429,000 in 1951. In contrast, West Indian ex-servicemen were given no official or unofficial encouragement to settle in Britain, nor was any attention paid to the ex-servicemen in India or Pakistan. Instead of helping West Indians who had come to Britain under the wartime Overseas Volunteers Scheme to stay, the government encouraged them to return home, and finally wound up the scheme in 1947.

When, in June 1948, nearly 500 West Indians boarded the SS *Empire Windrush*, 'the news of the passenger list began to worry both Whitehall and the House of Commons'.[2] Their arrival in England became a subject of debate in the Commons. 'Merely to read the House of Commons debate of June 1948,' wrote Professor Gordon Lewis, 'is to be made to appreciate how British political leadership, including Labour, managed to see it [the arrival of the SS *Empire Windrush*] not as a free movement of voluntary labour but as a sort of slave transportation engineered by evil agencies somewhere in the Caribbean.'[3]

The old fears and prejudices associated with dark skin were revived and expressed not only in Parliament but in the popular press as well. Apprehension on this subject was never fully dispelled. Meanwhile the labour scarcity persisted, even grew worse, thus providing an economic magnet for West Indian migrants. By the early 1950s, as post-war reconstruction got under way in continental Europe, the European sources of manpower had dried up. In contrast, the 1952 McCarran–Walter Act began diverting West Indian emigrants from America to the United Kingdom. Consequently, apprehension in Britain at the rising 'black tide' grew. And, with it, voices of alarm.

One of the politicians to raise the alarm was Sir Cyril Osborne, a Conservative MP. Even before the McCarran–Walter Act came into force he had started to demand control of coloured immigration. The five-fold increase in the West Indian intake – from 2000 in 1953 to 10,500 in 1954 – strengthened his case. He received support from the Central Council of the Conservative and Unionist Associations, the policy-making organ of the party then in power. In 1955 the Central Council demanded that the laws pertaining to aliens be applied to Commonwealth immigrants. Demands for coloured immigration control also came from the Labour-dominated Birmingham City Council and some of the Labour MPs representing constituencies in Greater London.

But the government did not yield to these pressures for internal and external reasons. The leaders of both major parties regarded the Commonwealth as 'one of Britain's principal sources of diplomatic influence'. This source was impressive not only in its magnitude – it covered nearly a quarter of the world's population spread out from Australasia to northern America and the Caribbean through Asia and Africa – but also, more importantly, in its unique exemplary nature. As the head of the Commonwealth, routinely described as a 'multiracial society',[4] Great Britain was seen as a first-rate moral leader, setting an example to the world at large.

The 1950s were notable for high idealism in regard to the New Commonwealth, blended with a self-congratulatory mood. To have transformed Britain's hitherto imperial role into moral leadership of its former colonies – freely bestowed upon it by the latter – pleased and excited its leaders. Never before in the history of empires, they often proclaimed, had there been such a development. They felt that for the New Commonwealth to be meaningful there had to be at least one common element, and that was to be the opportunity for *all* Commonwealth citizens freely to enter or leave the mother country. To limit that right was to undermine the very foundation upon which this institution was built, and to cast a shadow on the quality of moral leadership expected of the mother country.

At home, coloured immigration was a local issue, limited only to some parts of London and the Midlands. It had not yet impinged on the national mind. However, the 1958 race riots altered the domestic situation considerably. The British public at large became aware of the coloured immigrants' presence. Once that happened, the task of the proponents of immigration control became easier. It was the presence of blacks that had created a 'colour problem', they argued. So the solution lay in banning, or severely restricting, non-white immigration.

George Rogers, the Labour MP for North Kensington, London, where the Notting Hill riots occurred, demanded quick legislation to end 'the tremendous influx' of coloured immigrants. Lord Home (later Sir Alec Douglas-Home), then a junior minister for Commonwealth Relations, said in a speech in Vancouver, Canada, that 'curbs will have to be put on the unrestricted flow of immigrants to Britain from the West Indies'.[5] In this he was supported by the delegates to the Conservative Party Conference later that year who, by a substantial majority, passed a motion demanding control of Commonwealth immigration. The conference was well in tune with the popular mood on the issue: a public opinion poll had earlier shown that 75 per cent of those questioned wanted coloured immigration to be controlled.

It was the first time the general public had been polled on this subject. And the result revealed a conflict between the external and internal interests of the country: between the ideal of free entry into Britain of all British subjects, irrespective of colour or race, and the unfavourable reaction of most white Britons to black and brown citizens in their midst. This conflict ran straight through Whitehall. There, it was symbolized by the opposing stands taken by the Commonwealth Relations Office and the Colonial Office on the one hand, and the Home Office on the other.[6]

Besides this matter of principle, the government was faced with a genuine administrative problem. Most of the coloured immigrants then were from the colonies in the Caribbean and as such were citizens of 'the United Kingdom and Colonies'. To subdivide further this category would probably have necessitated new legislation, a step which would certainly have exposed the government to charges of racism by critics at home and in the coloured Commonwealth countries.

The timing was awkward, too. In 1958 the West Indian colonies were being federated, and the Federation was to be groomed for independence. It was hoped that once the Federation was on its feet, it could be persuaded, like India and Pakistan, to restrict emigration at source.

All these factors combined to make the government stand firm on the principle of free movement when Sir Cyril Osborne's motion calling for immigration control was discussed in Parliament in December 1958. The motion was defeated, but the debate revealed more clearly than ever before the reasoning of many of those demanding controls. Sir Martin Lindsay, a Conservative MP, warned that: 'A question which affects the future of our own race and breed is not one we should merely leave to chance.' Frank Tomney, a Labour MP, said: 'The coloured race will exceed the white races in a few years by no less than five to one. This will be a formidable problem for the diminishing members of the white races throughout the world.'[7]

Contrary to its public posture the government was not totally unresponsive to popular feeling. Just a week before the Commons debate on immigration a well-briefed staff writer on the *Economist* wrote: 'They [i.e. officials] think that the liberal line – uncontrolled immigration – can be held for a few more years, but not indefinitely ... This school in Whitehall and beyond feels that when the tide of colour rises to a ceiling yet unspecified ... British voters will demand that some checks be imposed.'[8]

But when a general election was announced a year later the Conservatives were eminently successful on the hustings in generating a euphoric feeling among the voters summed up by the slogan: 'You never had it so good'. It was therefore in the interests of Conservative candidates, individually and collectively, not to bring up the unpleasant and controversial subject of coloured immigration in their speeches and thus tarnish the happy, affluent image. As supporters of the 'open-door' policy, the Labour leadership were only too willing to oblige by keeping quiet on the subject.

Once the election was over, with the Conservatives retaining office, the issue was revived. Undeterred by the statement of R. A. (later Lord) Butler, the Home Secretary, in July 1960 – 'It is very unlikely that this country will turn away from her traditional policy of free entry' – Sir Cyril Osborne kept up the pressure to restrict Commonwealth immigration. In this he was now actively supported by a group of newly elected working-class and lower-middle-class Conservative MPs from the Midlands. Aware of the value of grassroots support, these lobbyists tried to direct mass opinion in such a way as to produce the maximum pressure at the right places. The establishment of the Birmingham Immigration Control Association in October 1960 proved an additional lever to them as it encouraged its members and sympathizers to secure signatures for a mass petition and deluge MPs with letters.

Soon thereafter R. A. Butler directed an interdepartmental committee to re-examine the mechanics of immigration control. It favoured control based on the availability of jobs in Britain. The details were leaked to the press in January 1961 by ministers anxious to test public opinion.

On 9 February the *Birmingham Evening Mail* reported that the Home Secretary had told senior ministers that Commonwealth immigration would be controlled. The government duly denied the report, and once again opposed Sir Cyril Osborne's bill to restrict the inflow from the Commonwealth. In May it let every MP know through a circular that there would be no immigration control legislation 'for at least a year'.[9] Nevertheless, by July 1961 the *Observer* was confidently forecasting an outline of future legislation: a labour permit would be the prerequisite for settlement in Britain.

A Gallup poll taken in June showed 67% in favour of restrictions and another 6% for a total ban, with only 21% for continued free entry. The figures had hardly changed since the 1958 riots. But there was one crucial difference. Now both the Conservative Government and party were more than willing to fall in line with the public mood, and did so with speed.

On 11 October the Conservative Party Conference passed a motion in favour of immigration control. On 31 October came the official decision in the text of the Queen's speech to the opening session of Parliament 'to control the immigration to the United Kingdom of British subjects from other parts of the Commonwealth'. The appropriate bill was published the *next day*. The second reading of the bill began on 17 November, with the committee stage and the third reading commencing after the Christmas recess. On 27 February the bill was passed by 277 to 170 votes, with Labour opposing it. The Act became operative on 1 July 1962.

This Act restricted entry to those Commonwealth citizens who had current work vouchers issued by the Ministry of Labour (later the Department of Employment and Productivity). Very shrewdly, the Conservative Government did not include the actual scheme of control in the Act. Thus the procedures could be changed through the administrative decisions of the Ministry without reference to Parliament.

In 1962 the Ministry of Labour designed a graded system of work vouchers: category A, for those Commonwealth citizens who had specific jobs to fill; category B, for those who possessed special skills or qualifications; and category C, for unskilled persons without definite prospects of employment. Right from the beginning, the Ministry indicated that it might impose limits on the C category. Actually, this category was abolished altogether in August 1964. A year later ceilings were to be imposed on the number of A and B vouchers – and by a Labour administration.

Throughout the late 1950s and early 1960s, when the issue of immigration control was raised and publicly debated, Labour consistently opposed restrictions. Popular sentiment and opinion polls notwithstanding, the party stuck firmly to its position. But in the end it bowed before public opinion. It took much longer than the Conservatives to yield to the electors' pressure. But when it did, it did so completely.

There were various reasons for the delayed change in Labour's position on Commonwealth immigration. The party had come into existence in 1900 to fight for the underdog. So it identified, at least emotionally, with the exploited millions in the colonies. It was favourably disposed to the idea of self-rule for India. It was also committed to the socialist doctrine of the 'Brotherhood of Man'.

More specifically, the New Commonwealth was the creation of the post-war Labour Government. Therefore the party, even when in opposition, remained deeply attached to the concept of a multiracial Commonwealth. When the demand for controls first arose in 1955, it was the

Commonwealth Sub-Committee of the party's National Executive Committee which stated publicly that it had no doubt that 'the [immigration] problem is based on colour'. Following the 1958 race riots, Labour stated that 'any form of British legislation limiting Commonwealth immigration into this country would be disastrous to our status in the Commonwealth and to the confidence of Commonwealth people'.

Until then appeals to the 'Commonwealth ideal', like the 'Brotherhood of Man', had the advantage of what Paul Foot, a British journalist, called 'electoral irrelevance'.[10] But as the ideal began to be associated by more and more Britons with increasing numbers of black faces in streets, pubs and factories, it became relevant. Indeed, it became an electoral liability. This was illustrated by the outcome of a by-election in a Birmingham constituency in April 1961, when the Birmingham Immigration Control Association's candidate secured twice as many votes as his Labour rival.

Yet Labour's national leadership remained firmly committed to the 'open-door' policy. To them – and particularly to Hugh Gaitskell, the party's leader in Parliament – upholding a moral principle was more important than short-term electoral popularity. Labour opposed the second reading of the Commonwealth Immigrants Bill in November 1961 because it introduced control and because 'it was widely held to introduce colour bar into our legislation'. The latter was a valid claim, and was confirmed when the Home Secretary stated during the parliamentary debate that controls would not apply to the Irish Republic because of 'practical difficulties'.

But the question still remained: how long could a mass organization, such as the Labour Party, continue to disregard popular opinion on a subject that mattered to British voters on a direct, personal plane? During the final debate on the bill Labour softened its opposition. Summarizing the party's modified stand, its spokesman on colonial affairs, Denis Healey, said: 'If the information collected by a serious survey of the whole problem revealed that immigration control was necessary, we should regard it as essential to consult the other Commonwealth governments ... to see how this could be achieved with the minimum of damage to their interests and to their confidence of our loyalty and good will.' Despite repeated questioning he refused to state whether or not a Labour Government would repeal the Act. Thus the party started to register – and yield to – popular feelings on the issue.

After the change of leadership, following Hugh Gaitskell's death in January 1963, Labour began smelling victory at the polls, and became more responsive to the voters' feelings. Some Labour MPs suggested giving unqualified support to the 1962 Act when it came up for renewal in November. But a complete renunciation of its previous policy, reiterated until recently with moral fervour, would have meant a politically embarrassing admission of poor judgement, which the Conservatives would probably have exploited to the hilt. So, in the end, Harold Wilson, the new leader, spelled out a compromise in Parliament. 'We do not contest the need for control of immigration into this country,' he said, and then went on to suggest that certain loopholes in the Act must be eliminated. He offered a bargain to the Home Secretary: if the government would initiate consultations with the Commonwealth governments to get control from their end, his party would not oppose the renewal of the Act. The proposal was disparagingly rejected by the government. Labour therefore had no choice but to vote against the Act. This was madness, or so thought many Labour supporters up and down the country.

Letters began arriving at the party's London headquarters warning that Labour would probably lose the general election (expected at any time) on the issue of coloured immigration. Most of the letters from the provinces pointed out that 'it was easy to sit back in London and be idealistic about the matter, but that living with the problem was a more serious business'.[11] The point was not lost on the drafters of the Labour Party's manifesto for the 1964 election. It stated: 'Labour accepts that the number of immigrants entering the United Kingdom must be limited. Until a satisfactory agreement covering this can be negotiated with the Commonwealth, a Labour government will retain immigration control.'

During the campaign some Labour candidates blamed the Conservatives for 'the whole wave of immigration'. The Smethwick Labour Party issued a leaflet on Patrick Gordon-Walker's behalf: 'Immigrants only arrived in Smethwick in large numbers during the past ten years – while the Tory government was in power.' None of this cut much ice with the local electors. Gordon-Walker's vote fell from 20,670 to 14,916. He lost. And his defeat was greeted with chants like 'Where are your niggers now?' He was made to pay a price for his anti-immigration-control speech in Parliament three years earlier which had, it seemed, earned him the label of 'Nigger Lover'.

This epithet remained with him even when, in January 1965, he contested a very safe Labour constituency in Leyton, east London, specially vacated for his benefit. He lost again, reducing the Labour administration's majority to three. About that time a private poll indicated that 95 per cent of voters favoured stringent control of coloured immigration. The Labour Government was visibly shaken. It seemed to have realized that simply being in favour of immigration restrictions was not enough: controls had to be tightened. Moreover, the government had to be *seen* to be getting tough on the issue.

The Conservative Opposition was competing with the government in its enthusiasm for further restrictions. In February 1965, as Leader of the Opposition, Sir Alec Douglas-Home demanded a reduction in the number of Commonwealth immigrants and the inclusion of dependants in the overall quota.

Not to be outdone, first the Home Secretary and then the Prime Minister stated that 'evasions' were almost totally eroding the Act. In a speech at a Labour Party rally in March, Richard Crossman, the Housing Minister, criticized the Conservatives for instituting 'completely ineffective controls'. To prove the point the government announced that in 1963 and 1964 some 10,255 New Commonwealth citizens had 'evaded' immigration controls.

This figure was obtained by subtracting the 'total deliberately admitted for settlement' from the 'net overall gain'. A similar exercise for the Old Commonwealth (Canada, Australia and New Zealand) showed a difference of 15,538. But a footnote to the table of 'Evasion Figures' stated: 'It is doubtful whether most of these have the intention of permanent settlement.'

It seemed the government's associating of evasions with coloured immigrants had a dual political purpose. It demonstrated that the Labour administration was ever vigilant and had detected evasions during the preceding Conservative rule. Secondly, the constant refrain of 'evasions' was meant to demoralize the liberal lobby expected to attack the impending tightening of immigration controls.

The White Paper presented to Parliament in August 1965 increased the immigration officer's discretionary powers. It gave the Home Secretary authority to deport a Commonwealth citizen. It placed a limit of 8500 on work vouchers, a reduction of 11,500 from the current annual intake. Finally, the permissible age for the entry of dependent children was lowered from eighteen to sixteen.

Among those who approved of the White Paper were Sir Cyril Osborne and Peter Griffiths, the victor of Smethwick. Their stand had been vindicated, they stated triumphantly. More significantly, a Gallup poll showed that while 88 per cent of the population backed the White Paper only 5 per cent opposed it.[12] So the government action was well in step with the popular feeling on the subject. In contrast, the national press, particularly the quality papers, condemned the document, pointing out the immorality of slashing Commonwealth intake while leaving untouched Irish immigration (amounting to 30,000 in 1965) as well as European.

This was a measure of the chasm that lay between the British masses and the liberal, intellectual minority. Though small in size, the liberal lobby was quite vocal. In criticism of the White Paper, the National Council for Civil Liberties came out with a publication, *Prejudice or Principle*; the Campaign Against Racial Discrimination produced *A Spur to Racialism*; and the Young Fabians, *Strangers Within*. Plans were made to raise the issue at the impending Trades Union Congress conference; but TUC leaders adroitly managed to avoid a debate on the subject.

Liberal hopes were then pinned on the emergency motion at the forthcoming Labour Party Conference asking the government to withdraw the White Paper. These were never realized. The motion was lost. The only major block of votes for the resolution came from the Transport and General Workers Union; but that was not enough to win an overall majority. 'The representatives of the British working man faithfully reflected his aversion to any spirit of universal brotherhood which touched him too closely,' commented the *Economist*.[13]

Defending the White Paper, Harold Wilson repudiated 'the libel that government policy is based on colour or racial prejudice'. But had not the Conservative leaders too rebutted the label of racism thrown at them by critics at the time of the 1961 Commonwealth Immigrants Bill? What, then, was the fact? It was spelled out by William Deedes, the Conservative Minister without Portfolio, in 1968. 'The Bill's purpose was to restrict the influx of coloured immigrants,' he wrote. 'We were [then] reluctant to say as much openly.'[14]

However, this time the Conservative leaders were in no doubt about the real purpose of the 1965 White Paper. They fully supported it. At their party conference later in the year they harped on the fact that the Labour Government had been so quickly, and so thoroughly, converted to their viewpoint. Satisfied with this achievement, they refrained from making further demands for controls. It seemed the 'Dutch Auction on Restrictionism' was over – for the time being at least.

From a historical perspective, the period 1961–5 saw the collapse of *laissez-faire* policies regarding coloured immigrants as well as their settlement. A *laissez-faire* policy was very comfortable to follow: it meant doing nothing. And this was clearly what the Conservative Government did regarding coloured immigration until popular anxiety forced its hand in 1961.

Simultaneously, however, another problem had grown. It concerned black settlers. They were being denied equal opportunity in jobs and housing, and equal access to public places. The *laissez-faire* stance in this case meant refusal by the authorities to admit that such problems existed. But as the traditional 'open-door' policy regarding Commonwealth citizens became vulnerable, slightly more attention was paid to the problem of their settlement. For instance, from 1961 onwards, Fenner (later Lord) Brockway's bill against racial discrimination – submitted to Parliament almost every year since 1951 – began to receive bipartisan support.

2 Coloured Immigration and Race Relations: A Composite Policy

Nobody thinks prejudice can be cured by legislation ... But legislation can check open and offensive manifestations of prejudice.

TOM DRIBERG, Labour MP, 6 October 1967.

This [1968 Commonwealth Immigrants] bill ... must be considered at the same time, and in accordance with, the [1968] Race Relations bill ... which is to be introduced during the next six weeks.

JAMES CALLAGHAN, (Labour) Home Secretary,
22 February 1968.

The [race relations] legislation may originally have had an effect as a moral declaration, but by now [the mid-1980s] it can have no additional effect of that kind.

COLIN BROWN and PAT GAY[1]

Fenner Brockway's views on race and immigration were in total contrast to Sir Cyril Osborne's. Whereas from the early 1950s Osborne devoted himself to getting coloured immigration stopped, Brockway concentrated on redressing the problem of racial discrimination. He first introduced a private member's bill on the subject in 1951. Nothing came of it. He made the next attempt in 1953, but in vain.

By then, however, the Commonwealth Sub-Committee on the Labour Party National Executive showed enough interest in the issue to invite an opinion from Kenneth L. Little, the author of *Negroes in Britain*. In his memorandum, Little concluded that there was 'a good case both in principle and in fact for enactment ... of ... legislation ... as a means of stirring the national conscience and of creating a new standard of public behaviour in relation to coloured people'.[2] But the Labour Party took no further action.

As for the Conservatives the problem was non-existent. In 1954 the Prime Minister, Sir Winston Churchill, refused to instruct ministers to prevent the operation of a colour bar because 'the laws of this country are well known, and ... there is no need for new instructions'.[3] A similar sentiment was echoed two years later by Gwilym Lloyd-George, Home Secretary. 'I have no information that there is any particular problem as far as these people [Commonwealth immigrants] are concerned,' he said.[4] That this view was shared by most legislators became apparent when, in 1957, Brockway's bill on racial discrimination was talked out in Parliament because less than forty members out of a total of 630 were present.

Even in 1958 race riots did not shake the complacency of the Conservatives. Their government perceived the rioting in terms of a breach of the peace and restoration of law and order. British law was quite unambiguous about that; and the stiff sentences imposed on the rioters amply illustrated it, Conservative leaders argued. However, Labour was sufficiently perturbed by the event to demand that the government outlaw 'the public practice of discrimination'. In response Lord Chesham, a Conservative leader, argued that an Act 'would run the risk of recognizing the existence of discrimination in a way that might draw attention to it, and would tend rather to foster it than do away with it'.[5]

The Conservative administration's wish to leave the *status quo* undisturbed was much too strong. And despite the 1958 riots, it persisted. The government resisted the demands for immigration restrictions as firmly as it did those for legislation against racial discrimination. But as practical considerations and popular opinion began undermining the 'open-door' doctrine, realism began creeping into the assessment of the coloured settlers' position in British society.

Indeed, following the 1962 Commonwealth Immigrants Act, a composite doctrine gradually emerged: regulate the number of coloured immigrants coming in, and assure equal rights to those already here. Labour showed distinct signs of following this pattern of thinking. It combined its shift towards immigration control with a stronger commitment to legislation against racial discrimination and incitement.

When elected to power in October 1964, the Labour administration announced its intent to introduce a Race Relations Bill. But before its publication in April 1965 the government had dropped enough hints about further restrictions on Commonwealth immigrants to cancel, in advance, much of the enthusiastic support this bill would have otherwise received from the liberal lobby. Now many of its members considered the bill more an example of political tightrope-walking rather than proof of Labour's positive commitment to racial equality.

The Race Relations Bill's declared intention was 'to prohibit discrimination on racial grounds in places of public resort...; to penalize incitement to racial hatred; and to amend Section 5 of the Public Order Act, 1936'. The absence of the vital areas of housing and employment from the bill was criticized by liberal opinion both inside and outside

Parliament. The only consolation it had was that the practice of racial discrimination was classified as a criminal offence. But this was precisely where the Conservative Opposition found the legislation objectionable, and they opposed its second reading in May 1965. Its spokesman offered to tolerate the measure if the Home Secretary drastically cut Commonwealth immigration, and withheld the bill until conciliatory procedures regarding racial discrimination had been thrashed out. This offer was rejected, and the bill was given a second reading by 258 votes to 249.

But then, suddenly, Home Secretary Sir Frank Soskice retracted his position to accommodate the Conservative viewpoint before the start of the committee stage of the bill. He replaced criminal sanctions against the discriminator with conciliation between him and the discriminated party to be undertaken by a special body to be called the Race Relations Board. His gambit paid off: Conservative co-operation on the parliamentary committee was secured. In early August 1965 the government established its restrictionist bona fides on immigration by publishing the White Paper, thus winning further Conservative approval. So, when the bill was finally passed into law in September, it had the stamp of a bipartisan measure.

Taken together, the 1965 White Paper and the 1965 Race Relations Act signalled the convergence of the two major political parties on the issues of immigration control and racial justice. An advance, albeit minor, on the front of racial equality for ethnic minorities was conceded by the Conservatives in exchange for a retreat by Labour in the matter of immigration restrictions. Conservatives tempered their opposition (expressed as late as 1964) to a law against racial discrimination; and Labour committed themselves to 'realistic goals, flexibly administered', as their 1966 election manifesto stated.

By the March 1966 general election Labour had established its restrictionist bona fides with electors. As a result many traditional Labour voters in the areas of racial minority settlement, such as Smethwick, who in 1964 had abstained from voting in protest at Labour's softness on coloured immigration, returned to the fold, thus enabling Labour candidates to regain their seats or improve their majorities, making the likes of Peter Griffiths redundant. The Labour victor over Peter Griffiths became so effusive over the result that he declared jubilantly, 'We've buried the race issue!' But this was not to be the last laugh, as subsequent events were to show.

The Conservative Party wanted to tighten controls even further. Its manifesto proposed that new entrants be allowed in only on a probationary basis for two years, and that they be required to register the number of dependants they wished to bring over. More significantly, the idea of government financial assistance to immigrants wishing to return home, first mooted by Sir Alec Douglas-Home in February 1965, was enshrined in the document. However, these proposals were not flaunted with much enthusiasm during the election campaign because of the realization among Conservative leaders that, since the previous parliamentary election of October 1964, British voters had been subjected to a continual barrage of argument and counter-argument on the immigration issue, and that it was time to let passions cool.

Following the election a comparative calm prevailed in this field. It seemed that the leaders of the two main parties had reached a tacit understanding to keep race and immigration out of party politics. In any case, they were generally agreed on a common prescription of minimum coloured immigration and maximum integrative effort. 'For the moment,' wrote Enoch Powell, an eminent Conservative MP, in early 1967, 'there is a feeling of stabilization and the subject has disappeared below the surface of public consciousness.'[6]

But the calm was brittle. Any indication of a reversal in the downward trend in the coloured immigration was likely to revive public unease. This happened with the issue of the Asians from Kenya: The central question was whether those with British passports could enter Britain freely. That is, were they exempt from the 1962 Commonwealth Immigrants Act, or not? When this question was raised publicly in February 1967 it was answered unambiguously by, *inter alia*, Donald MacColl, a former deputy passport officer in Kenya: Yes, they were exempt.[7]

This was in contrast to the official silence on the subject. 'British officials [in Kenya] had made no attempt to apprise us of our rights, unless they were asked point blank whether a particular person was free to come here,' said a Kenya Asian recently arrived in Britain. 'The position has been deliberately obscured.'[8] This continued until the Court of Appeal ruled that the 1962 Act did not apply to the residents of former British colonies with passports issued by the British government.[9] Then the fear of yet another 'black tide' gripped those Conservative leaders who had made it a point to safeguard Britain's racial interests. Enoch Powell was one of them. 'Hundreds of thousands of people in Kenya, who never dreamt they belonged to this country, started to belong to it like you and me,' he said in a speech at Deal, Kent, on 18 October. 'It is monstrous that a loophole in legislation should be able to add another quarter of a million to that score [of Commonwealth immigrants].'

There was no loophole in the 1962 Act. It applied to the nationals of independent Commonwealth countries and overseas British subjects whose passports were issued by the colonial governments, such as the one in Hong Kong. But the passports of Asian and European settlers in

Kenya originated with the British government through its agent – the British High Commission. This had happened because of the pledges given to *both* these groups of settlers by the Conservative administration at the time of Kenyan independence in 1963. They could, if they wished, retain British citizenship after independence and receive British passports. The main reason for this offer was to save them from becoming stateless.

As for numbers, Enoch Powell was exaggerating. On the eve of its independence Kenya had 185,000 Asian and 53,000 European settlers. Of these, some 60,000 Asians automatically became Kenyan citizens since they and their fathers were born in the country. Another 10,000 were citizens of India or Pakistan. The remaining 115,000 were offered Kenyan citizenship if they applied within two years of independence. Some 20,000 did so (compared to 975 Europeans). That left 95,000 Asians in the category which either had, or was entitled to have, British passports. These documents carried a distinct label: 'Exempt UK Citizens', and their holders were counted as they entered Britain. In 1965 they totalled 6149; and in the following year, 8846.

In 1967 the Kenyan government, in pursuance of its Kenyanization policy, passed a law according to which non-citizens could work and live in the country only on a temporary basis. This caused a rise in the migration rate of the Asians with British passports. By September of that year another 8443 had entered the United Kingdom. It was at this stage that Enoch Powell blew his policeman's whistle.

As it was, the government was monitoring the situation closely. Its problem was that it did not know how to resolve its moral dilemma. This was spelled out by the *Sun* in its comment on Enoch Powell's speech at Deal: 'No feasible way of legally differentiating between them [European settlers in Kenya] and Asiatics who were granted passports by the High Commission in Nairobi had been devised.'[10]

The situation paralleled that in 1961. Then too the Conservative administration had to design a bill which would control coloured immigration without being labelled racist. But at least it had stated publicly then that Commonwealth immigration would not be restricted for a year. In contrast, this time the Labour Government just kept quiet.

However, repeated statements by right-wing Conservatives were beginning to draw public attention. What they needed to capture popular imagination was a dramatic news item. It came. In January 1968 there were front-page reports in the press of clandestine arrivals of Pakistanis. Public anxiety on coloured immigration, never fully dormant, was revived; and the drama of 1961–2 was re-enacted. Just as the smallpox cases in December 1961, attributed to the arrival of an infected Pakistani girl immigrant, had led to public hysteria, the illegal arrivals followed by arrests of the Pakistanis had similar effect now. In that climate the Kenya Asian issue was soon blown up into a major crisis.

By early February, Enoch Powell was speaking of 'the cloud no bigger than a man's hand, of communalism and communal agitation in Britain'. Sir Cyril Osborne predicted ominously: 'If we go on like this, there will be more blacks than whites in seventy years' time.' In mid-February Duncan Sandys, another prominent Conservative MP, introduced a motion in Parliament containing a provision for tighter restrictions for Commonwealth immigrants.

Outside Parliament panic seemed to seize the mass media. In a front-page editorial, the mass circulation *Daily Mirror* warned that 'The country now faces the prospect of an *uncontrolled* flood of Asian immigration from Kenya.'

In reality, the size of this potential 'flood' was 66,000 people: of the 95,000 Kenya Asians entitled to settle in Britain, 29,000 had already done so. Even if all of the remaining 66,000 had come in 1968, they would not have made up the net loss of 84,000 that Britain had suffered in the previous year due to the excess of emigration over immigration.

But in the emotional climate of mid-February 1968, the number of those who could arrive in Britain 'tomorrow' was inflated from the original quarter-million to a million, and then to two million. 'Fearing betrayal, the Asians are coming faster,' stated a *Sunday Times* editorial on 18 February. 'Fearing a deluge, the British, led by politicians, who exaggerate its proportions, are running daily more scared.'

Two days later the bipartisan policy on coloured immigration collapsed. The Conservative shadow cabinet demanded a tightening of existing controls, return of illegal immigrants, registration of dependants by applicants for work vouchers, and financial help for those wishing to return home. It was the first time since the 1966 parliamentary election that the Conservative shadow cabinet had issued a public communiqué on this subject. On Kenya Asians, it proposed that the entry of British passport holders be phased.

The Labour Government went much further. Its bill, introduced two days later, limited the right of entry *only* to those British passport holders who had substantial connections with the United Kingdom by virtue of birth, or their fathers' or grandfathers' birth, in the UK. Thus a non-racial device was employed to make a racial distinction between Asian and British settlers in East Africa. As for the rest, they were to be allowed in at the rate of 1500 special vouchers a year.[11] For the Commonwealth immigrants already here, there were further restrictions on the ages of dependent children and parents wishing to join them.

There was strong protest against the bill, especially its 'grandfather' clause, from liberal quarters. But on the whole Labour backbench MPs evinced little interest or concern. At the Parliamentary Labour Party meeting on 22 February, there was a greater outcry against the location of a new airport near London than against this bill.[12] This provided a dramatic contrast to the 1961–2 period. The 1961 Commonwealth Immigrants Bill had aroused strong passions, with the public controversy on it continuing for months; the parliamentary debate had dragged on for weeks. The 1968 Commonwealth Immigrants Bill was presented, debated and passed through both Houses of Parliament in a week. The Act became law immediately – on 1 March 1968.

From both legal and moral standpoints, the 1968 Act was far more objectionable than the 1962 Act. The earlier law curtailed the rights of Commonwealth citizens; but then the British Commonwealth was not a national or supra-national entity. As for the 1968 Act, it curtailed rights implicit in a document issued by the British government. It denied, in the words of the International Commission of Jurists, 'the right of every person to enter the country of which he is citizen, which has been recognized in the universal declaration of human rights and all other human rights conventions that have been adopted by the international community since the war'. Furthermore, the Commission pointed out, 'The fact that these citizens are non-white inevitably gives the legislation a racial character'. Later, in October 1970, the Commission of the European Convention on Human Rights declared the complaints of 25 East Africa Asians to be admissible. Referring to Article Three of the Convention regarding 'degrading treatment', the Commission stated that 'publicly to single out a group of persons for differential treatment on the basis of race might, in certain circumstances, constitute a special form of affront to human dignity'. This, and the British government's admission that 'the intentions and effects of the Commonwealth Immigrants Act of 1968 were discriminatory', led to the Commission's judgement against Britain.[13]

The overriding factor in both cases, however, was the same: to keep the inflow of coloured immigrants to an absolute minimum. If it became necessary to devalue British passports to achieve this objective, so be it. That seemed to be the general feeling among British legislators. Only 62 of the 630 MPs voted against the 1968 bill, and only 31 against its third reading.[14]

The bill was introduced and passed in such haste that no opinion surveys could be undertaken. However, polls taken after the bill's passage showed overwhelming backing for restrictions on coloured immigration: 81 per cent among Labour voters; 78 per cent among Conservative supporters; and 73 per cent among Liberal electors (whereas all the Liberal MPs opposed the bill). Overall, 39 per cent were for a total ban on coloured immigrants. This section of society seemed unable, or unwilling, to register the fact that work vouchers for Commonwealth immigrants during the period 1963–7 had been cut drastically, from 28,678 to 4721. If the 1967 coloured immigrants figure remained about the same as the 1964 figure (at 53,000), it was due to an increase in the number of dependants of the settlers already here. An immediate drastic cut in absolute numbers was impossible without a legislative bar on the reunion of families. Such a law, besides being unquestionably inhuman, would have contravened the European Human Rights Declaration, to which the United Kingdom was a signatory.

As it was, Labour had some moral qualms about the 1968 bill. Anticipating an outcry from the liberal lobby, James Callaghan, the Home Secretary, had pleaded, while moving the bill's second reading, that it must be considered in conjunction with the (liberal) race relations legislation to be introduced in Parliament soon, and both these bills were, in his view, parts of 'a fair and balanced policy on this matter of race relations'.

Viewed rationally, immigration – from whatever quarter – should be a subject in itself. It should be considered as part of a population control policy and its rate tied to the economic state of the country. Social justice for racial minorities should be a separate issue. But since the presence of black and brown peoples in Britain was related mainly to the immigration of the past generation, the two subjects had become hopelessly entangled. And this interlinking was given official recognition, the latest example being the establishment in November 1968 of the Select Committee on Race Relations and Immigration in the House of Commons.

A generation of coloured immigration (1948–68) also gradually translated the previously latent contradiction in British society between regard for 'human dignity' and a general contempt for poor, dark humanity into an open conflict between the moral principle of equality for all British subjects and the very real social fact of racial antagonism towards racial minority settlers in their midst.

When, in 1958, racial hatred against black immigrants erupted into violence, the Conservative Government, for all its public disclaimers, registered the intensity of public feelings which led it in 1961 to compromise the hitherto sacrosanct principle of freedom of movement for all British subjects born in or out of the United Kingdom. This measure had a calming effect, but not for long. As racial antagonism began to rise again, the Labour Government slapped further restrictions on (predominantly coloured) Commonwealth immigrants in the form of the 1965 White Paper. It also passed the 1965 Race Relations Act to assure members of racial minorities equal access to places of public resort.

The calm that followed proved, once again, short-lived. To defuse a potentially violent situation in early 1968, the government now deprived a class of *British* passport-holders of their rights. It resolved the conflict between popular pressure and a moral principle by yielding to the former at the expense of the latter: a familiar pattern of behaviour. Yet, despite the haste with which it implemented the appropriate legislation, the British voters were not reassured as the opinion polls clearly indicated.

Fed by alarm and rumour, the public mood had grown irrational. It was hardly likely to accept the official view that the impending Race Relations Bill – meant to assure equal opportunity to coloured immigrants in employment and housing – was a part of 'a fair and balanced policy on race relations'.

After all, only three years earlier the Labour administration itself had not regarded racial discrimination in housing and jobs as serious enough to include it in its 1965 Race Relations Act. It had thus placed the onus on those who disagreed with its judgement to produce hard evidence to the contrary, and also to convince the populace at large. It was in that spirit of challenge that (backed by a grant from a private trust) the National Committee for Commonwealth Immigrants and the Race Relations Board jointly commissioned a private research organization, Political and Economic Planning Ltd (PEP), to undertake a survey on racial discrimination in Britain.

The survey was conducted in late 1966 and early 1967 in six different areas of coloured settlement: Brent (London), Islington (London), Keighley, Sheffield, Slough and West Bromwich. It included interviews with almost 1000 immigrants (West Indians, Asians and Cypriots); with 500 potential discriminators (that is, employers, trade union officials, employment bureaus, accommodation agencies, estate agents, local housing authorities, car insurance firms, etc.); and conducted 400 tests of 'situations' in employment, housing and personal services. The report was published in April 1967.

Its conclusions could be summarized thus. Firstly, West Indian and Asian settlers consistently under-reported racial discrimination. Only 36% of them claimed personal experience of discrimination in jobs, whereas a 90% discrimination-factor against coloured applicants was revealed in a series of 'situation tests'. A similar under-reporting occurred in private housing. Secondly, the thesis that the problems faced by coloured newcomers were due to their immigrant status was disproved. Only 6% of the Cypriots, who had been arriving in Britain during the same period as the West Indians and Asians, experienced discrimination in jobs whereas 43% of the West Indians, by far the most anglicized group, did so. Similarly, only 11% of the Cypriots, compared with nearly 66% of the West Indians and Asians, encountered discrimination in private housing. Thirdly, discrimination was higher among the educationally qualified coloured settlers than among the unqualified. Of those who did not speak English, only 25% claimed personal experience of discrimination in employment whereas 70% of the English-speaking coloured people with *British* qualifications did so. This, indeed, was the most disturbing discovery made by the survey, for it was an ominous pointer towards the pattern of the future.

The PEP report received wide publicity and seemed to have established the point that racial discrimination was widely prevalent. A national opinion poll taken soon after showed that 66% of the respondents thought there was 'a great deal' or 'quite a lot' of discrimination against coloured people; another 30% thought 'not very much'; and only 1% said 'not at all'.[15]

The proponents of a law against racial discrimination in housing, employment and personal services felt they had won their case – particularly when in the same month (April 1967) the Race Relations Board stated in its annual report: 'No effort should be too great to prevent the development of American patterns of *de facto* segregation in this country. Similarities in housing patterns and employment already exist in fact.'[16]

The comparison with America was pertinent and timely. What could happen in Britain if matters were allowed to drift, out of neglect and complacency, became frighteningly clear to the government when racial violence flared up first in Newark, New Jersey, and then in Detroit, Michigan, in July, resulting in the loss of many lives and hundreds of millions of dollars' worth of property. As chance would have it, black audiences in London were at that time being stimulated to greater political awareness by the speeches of Stokely Carmichael, a young, militant black American leader. These events seemed to jog the British government out of its lethargy. On 24 July, when rioting in Detroit was at its most severe, Home Secretary Roy Jenkins, speaking in Parliament, committed the government in principle to legislation against racial discrimination in housing and employment.

From then on, liberal lobbyists never seemed to tire of scaring their white audiences by pointing out the American example. Anthony Lester, a white official of the Campaign Against Racial Discrimination, for instance, warned the Labour Party Conference in October: 'Unless the victims of discrimination are given an effective remedy the coloured population in this country will have no alternative but to take its remedy in the way it has been taken in some cities of America.'[17] This tactic proved effective. The conference unanimously endorsed a resolution calling for extension of the current legislation against racial discrimination to housing and employment.

However, outside the Labour Party there was still much opposition to such a law. It came not only from the Conservatives and the Confederation of British Industries, but also the Trades Union Congress. The Labour administration itself seemed over-sensitive about the prospect of engendering fears of 'persecution' among white voters. Its spokespersons constantly reiterated that the forthcoming legislation would be 'exhortative' and 'declaratory'. There was also much delay in publishing the appropriate bill.

It was not until April 1968, nine months after the government's commitment to it in principle, that the bill was finally published. It covered housing accommodation, business premises and land. In employment it included hiring, training, promotion and dismissal. It also encompassed the provision of goods, facilities and services in banking credit, education, entertainment and travel. It outlawed discriminatory advertising such as 'No Coloureds' and 'Europeans Only' signs.

The proponents of the bill argued that legislation had an important role to play in combating racial discrimination. As the embodiment of public policy it gave a prop to those who did not want to discriminate but were unable to withstand social pressures to do so: for example, those white landlords who did not wish to upset their present tenants and/or neighbours by taking in coloured tenants; and white shop managers who refused to hire black or Asian shop assistants for fear of offending white customers. As for the discriminated against minority, a law provided it with a means of redressing its grievances, thus relieving social tension which, if allowed to build up, could explode violently. Anti-discriminatory legislation would thus help to effect change gradually and peacefully, and preserve the liberal image of British democracy.

Furthermore, the bill's supporters argued that it was not designed to make prejudiced thinking illegal, but only discriminatory behaviour and actions which were considered undesirable by any humane, civilized society.

The opponents of the bill criticized it for the following reasons: it put the blame on the wrong party, the indigenous population; it entailed unprecedented interference by Whitehall in the daily life of citizens; it severely circumscribed individuals' freedom of action; it would, by virtue of these points, worsen the situation by causing further resentments against blacks and Asians; it created a privileged minority; it was unworkable; and, most importantly, it could not alter the attitudes from which discriminatory action and behaviour stemmed.

The concept of British culture was at the centre of the first argument. Duncan Sandys, a prominent Conservative, enunciated it thus: 'If the newcomers wish to be treated without distinction, they must make a greater effort to conform to British standards and the British way of life.'[18] Cypriot immigrants had made little effort to conform or anglicize themselves, and yet they met with minimal discrimination; whereas West Indians, culturally nearest to the British, had met maximum discrimination. This meant that race, not culture, was the overriding factor. And the racial stock of a person could not be made to conform to an extraneous standard. In any event, the 'cultural case' argument did not prove sufficiently weighty to be accorded the central position by the bill's opponents. Nor did the argument that the bill created a privileged minority – though both Enoch Powell and the conservative *Daily Telegraph* advanced it. The latter predicted: 'Those who feel obliged to give actual privilege to coloured clients or employees may be inclined to find lawful ways of avoiding contact with them.'[19] This was a curious statement to make. Whites possessed all the advantages that numbers and long settlement conferred. Black and Asian immigrants, on the other hand, were numerically small, economically depressed and psychologically insecure. It was hard to visualize the racial minority being elevated to a privileged position.

Another major argument concerned the practicability of the legislation. A body of Conservative lawyers, for instance, called the bill 'unworkable legal nonsense likely to bring the law into contempt'. But this was begging the question. If it was agreed that racial discrimination existed and that it was a social ill, then it was a challenge to legislators to design a law that would work. However, this criticism provided a politically convenient escape hatch for those who held a morally ambivalent attitude towards the bill. Among those who took this way out was the Conservative shadow cabinet. It reaffirmed its 'condemnation of racial discrimination' and accepted 'the need for steps to improve the situation', but opposed the second reading of the bill because 'on balance [it] will not in its practical application contribute to the achievement of racial harmony'.

This in turn led to the central core of the opposition's standpoint: the bill entailed excessive Whitehall interference in everyday actions of citizens and circumscribed their freedom. The argument caught the popular imagination. Its essence and effect on society at large were expressed by Ronald Bell, a Conservative MP, thus: 'The bill deeply encroaches upon the proper sphere of the freedom of the individual and, by exacerbating ill-feeling between people of different races in this country, will lead to permanent hostility and endemic violence.'[20] This was a valid point; but it raised a moral dilemma. If freedom of choice for one person led to the diminution of the freedom of another individual (for reasons beyond the latter's control), how was one to resolve the conflict, especially when the latter – being a member of a numerically small and economically weak group – was unable to counteract? However intellectually stimulating this line of argument and counter-argument might be, its practical value and importance during the public debate on the bill was negligible.

What actually happened was that reiteration of Bell's viewpoint by many others, backed by vocal demonstrations, had a profound impact on the government. It refused to yield to pressure from many white liberals and racial minority leaders to strengthen the bill's enforcement clauses.

As parliamentary discussion on the bill proceeded, the enthusiasm of its backers, never too high, waned. When the final vote was taken on 9 July 1968, no more than 182 out of nearly 360 Labour and Liberal MPs could muster enough courage to vote for it. Even the liberal press, which had no white constituents to face, considerably moderated its support for the measure. 'The fear of the white community that there will be too much interference by authority into their ordinary way of life is much more acute in these new areas of legal concern,' wrote *The Times*, a consistent standard-bearer of enlightened policies on race. 'So ... the Conciliation Committees [of the Race Relations Board] would provide an assurance of realism as well as of a moral conscience. It is true that the coloured population needs to be reassured as well, but with the public opinion in its present mood the first essential is to prove that the law will be applied in a practical fashion.'[21]

So 'realism' blended with 'a moral conscience' was the formula *The Times* recommended to the Race Relations Board. But the advice was superfluous. For, since its inception in 1966 to enforce the 1965 Race Relations Act (concerning access to public places), the Board had always followed the principle of persuasion and conciliation. Indeed its administrative organs were called conciliation committees.

The Board now enforced the second Race Relations Act, which went on to the statute book in November 1968, in the following way. On receiving a complaint the Board instructed one of its regional conciliation committees to investigate, hear evidence, discuss and form an opinion; and – if discrimination[22] was proved – to conciliate the parties within four weeks: that is, to secure from the proved discriminator an undertaking of future compliance with the law. If the discriminator refused, the

Board had the authority to take the respondent to the county court. If found guilty, the respondent was liable to pay damages to the victim for 'loss of opportunity' due to discrimination. However, the theoretical threat of court action meant very little in practice. Of the 697 cases investigated by the Board in its first year under the 1968 Act, court proceedings were taken only once, and that unsuccessfully.

The make-up of the complaints investigated from 1 April 1969 to 31 March 1970 was: employment, 52%; housing, 9%; public places and general facilities and services, 23%; and discriminatory advertisements, 16%.

Unsurprisingly, the Board upheld 94 per cent of the complaints regarding discriminatory advertising. After all this was the one area which, by virtue of its explicit nature, lent itself to straightforward judgement. It was easy to conclude whether the Act had succeeded in its intent on this score. It had. The fact that discriminatory advertisements had fallen to 6 per cent of the total complaints to the Board in 1971–2 provided further evidence of the effectiveness of the law.

But in employment, of the 1241 complaints investigated up to January 1972, only 10 per cent were upheld as discriminatory. So either racial discrimination in British industry and services was indeed minimal or the Board was finding it difficult to prove discrimination.

As extensive surveys undertaken by Political and Economic Planning Ltd during the period 1973–5 were to demonstrate, substantial discrimination in employment existed. So the problem apparently lay mainly in proving discrimination. Either that was difficult to do in employment or the Board had set very high standards for accepting evidence; or both. That the Board was following a very cautious policy in pronouncing discrimination became clear when a West Midlands conciliation officer, Bob Harrison, publicly urged the Board to be 'more easily convinced of discrimination' than was the case then.[23]

Next there was the ambivalent attitude of the victim of discrimination towards lodging a complaint. 'Those who are aware of the humiliation of being discriminated against prefer to forget it and get on with life, taking care in future to avoid situations where they are likely to encounter so degrading a rebuff,' noted the Board in its 1968–9 report. So, by and large, coloured immigrants continued to 'play safe' by 'confining themselves to areas in which there is little risk of discrimination, or to areas in which large numbers of immigrants are already employed'. As a result, there were 'very few complaints against firms who do not employ coloured immigrants or who only employ them in certain jobs'.[24]

The net effect of a low score on proved discrimination was twofold: it made most white people and politicians feel, 'After all we're not prejudiced'; while it made most black and brown citizens think that it was no use complaining.

As it was, the Board had the authority to initiate complaints of its own, a right it used sparingly – only in 3–8 per cent of the cases. Political events and milieu seemed actively to dictate its stance. During the Conservative Government of Edward Heath, from 1970 to 1974, Board officials considered it prudent not to pursue discriminators vigorously for fear of creating a white backlash.

The Heath administration passed the Immigration Act of 1971 (effective from 1 January 1973), which introduced the concept of 'patriality' when it came to exercising the right of abode in Britain. For all practical purposes, the patriality measure transformed the citizens of the non-white Commonwealth into aliens by specifying that only those holding British passports and with evidence of their birth or their parents' birth in Britain had the right of abode in the United Kingdom. Those arriving in the UK from the Commonwealth countries with a work permit lost their automatic right to settlement, and were required to renew the document annually. Only after four years of working in approved jobs could they apply for the lifting of restrictions and settle here. The opposition to this bill brought numerous black and Asian immigrant organizations as well as others to form the Joint Council for the Welfare of Immigrants in 1971.

The official restrictionist pattern was broken briefly by the crisis created by the threat of expulsion of Asians from Uganda by its military ruler, General Idi Amin. On 4 August 1972 Amin declared that all Asians must quit Uganda within three months.[25] He mentioned a figure of 80,000 Asians which turned out to be an exaggeration. In the event, about 50,000 Asians left Uganda by the deadline. Of these, only a little over a half landed in Britain.[26]

Yet popular feelings ran high in Britain. And Enoch Powell was ready to stoke them up. The Uganda Asians were the proverbial 'thin end of the wedge' comprising British Asian citizens throughout the world to whom Britain had no legal obligation, he stated. The responsibility accepted by the Heath administration, he went on, constituted a breach of the election promises because the Conservative manifesto had specifically pledged 'no further large scale immigration'.[27] His views were widely shared.

'The prejudice against black people which manifested itself in August, September and October 1972 was so widespread and powerful that it eclipsed the feelings which arose during Enoch Powell's 1968 campaign[s] against the Kenya Asians, and the passing of the Race Relations Act later in the year,' noted Derek Humphrey and Michael Ward. 'The surface evidence of this feeling was in the newspapers – both in journalists' and readers' contributions – and on radio and television, but more markedly in people's everyday conversation.'[28]

But popular sentiment was not reflected in official circles, whether government or opposition. Having decided to accept the Asians from Uganda, the Heath administration presented a convincing case to the public for shouldering Britain's moral responsibility as a civilized nation. In this it received the backing of the Labour Opposition. At its annual conference in early October 1972 the Labour Party unanimously supported the government's decision to accept the Uganda Asians. At the Conservative conference that followed a week later, Powell moved a resolution attacking the government for contravening its declared policy on immigration through 'the precipitate acceptance of an unqualified duty'. He lost by 1721 votes to 736.[29]

Unlike the 1968 crisis, this time certain factors emerged to buttress the anti-racist position of the government and the official opposition. The leading one was the persona of Idi Amin. He came through as unintelligent, unlikeable and unpredictable, part-dictator and part-clown. He united the British media against him when, following the assassination of several Israeli athletes at the Olympic Games in Munich in September 1972, he despatched a cable to the United Nations secretary-general in which he *inter alia* praised the German dictator Adolf Hitler for killing Jews. This created sympathy for his victims – the Asians facing mass expulsion. The government tried to help the process by constantly stressing that this group of immigrants was educated and middle class with commercial and other skills. It also succeeded in reassuring an initially sceptical public that this one-off concession to let in about 30,000 Asian immigrants did not alter the current legislation on immigration, and that the arrival of this limited number could not possibly change the nature of British society. The precipitate fashion in which Amin acted and brought the matter to the boil did not allow much time for the opponents of government policy to mobilize their forces fully. Finally, the government stage-managed the reception and settlement of the refugees through the Uganda Resettlement Board (formed on 18 August 1972) in a low key so as to avoid any measures that might prove electoral liabilities. When several Labour-controlled city and borough councils refused to accept the refugees for settlement in their areas on the grounds of the insufficiency of local services, the government did not press them.

Later, when most of the Uganda Asians had managed to find their feet on their own and secured accommodation in the private sector, the government was only too pleased to disband the Uganda Resettlement Board in January 1974.

Overall, the Conservative administration performed better in resolving the wholesale Uganda Asian expulsion than did the preceding Labour Government in diffusing the Kenya Asian crisis. This fact weighed heavily on the conscience of the Labour Party when it was returned to power in early 1974, and it tried to give some impetus to the goal of achieving racial justice.

In this respect the Heath government had made only marginal progress. The national surveys undertaken by Political and Economic Planning Ltd between 1973 and 1975 showed that racial discrimination was still widely prevalent. In unskilled jobs West Indians and Asians encountered discrimination in nearly half of the cases (see Part I, Chapter Seven). In general the PEP surveys established that in the same social class coloured immigrants lived in worse housing than whites, with two-thirds of them living in terraced dwellings, more than double the proportion for whites. More particularly, these reports established that in south-east England (accommodating the majority of racial minority settlers) blacks and browns were five times more likely to be living in shared accommodation than whites. Whereas 11% of white households suffered overcrowding (i.e. two or more persons per bedroom) the figure for West Indian households was 34% and for Asian 40%. While only one-sixth of white families lacked an inside lavatory or hot water, nearly three-fifths of all Pakistani/Bangladeshi families did so.[30]

Britain had to wait for another Labour Government to assume office before further progress could be made to combat racial discrimination lawfully. This happened first in February 1974 when Labour was returned to power with a narrow majority, and again in the following October when the party, led once more by Harold Wilson, improved its parliamentary majority.

In 1975 the Wilson government offered its assessment of the 1968 Race Relations Act in a White Paper. 'Generally, the law ... gives support to those who do not wish to discriminate but who would otherwise feel compelled to do so by social pressure,' it stated. 'It has also made crude, overt forms of racial discrimination much less common. Discriminatory advertisements and notices have virtually disappeared both from the press and from public advertisement boards. Discriminatory conditions have largely disappeared from the rules governing insurance and other financial matters and they are being removed from tenancy agreements. It is less common for an employer to reject any coloured workers and there has been some movement of coloured workers into more desirable jobs.'[31]

The new Race Relations Bill published in February 1976 was much stronger and more extensive than its 1965 and 1968 antecedents. It categorized racial discrimination as direct and indirect. Direct discrimination occurred when a person treated another person less favourably on 'racial grounds' than he treated, or would treat, someone else, with 'racial grounds' referring to 'colour, race, nationality (including citizenship) or ethnic or national origins'.

Indirect racial discrimination referred to treatment which might be described as equal, in a formal sense, as between 'racial groups' but discriminatory in its effect on one particular 'racial group', with a 'racial group' identified by the same set of characteristics as those employed to identify 'racial grounds'. For example, if an employer specified passing a certain test as a prerequisite for a job, and if that test resulted in the exclusion of racial minority applicants, and if it could be proved to be unrelated to the job performance, then prescribing that test amounted to practising unlawful racial discrimination. Also, victimization of a person for asserting his rights under the Act was declared unlawful.

Significantly, the bill defined segregation on racial grounds as racial discrimination, and therefore unlawful.

It applied to local government, which was also required to ensure that the task of countering unlawful racial discrimination was combined with promoting equal opportunities and harmonious relations between different 'racial groups'.

The bill replaced the Community Relations Commission and the Race Relations Board with a single organization to be called the Commission for Racial Equality (CRE).

Regarding the enforcement of the Act, there was a remedy for individual complaints as well as a means for a strategic attack on the racist practices of companies and institutions through the Commission for Racial Equality. An individual suffering racial discrimination was entitled to approach the county court in all cases, except in employment and education. In education, he was required to notify the education ministry before taking the matter to the court. In employment, he had to take his case to an industrial tribunal. The victims were provided with redress by way of compensation.

Section 43 defined the functions of the newly formed CRE thus: to work towards eliminating racial discrimination; to promote equality of opportunity; to influence policy, and promote and encourage research in race relations; and to keep the functioning of the Act under constant review. The CRE was empowered to help individual complainants and act where persistent discrimination occurred. It was the only authority to take action in cases of indirect or suspected discrimination as well as discriminatory advertisements. In short, the CRE was entitled to enforce the law in the public interest by focusing on identifying and countering discriminatory practices by companies, industries and institutions. It did so by issuing notices requiring unlawful practices to stop; if they continued then the CRE could apply for injunctions from civil courts, thus laying the ground for imprisonment for contempt of court by persistent offenders. It was also authorized to allocate financial and other resources to organizations promoting harmonious race relations and equal opportunities.

The bill strengthened the racial incitement aspect of the previous law. It did so by inserting into the Public Order Act of 1936 a section which made it a criminal offence either to publish or distribute written material, or use in any public place or at any public meeting language which was threatening, abusive or insulting and which, taking into account all of the circumstances, was *likely to encourage* hatred against a 'racial group'. This was an improvement on the provision in the 1965 Act which required evidence that the accused *intended to create* racial hatred. However, as before, incitement to racial hatred continued to be a criminal offence to be handled by the criminal courts, and subject to the consent of the Attorney General to prosecute under the aegis of his office.

The Labour Home Secretary Roy Jenkins introduced the bill. And the Conservatives decided not to oppose it.

The Commission for Racial Equality was formed in June 1977, when the new Race Relations Act went into force. During the first year of the Act, the CRE received 862 applications for assistance, with industrial tribunals entertaining 123 complaints of racial discrimination, and returning only four verdicts in favour of the plaintiffs, who were awarded compensation of £75 to £250. Its performance was, to put it mildly, lack-lustre.

However, its progress in the field of tackling indirect discrimination was noteworthy. By April 1979 it had initiated thirty formal investigations. Of these, two had been finished, resulting in the issuance of non-discrimination notices.

Regarding incitement to racial hatred, the Attorney General announced that of the eleven police reports concerning their investigations of alleged offences by the end of 1978, some action had been taken in four cases. In three instances the Director of Public Prosecutions had concluded that the evidence was insufficient to justify initiating proceedings; and only in one case had the Attorney General granted permission to proceed with prosecution.

The poor performance of the CRE in combating racism, and the marked reluctance of the Director of Public Prosecutions to prosecute inciters of racial hatred, stemmed primarily from a socio-political milieu which was antithetical to the emergence and implementation of a nationally directed, coherent race relations policy. 'Even if both parties were in favour of extensive anti-racialism laws – and the Conservative Party is not – progress on this front would be inhibited by their belief that the white population would be antagonistic to such policies,' wrote Malcolm Cross, a British sociologist, in the *Yearbook of Social Policy 1981*. 'Whether or not this assumption is valid is difficult to gauge, but it is clear that the work of the CRE is severely constrained by this assumption.'[32]

That all was not well with the Commission for Racial Equality became clear when it came under scrutiny by the Home Affairs Committee of the House of Commons in 1981, the second year of the Conservative administration under Margaret Thatcher. It was a three-prong enquiry, focusing on the Commission's operational efficiency, its grant-giving powers and its part in race and community relations.

CRE witnesses were uniformly critical of the government for its lack of political will to implement more positive policies to promote harmonious race relations. The Home Affairs Committee concurred with this view, pointing out that Whitehall had reacted unfavourably to both equal opportunities policies within the Civil Service and to the CRE's draft code of practice on employment.

But, on the whole, the Committee's report was far more critical of the CRE on various points. The CRE lacked priorities or any clearly stated objectives, it said. Part of the reason for this lay in the dualistic character of the organization, concerned as it was with both legally enforcing non-discriminatory practices and promoting good race relations. It had, wrongly, allowed the promotional function to dominate its existence. 'Whilst they [the CRE] have a significant part to play, the task of promoting race relations lies mainly with [central] govt and local govt,' the report stated. 'Only they have the power and resources to make the necessary impact.' It recommended that the CRE should limit itself to that side of promotional work which is dictated solely by the need to eradicate racial discrimination.[33]

Following this report the CRE concentrated on the following areas: employment, with especial stress on jobs for young blacks and Asians; education, with particular emphasis on developing the school curriculum to reflect more positively the multicultural character of contemporary society; improving relations between young blacks and the police; producing ethnic profiles of different areas; and aiding rapid development of black businesses.

The CRE's increased interest in multicultural education strengthened the hands of its proponents. Thanks to the initial work done by such bodies as Teachers Against Racism, the Afro-Caribbean Educational Resource Project and the National Association for Multi-Racial Education, the matter had aroused enough interest to engage the attention of the Inner London Education Authority, which was concerned about the poor performance of West Indian pupils. A study conducted by Raymond Giles examined the particular needs of West Indian children at school in the deprived areas of the ILEA. Having recognized that these pupils suffered educational disadvantage – emanating cumulatively from being working class and being black – the Giles Report stressed the need for developing a positive self-image among Afro-Caribbean children. It recommended setting up fresh courses and programmes in schools with a substantial proportion of black pupils. This involved curriculum revision to shift the stress away from studying the culture and lifestyle of the overseas communities in favour of tackling themes and topics which related directly to multi-ethnic Britain. There was a further suggestion of creating socio-cultural compatibility between the domestic and school environments of black children by engaging specialists to teach Black Studies and introducing supplementary extra-curricular activities.

What was revealing about the Giles Report was that it made no mention whatsoever of making Black Studies compulsory for whites. Typically, it focused primarily on solving the problem of black under-achievement without sparing any thought for efforts to dissipate the deeply ingrained racism of many white pupils as well as teachers.

Those who advocated incorporating Black Studies into all school curriculums with a view to exposing white students to non-white perspectives pointed out the advantages that would follow. The primary one would be the injection of objectivity. Such courses would present the European colonizers in Africa not as benevolent bearers of the white man's burden, set on improving the socio-economic and moral condition of African pagans, but as rapacious exploiters and profiteers engaging in the slave trade and carving out colonies with borders which ignored the long-established patterns of tribal settlements. Furthermore, the positive aspects of life in Africa would be highlighted, and the current under-development of the continent would be related to the present and past policies and actions of the dominant European nations.

Along with this way of thinking went the assessment that racial disadvantage stemmed from institutional racism, that is, racism which permeated normal practices and procedures followed by the education authorities. These ranged from the allocation of children to schools to sending out letters to parents solely in English, and from streaming in classes, to discipline, to advertising for teachers in publications read only by whites. As white teachers and administrative staff were perpetuating traditional practices and procedures they needed to be targeted for a course of Black Studies as much as white pupils.

Both these remedial prongs were seen as emanating from the ideology of anti-racism. Its followers argued that since racism was a white problem there was greater need for anti-racist education in all-white schools than in racially mixed ones. They argued, furthermore, that links must be made between countering oppression stemming from race and that originating in gender and class.

By the early eighties, when the CRE decided to concentrate on education, the idea of anti-racist education had taken shape, and was being advocated by, among others, Professor Chris Mullard of London University. It involved countering racist bias not only in formal education but also in institutional practices as well as in teachers' attitudes. This meant challenging a whole host of perceptions of white Britons. Mullard was critical of the multicultural variety of multi-ethnic education, which consisted of nothing more than bits of non-Western faiths, cultures and languages to broaden the base of knowledge for the pupil. He described it as 'rag-bags of good intentions, bits of ideology, strips of anger and cotton-wool balls of love'.[34]

As for the anti-racist version of multi-ethnic education, it was not taken seriously by education authorities anywhere in the country until 1983, when Frances Morrell, a Labour left-winger, became head of the Inner London Education Authority. Since the ILEA was part of the Greater London Council (GLC), and since the political environment in the GLC changed with the election of Ken Livingstone, a Labour radical, as its leader in 1981, the ILEA became receptive to anti-racist ideas and actions.

Such a commitment by an entity which included seventeen Local Education Authorities (LEAs) enabled the CRE to claim in 1983 that, nationally, twenty-nine LEAs were imparting multicultural education to pupils. It received impetus from the Swann Committee report, *Education for All*, published in March 1985. Endorsing the idea that teachers must prepare students for a multiracial society, the report called for action to remedy under-achievement of minority pupils, increase the number of ethnic minority teachers and expand anti-racist education in the curriculum. The CRE sponsored a seminar of senior LEA officers and others to forge a strategy for implementing these recommendations. By so doing the CRE reinforced the commitment of those LEAs already imparting multi-ethnic education and made this policy more palatable to those LEAs which had hitherto been wavering. Little wonder then that within three years the number of LEAs which had adopted multi-ethnic education rose to 77 (out of a total of 115).

As for its activity in the field of young blacks and Asians, in the aftermath of the 1981 riots the CRE increased its project funding from £1.14 million in 1982 (amounting to about one-eighth of its total budget) to £1.41 million in the following year. Of this about £750,000 was given to such bodies as the Southall Youth Movement, the local Harambee Associations and the Federation of Bangladeshi Youth Organizations. The CRE also strengthened its links with the Manpower Services Commission and the Youth Training Scheme.

During 1983 the CRE placed before Parliament its *Code of Practice for Employers*. It received the Employment Secretary's sanction, and came into force on 1 April 1984. Among other things the Code enabled trade union officials to protect basic rights of their members in race-related issues. In 1985 the CRE submitted two reports to the Employment Committee of the House of Commons on the effectiveness of the Code. These stated that while some progress had been made in the private sector in having companies adopt Equal Opportunity Policies (EOPs), most of them had not progressed beyond promising non-discrimination in hiring. Given this, the CRE decided to stress other aspects of the Code such as encouraging racial minority job applicants, and the monitoring of the ethnic make-up of the present workforce as well as the success rate of ethnic job applicants.

In the mid-1980s, according to the CRE, the balance between finding out what was wrong and why, and putting it right, began to change. 'Increasingly,' stated the Annual Report of the CRE, 1986, 'the questions asked of any set of practices or an institution have been less concerned with how they have come to be in the situation they are in – or what procedures have or have not been adopted in the past – and more with what can be done, within what time-scale, to put things right.'[35] In professions this meant having to concentrate on entry to higher education, and in the job market in general on such potentially large employers as new shopping centres. In education it amounted to focusing on such policies as channelling non-English-speaking children into special centres.

Employment remained the major area of concern. As the CRE's 1987 report stated, the black jobless rate was twice that of whites, with the figure being much higher in many inner-city areas. While large establishments in the public sector had made progress in providing equal opportunities to black and brown employees, most employers in the private sector had yet to implement the recommendations of the *Code of Practice for Employers*. The number of job-related complaints lodged with the CRE showed that it had failed to win the confidence of racial minorities. In 1986 the figure was 619 and in the following year 827.[36]

These statistics were only a fraction of the 'tens of thousands of acts of racial discrimination in job recruitment every year', as estimated by the Policy Studies Institute (PSI) after an investigation into the matter in 1984–5. 'For many of them [employers] the fact that discrimination is illegal does not make the avoidance of discrimination a moral imperative,' noted the PSI report. 'They continue to discriminate because there is only a minimal risk of detection ... The heart of the problem is that employers know that cases rarely get as far as legal action because the victim is very unlikely to be aware that he or she has been discriminated against.'[37] The only way to establish whether a company or an institution had been discriminating or not was by scrutinizing its records, something the CRE was entitled to do. But, given its limited resources, it could undertake only a few such investigations, limiting itself to large institutions or companies.

Not surprisingly, summarizing the overall situation, the 1987 report of the CRE itself stated: 'Each case won and each formal investigation completed seemed only to expose the sheer weight and pervasiveness of the discrimination facing black people, whether in their search for jobs, skills, homes or public services.'[38] Yet the changes in the 1976 Race Relations Act proposed by the CRE in 1985 to improve the effectiveness of the law were unlikely to be accepted by the government. So, in the final analysis, the CRE had little choice but to tread softly.

However, as Duncan Sandys and Tom Driberg among others pointed out in the late 1960s, there was a limit to what could be achieved through legislation. The race relations field was so wide and varied in its social, economic, political and psychological ramifications that no single law, organization or approach could fully cover it. Various approaches and organizations at different levels could co-exist and complement one another. For instance, the enactment of the 1968 Race Relations Act did not make redundant the local voluntary organizations established earlier to foster harmonious race relations. These local bodies had always been considered by the liberal lobbyists as complementary to their own efforts for an anti-discriminatory law. Indeed, voluntary local organizations, such as (inter-racial) liaison committees, had started springing up at just about the time that Fenner Brockway began his efforts in Parliament to have racial discrimination outlawed – in the mid-1950s.

3 Inter-racial Harmony and Integration

I would accept a coloured man as a friend inside the works but not outside.

A white worker, Pentland Alloys Ltd.[1]

You meet each other outside the squadron, you wouldn't believe that ten minutes earlier you had been in the Training Corps talking to each other as friends. Outside, your attitude [towards coloured cadets] is quite different.

A white student in Southall, member of the Air Training Corps, in a BBC television documentary.

The local liaison committee is a smoke-screen: fashion parades, food plates, steel bands. It's just a show. The Liaison Officer gets a steel band on stage, and they think they've got integration.

A Pakistani member of the local liaison committee, Nottingham, 1969.

In the early days of coloured immigration the initiative to form inter-racial liaison committees often came from the local Council of Social Service (CSS). This happened, for instance, in Nottingham in 1954. There the CSS initiative was supported by the local Council of Churches. The result was the Nottingham Consultative Committee for the Welfare of Coloured People, soon to be renamed the Nottingham Commonwealth Consultative Committee.

Though the name was changed, the Committee's main function remained the same: social welfare work for immigrants, for whom the CSS set up in its building a private counselling and employment advisory service. Whatever liaison took place was between social and religious welfare bodies, and not between black and white communities. Indeed racial categories did not even exist, as Robert A. Burt, a social researcher, pointed out: 'The dominant response of the formal social organizations dealing with the West Indian immigrant population has been the refusal to view the social problems within racial categorizations.'[2]

Even the 1958 race riots did not significantly alter this attitude, prevalent among social workers and the few interested civic leaders. Generally speaking, local councillors seemed reluctant either to help form local liaison committees or to support, morally or financially, multiracial bodies already in existence. They felt that establishing such committees was an admission that race relations in their boroughs were bad. So they thought it best to claim 'No problem here', or at most to say: 'We're watching the situation carefully.'

Despite this myopia, the issues of racial and communal relations began to engage the attention of those involved with local liaison committees. Also, more such organizations were formed. But the majority of these proved short-lived. They collapsed because of the 'tea and bun' approach, whereby at the opening party – attended by a few local dignitaries and some West Indians and 'Singhs' (chosen from the electoral rolls) – there were a few speeches, followed by applause and a few cups of tea; then everyone went home.[3]

The Conservative administration, wedded to a *laissez-faire* policy, took no notice of, or interest in, these local committees. Even the Commonwealth Immigrants Advisory Committee, appointed by the government after the 1962 Immigrants Act, waited two years before appointing a full-time secretary and instructing her to help bring about 'integration' of Commonwealth immigrants on an annual budget of £6000.

Little wonder that, of the thirteen local committees only four, partly supported by local government, were operational; the rest were paper organizations. The active committees were engaged in (a) collecting information regarding Commonwealth immigrants – how many there were, from where they came and their pattern of settlement; (b) informing the newcomers on such subjects as house purchase, rent control, electoral registration and social welfare services (i.e. generally acting as a 'coloured citizens advice bureau'); and (c) fostering better 'immigrant-host' relations through multiracial parties and the like which were generally unsuccessful.

Yet the 1965 White Paper on immigration from the Commonwealth singled out the 'International Friendship Councils' and the 'Commonwealth Citizens Consultative Committees' for creating 'a climate of mutual tolerance in which the stupidity of racial prejudice cannot survive'.[4] This was all the more ironic because, despite the existence of a local liaison committee, Nottingham had experienced a racial flare-up in 1958.

But at least Whitehall noticed the existence of such committees and recognized a 'need for a wider sharing of experience' in this field. It committed itself to setting up a National Committee for Commonwealth Immigrants (NCCI) 'to build up a comprehensive body of doctrine which can be flexibly applied to a variety of local solutions'. It also prescribed the following criteria for the success of present or future local liaison committees: they had to be non-sectarian and non-political projects involving the immigrants and the host community, with the full backing of local authorities.[5]

The NCCI interpreted the 'non-sectarian and non-political' condition so rigidly that it disqualified (from official recognition and financial support) those local inter-racial committees which could possibly be termed 'campaigning' committees simply because they did not preclude the use of protest to combat racial discrimination. In other words, the old school of 'social-welfare-for-the-newcomers' was once again in the saddle, backed now by government money and prestige. The only difference was that the local Councils for Social Service lost the initiative. Now the NCCI became the prime mover.

The NCCI adopted existing social-welfare-type inter-racial organizations, and formed others. It evolved a formula for establishing new committees, which was to involve social workers, churchmen, local councillors, trade unionists and the New Commonwealth immigrant leaders, and set up an inter-racial committee, to be categorized generally as a voluntary liaison committee (VLC – later called a community relations council, CRC). The NCCI also encouraged town halls to appoint full-time liaison officers by underwriting their salaries. In this it was not always successful because the enthusiasm of the NCCI, or the national government, was not generally shared by local authorities. Yet the attitude of the town hall was the most important element in the success or failure of the local VLC/CRC.

In spite of the continued efforts of the hierarchy of the NCCI and its successor (after the 1968 Race Relations Act), the Community Relations Commission, to isolate the social welfare of racial minority citizens from 'politics', this subject remained, in the final analysis, political. After all, their welfare depended on the political decisions of local councillors. And it was for political reasons that, with a few notable exceptions, local councils were unenthusiastic about liaison committees and community relations councils.

Local authorities showed their stepmotherly attitude towards the CRCs in such ways as starving them of monetary and secretarial help. They tried to stress their dissociation from the CRCs by allocating them office accommodation away from the town hall, or by letting them stay in the office of the local Council of Social Service.

The position of the liaison officer was hardly enviable. At worst, he was treated as no more than a paid secretary to the CRC executive committee; at best, as a 'minister for Bantu Affairs', specializing in handling black and Asian citizens with grievances against the town hall.

As for the CRC itself, whether it functioned as a mere talking forum or an active adviser to the town hall depended on three factors ranked according to their importance: the attitude of the councillors; the diplomacy and aggressiveness with which the liaison officer conducted his job; and the calibre and influence of its committee members, especially those representing racial minority citizens.

Many black and Asian organizations affiliated themselves to the local CRC solely because their leaders realized that they had no other channel through which to express their community's problems and grievances with regard to housing, education, relations with the police, and employment. But then a close association with the CRC exposed ethnic leaders to a trap: many shrewd councillors on the CRC committees attended to the personal grievances of the racial minority leaders and their friends while continuing to neglect the general problems of their community. 'There is a tradition among power-wielders in Britain to try to detach the leaders of a protesting minority from their ranks through acts of patronage,' said a perceptive Pakistani leader in Slough. 'The local white leaders have the power to place a coloured man in a job, to make sure that his children get accepted in a school right away, even make a discreet phone call to his building society or bank ... They try to separate me from my people by telling me that I'm different. And I know it. But not all of us are so self-aware.' In other cases, many councillors considered appointing a coloured liaison officer as *the* answer to the local 'colour problem'. In practice, this often ended up as a symbolic act, leaving the core of the problem untouched.

The major weakness of the local liaison committees lay in the fact that they were non-elected bodies and had to be non-political. Literal subservience to the latter condition sometimes led to ludicrous situations. For instance, in its annual report in June 1968, the Wolverhampton liaison committee made no reference at all to the 'river of blood' speech by Enoch Powell, one of the local MPs, or even to its own executive committee's decision to draw the Attorney General's attention to that speech as material 'likely to lead to racial hatred' (see Chapter Four).

Because local CRCs were not under any popular pressure from black and Asian citizens, they did not feel obliged to show positive results despite the fact that over the years they became quite businesslike. By the early 1970s, when there were eighty CRCs, most of them operated through sub-committees – on housing, education, employment, community-police relations and integration. That these CRC sub-committees had almost no impact on local government policies became apparent when the PEP surveys of the mid-1970s showed that racial discrimination was widely prevalent in employment and housing.

As for promoting 'peaceful integration', the local CRCs performed this function by organizing inter-racial dances, international exhibitions of food and dress, and the like. At these occasions, the mere presence of the mayor or a local MP was construed as a token of the white community's goodwill. Commenting on such social gatherings, the authors of *Colour and Citizenship* stated: 'They could become a matter of non-representative English meeting non-representative immigrants, a dilemma familiar to many middle-class voluntary workers in the field.'[6]

That deliberate efforts had to be made by a quasi-official body to help the 'mixing' of races, and that these efforts attracted only 'non-representative' members of different races, in a country that did not have segregated schools, factories or public services, proved one thing: contacts between people of different racial stock which occurred in the structured world of work and education did not extend into social life. It was a sad situation, but it did exist, as a close examination of the racially integrated factories and educational institutions clearly showed.

As regards integration, there was a common tendency among the British to think of it in a general, undefined way. One often heard such statements as 'Are the immigrants integrating?'; 'If Sikhs want to integrate they must discard their beards and turbans'; 'It takes two to integrate, and one side hasn't even begun'; 'They don't want to integrate' (said across both sides of the colour line). This was misleading and imprecise. To be precise one needed always to specify the kind of integration one had in mind: economic, educational, social, political.

Since the size of coloured immigration was related to the labour needs of Britain, the economic integration of black and Asian immigrants occurred almost immediately. These newcomers became an integral part of the British economy. 'Building, engineering and heavy foundry works to a high degree depend on immigrant workers,' wrote Roy Perrott and David Haworth, industrial correspondents of the *Observer*, in April 1968. 'So do many menial but essential jobs that whites do not care for. The cotton industry's revived fortunes would not be possible without the ready supply of Asians in the North ... Foundries, which demand heavy work in hot conditions, would be lost without coloured workers.'[7] To this list had to be added glass factories, paper mills, rubber works, bakeries, hospitals, post offices and public transport.

Had racial minority workers withdrawn, hundreds of factories, hospitals and public transport systems would have been severely crippled or forced to close down. But then, were blacks to withdraw their labour in South Africa, the country's economy would grind to a halt: economic integration of races can co-exist with educational, social and political apartheid. We are therefore led to examine the social implications of the employment of non-white labour in the British economy, and to ask

(a) whether the black or Asian worker has been accepted socially by his white colleagues, and (b) whether personal relationships have resulted through formal contact at work.

The introduction of racial minority workers into Britain was of course gradual, and was pioneered by English-speaking West Indians. This development appeared, superficially at least, conducive to their social acceptance. It was also in tune with the theory popular among white Britons that the smaller the number of coloured settlers the better their chance of acceptance. But available evidence did not support this thesis.

In his study of coloured workers in the Midlands and the North in the mid-1960s, Peter Wright described the case of Grange Graphite Company, where only 8 per cent of the employees were black or Asian. And yet, in the words of the firm's personnel manager, 'They [the white workers] don't like them ... but they try to pretend they [coloured workers] aren't there.' One would expect that when the proportion of coloured workers became preponderant in a factory the remaining whites would accept the situation with a certain resignation. But this was not always the case. Consider, for instance, the Muirhead Foundry with three-quarters of its workforce coloured. Yet, noted Peter Wright, 'the white employees in general were still strongly opposed to the employment of coloured labour'. His interviews with white workers revealed that though only 12 per cent were not prepared to accept coloured immigrants as co-employees, 60 per cent would, 'other things being equal', prefer to work where only white people were employed. His overall conclusion was that the acceptance of coloured workers by the whites in companies already with black or Asian employees was 'largely of a negative nature'.[8]

The prevalent attitude among white workers could then be summed up as a negative acceptance blended with avoidance. Negative acceptance was the dominant element when the overriding demands of production imposed a certain discipline and elicited co-operation. But once this pressure was off – as, say, during tea- and meal-breaks – the element of avoidance projected itself fully and led to voluntary racial separation. 'You never see English and coloureds sitting together in the company's bus,' said a personnel manager. 'You don't see them walking down the yard together either. The situation hasn't changed at all since 1956, and [ten years later] it shows no sign of changing.'[9]

What about social contacts beyond the factory gates? Interviews on this subject with white workers led Wright to conclude that the majority did not wish to associate socially with blacks or Asians. 'Even those white workers who were willing to accept coloured immigrants as friends at work were, in the main, unwilling to do so outside,' he stated. Some of the statements by white workers were: 'We shouldn't really pal with them'; 'Once my day's work is done, I don't want anything to do with them'; 'If I had money, I would go to Australia or New Zealand where they're not permitted'.[10]

It may be argued that we are dealing here with adults whose opinions and attitudes are, for better or worse, firmly set and unlikely to change. After all, until the early 1950s half of the British population had not even seen a black or brown person, much less dealt with him or her as a bus conductor, nurse or factory workmate. One must therefore place one's hope in the succeeding generations. Let schools be kept integrated; let children of different races mix freely in school, know one another, become friends and racial antipathy and separation would disappear. This seemed a fair and logical proposition.

Also, since education was the responsibility mainly of public authorities, it was quite different from, say, industry which was chiefly in private hands. This therefore required an examination of governmental policies, or lack of them, at local and national levels.

It was not until October 1963 – when white parents in Southall demanded separate classes for their children on the ground that the presence of coloured pupils was retarding their children's progress – that the local authority and the national government found themselves compelled to devise a policy on educating white and non-white children together. Whatever may have been the motives of the protesting parents, their action at least made the authorities realize that the 'integration through schools' concept would not automatically be translated into reality, and that they would have to design and implement specific policies to achieve the desired end.

The events in Southall also highlighted the fact that 'predominantly immigrant schools' were emerging there, and elsewhere, not only because of the increase in the number of coloured children but also because of the tendency among 'some [white] parents ... to take native-born children away from schools when the proportion of immigrant pupils exceeds a certain level which suggests to them that the school is becoming an immigrant school'.[11] This was an example of white adults' attitudes intruding into the world of children, and white parental decisions paralleling those of white workers who stopped seeking employment with companies which, they felt, were 'going coloured'.

However, the functions of factories and schools were quite divergent. Besides teaching the child how to read and write and express himself, an important function of primary and secondary education was to socialize the child, to ease his way into adult society. For children of immigrants, school was also an important tool of acculturation.

Evidence received by the Commonwealth Immigrants Advisory Council in 1963 suggested that 'if a school has more than a certain percentage of immigrant children among its pupils the whole character and ethos of the school is altered'. In that case, the Council felt, 'Immigrant pupils ... will not get as good an introduction to British life as they will in a normal school'.[12] In other words, a substantial presence of black and Asian children in a particular school would minimize their contacts with white British pupils, thus simultaneously retarding the acculturation process and weakening the foundation on which a racially integrated society was expected to be built. Hence the Council recommended that the catchment areas of schools be so planned as to keep schools (racially) mixed, and if that failed or proved unfeasible, a dispersal of children should be implemented rather than let *de facto* segregation set in.

The Council's recommendations were apparently well-intentioned and 'non-political'. But, with white parents protesting vocally, the issue acquired a political slant. Whitehall became more concerned with reassuring white parents than with ensuring a 'good introduction to British life' for coloured children. When the Department of Education and Science recommended the policy of dispersal of 'immigrant children' to the local education authorities in June 1965, the only italicized paragraph in the circular read: 'It will be helpful if the parents of non-immigrant children can see that practical measures have been taken to deal with problems in the schools ...'[13] Yet the 'integration of immigrant children' was not totally ignored by the national government. Its White Paper on Commonwealth immigration, published two months later, stated that '[it can be] more easily achieved if the proportion of immigrant children in a school is not allowed to rise too high'.[14]

As always, the word 'integration' was not qualified or properly defined. If it meant the absence of segregation, then the question of proportions did not arise. So long as there was *one* white child in a school which had otherwise become all-black, that school still remained, technically speaking, 'integrated'. If it meant social integration, then such a statement had by 1965 acquired a ring of irrelevancy. By then enough evidence had become available to prove that the concept of 'social integration through schools' was fallacious, as was the idea that smaller numbers of black or Asian students in schools led to social integration.

In 1962 the London Council of Social Service (LCSS) conducted a broad survey of the position and problems of younger or second-generation immigrants in Brixton, Hackney, Notting Hill, Paddington and Willesden. '[We] noted with disquiet that these good [race] relations often did not extend beyond the structural world of the school or beyond the early years of puberty and school leaving,' noted the authors of *Immigrants in London*, the LCSS's report published in 1963. 'When children left school they seemed to slough off the school pattern completely and to accept the values and norms of the place of work, the youth club and the neighbourhood.'[15]

The adults most favourably placed to observe and judge the situation in schools were those directly in touch with pupils, namely teachers. So their observations deserved to be taken seriously. 'There appears to be very little real integration of races,' stated a headmaster in Birmingham. 'Toleration, acceptance, some respect for each other's ability, team partnership and an occasional friendship, but little more.'[16] This precise statement was probably the most accurate assessment of the situation.

'Boys of one race tend to sit together in the classroom, to play together, to go around together,' wrote a London schoolteacher in *New Society* in June 1966. 'This has no harmful effects unless the heat is on. Occasionally, there is a bust-up in the street after school – 100 boys may be involved, tension is at a snapping point, noses are broken: it always so happens that whatever started the fight, it always finishes as black versus white, two clearly divided factions.'[17]

If these occasional punch-ups did not occur within school premises it was because of the general understanding among pupils that school was not the place for them. Just as the demands of production in a factory elicited tolerance and co-operation among whites and blacks, so the disciplinary aura of an educational institution helped to keep racial antipathy at a low level. Outside the school gates, however, this antipathy translated itself into racial separation.

The study group of the London Council of Social Service ascribed the phenomenon of racial separation primarily to parental influence. But even if there were no directives by parents, children would find no model of social integration among adults to emulate. 'Children learn the great things of life by the examples set by adults around them, and relationship to people of other races is no exception,' stated the Wolverhampton Association of Schoolmasters. 'It would be presumptuous for a small body of teachers to pretend that they could overcome fears and prejudices built up over generations.'[18]

If there was a single national body given to assisting the public and politicians to 'overcome fears and prejudices built up over generations', it was the Community Relations Commission and its successor the Commission for Racial Equality (CRE), formed in 1977. The 1976 Race Relations Bill, which created the CRE, allowed it to fund not only the local quasi-official Community Relations Councils but also other voluntary bodies given to improving community relations. The sums involved were modest. None the less, in the 1970s the network of CRCs, integrated into the town halls at the local level and the Home Office at the national level, provided a useful channel for a large constellation of West Indian and Asian organizations to participate in the decision-making of the CRCs, and thus influence local community relations policies. Their association with the local CRC made such bodies serious candidates for funding by the national Commission for Racial Equality for specific projects.

A major test of the CRC–CRE network came in 1981 in the wake of the urban disturbances. The eruption of riots in itself underlined the failure of the CRE so far as creating harmonious community relations was concerned. The deepening hostility between the police and young blacks was another major blot on the performance of the CRE. Not surprisingly, in its annual report the CRE conceded that 1981 was 'in some respects our hardest year yet'. It referred to 'strains in race relations' intensified by economic downturn and high joblessness among racial minorities. On the other hand, it maintained that but for the CRE–CRC network actively working to lower tempers, the rioting would have been more severe. It could claim that the existence of an extensive and interlocking system of voluntary and quasi-official organizations enabled the law enforcement agencies at the local and national levels to establish an immediate two-way communication. What proved particularly fruitful were the contacts between the black community leaders and the local police force through the Community Relations Council.

Like the police, the CRE had a narrow view of what constituted good race relations: it meant absence of open conflict or racial discrimination. To achieve this limited objective the CRE stressed a need for a determined policy to enforce the 1976 Race Relations Act and encourage moderate community leaders to engage in effecting reconciliation. Its leading officials were by no means thinking in more ambitious terms of attacking racist ideology and practices through education, propaganda and national campaigns. They were constantly aware of the right-wing lobby within the ruling Conservative Party, which had never really accepted the concept of race relations legislation, and which was anxious to undermine the CRE as a first step towards abrogating the race law on the basis of the traditional argument that no piece of legislation could bring about harmony between diverse races.

But even if the CRE officials had their plans for attacking the roots of racism, these would have been crushed by the parliamentary enquiry of 1981. The House of Commons committee criticized the CRE for overstressing its promotional aspect, pointing out that the local and national governments were primarily responsible for promoting race relations.

This made sense. Even when considering merely financial support for the local CRCs, the town halls' contributions were higher than the CRE's.[19] Despite the convulsions of 1981, or perhaps because of them, many black and Asian bodies continued to co-operate with local CRCs and the national CRE. And this made an impact on the ordinary Asian or Afro-Caribbean. The 1982 Policy Studies Institute survey showed that 68 per cent of West Indian men and 62 per cent of Asian men knew of the CRE, and a little over half of West Indian and Asian men were aware of the local CRCs.[20]

Part of the reason for this was that co-operation with the local CRC smoothed the way for a particular ethnic organization to participate in projects financed by Section 11 of the Local Government Act of 1966. The Whitehall allocations, intended specifically for race-related activities, provided grants to the town hall to cover staff expenditure as and when it made special provisions for minorities in areas with 'substantial numbers of immigrants'. These subsidies amounted to three-quarters of the total eligible expenditure. In 1978–9 Section 11 funding nationally was £40 million[21] compared to £6 million annual budget of the CRE.

Shaken by the violence of 1981 the Conservative administration promised in 1982 that important provisions of the Section 11 scheme would be revised within the limits of the current law. The subsequent revision allowed the town halls to expand their race specialist staff to include race relations advisers, as well as to set up special units to develop new race-related administrative practices. These policy units enabled the local government to monitor the impact of certain policies on ethnic minorities, and determine priorities for financial allocations to improve public services in areas with substantial black and Asian populations. Moreover, as a result of an overall review of Section 11 by the Home Office, the section was upgraded from being a supplementary provision into something more substantial and capable of bringing about positive and administrative changes at local government level. Little wonder that in 1983–4 Section 11 funding rose to £90 million.[22]

Even the more general Urban Programme registered a steep jump in the wake of the 1981 riots. This programme allowed Whitehall and town halls to link up with private sector and voluntary agencies to fund projects which would not normally be financed through the local government's service departments. In practice most of the money went on recreational and cultural projects. Within this general framework ethnic programmes accounted for only 4 per cent of the total of £8 million in 1981–2, the financial year of widespread rioting. Two years later the aggregate stood at £27 million, with ethnic programmes consuming 9 per cent of the total.[23]

One interpretation of this increase in Section 11 and Urban Programme expenditure was that, contrary to its public stance of labelling the 1981 riots as matters of law and order, the Thatcher government privately accepted the analysis that violence was related to the deprivation that the inner-city areas had come to suffer. Another interpretation was that an increase in Section 11 and Urban Programme was an inadequate substitute for the general cutbacks, restraints and reductions in the quality of services provided to the old and unemployed as well as the racial minorities.

However, by the mid-1980s, most black and Asian organizations based in the inner-city areas seemed to have concluded that besides the local CRC there were other forums and channels of communication to influence town hall policies with a view to securing better resources for ethnic minorities.

This happened at a time when many local councils began establishing policy and advisory units on race, with councillors and their officials actively co-operating with these units to encourage the local administration to meet the needs of racial minorities. At the same time, more and more town halls committed themselves to providing equal opportunities within their own bureaucracy. Several boroughs in Greater London were in the forefront of this movement, particularly Hackney and Haringey. Hackney set up a Race Relations Committee with its executive arm, called the Race Relations Unit, functioning as part of the Chief Executive's directorate. It performed its job of countering racism and ensuring racial equality by overseeing the specific areas of employment, service delivery, grants and support to community organizations. Haringey implemented a somewhat different system to monitor execution of its race-related policies and programmes. It appointed race equality officers in its major service departments, with the Central Race Equality Unit co-ordinating their activities.

Such steps, designed to further the welfare of racial minorities, were by no means typical. These applied to certain areas in Greater London. The overall view of life for ethnic groups was well summed up by the 1982 Policy Studies Institute survey. When asked if life for West Indians and Asians had grown better or worse over the past five years, more than half of the respondents replied 'worse' compared to 20 per cent of West Indians and 15 per cent of Asians who replied 'better'.[24]

The tardiness of progress towards racial equality could only be understood in the context of 'fears and prejudices [of whites] built up over generations', as the report by the Wolverhampton Association of School-teachers had put it in the late 1960s. In other words, white Britons in general were meeting black and brown peoples in their midst, not with an open mind but with preconceived notions. This prejudice seemed to have emanated from historical contacts of Europeans with people of different races, which almost always led to a relationship of dominance–subservience, and which continue to bedevil inter-racial relations.

4 White Powell, White Power

To trust people means for an MP not to be afraid to voice their anxieties, their instincts and their aspirations.

ENOCH POWELL

Not in living memory have groups of workers across the country gone on strike in favour of a Tory politician, as they did for Enoch Powell ... a Tory whose views on every aspect of politics apart from race and immigration they barely understand, and would reject even if they did.

Economist, 26 April 1968

One down – a million to go.

JOHN KINGSLEY READ, leader of the British
National Party, on the murder of a Sikh youth in
Southall in 1976.[1]

No one expressed the thoughts and feelings of the majority of white Britons on race relations and coloured immigration as well and as lucidly as Enoch Powell did in his speech in Birmingham on 20 April 1968. And no one else has since then equalled Powell's performance in this respect.

After stating that 'the supreme function of statesmanship is to provide against preventable evils', Powell illustrated the evil, indirectly, by quoting a white middle-aged constituent: 'In this country in fifteen or twenty years' time the black man will have the whip hand over the white man.' By then, 'on present trends', there will be in this country 'three-and-a-half million Commonwealth immigrants and their descendants ... the official figure given to parliament by the spokesman of the Registrar General's office'.[2]

Having posed the 'danger', he suggested remedies to reduce it. Stop, or virtually stop, further inflow, a process he likened to 'watching a nation busily engaged in heaping up its own funeral pyre'. But that was not enough because, even then, 'the prospective size of this element in the population would still leave the basic character of the national danger unaffected'. He therefore urged the implementation of the 'second element of the Conservative Party's policy: the encouragement of re-emigration'. A determined pursuance of such a policy could then 'appreciably alter the prospects for the future'.

Though he agreed with 'the third element of the Conservative Party's policy' that 'there should be no discrimination or difference made between them [white and coloured citizens] by public authority', he emphasized that it did not mean that 'the immigrant and his descendants should be elevated into a privileged or special class or that the citizen should be denied his right to discriminate in the management of his own affairs between one fellow-citizen and another ...'

However, according to Powell, 'the discrimination and the deprivation, the sense of alarm and resentment, lies not with the immigrant population but with those among whom they have come and are still coming'. He illustrated this with the case of an old-age pensioner, the only white left in a respectable street (in Wolverhampton), now filled with negroes. Her story is that, 'She is becoming afraid to go out. Windows are broken. She finds excreta pushed through her letter box. When she goes to the shops, she is followed by children, charming, wide-grinning piccaninnies. They cannot speak English, but one word they know. "Racialist", they chant.' Under the circumstances, to enact the 1968 Race Relations Bill (then before Parliament) was to 'risk throwing a match on to gun powder'.

'As I look ahead,' concluded Powell, 'I am filled with foreboding. Like the Roman, I seem to see "the River Tiber foaming with much blood".'

The next day his speech was termed by Edward Heath, the Conservative Party leader, 'racialist in tone and liable to exacerbate racial tensions'. Colin Jordan, leader of the neo-fascist British National Party stated: 'What Enoch Powell said in his speech constitutes what I said in a pamphlet – for which I got 18 months [imprisonment] under the [1965] Race Relations Act [for incitement to racial hatred].' Its moral distastefulness was underlined by Dai Francis, a miners' leader, who pointed out that 'If you substitute the word immigrant for Jew, and read the speeches of [Adolf] Hitler and [Josef] Goebbels there was no difference between them and Mr Powell.' But, according to Powell, moral right or wrong did not enter the picture: for an MP, trusting 'people' meant voicing their aspirations, instincts and anxieties. This he had apparently done very well in his Birmingham speech. His use of highly charged phrases and images – 'foaming with much blood', 'match on to gun powder', 'heaping up its own funeral pyre', 'whip hand over the white man', 'excreta pushed through her letter box' – was probably intended to capture popular imagination. And it did.

Over 110,000 letters poured into his office, a record in the history of Parliament. All but 2300 supported him. One national poll showed that

82 per cent considered Powell right in making his speech. Another revealed that 74 per cent agreed with him 'in general'. His support came from all sections of society, stated the pollsters: from all parts of the country; from those who lived near or worked with blacks or Asians, and those who did not. Captain Henry Kirby, a Conservative MP, claimed, 'At last the nation has found a leader brave enough to break the all-party conspiracy of silence which for too long has shrouded this sinister and festering issue.' If so, the silence was broken with a vengeance.

Thousands of workers went on token strikes and staged pro-Powell demonstrations up and down the country – in Birmingham, Coventry, Gateshead, London, Norwich, Nottingham, Preston, Southall, South- ampton, Tilbury and West Bromwich among other places. By most accounts these actions were initiated by people who were not normally politically active. The demonstrators marched either to their town halls or to local newspaper offices. These continued until 26 April, three days after the start of the parliamentary debate on the 1968 Race Relations Bill, with London dockers and Smithfield meat-porters playing a promi- nent and much-publicized role.

Of course, there were trade unionists who expressed opposition to Powell's speech. Shop stewards at the Ford car factory in Dagenham, east London, for instance, pointed out that 'Historically, attacks on racial or religious minorities are attempts to divert attention from major problems in an era.' The National Union of Railwaymen and the Association of Scientific, Technical and Managerial Staff (ASTMS) condemned Powell's speech. But in no case were these resolutions or press statements translated into demonstrations by ordinary workers against Powell.

Furthermore, almost every condemnation of Powell from leaders brought a backlash from the rank and file. When an ASTMS official in Birmingham issued an anti-Powell statement to the press, he was immediately upbraided on the telephone by union members, who asked him to 'mind the union business instead of looking after those nig-nogs'. Edward Heath's dismissal of Powell as a result of his speech was disapproved by 61 per cent of those questioned by pollsters.

For the first time, it seemed, the rank and file were sufficiently incensed by the moralizing tone of their leaders to speak up in contradiction. They expressed themselves freely. Whites discussed immigration and blacks and Asians openly in buses, pubs and work canteens, without regard for the feelings of the coloured people present. Voices were no longer lowered. Individual West Indians and Asians were often taunted by white workmates with 'When are you going back home?' In some places white hostility turned violent. In Sheffield the windows of practically all Indian and Pakistani restaurants were broken. In Wolverhampton, within a fortnight of Powell's speech, there were at least a dozen assaults on West Indians and Asians and their properties.

Expression of mass anxiety on coloured immigration was nothing new. What was new was the fact that the vehement protesters now had an eminent and respected leader, Powell, to rally around. By speaking the (hitherto) unspeakable, Powell emerged as a man of courage. His dismissal from the shadow cabinet won him the status of a martyr. 'Free Speech' was prominent among the placards used by his supporters. The events and statements following Powell's speech were prominently and meticulously reported in the press. This in turn had a liberating effect, and made many white Britons speak and behave without their customary inhibitions. And this had an immediate political impact on the fate of the 1968 Race Relations Bill, published in early April.

The all-inclusive nature of the Race Relations legislation enabled its opponents, such as Powell, to engender fear in the public mind. 'We won't be able to say a "boo" to a nigger without being reported,' said a London docker marching for Powell.[3] Consequently popular support for the bill plummeted. An opinion poll taken after the Powell speech showed only 30 per cent approving the bill in contrast to 58 per cent support for it a year earlier.

By delivering his speech three days before the parliamentary debate on the race legislation, Powell succeeded in torpedoing the liberal lobby's efforts to get the bill's enforcement clauses strengthened. He managed to divert popular attention away from the constructive measures to improve race relations to the old premise of immigration restrictions. On that front it seemed almost impossible fully to reassure the public. Despite the restrictive Commonwealth Immigrants Act enforced in March, 75 per cent of those polled in an opinion survey in mid-April felt that immigration controls were not stringent enough, with the percentage rising to 83 after Powell's speech.

Throughout the summer Powell kept up his campaign on race and immigration, giving rise to speculation that Powellite forces would challenge Edward Heath's leadership at the forthcoming Conservative Party Conference. This led Heath to demand that a check must be kept on the whereabouts of the Commonwealth immigrants during their first four years before they were allowed to become permanent residents, and to reaffirm the party's policy of financial assistance to those Commonwealth immigrants who wished to return to their countries of origin.

At the party conference in October, in the most frequently applauded five-minute speech, Powell devoted himself exclusively to airing his anxiety about the future of England which, he prophesied, would be changed 'beyond recognition' due to the settlement of coloured immigrants and their 'offspring'. The following month he delivered another major speech, calling for 'a programme of large scale voluntary but organized, financed and subsidized repatriation and re-emigration' of racial minority settlers. This was to be undertaken 'preferably under a Ministry of Repatriation or other authority charged with concentrating on the task'.

In January 1969, Edward Heath demanded that the government should take powers by next August to enable it, if it so wished, to stop all immigration. As for the immigrants already here, the administration should acquire the authority to restrict the entry of their dependants.

The Labour Home Secretary James Callaghan called Heath's speech 'slick and shifty'. Three days later he proceeded to bar male Commonwealth citizens from entering Britain to marry their fiancées and settle here 'unless there are compassionate circumstances'. The previous year only 1676 such males had entered Britain; but even that number seemed excessive to the Labour administration. A few months later it did not shirk from passing a law which considerably reduced the freedom of dependants to join the Commonwealth immigrants settled here. To avoid embarrassing publicity, it juggled the legislative procedures. After the liberal Immigration Appeals Bill, 1969 – which entitled an immigrant to appeal to a judicial authority if dissatisfied with the governmental decision – had passed the Commons and reached the committee stage in the House of Lords in May 1969, the government introduced an amendment requiring dependants of Commonwealth immigrants to obtain entry certificates (equivalent to visas) before coming to Britain.

This law severely reduced the inflow of dependants, which was of course the unexpressed objective of the Labour administration of Harold Wilson. The number of dependants from East Pakistan fell from 225 a month during February–April 1969 to 32 a month during June–July 1969. Thus, without openly saying so, the Wilson government conceded one of the important official Conservative demands on immigration control.

By then, however, Powell's mind was fixed firmly on repatriation. In June came his estimated cost of the scheme: 'To give each family £2000 for passage and resettlement would cost £260 million assuming that 600,000 to 700,000 coloured immigrants are involved. Raise this to £300 million to include all the costs of administration.'

The Wilson administration responded by slapping on yet another restriction, this time on 'A' category work vouchers for Commonwealth citizens, requiring the British employers to prove that no suitable local labour was available before the Department of Employment issued them this type of work voucher. Clearly, the Labour Government tightened the screw on the entry of black and Asian immigrants as far as it thought possible, through both administrative and legislative means.

Not satisfied with this, the Conservative manifesto for the June 1970 general election proposed still tighter control on Commonwealth immigrants along the lines proposed by Heath earlier. Indeed, when returned to power, the Conservatives passed the Immigration Act, 1971, incorporating these principles.

This was a comprehensive law, and replaced the Aliens Restrictions Act of 1914, the Commonwealth Immigrants Acts of 1962 and 1968, and the Immigration Appeals Act of 1969. It covered the immigrant's entry, residence, deportation, repatriation and acquisition of citizenship. It restricted 'the right of abode in the United Kingdom' to 'patrials', that is – to put it simply – those who were either born here, or Commonwealth citizens whose parent(s) were born here. The 'patrial' concept stemmed directly from the clause in the 1968 Immigrants Act, which allowed the right of entry to those British passport-holders who had substantial connection with Britain by virtue of birth, or their fathers' or grandfathers' birth, in this country. (It was this clause which earned the latest bill the label of 'racist', and rightly so.) As for a non-patrial, he was required to obtain a work permit to get in. This was to be issued only for a specific job and a specific period. On arrival he had no right to settle in Britain until controls on him were removed – normally after four years. The sections pertaining to non-patrials were full of such unspecified powers as 'if the Home Secretary deems it conducive to the public good', 'any person appearing to an immigration officer', 'if he is ... of good character and has a sufficient knowledge of English', and so on. The Act made a provision for 'voluntary repatriation' for those immigrants who had not succeeded in Britain by allowing them to return home on government-assisted passages.[4]

In general, wherever there was a choice between the provisions in the Aliens Act and the Commonwealth immigration laws, the harsher one was chosen. In particular, the new Act empowered a police constable or immigration officer to 'arrest without warrant anyone who has, or whom he, with reasonable cause, suspects to have, committed or attempted to commit an offence under this section (24)' – that is, to enter Britain illegally, to stay beyond the allowed period or to fail to observe any restriction imposed on him. This meant, in theory, every black or Asian citizen, no matter how long he had been a resident in Britain, was liable to be arrested: a situation that could hardly help to improve race relations. The police showed an unusual proclivity to exercising its new powers. With a freshly installed Illegal Immigration Intelligence Unit at Scotland Yard at its command months before January 1973, the Metropolitan Police carried out 219 enquiries and arrested 73 people during that year. Between October 1973 and April 1978 police and immigration officers conducted twenty-five major passport raids.[5]

If the government's intention was simply to reduce the number of immigrants into Britain it was unnecessary to pass a new bill. After all, the already existing legislative and administrative powers had enabled successive administrations to cut the number of work vouchers from 28,678 in 1963 to 3052 in 1970. Passing a new piece of legislation was a means to still 'the fears of *our* people' (as Prime Minister Heath once put it) regarding 'inadequate control' over coloured immigration. It was the same fears that dominated Enoch Powell's thinking.

The only difference was that, unlike other political leaders, Powell's sights were fixed on the future – a future of '"a large alien wedge" in our towns and cities'. This he was determined to avoid not only for the sake of white Britons but, as he often claimed, also for the welfare of coloured immigrants and their descendants. For he argued: 'If those who are concerned, think that this fact [of the development of a "large alien wedge"] is being deliberately ignored and overlooked, the danger will be that there will be a tendency for people to be treated differently.'[6]

This statement implied that when the size of the coloured community in Britain was small there was no tendency for the racial minority 'to be treated differently'. Where was one to find the evidence to support this view? In those cities where small numbers of black and brown peoples had first settled half a century ago. Liverpool and Cardiff were examples.

A study of the second and third generation of black youths in Liverpool was conducted by the Working Party of Liverpool Youth Organizations Committee, and published in October 1968. Its findings were summed up by the authors of *Colour and Citizenship* thus: '[Black youths] meet discrimination in employment, and when they move outside the coloured quarter they feel insecure ... The long-standing myth in Liverpool of non-discrimination between people of different racial characteristics ... is a cloak for indifference and lack of understanding ... [There is] evidence of hostility to colour in white downtown areas.'[7]

This summary was in tune with the statements of Lord Simey in the Lords in December 1966. 'I come ... from Liverpool where our coloured citizens are nearly all locally-born,' he said. 'They have been educated in our schools, they speak the common language of Liverpool, but because of their colour they are given unskilled jobs. They are the first to become unemployed in a slump; they have the worst accommodation, the worst social services, and the worst neighbourhood to live in.'[8]

A more detailed and scientific study of Bute Town, Cardiff's dock area, was conducted by Leonard Bloom in 1966–7. He compared and contrasted three generations of black settlers and some post-war black and Asian settlers with a sample of Italian and Greek immigrants of first and second generation. He discovered that the Italians and Greeks who had first settled in Bute Town had by the mid-1960s dispersed throughout Cardiff where they could easily find employment: they had been more or less socially accepted. But not so the black and Asian settlers. His general conclusion, summarized by the authors of *Colour and Citizenship*, was: 'We see a second and third generation [of black settlers] which lives in a quasi-ghetto, is denied the opportunities available to white English-speaking immigrants, is less ambitious, and achieves less than they [the white immigrants] do.'[9] The author's study of Bute Town revealed that over the past two generations the black community of 4000–5000 had produced only four professionals: two teachers, one architect and one civil engineer – who was working in America.[10]

But none of these arguments had any impact on the Powellite forces in their campaign for the introduction of repatriation for coloured immigrants.

However, the influence of Enoch Powell within the ruling Conservative Party waned as he took a strong stand against Britain's joining the European Common Market, then encompassing nine continental countries. The government was led by Edward Heath, an early and staunch believer in the idea that Britain's future lay with Europe. Britain formally joined the European Community on 1 January 1974. The Heath government's decision was opposed by Labour, which captured power in the February 1974 election against the background of a ruinous coal miners' strike, electricity cuts and a three-day working week. In this election Powell defected from the Conservatives, backing Labour's anti-Europe stance. He thus lost his supporters in the Conservative Party, the natural home for the (respectable) anti-immigrant forces within society.

Powell was adopted as a candidate by the Unionists in Northern Ireland, and was elected to Parliament from that province. This created a vacuum in the right-wing, anti-immigrant political spectrum of the British Isles. It was soon to be filled by small rightist groups, particularly the National Front.

Among the political groups that benefited greatly by Powell's unrelenting campaign against black and Asian immigrants, the National Front was the best known. Powell's breaking of the taboo on frank and uninhibited public discussion of race and immigration – coupled with the media's projection of a negative image of ethnic minority citizens and the government's racist bias in controlling immigration – improved the climate for the ultra-right National Front (NF) to win supporters.

The Front was a direct descendant of the ultra-right-wing movements of earlier periods: the British Union of Fascists and the Imperial Fascist League of the inter-war era; and the League of Empire Loyalists, the Racial Preservation Society and the British National Party of the post-war period. The amalgamation of the League of Empire Loyalists, the British National Party, and a section of the Racial Preservation Society in late 1966 led to the formation of the National Front. The next year its ranks expanded when the Greater Britain Movement (GBM) merged into it. Led by John Tyndall, the GBM was a breakaway group from the National Socialist Movement founded in 1962 by Colin Jordan, who was to serve a jail sentence for inciting racial hatred (see p. 247). The National Front was led by A. K. Chesterton, a former editor of the *Blackshirt*, the journal of the British Union of Fascists before the Second World War. Thus the newly formed National Front included various political trends within British politics, ranging from racist nationalism to Conservative imperialism to National Socialism.

Among other things the National Front enthusiastically adopted the Powellite idea of repatriating black and Asian immigrants. Like Powell it was opposed to Britain's entry into the European Community. However, as an organization, it was still in its infancy at the time of the 1970 general election. The Conservative Government's agreement to accept Uganda Asians on a large scale in 1972 provided an opportunity for the NF to widen its appeal in an atmosphere where Robert McCrindle, a Conservative MP from the Home Counties, could unashamedly declare: 'I won't worry if I am branded a racialist by political opponents. I shall at least know I am in extensive good company.'[11]

In the by-elections of late 1972 and 1973 the anti-immigrant candidates did well, with the National Front winning a record 16.2 per cent vote in the West Bromwich parliamentary election in May 1973. Since the late 1960s the National Front had concentrated most of its fire on the Asian immigrants, portrayed as a major threat to the British way of life for demographic and cultural reasons. They came from the Indian sub-continent of teeming millions, which could supply an unending stream of immigrants. Their cultural differences from the British were so acute as to place them beyond the pale so far as mainstream Britons were concerned. Their food smelled, their music was a caterwauling whine, and their women, draped in strange costumes, never took the trouble to learn English. It was unbearable for National Front followers to see foreign people settled in Britain clinging to their distinct traditions and thus, implicitly, challenging the superiority of the white British way of life. The events of the early 1970s provided further ammunition for National Front propaganda against the Asians.

The National Front's electoral performance in West Bromwich boosted its morale. Little wonder that it did better in the February 1974 general election than in the previous one, and further improved its performance in the October poll.

In two constituencies of London's East End its candidates secured 7.6 and 9.4 per cent of the vote, a respectable performance. Buoyed by this, its leaders decided to focus on the East End, a mainly working-class area. They had by now devised a strategy of pinning rising crime, particularly mugging, and unemployment on to the racial minorities. In this they were aided by the figures contained in a top-secret police report on street crime in south London, submitted to Home Secretary Roy Jenkins in early January 1975. The report was never published, but some details leaked out. Among these was one which stated that while 80 per cent of the muggings in Brixton were done by young blacks, 85 per cent of the victims were white.[12] The National Front exploited the propaganda value of this figure, and also warned 'true Britons' to guard against the 'rising red tide swamping British society'. Its activists infiltrated some schools, churches, community groups and trade union branches. The high-profile propaganda and infiltration of established institutions paid off. The NF-organized anti-mugging march in the East End in September 1975 drew substantial support.[13]

In Parliament, Enoch Powell was in the forefront in attacking any liberalization of the immigration rules that came from Roy Jenkins. In April 1974 he opposed the amnesty for illegal immigrants from the Commonwealth and Pakistan, who were adversely affected by the 1971 Immigration Act which came into force on 1 January 1973. Again Home Secretary in the Labour Government that followed the October 1974 general election, Roy Jenkins tried to soften some of the harsher measures taken by his predecessors. In June 1975 he increased the quota for British passport-holders in East Africa from 3000 to 5000. He rescinded the entry bar imposed by the earlier Labour administration in 1969 on fiancés and husbands of women settled in Britain. Three months later he introduced the new Race Relations Bill. All of this made Jenkins a prime target of attacks by Enoch Powell and right-wing Conservatives inside Parliament and by the National Front outside.

Powell repeatedly pressed Jenkins to furnish detailed immigration figures. In December 1975, Jenkins announced in Parliament that 'for a number of years' these statistics had been 'incorrectly collected'. With this, Powell and other MPs of a similar ilk redoubled their assaults on the government, arguing that growing immigration was harmful to the objectives of the Race Relations Bill scheduled to receive its second reading in early 1976 – and focusing their fire particularly on Alex Lyon, the Home Office minister responsible for immigration. Yielding to these pressures, Jenkins stated in early March: 'There is a limit to the amount of immigration which this country can absorb and that it is in the interests of the racial minorities themselves to maintain a strict control over immigration.'[14]

In early May 1976 the discovery by a British tabloid that a few Asian families from Malawi had been accommodated in a four-star hotel near Gatwick Airport made a sensational impact on the British public. Instead of highlighting the administrative bungling by the local and national authorities which had led to the anomaly, the media pointed up the event as an example of official generosity to Asians from abroad at the expense of the public exchequer. The National Front and the British National Party (BNP) exploited the episode for partisan purposes, and improved their popular standing. In the local elections the BNP won two seats on the district council in Blackburn in north-west England.

The Malawi Asian event provided a dramatic handle to the anti-immigrant MPs. Their offensive mood intensified when, during a parliamentary debate on immigration in late May, Powell leaked a confidential document compiled by a Foreign Office official. A summary of the reports from British immigration officers based in the Indian sub-continent, this document stated that (a) the immigration procedures being followed in India for intending migrants were lax; (b) an illegal network for aiding Indians to settle in Britain had emerged; and (c) the Home Office figure for dependants entitled to come to Britain was a gross underestimate. This was enough to put the Home Secretary on the defensive.

In the face of a continued onslaught from the anti-immigrant MPs, in early July 1976 Roy Jenkins appointed a parliamentary committee under Lord Franks to examine the feasibility of establishing a register of dependants for the immigrants already here.

Outside Parliament, National Front activists accelerated their plans to project a high profile of their organization in London's East End. They did so mainly by covering the walls with NF symbols and racist graffiti. They also concentrated on recruiting youngsters, with the Young National Front printing and distributing a quarter of a million copies of the leaflet entitled 'How to Spot a Red Teacher' in 1977.

The apparent success of the NF and the BNP strengthened the hands of those left-wing Labour leaders who had all along advocated a campaign against racism. In September 1976, Labour's National Executive Committee decided to mount a campaign in conjunction with the Trades

Union Congress to highlight the dangers of rising racism and neo-fascist politics as represented by the NF and the BNP. The party conference demanded the abrogation of the 1968 and 1971 Immigration Acts.

But the initial actions of anti-racist Labour supporters and trade unionists proved inadequate to stem the steady rise of ultra-right-wing politics. In the 1977 Greater London Council election, when the National Front contested 91 of the 92 seats, the East End provided nearly a third of its total vote. Moreover, in some GLC constituencies the NF vote went above 20 per cent. Encouraged by their strength, NF leaders took to expounding National Socialist concepts and demands. This acted as a damper on both the current and potential membership. Then in January 1978, Margaret Thatcher, the leader of the Conservative Opposition since 1975, made a statement which had the inadvertent effect of undermining popular backing for the NF.

On 30 January 1978, Thatcher stated in a television interview that '[British] people are really afraid that this country might be rather swamped by people with a different culture.' She added that her party should hold out the prospect of an end to immigration except in compassionate cases. Stating that the neglect of the immigration issue was driving some people to back the National Front, she expressed a wish to attract such voters to the Conservative Party.

It was obvious that Margaret Thatcher had made a calculated move after having concluded that the Conservatives stood to profit politically by voicing the anxieties of the white electorate regarding coloured immigration, rather than by striving to attract racial minority voters. The ploy worked. There was a notable shift in public opinion. Between mid-January and mid-February the Conservatives improved their electoral support from 43.5 per cent to 48 per cent whereas Labour backing fell from 43.5 per cent to 39 per cent. The percentage which regarded immigration as one of the urgent problems shot up from 9 to 21. 'By exploiting the immigration issue so dramatically Mrs Thatcher regained the political initiative which at this time appeared to be slipping away from the Tories to the Labour government,' noted Zig Layton-Henry, a British race relations specialist.[15]

Her statement had an immediate impact on Parliament. In March the parliamentary Select Committee on Immigration and Race Relations recommended stricter controls on immigration from the Indian sub-continent, an end to amnesties to illegal immigrants, and an official register of dependants for those already settled here. The last recommendation had indeed been rejected a month earlier by the government as impracticable and undesirable, following the submission of a report by the Franks Committee. The other two Select Committee recommendations, too, were to be rejected later.

Outside Parliament, Thatcher's statement drew back those Conservative supporters who had defected from the party in favour of the National Front and the British National Party. The results of the local elections in May 1978 showed that clearly: there was a steep decline in the votes for these groups.

The position of the Parliamentary Labour Party, which enjoyed a narrow majority in the Commons, deteriorated as the country underwent an epidemic of strikes in 1978–9, popularly called 'the winter of discontent'. Labour managed to govern only by entering into a pact with about a dozen Liberal MPs. In April 1979 the Labour administration led (since March 1976) by James Callaghan fell by one vote because of the absence of an MP from the treasury benches during a crucial vote.

In the ensuing election campaign the excessive power of trade unions was turned into the leading issue by the Conservatives. With this, and a strong anti-immigrant stance written into the Conservative manifesto, the National Front did badly. In the ten Greater London constituencies scattered from Islington Central to Dagenham through the East End – where the National Front had secured a respectable number of votes in the previous parliamentary election – the swing to the Conservatives was 14.2 per cent. And this was obtained by garnering National Front voters. Labour's electoral chances were seriously dented by its administration's failure to rein in the trade unions. This, coupled with the party's commitment in its election manifesto to strengthen and widen the 1976 Race Relations Act, promote equal opportunities in the public sector and monitor the local and national government bureaucracies for fair treatment to racial minorities, reduced the party's popular appeal among whites. As such, the May 1979 poll placed the Conservatives in power with a comfortable majority.

The National Front did not recover from that débâcle. The political territory that the NF, its breakaway faction called the British Movement, and the British National Party occupied was virtually taken over by the Conservative Party as it moved rightwards radically under the stewardship of Margaret Thatcher, who sugar-coated her authoritarian style with petty-bourgeois populism.

But there was no drop in the support for the National Front, the British Movement or the British National Party among young whites. In fact, with unemployment rising sharply during the early 1980s, white youths turned increasingly racist, believing that enforced expulsion of non-whites – as advocated by the extreme right-wing groups – would lead to an increase in job vacancies. Summarizing the findings of six studies of young people during the period of 1978–86, *What Next?*, a booklet published by the Economic and Social Research Council, established this conclusively. In 1979, it stated, just under 7 per cent of those interviewed said they supported the National Front or the British Movement. Three years later this figure had risen to 14 per cent.[16]

Given this, there was no let-up in racist assaults on blacks and Asians, particularly in London's East End. The logic behind such acts was articulated by a group of skinheads in a BBC Radio programme broadcast in February 1981. In it they openly admitted that a lot of violence was being perpetrated against blacks. 'White European race, right, is the superior race and always will be,' said a skinhead. 'They [blacks] are not people, they're parasites, they're just poncing off us. It takes ten years for a bill to go through parliament, right, and nothing happens. So if you give them a good dig and all that like, it might send a couple of them home … They might think, oh, you know like, we've had enough, we're going home. So we're doing our bit.'[17]

Racist violence increased when, on assuming office, the Conservative administration found itself unable to halt ethnic immigration, a popular expectation that Thatcher had aroused before and during the election campaign. The fact was that the controls were already as stiff as was possible within the framework of the European Convention on Human Rights.

The government implemented its pledge to replace the British Nationality Act of 1948 which, *inter alia*, was full of administrative confusions. It did so with a view to linking the right of abode in Britain with an unambiguous definition of citizenship, and thus achieving two major objectives: avoiding charges of racism in the administration of its immigration policy, and making immigration control less controversial.

In January 1981 the Home Secretary, William Whitelaw, introduced the British Nationality Bill in Parliament. It categorized citizenship thus: British, British Dependent Territories, British Overseas. British citizenship was to be awarded to those with close connection with the United Kingdom either by virtue of the birth of their parents or grandparents in the UK or their own permanent settlement here. The bill proposed that British citizenship would pass on only to the children born overseas to British citizens born in the UK, thus discriminating against those citizens not born in the UK (which meant all of the first-generation West Indian and Asian settlers). A person marrying a British citizen was required to acquire three years' residence before applying for citizenship.

Roy Hattersley, Labour's Shadow Home Secretary, called the bill racist and sexist, an Immigration Control Bill dressed up as a Nationality Bill. 'What we need is a positive statement of nationality based on objectively defined principles, clear of all racial considerations,' said Hattersley. 'From that statement of nationality a non-discriminatory immigration policy should then flow.'[18] He urged that the bill's provision to deny automatic citizenship to the children born in Britain to the parents of 'uncertain status' – that is, illegal immigrants or those staying beyond their period of residence – be changed to automatic citizenship for all the children born in the UK. He also argued that the residential requirement for prospective spouses wishing to acquire citizenship discriminated against women from the Commonwealth who might have to wait a long time before being let into Britain.

In response Whitelaw announced amendments which enabled a UK-born child denied citizenship at birth to acquire it after ten years of continuous residence, irrespective of the status of the parents, and which allowed naturalized British citizens to pass on citizenship to their children born abroad. But this was not enough to pacify numerous Civil Rights groups and racial minority organizations as well as the Commission for Racial Equality and the Joint Council for the Welfare of Immigrants. The Act came into force in late 1981.

In one sense the 1981 British Nationality Act was a logical evolution of the process which began in 1962 and which could be summarized as 'control and preserve'. In another sense, the Conservative Government's attempt to rationalize the nationality provisions needed to be viewed against the background of growing integration of Britain into the European Community which it had joined in 1974.

Britain had first turned its thoughts seriously towards some sort of union with continental Europe soon after the end of the Second World War in 1945. This was partly because post-war Britain was in dire need of labour and saw much potential in tapping Europe's large human resources, still in an unsettled state.

Historically, Britain's economic requirements have regulated the flow of immigrants. Industrial Britain has been drawing poor, unemployed men from mainly agrarian Ireland since the nineteenth century. Irish workers played a crucial role in the construction of canals, railways, roads and houses, as well as providing manpower for mining; and they still do in the construction industry.[19]

5 Room at the Bottom

After the [Second World] War there was firstly a shortage of workers ...
[Secondly] they felt that because they had fought for freedom, they deserved
a job, and could pick and choose, so they didn't like settling down. We tried
employing continentals and refugees, but it didn't work out ... in 1950
[we] employed Indian workers.

Labour Manager, Edge Tools Ltd.[1]

We do find they [coloured tenants] are happier in the older properties which
are very often in the districts where many of them live.

An official of a local housing department and member
of a housing committee.[2]

But for the intervention of the law, constant exposure of racism by
individuals and agencies, and organized protests by blacks, the situation
would have been much worse.

BHIKHU PAREKH[3]

Post-war Britain was afflicted with an acute manpower shortage.
Demand for labour was high owing to a massive backlog of postponed
projects and post-war reconstruction, and the reduction of the size of the
national workforce by war casualties. Furthermore, there was heavy
emigration from Britain during the post-war years. Even the arrival of
tens of thousands of immigrants from Europe, Ireland and the Commonwealth failed to balance this loss of manpower. For instance, in 1953
emigration exceeded immigration by 64,000. During the period
1946–56 (with the exception of 1952) there were more unfilled vacancies
than unemployed workers, the excess being 174,000 in June 1956.

Some industries and services were worse hit by the labour shortage
than others. 'In 1954,' recalled the works manager of a Midlands
foundry, 'you couldn't get an armless, legless man, never mind an
able-bodied one.'[4] Many employers paid regular visits to Ireland, and
even Italy, to recruit labour. But these visits were not always fruitful. The
same foundry, for example, hired thirty-six men in Ireland; but only eight
took up their jobs, and only one stayed for any length of time.

West Indian workers, appearing on the British labour market in the early 1950s, on the other hand, offered certain advantages to employers. They were already here; they were English-speaking; and they were anxious to work. But personnel managers hired them only as a last resort. 'We had no alternative, really'; 'We couldn't get enough non-coloured labour'; 'Shortage of white labour' – such were the statements frequently made by employers in the Midlands and North. In fact, 70 per cent of the firms surveyed by Peter Wright, a British researcher, attributed the employment of black and Asian workers to labour scarcity. 'Coloured workers are not employed unless they are urgently needed for specific jobs ... unless absolutely essential,' said a personnel manager. 'We get a lot of coloured people coming up for jobs and we have to turn them away.'[5]

A more scientific study of discrimination against racial minorities was conducted by Political and Economic Planning Ltd in 1966–7. Using a sample of forty firms, PEP surveyors directed a set of applicants – an Englishman, a Hungarian and a West Indian – with identical qualifications to apply for the same vacancy. The English applicant was offered a job or kept in mind in thirty cases; the Hungarian in seventeen; and the West Indian in three. That is, 90 per cent of the thirty companies discriminated against the black applicant.

Those establishments which were driven to consider racial minority applicants by the unpopular nature of their work (such as foundries and rubber mouldings), or low wages (such as bakeries and textiles), or shift work (such as paper manufacture, glass works, bakeries and public transport) were generally apprehensive of their white employees' reactions. Hence they considered it necessary to consult their workforce. When they did not, strikes often ensued. For instance, the operating staff on the West Bromwich buses went on strike in 1955 when an Indian was recruited as a trainee bus conductor. Twelve years later, in the same town, workers at a light engineering company went on strike when a West Indian woman was hired as a trainee press-operator. A few of the typical examples of this nature during 1962–5 were: employees of a cartage firm refused to work with a British-born coloured fitter; 49 workers at a north London company went on strike in protest at the recruitment of three new coloured persons; and following the hiring of a Pakistani by their firm in Banbury, its workforce voted for a 'colour bar'.[6] If, as was often the case, white workers' representatives opposed the idea of coloured recruitment, managements reassured them that only those jobs for which white labour was unavailable would be given to non-white applicants. Since local workers were most difficult to get for dirty, tedious, dead-end, low status, unskilled jobs, employers placed West Indian and Asian applicants in these positions irrespective of their skills and experience. In short, racial minority labour was taken in to fill the vacuum at the bottom.

Peter Wright's analysis of thirty-eight companies in the Midlands and North showed that 58 per cent of coloured workers were employed in unskilled jobs compared to 10 per cent of white. 'Generally speaking,' he concluded, 'the coloured worker tended to obtain the jobs white workers valued least.'[7] This resulted in considerable job downgrading for black and Asian immigrants. It meant that employers were able to serve their economic interest while sustaining their own, and their white employees', prejudice against racial minorities by keeping them 'in their place'.

The other restriction that managements, in (unofficial, unrecorded) consultations with the unions, imposed on the hiring of coloured workers was that of quotas. However, in some cases managements were unable to maintain quotas at the agreed levels because of a perennial dearth of white labour, and also because they found it cheaper and less troublesome to engage black or brown labour. They let their economic interest become the sole guiding factor. Hence the emergence of factories with more coloured labour than white. But, taking British industry as a whole, such plants were a tiny minority. The vast majority of companies continued to limit the number of racial minority employees. As the personnel manager of a west London firm admitted in 1965: 'Twice we have reduced or stopped taking coloured people on, temporarily, in order to maintain a balance, say, of 20 to 30 per cent coloured.'[8]

More typical still was the company which managed to keep coloured workers at the lowest job level by barring them direct recruitment to skilled jobs, and by refusing to promote senior black or Asian employees to better jobs (in terms of pay and work conditions), or to supervisory posts. Managements almost invariably refused to treat the West Indian or Asian immigrants' experience and skills on a par with the British. Also, available evidence suggested that the higher the skill required for a job, the greater the resistance among white employees to the hiring of blacks or Asians. In many cases white skilled workers took militant action to force managements to fall into line with their feelings. For instance, 64 workers in the machine shop of a Keighley, West Yorkshire, factory downed tools when two Pakistanis were engaged as machine operators. The management backed down, and agreed not to employ coloured workers for skilled jobs.[9] Not surprisingly, many firms placed a limit beyond which a black or Asian employee was not to be allowed. 'The highest job done by any coloured worker (with us) is fork-lift operator,' stated the personnel manager of Grange Graphite Co.[10]

Prejudice on the part of white employers and workers against racial minorities manifested itself most strongly when it came to supervisory posts. The idea of recruiting black or Asian candidates as supervisors was seldom seriously considered by managements. But as the proportion and seniority of racial minority workers in certain companies increased, the question of promoting a few to supervisory positions arose as a matter of course. 'Now with 32 per cent of the workforce coloured,' said the personnel manager of an asbestos company in north-west England, 'we could well promote one or two of the senior ones, but we are not sure of the reaction [of white workers].'[11]

Even a temporary situation of subordination to a black or Asian supervisor seemed unbearable to most white workers. When, for example, a senior coloured employee stood in as a foreman at a Lancashire firm, white workers refused to take orders from him. 'We have no objection to working alongside with them,' said a white worker to a reporter. 'But we do object to taking orders from them.'[12] Such instances corroborated the findings of Clifford S. Hill, a British social researcher. His survey of the attitudes of whites in north London showed that 83 per cent of those interviewed objected to working under a black person.[13]

No wonder, then, that most of the racial minority supervisors in British industry in the late 1960s were to be found only 'at the manual worker level', and exercised authority 'over only coloured workers'.[14] Even that became possible only because certain departments or sections of some factories had become all-coloured. However, this practice was by no means widespread. Night shifts at many textile mills in West Yorkshire were all-coloured, and yet the supervisory staff remained almost all-white.

Reluctance to promote racial minority employees to supervisory positions was strong even among the managing authorities of such public services as hospitals and transport. Through the National Health Service (NHS) the government had emerged as an important employer of coloured settlers. Of the 250,000 nurses and midwives working in British hospitals in the late 1960s, at least a third were from the New Commonwealth. Yet no more than 5 per cent of the senior nursing staff was coloured.[15] A similar pattern was discernible among doctors in NHS hospitals. Nearly half of the junior doctors were born outside the UK and Eire (that is, primarily in the New Commonwealth), but only one-sixth of the senior registrars.[16]

Public transport authorities resisted promoting coloured drivers or conductors to inspectors. In 1967 the West Indian Standing Conference in London pointed out that in the preceding year not one of the twenty-one West Indian bus conductors who had applied for promotion had succeeded. Some of them had a record of ten years' unflawed service.

At the grassroots level, trade union leadership generally tended to reflect the racial prejudice of the rank and file. This was in direct conflict with the purported policy of the Trades Union Congress which, in 1955, condemned 'all manifestations of racial discrimination or colour prejudice whether by governments, employers or workers'. But to pass lofty resolutions at the annual conference was one thing; to put them into practice in everyday situations quite another. In any event, the TUC represented only two-fifths of the total labour force in Britain.

Indeed, trade unions at the factory level worked in league with management to restrict equal opportunity for black and Asian settlers – in recruitment, types of jobs available, promotion and redundancy. One of the earliest exposures of union collusion with management occurred in Birmingham in 1954. The local Transport and General Workers Union had banned the hiring of coloured people as bus crews, in spite of the fact that the transport authority was 900 workers short.[17] A few of the reported cases of union officials initiating action to restrict the rights of black and Asian citizens were: led by a union secretary, 40 dustcart drivers threatened to strike on public holidays if a coloured employee was promoted to dustcart driver; a chapel of a union branch voted by 38 to 24 to oppose the recruitment of coloured people; and a personnel manager in west London was reported as saying: 'Officially there is no colour bar in unions. But you get pressure from the shop-floor ... They do a bargain, the same with wages. They say, "Get the proportion of coloureds down to 10 per cent".'[18]

This is only a minute sample of the cases reported in the press which in turn was a small proportion of the numerous informal, oral agreements made between union officials and company managers. However, these instances faithfully reflected the general attitude of union members and officials.

Unsurprisingly, very few, if any, local union officials took the trouble to enrol coloured workers. This was so, in spite of the evidence that blacks and Asians were as willing to join unions as whites. Indeed, in many factories where ethnic workers found themselves in the majority they introduced unions where none existed before. West Indian wage-earners, for example, formed a union at a confectionery company in High Wycombe. Afro-Caribbean and Asian workers established a union at a foundry in Wolverhampton. And so on.

Indian workers, guided by the local Indian Workers' Association, were particularly active in this field (see Part II, Chapter Five). For example, they established a T&GWU branch in a rubber factory in Southall and in December 1965 declared an unofficial strike in protest against the management's policy of victimizing trade union activists. Later the strike received 'industrial support' from the regional office of the T&GWU, but not 'full official support'. The union's regional secretary refused to blacklist the companies which continued to deal with the rubber factory because, he argued, 'It will put a lot of people out of work in a few days.' The industrial action failed.

As coloured workers realized more and more that they were not receiving the expected help from trade unions, and that union officials were unresponsive to their special needs (such as a long, unpaid holiday every three years to visit the home country, etc.) they were driven to the conclusion that unions were beneficial only to white workers.

'In practice,' stated the authors of *Colour and Citizenship*, 'they [unions] have often acted in ways which have alienated the coloured worker ... They have failed, with a few notable exceptions, to organize and involve coloured workers ... [they] have failed to educate their members to face the challenge presented by the presence of the coloured workers in British industry.'[19]

White trade unionists' lack of interest in racial equality for black and Asian citizens became apparent when major unions at the local and national levels failed to respond positively to the repeated appeals by the leaders of the Campaign Against Racial Discrimination to affiliate to their organization. Excepting the T&GWU, all major unions stayed away from the Anglo-American conference in February 1967 on 'Racial Equality in Employment', sponsored by the National Committee for Commonwealth Immigrants (NCCI), a quasi-official body. Only eighteen trade unionists attended the conference.

Employers and their associations showed a similar lack of interest in this gathering. The NCCI had to despatch 600 invitations to fill 50 seats allotted to industry. At the conference, a spokesman for the Confederation of British Industry stated: 'Our experience is that up to now no serious problems have arisen.' The Director of the Engineering Employers' Federation made a similar statement.[20]

It seemed that far too many employers and managers felt virtuous in having a few black and brown faces among their workforces. They were unconcerned about the distance that lay between what a coloured employee could do and what he was actually doing. They were unaware of the frustration felt by many competent racial minority workers denied promotion out of (unstated, but known) racist considerations, and of the rising expectations of black and Asian school-leavers.

However, as in the case of unions, there were notable exceptions. The Junior Chamber of Commerce (JCC) in Keighley was one. Concerned with future prospects for coloured school-leavers, educated totally in Britain, the JCC conducted a survey of local employers in 1966. It found the results depressing. It could not find a single white-collar job for West

Indian or Asian school-leavers. It summed up the employers' attitudes as ranging from 'wooden indifference to frank hypocrisy'. Some of the recorded responses from employers were: 'A large textile firm, "Not prepared to employ any Pakistani men or women"; a large firm ancillary to the textile industry, "It is not the policy of our company to employ immigrants"; a printing firm, "We are not anticipating employment of coloured personnel ... Unions would not take kindly to their introduction"; and a large bank, "We cannot foresee any possibility of employing these people".'

Undoubtedly the same employers, if questioned in public, would have begun their answers with, 'Let me make one thing clear: we are absolutely against racial discrimination ...' It was rare to encounter the frankness with which the secretary of the Woolcombers' Association in Bradford expressed himself to the *Guardian*: 'He [a coloured person] has to be twice as good as an Englishman for the same job'.[21] This was the true attitude of most white employers and trade unionists.

And it was this attitude which within a generation led to the creation of 'industrial ghettoes' for racial minorities. In the late 1960s coloured workers were concentrated in comparatively few, generally unpopular factories and services. Even where black and Asian workers formed a substantial minority (say, 30–35 per cent) of the total labour force they were to be found in the least liked jobs, departments or shifts. Resistance to hiring or promoting blacks or Asians to skilled jobs or supervisory posts remained strong, as did the resistance to appointing them to white-collar jobs.

This could be read as a summary of the housing conditions of coloured settlers if one were to replace 'few, generally unpopular factories and services' with 'the decaying inner rings of British cities', 'the least popular jobs or departments' with 'old, slum properties', and 'skilled jobs or supervisory posts' with 'houses in the suburbs'.

So far as the general attitude of whites towards blacks went, the statement 'A coloured person has to be twice as good as an Englishman for the same job' ran parallel to 'In both the public and private sectors [in housing] a coloured applicant has to be superlatively respectable in order to receive the same treatment as an ordinary English person'. That was the conclusion of Elizabeth Burney, the author of *Housing on Trial*, published in 1967.[22]

The designers of the 1966–7 PEP survey were aware of the widely-held opinion which attributed the problems faced by coloured immigrants to their being immigrant rather than being coloured. Hence, for their tests of housing (as well as employment) situations, they used a set of three applicants: an Englishman, a white immigrant (a Hungarian) and a black immigrant (a West Indian).

Of the 60 applications made in response to advertisements for accommodation to let, which did not specify a colour bar, the West Indian was discriminated against 45 times (that is, 75 per cent); the Hungarian, three times (5 per cent); and the Englishman not at all. In other words, only 25 per cent of the white landlords were prepared to give equal treatment to the black applicant. But since, according to the Milner-Holland Report, advertisements without a colour bar constituted only 11 per cent of the total accommodation vacancies, it meant that, in absolute terms, only 3 per cent of white landlords acted in a non-discriminatory manner.

Follow-up interviews with the discriminating landlords produced such comments as: 'Nobody wants this to become little Jamaica, do they?'; 'I don't think it's good for the children ... to have them [coloured people] around'; and 'My wife doesn't go for them much, and anyway it would look bad with neighbours. And, come to think of it, give me a good reason why should we?'[23]

An overwhelming number of accommodation agents were found to be discriminating, and they blamed the landlords. 'I'd like to fix them [coloured accommodation-seekers] up,' said one agent. 'I make more money that way, and it's no skin off my nose what colour they are ... [But] nine times out of ten you can't do a thing for them.' Another agent stated: 'If you send a coloured person around, the landlords go berserk. The phone never stops ... They certainly never expect them.'[24]

In the case of house purchase, the discriminatory estate agents, forming two-thirds of the sample, advanced a compounded reason. 'To begin with,' said one agent, '[white] people are reluctant to sell to them [coloured people]. They are under pressure from their neighbours and so on. Secondly, there are great difficulties in getting mortgages: either they are asked for higher deposits, or the interest rates are higher – or they aren't given loans at all. That's the way building societies do it.'[25]

Since building societies financed three-quarters of all house mortgages, their policies and attitudes in this matter were crucially important. Their officials spelled out the criteria for granting mortgages: age, income and the reliability of the applicant regarding the price, value and age of the house. They argued that if black and Asian immigrants fared badly it was because they failed these 'objective' criteria. But how objective was the rating of the applicant's reliability, particularly when it was stretched to include the reliability of his weekly wages as well? The fact that many West Indian and Asian immigrants were able to obtain mortgages by bribing building society officials (directly or through the agent) proved the subjectivity of the 'reliability rating'. Subjectivity also entered the judgement of most professionals that the arrival of a black or Asian family into an all-white street led to a depression in the value of property in general.

A series of decisions like this by building societies and estate agents, coupled with their efforts to steer the socially mobile racial minority settlers away from better residential areas, led to a *de facto* segregation in housing. The only chance in the future of breaking this pattern – which showed signs of developing along American lines – lay in the field of public housing. But the PEP findings in this sector were equally depressing.

In the six areas covered by the PEP survey, 26 per cent of the white residents rented accommodation from the local council compared with 1 per cent for the racial minority groups. This was the situation two years after the 1965 White Paper, *Immigration from the Commonwealth*, had sanguinely declared: 'Local authorities already have a wide range of powers which, if judiciously used, can make a major contribution to this end [of relieving the immigrants' housing problems].'[26]

In public housing, the demarcation of powers between local authorities and the national government was such that the latter could at best only play a passive role. Local councils had the sole right to select their tenants, allocate them dwellings they considered suitable, and operate differential rent schemes. They also had a more or less free hand in demolishing buildings considered 'unfit for human habitation', and in enforcing public health rules. Above all, they exercised sole authority over the allocation of funds and the administrative machinery that executed their redevelopment and housing policies.

Judicious use of this 'wide range of powers' to relieve the immigrants' housing shortage implied that the local councils recognized the existence of a problem. This was hardly the case. Because, as Elizabeth Burney pointed out, 'Most Labour councils make it a habit of resolutely ignoring the subject of immigration, to the extent of, wherever possible, ignoring the presence of immigrants.'[27] In the major industrial conurbations, where most of the black and Asian immigrants had settled, local councils were generally Labour-controlled.

In a few cases, such as Lambeth, London, the local authority did take notice of the inflow of black immigrants, but refrained from acting on the premise that 'any action it took would be regarded by the public as giving unfair priority to "coloured folk"'.[28] This was a real dilemma for most civic leaders. For, as a governing institution, the local council was the nearest and most accessible to ordinary citizens. As such most councillors, like the leaders of many local trade union branches, found that they had little choice but to reflect the views and biases of the majority on this sensitive issue. To act otherwise was to invite sharp and direct criticism from white voters. Furthermore, there was the economic fact that, apart from a slum house, a council dwelling provided a working-class family with the cheapest possible accommodation. So in practically every town and city the waiting list for council accommodation was long, and the conditions for securing it often stiff.

Basic criteria for the allocation of council housing were: length of residence, period of waiting on the Housing Register, and the urgency of 'housing need'.

Residential qualification could range from one to ten years and was, as the town halls repeatedly pointed out, equally applicable to all. Nevertheless, the net effect of this stipulation was to handicap coloured settlers. 'That may be so,' argued many civic leaders, 'but we certainly do not discriminate on racial grounds. How could we? We don't know whether the applicant is coloured or not.' But they did – if one was to believe the findings of an independent investigative body such as the PEP. 'When someone was in the process of being housed by the council his colour was usually known,' the PEP report stated. 'This may be a result of a discreet pencil mark in a margin subsequently rubbed out, something the sophisticated reader can tell from the housing visitor's report, or a straight record of "country of origin".'[29] Under 'country of origin' those Afro-Caribbeans born in Britain were unlikely to be noticed. On the other hand an Asian, identifiable and alien by virtue of his name, was sure to be detected, irrespective of his country of birth.

Awareness and acceptance of widespread discrimination at the town hall made most blacks and Asians reluctant to apply for a council house. The PEP survey established that only 10 per cent of the West Indians (and even fewer Asians) had registered for a council dwelling even though most of them belonged to the economic class in which such registration was common. They felt that their chance of securing council housing was 'poor' to 'non-existent' – a feeling that dovetailed with Elizabeth Burney's observation that 'Authorities were inclined to regard coloured tenants as an embarrassment.'[30]

There was another route by which a racial minority settler could, or should, become a council tenant: through slum clearance or redevelopment plans. But this method was not as simple as it seemed at the outset.

First, a local council had to decide which neighbourhood was to be declared a slum clearance or redevelopment area. Second, broad principles regarding rehousing had to be laid down. Third, every household so qualified had to be visited by a housing visitor. Finally, if recommended, a householder was to be offered one of the various types of council houses or flats available. At each juncture of this elaborate procedure the dice were, or could be, subtly but definitely loaded against racial minority slum-dwellers.

The broad principle sacrosanct with local authorities, that redevelopment should begin where there would be the highest gain in persons rehoused per unit of space redeveloped, was often translated as: areas of high density population should be kept out of redevelopment plans. This meant that neighbourhoods with a high proportion of black and Asian residents tended to be bypassed.

Since such decisions were taken *in camera*, hard evidence was difficult to produce. But, as in the case of employment practices, someone occasionally spoke his mind freely and revealed the facts. In August 1965, for instance, Professor John Rex and Robert Moore pointed out in the *Sunday Times* that, 'A few weeks ago a plan to redevelop part of Sparkbrook [in Birmingham] by the council was rejected by the council because, according to a member of the public works committee, "600 immigrant families would have been rehoused".' It would probably be more accurate to attribute this statement by a councillor to a desire to reassure the white electors rather than to an unfortunate slip of discretion. In other words, in the ever-present conflict between according equal treatment to a disliked minority and reflecting the popular prejudices of the white majority, many local representatives opted for popularity, or sheer political survival.

In deciding who was to be rehoused, the principal guidelines could be so formulated as to preclude a large majority of racial minority residents. One Inner London borough (later identified as Islington) ruled that those living in furnished accommodation would not be rehoused. This automatically excluded a vast proportion of its West Indian and Asian residents. The housing manager of a large town told the leaders of his local coloured community: 'Dirty people will not be rehoused.' He did not make this point to the leading white citizens. Who was to decide who was 'dirty'? The council's housing visitors, who were qualified 'by experience'.

Which brought the matter to the third step of slum clearance and rehousing procedures: the housing visitor's report. The function of a housing visitor was to collect 'objective' information – namely, household income, rents or rates paid; to pass 'subjective' judgement on cleanliness, furniture and the general state of the household, and on the 'type' of applicant – good, fairly good, fair or unsuitable; to record the householder's preference regarding the location and type of accommodation desired; and, finally, to make his/her own recommendation.

Almost all housing visitors were white and quite unfamiliar with

Afro-Caribbean and Asian settlers' cultural backgrounds. This fact alone put most racial minority residents at a disadvantage. 'There is, for example, the woman investigator who plainly gives higher marks for newly polished furniture than for a well-cared-for baby in a shabby cot,' noted Elizabeth Burney. 'There are others who are quite obviously biased, or baffled, or both, in dealing with coloured people, and therefore play safe by giving low marks ... When all the evidence showed a bright, spotless room ... a good mark was sometimes justified with the comment "Although she's coloured she does seem very clean".'[31]

Supposing an ultra-clean, respectable black or Asian resident found himself qualified for council housing, what kind of dwelling was he likely to be offered out of the large public housing pool, consisting of modern houses and flats; older houses and flats; and old, reclaimed houses? Most probably another run-down house with a further useful life of barely a decade or two – or, at best, a dwelling in an older, pre-war housing estate.

An official of an Outer London borough (later identified as Brent) revealed to the PEP investigators that 'They [coloured tenants] have been housed in acquired properties which came on to the market in slum clearance areas and [which] the council buys'.[32] This was the truth as revealed privately by an insider. But no spokesmen for local councils would publicly admit that racial minority tentants were being treated in a discriminatory way.

Local authorities explained the concentration of racial minority tenants in old council properties on the following (non-racial) grounds: 'The immigrants themselves show such preference'; 'They have large families, and only old houses are large enough to accommodate them'; 'They like to live in areas where they find their "own people", they're happiest there'; and, 'In any case, it is our policy that those who have lived longest in the borough should get the best property'. But, characteristically, the real and most important reason remained publicly unstated. It was that, when West Indian or Asian tenants were accommodated in old dwellings, 'they are not noticed as being housed by the council, which means that [white] people who do not qualify for public housing do not nurse resentment against them'. This is what a local councillor told PEP researchers in private.[33] In other words, allotting new dwellings to racial minority tenants was considered damaging to electoral popularity. No wonder then that the Birmingham Labour conference in 1966 rejected a motion that the (Labour-controlled) council allocate houses on new estates to coloured applicants, and that the Labour group in the council, most exposed to the (white) electorate, opposed the motion.[34]

Those councils which had allotted new houses to racial minority applicants had done so grudgingly. This was well illustrated by the case of a West Yorkshire town (later identified as Keighley) which in 1966–7 was nearing a position where applicants could secure a key to a house immediately. Yet its performance in rehousing its coloured residents involved in slum-clearance plans was tardy. 'Out of the last block of 200 houses we cleared, twelve or fifteen we knew had Pakistanis in them,' a housing official told PEP investigators. 'We eventually agreed to rehouse ... five families ... We try to keep them away from blocks of flats ... [and put them] on the edges of open estates – in cul-de-sacs ... Over the years we have rehoused perhaps a dozen or more coloured families.'[35] And this was a town of 56,000 where coloured immigrants, having first arrived in the mid-1950s, now constituted 4 per cent of its population, and where 120 council houses lay vacant in March 1968 due to lack of demand.

This case provided a textbook example of how – when caught in a cleft stick of the moral wrong of racism and the political expediency of reflecting white voters' bias – the councillors managed to wriggle out of it by manipulating administrative procedures and decisions effectively to keep black and Asian residents out of new public housing while simultaneously claiming a non-discriminatory policy. Not that policies themselves were fixed for all time.

Time and again local councillors argued that major policies had to be in line with the views of the electorate. Among them was Alderman Peter Farmer, chairman of the housing committee of Wolverhampton council. Justifying the housing policy which discriminated between the native-born and the immigrant, he said in late 1969: 'We believe we have pursued a policy backed by the vast majority of people in Wolverhampton.'[36] This belief was well borne out by the research of Danny Lawrence, a British academic, in Nottingham in 1967–8. He found that 62 per cent of the white respondents felt that (white) British families should be given preference in the allocation of council accommodation.[37]

Extensive national surveys by Political and Economic Planning Ltd in 1973–5 provided a full picture of the way racial minorities were treated by white Britons and white-dominated organizations and institutions.

In the private housing sector there was a change for the better. Between the PEP surveys of 1966–7 and 1974, the proportion of West Indians who had personally experienced racial discrimination dropped from 39 per cent to 21 per cent. There was a similar decline in the case of Indians.[38]

For the public sector housing the PEP surveyed ten local councils. Its general conclusion was similar to the one reached in 1967 – namely, 'very few Asians have penetrated into council housing, and the proportion of West Indians who have done so is low when their job levels are taken into account'. The actual figures were 4 per cent for Asians and 26 per cent for

West Indians. The low figure for Asians was due to an inordinately high proportion of home-owners in the community, estimated to be around 65 per cent. When it came to the quality of accommodation, the West Indian and Asian council tenants did much worse than white. Compared to the 0.6 per cent of the white council tenants who lived in shared dwellings, 18 per cent of the Asian and 10 per cent of the West Indian tenants did so. In contrast to the 28 per cent of the white households which scored below 11 on the housing amenity chart, 69 per cent of the West Indian and 51 per cent of Asian households did so. These figures stemmed from the fact that West Indians and Asians were often placed in sub-standard council properties. The other major discrepancy was in the occupation of houses or flats. Only one out of five white tenants was placed in a flat; whereas the proportion for racial minority tenants was one out of two. That is, the chance of being accommodated in a flat was two-and-a-half times higher for West Indians and Asians.[39]

A similar inequality could be discerned in the owner-occupier sphere. While a little over a quarter of white owner-occupiers lived in terraced houses, more than three-quarters of black and Asian owner-occupiers did so. The contrast was even sharper when it came to those living in detached houses: 34 per cent of whites versus a mere 1 per cent for racial minorities.[40]

However, a national survey conducted by the Department of Environment in 1977, and published a year later as *National Dwelling and Housing Survey 1977*, put the proportion of West Indian and Asian households in council housing at 45 per cent and 10 per cent respectively: a substantial improvement on the PEP survey figures of four years earlier. The national statistic was 30 per cent.[41] Obviously the mid-1970s was a period of perceptible change in public housing for black and Asian citizens. This happened because during these years a substantial number of them came to meet the residential requirement and became entitled to council accommodation. Secondly, as a result of wide-scale slum-clearance programmes, which were implemented in almost all industrial areas, a certain proportion of racial minority residents found themselves rehoused in public housing.

Given that both West Indian and Asian communities contained a higher percentage of working-class households than the national average, the proportion of council tenants among them was expected to be higher. The 1977 national housing survey as well as the 1982 Policy Studies Institute survey demonstrated that this was the case with the West Indians: at 45–6 per cent they were above the UK average of 30 per cent. During the five-year interval between these surveys the proportion of council tenants among the Asians nearly doubled from the base of 10 per cent. But this change occurred at the expense of private tenants. At 70–72 per cent, home ownership among Asians was still much above the national 55–9 per cent. On the other hand, at 41 per cent, ownership among West Indians was lower than the national average.[42]

As for the policies and procedures followed by the housing departments of local authorities there was overall progress towards the goal of racial equality. Yet there was much room for improvement. 'While several housing authorities have introduced ethnic record systems over the years, few have checked that their policies are actually being carried out by analysing the records or producing reports on them', noted the *Annual Report of the Commission for Racial Equality, 1986.*[43]

Some metropolitan boroughs even continued to discriminate against ethnic minorities. London's Tower Hamlets was an example. In September 1987 the CRE found it discriminating against racial minorities in such areas as length of time spent by families in temporary bed and breakfast facilities and allocations to a certain housing estate in the borough. It served a non-discriminatory notice on the local authority requiring it to introduce a comprehensive ethnic record-keeping and monitoring system, review procedures regarding homeless and emergency applicants, and provide guidance and training to staff concerning equal opportunity issues.

All in all, however, it could safely be said that in housing, whether public or private, steady advance was being made towards racial equality. This was not the case in the field of employment.

The overall demand for jobs slackened considerably from the mid-1970s onwards as the economy was plagued by high inflation and low investment. Inflation reduced the value of £1 in 1970 to 27.5 pence in 1980. (In contrast, £1 in 1960 was worth 68 pence in 1970.) Due to tardy investment in new industrial processes during the previous decade the British economy did not grow fast enough in the seventies to absorb the labour that was shed by such older industries and processes as steel, coal and shipping. The jobless figure of 587,000 in May 1970 was a post-war record. Rising steadily from then on, it reached the million mark in December 1975. The arrival of the Conservative administration under Margaret Thatcher in May 1979 made matters worse. It was determined to reduce the powers of trade unions, and one of the important tactics in its armoury was to let joblessness rise and dampen the tempers of those in employment. Not surprisingly, during the first two years of the Thatcher government the number of unemployed doubled from a base of 1.4 million. The overall rate rose beyond 10 per cent, with the hitherto prosperous south-east England registering a record 8.4 per cent. The hardest hit were manufacturing plants, particularly those located in inner-city areas. Between 1971 and 1976 this sector of manufacturing industry lost a quarter of its workforce, with the rate of decline accelerating in the late seventies and early eighties. The fresh jobs being created in the cities were predominantly in the service sector or in new high-technology plants. The departure of industrial capital from the inner-city areas was combined with a squeeze on public sector spending imposed by Whitehall at both local and national levels.

Between 1979 and 1985 the absolute number of poor in Britain rose by more than half – from 6.1 million to 9.4 million. 'Increasingly,' noted Christian Wolmar, a British journalist, 'the line between the haves and have-nots is drawn by one factor – a job.'[44] Given that the jobless rate among racial minorities was much higher than among whites, the proportion of poor among black and Asian citizens was far above the national average.

'Unemployment grew steadily and struck hardest in the metropolitan areas and in manufacturing where ethnic minorities were disproportionately represented,' stated the Commission for Racial Equality in its 1987 report, surveying a decade of its existence. 'The overall unemployment rate of ethnic minorities rose to twice that of whites. Among young blacks the unemployment rate was even higher, peaking at 60–70 per cent in some London boroughs. The racial segmentation of the labour market, combined with persistent discrimination by employers, whether direct or indirect, made it difficult for black people to move into different jobs.'[45] In other words, while the first generation of black and Asian settlers had often been relegated to jobs below their qualifications, their children were being increasingly excluded from the labour market altogether.

Earlier, in 1985, the Policy Studies Institute published its survey of discrimination prevalent in non-manual and skilled manual jobs. Its February 1984–March 1985 study involved 550 employers in London, Birmingham and Manchester, and employed the technique of using three applicants (a white, an Asian and a West Indian) for an advertised job. 'The white applicant is over a third more likely to receive a positive response from the employer than either of the black applicants,' it stated. 'At least a third of the employers recruiting people to the jobs covered in this study discriminate against Asian applicants or West Indian applicants or both.' Comparing this investigation with the previous ones, it concluded that discrimination had not decreased over the past decade. 'The levels of discrimination found in this study are in fact higher than those found in the PEP study of 1973–4, but the differences are not statistically significant.'[46]

The investigations concentrating on young ethnic citizens produced similar figures. The Department of Employment's 1986 survey of the labour force revealed that 17 per cent of white youths aged sixteen to twenty-four were unemployed. The statistic for black youths was 32 per cent, and for Pakistanis and Bangladeshis 43 per cent.[47] A survey of large companies receiving public funds for training youngsters showed that in October 1987 fifty leading firms had no black trainees at all. Of the 2685 trainees in twenty-one large supermarkets only twenty-two were black or Asian. The figures for December 1988 were equally dismal. Of the 2411 trainees in seven nationwide supermarkets, only seventeen were black or Asian.[48]

To complement such studies the CRE initiated its investigations in such professions as teaching and medicine. Its reports, published in the late 1980s, portrayed a depressing picture.

A survey of ethnic minority teachers by Chris Ranger in 1987 established that over half of them believed that they had personally encountered racial discrimination in teaching. The sample of eight local education authorities included Brent and Newham (with over a quarter of their residents from the New Commonwealth and Pakistan) as well as Wolverhampton (with about a sixth of its citizens from the New Commonwealth and Pakistan). Yet Ranger found that ethnic minority teachers were 'few in number', that they were 'disproportionately on the lowest salary scales', and that they were 'concentrated in subjects where there was a shortage of teachers' such as mathematics and science, being grossly under-represented in modern languages, music, art and drama, where there was much competition. Also there was a tendency among their employers to marginalize them by hiring them for posts connected specifically with the special needs of racial minorities, which were often financed by Section 11 of the Local Government Act of 1966. This meant lack of security, for the jobs were subject to continual review. No improvement in the future was in sight since in 1986 black and Asian students about to graduate at teacher training colleges were only 2.6 per cent of the total – that is, about half of the racial minority proportion in the population at large.[49]

Another survey covered overseas doctors who had, by all accounts, been welcomed at the time of the expansion of the National Health Service in the sixties and seventies to fill the gap due to an insufficient number of British medical graduates. It showed that overseas doctors constituted about a third of all hospital physicians in England and Wales, and that they were concentrated in the low grades and in such unpopular specialities as geriatrics and psychiatry. Almost 84 per cent of the registrars in geriatrics were from overseas whereas only 9 per cent of the consultants in general surgery, the most popular speciality, belonged to this category.[50]

Furthermore, the study established that overseas doctors had to apply more often for posts, and took longer to gain promotion, than their white British-educated colleagues. Given their low status in the medical hierarchy and inadequate training opportunities, overseas doctors were set to remain at the bottom of the heap. Finally, and more disturbingly, even those black and Asian doctors fully educated in Britain were being put in the same pigeonhole as their overseas colleagues.[51]

The unequal treatment accorded to racial minority university students graduating from British universities was not limited to medicine. It applied to all other disciplines. This was borne out by a 1987 study by the CRE of university graduates during their first year after obtaining a degree in 1982. It demonstrated that, compared to their white contemporaries, a larger percentage of ethnic minority graduates were unemployed a year after graduating. Among those who were employed, the jobs held by black and Asian graduates were in many ways inferior to those secured by their white counterparts. In such vocation-oriented university degrees as pharmacy and electrical and electronic engineering, Asian graduates did much worse than their white classmates. In pharmacy, for instance, the Asians gained jobs mostly in small private sector firms, and not with large companies.[52] An enquiry by the Law Society in 1988 revealed that only one per cent of practising solicitors belonged to racial minorities.[53]

All in all, these surveys disproved the widely-held view that once the West Indian and Asian immigrants had settled down in Britain, with their children being fully educated here, they would be well on their way to achieving racial equality. That this had not come to pass *two* generations after the first West Indians arrived in 1948 – despite the assistance provided to the goal of racial justice by successive Race Relations Acts – only proved that the roots of racism were much deeper than most people, on both sides of the colour line, had realized.

And racism existed far beyond the actions and decisions of the officials of professional bodies or elected councils. It permeated the very fabric of society and manifested itself in many and diverse ways.

6 Contemporary White Attitudes and Practices

Well, I've never come across ... wealthy negroes other than the brothel-keepers.

White owner of a large garage.[1]

I've got black people in my family. I'm not a racist. But, you know, it's only natural that we should give jobs to our people.

A white trade unionist in Liverpool.[2]

Racism is deeply embedded in the cultural conditioning of the descendants of the British Empire.

ANGELA LAMBERT, a British journalist.[3]

Through a 1964 survey in north London, Clifford S. Hill discovered that 49 per cent of the respondents objected to having a coloured neighbour.[4] But nine years earlier, in a national survey of white attitudes, Professor Michael Banton had found that only 10 per cent of his sample – spread over three English towns, one rural district and two Scottish towns – objected to having a coloured neighbour. The reason for this discrepancy lay in the fact that in Banton's case the question had an air of theoretical irrelevancy: for most of his respondents the possibility of acquiring a black or brown neighbour was non-existent. In the case of Hill, however, with a substantial number of blacks and Asians living in north London, the question was visualized by his respondents in direct, personal terms.

This meant that either the settlement of coloured colonials in Britain had brought to the surface the submerged historical prejudice of the British, or the influx of black and Asian immigrants had *made* many white Britons racially prejudiced. Bearing in mind the historical background sketched earlier (see Part I, Chapter Two; Part II, Chapter One), the former conclusion seems valid. But, because of its simplicity as well as superficiality, the latter conclusion is more readily, and more widely, drawn and accepted. Moreover, it relieves most Britons of the stigma of being labelled inherently racially prejudiced.

Though a substantial minority, probably a quarter, of white Britons do not object to being labelled racially prejudiced,[5] the majority regard racism as morally wrong. So they tend to cloak their bias in a non-racist garb.

'I have nothing against coloured people but they suck the country's welfare system dry,' ran a popular rationalization. The prevalence of this feeling was clearly established by a national survey by the Institute of Race Relations (IRR) in 1966–7. As many as 62 per cent of the respondents thought that black and Asian immigrants took 'more out of the country than they put into it'.[6] The facts were to the contrary. A study by Mrs K. Jones, a British economist, showed that in 1966 the total social welfare expense per head among immigrants was £48.7 compared to £62.4 per head for the total population – that is, about one-fifth below the national average.[7]

According to the IRR survey, 91 per cent of the whites considered that coloured immigrants took more out of the National Assistance (Supplementary Benefits) service than they put into it; 70 per cent felt the same concerning the National Health Service; and 45 per cent regarding education.[8] It was ironic that the smallest proportion of whites named education as the service being over-used by the racial minorities. For, according to Mrs Jones's study, the per capita cost of education among immigrants was actually 15 per cent higher than the national average because many Asian children needed extra attention owing to their lack of English, and this necessitated hiring extra teachers.

But the appointment of additional teachers in schools did not impinge on the minds of white adults as much as did the presence of blacks and Asians, however few, at Labour Exchanges (Job Centres) and the offices of the National Assistance/Supplementary Benefits Board. Facts belied impressions. Mrs Jones found that the immigrants' demand on the National Insurance and Assistance benefits amounted to only 55 per cent of the national average. This was so because the black and Asian communities were younger,[9] and consequently more self-reliant than the indigenous population.

Also being younger, and therefore generally healthier, than white Britons, the racial minorities made less demand (5 per cent less, to quote Mrs Jones) on health services per head than the national average. Within that general context, they used maternity wards more often than whites. This was so because the proportion of persons in the 25–44-year-old age bracket among black and Asian settlers was one-and-a-half times the figure for the native population – respectively 42 per cent and 25 per cent. The actual demand on maternity wards was higher than the difference between the percentages. As more ethnic minority families lived in overcrowded conditions than indigenous whites, more of the pregnant women among them were advised to have their babies in hospitals.

The 1966 census showed the following density of population in the London and West Midlands conurbations: under 0.6 person per room for the indigenous population; over one person per room for coloured settlers.[10] The overcrowding was not due to the newcomers' own choice. It was, as shown in previous chapters, the end result of racial discrimination in both housing and jobs. However, many whites seemed to feel that blacks were inclined by nature to live in overcrowded and filthy conditions. Such remarks as 'They live like pigs', 'They live twenty-four to a room', and 'They sleep in shifts' implied that 'they' wished to live like that. What was once true of a section of the racial minority community had become the perceived truth about the whole of it.

But as the newcomers saved, bought houses and spread out, many whites started complaining in a different vein: 'They're taking over our streets'; 'One fine morning you wake up to find yourself living in Little Jamaica or Little Punjab'. This feeling was compounded by the growing presence of black and brown faces in streets, pubs and other public places. 'You go into the parks and you'll see that many [white] turbans it looks like a field of lilies,' said a white foundry worker in Wolverhampton.[11]

How prevalent this feeling of being 'swamped' by blacks was among whites was borne out by the IRR survey in 1966–7. At that time racist feeling in the country was generally quiescent and the prospect of a 'flood' of Kenya Asians was nowhere on the horizon. Yet, of those who guessed the number of coloured immigrants in Britain, nearly two-thirds overestimated it by a factor of three to seven-plus.[12]

Ours is a 'small and overcrowded island' was another remark which was repeated endlessly by many, including the national government.[13] Yet, in spite of this *general* overcrowding, the housing space per head in the country had increased steadily as living standards rose after the Second World War. Also, over the past generations more people had left Britain to settle abroad than had entered. So the immigrants could not have caused the housing shortage that had existed before the war and which still persisted in certain parts of Britain.

It is noteworthy that demands for control of immigration did not include incomers from white countries or continents such as Ireland, Europe and North America. Aversion towards immigrants manifested itself only when they were black or brown. For historical reasons, dark pigmentation had become associated in most white people's minds with such negative attributes as dirt, poverty, inferior social status, low intelligence, animal sexuality, primitiveness and violence.

Of these associations that of dark skin with dirt seemed to be strongest. In Victorian times soap manufacturers often advertised their product by showing a black boy turning white after he had used their soap. That such an idea persisted a century later was underlined by a statement made by George Hall, the middle-aged secretary of the North Wolverhampton Men's Club in 1968. 'My generation was always taught that black was dirty and white was clean,' he said.[14] Referring to a Somali worker, a white foreman told a (white) researcher, 'He [the Somali] *knows* he's coloured. You can say to him: "Why don't you come in early one morning and we'll take a scrubbing brush and see if it will come off." '[15] Black and Asian pupils in schools are often jeered by white classmates with 'You dirty wog [i.e. westernized oriental gentleman]' and 'Go, wash yourself'.

Almost always it was the dirty, unkempt multi-occupancy house, where racial minority lodgers or families resided, that was considered typical of 'them' rather than the well-kept, brightly painted house, owned and occupied by a single black or Asian family. A similar bias was shown by most whites in assigning social class to the ethnic settlers. The coloured manual worker or bus conductor was widely considered typical of his community.

Despite the growth of Asian businesses in their areas of settlement, and the impressive presence of ethnic minority doctors and nurses in hospitals, only 8 per cent of the whites, living within half an hour's walking distance of racial minority people, thought that coloured settlers could be middle class or skilled working class.[16] Many whites were prone to think of blacks as belonging to a sub-class, much below the white manual working class. On the eve of his marriage to a West Indian ticket collector, a cockney labourer was asked by a close friend: 'Fred, aren't you marrying beneath yourself?' No wonder whites resented the blacks or Asians displaying signs of material prosperity and upward social mobility. This feeling was often complemented by a tendency to attribute the material well-being of a West Indian or Asian to such illegal and criminal activities as 'drink rackets', 'gambling in the parks', 'drugs rackets', 'having white prostitutes on the game' and 'income tax dodging'.

A white coalman in Wolverhampton was incensed by the fact that coloured people were 'even opening their own pubs ... even buying up businesses'.[17] The sight of a black man as a publican or businessman clashed with the post-slavery image of him as, at best, a crooner, boxer or sportsman, complemented by the contemporary image of a bus conductor, mill worker or foundryman. None of these roles implied business acumen, or high intelligence, or ingenuity.

Most whites considered blacks and Asians less intelligent than themselves. A survey of white Brummies by John Darragh, a white researcher, in 1956 showed that 64 per cent of the respondents thought coloured people intrinsically less intelligent than whites, with only 17 per cent regarding them as equal.[18] The overall white view was aptly summed up by the following remark by the technical controller of 'Bradfield Foundry': 'The attitude [of the management] used to be: "You can't train them because they are Indians". I feel that they should be treated as intelligent children."[19] A national survey by the Institute of Race Relations in 1966 confirmed the results of Darragh's local enquiry of a decade earlier. Of those interviewed, 63 per cent considered the British superior to the Africans or Asians, with only 19 per cent placing the British on a par with them.[20]

The notion of the general inferiority and low intelligence of non-white races went hand in hand with a belief in their excessive sexuality and propensity to violence. That the negro male was more virile, and that his penis was larger than the white's, was probably the most prevalent notion among Europeans. The roots of this idea could be traced back to the times of slavery in the Western world.

In 1799, at the zenith of the slave trade and slavery, Charles White, a surgeon in Manchester, claimed that the fact that the genitalia of negro males were larger than those of whites had been demonstrated in every anatomical school in London.[21] This could hardly have been the case because four years earlier J. F. Blumenbach, a physical anthropologist, had stated that 'I have shown ... on the weightiest testimony that this assertion [of the larger penis of the negro] is incorrect.'[22] None the less, the notion persisted, and was reinforced by inductive logic. White planters and their assistants in the New World often indulged in sexual exploitation of slave women. Compared to their own generally guilt-ridden, inhibited women, they found negro women sexually uninhibited and exciting. Experiencing greater sexual pleasure with negro women, white men came to regard negroes – female and male – as sexually more virile than Europeans. Hence the undying image of male negro virility and the large penis.

At a subconscious level, excessive sexuality was associated with primitiveness. The primitiveness and violence of life in Africa was exaggerated and constantly reiterated by British merchants, planters and politicians in order to justify the slave trade and slavery. Later, as the British began conquering lands in Asia and Africa, they tended to downgrade the civilized and cultured aspects of the conquered people. In the battles between the intruding British and the local rulers, it was always the inhuman behaviour of the 'natives' which was emphasized. It was important to make the public in Britain feel that the 'natives' were indeed savage, uncivilized and undisciplined, and needed to be subdued, civilized and enlightened by the nation to whom Destiny had assigned this onerous, yet morally satisfying, task. There was little doubt that this strategy was successful, and that it left deep marks on the psyche of most Britons. 'We were taught about the Black Hole of Calcutta, the Zulu War and all the atrocities perpetrated by the coloured people,' said George Hall in Wolverhampton in 1968. 'That was what our education was about.'[23]

None of these atrocities could match, singly or jointly, the cruelty of transporting 24 million Africans in overcrowded, rancid ships ('floating coffins' as James Pope-Hennessy called them in his book *Sins of the Fathers*) to the New World, and 'losing' nine million in transit. Yet it is extremely difficult for many Europeans today to realize that the image of whites in the black person's mind was associated with chains, whips, branding irons, fetters, thumbscrews and mouth-openers, and with castration, mutilation and the gallows; or that white people can still strike fear among the blacks living in Britain and America. Describing his visits to black homes in the London of the 1960s, Clifford S. Hill wrote: 'The writer has more than once had the somewhat mortifying experience of calling at a house occupied by coloured people and having had the door opened by a small child who had immediately turned and run screaming back down the passageway shouting at the top of his voice, "Mummy! It's a white man".'[24]

A study of the history of Africans in the Western world establishes them as a people with a remarkable degree of forbearance and a capacity to suffer silently. 'The negro has loved even under severest punishment,' stated Marcus Garvey. 'In slavery the negro loved his master, he safe-guarded his home even when he [the master] planned to enslave him.'[25] Many blacks still showed this trait. 'I'd much rather suffer than protest,' said a much respected Afro-Caribbean leader in Luton in 1969.

It was as important to discuss fundamental attitudes and psychological undercurrents as it was to debate whether or not coloured immigrants drew more out of the social services funds than they deposited into them. There was a deplorable absence of discussion in basic concepts in race relations in the country. Most of the debate in the mass media, and even in serious journals, remained entangled in details, ignoring altogether the broader, more fundamental issues. 'We [British] have taken up the problem [of race relations] as it has appeared subjectively defined in our recent history,' noted Professor John Rex, 'or we have undertaken micro-sociological studies in abstraction from the real historical world.'[26]

The best explanation probably lay with the nature of British society, which is essentially reformist and pragmatic. The conscious or sub-conscious adoption of a reformist approach by the establishment since the 'Glorious Revolution' of 1688 has enabled it to contain the periodic pressures exerted by exploited or disaffected groups, thus successfully aborting the possibility of a violent, radical restructuring of society. This approach has thus become an integral part of the British way of life. Therefore, almost always, the stress has been on defining the symptoms of socio-political problems and gradually reforming the system to redress particular grievances, rather than on undertaking a thorough investigation of basic causes which might suggest a radical reordering of the social system. This trait is common to many liberal democracies; but given the unbroken continuity of the British political system for three centuries it is probably more deeply embedded into Britain than elsewhere. Another allied feature of contemporary British society is the strong grip middle-class values have over practically every facet of life – from accent to education to Parliament. Debate and research on race relations, too, came to be dominated by such values.

Though a numerical minority, the middle class is over-represented in the seats of power and persuasion – in Parliament, the Civil Service, the media and the universities. A study made in the late 1950s revealed that whereas 75 per cent of the population was working class,[27] less than 10 per cent of the students at Oxford and Cambridge – then providing nearly a quarter of all university graduates annually – had working-class backgrounds. Also, nearly 40 per cent of all MPs had Oxbridge degrees, a figure which remained intact into the late 1960s. In the parliament of 1970, only 61 of the 630 MPs were 'mineworkers, engineers, railwaymen and other manual workers'; the vast majority were 'barristers and solicitors (115), company directors (110), teachers and lecturers (65), journalists (60), landowners (42), managers and administrators (41), businessmen (36) and other professionals'.[28]

Even the trade union movement, a citadel of the working class, had not remained immune from middle-class influences. The upper ranks of the movement tended to manifest middle-class mannerisms, styles and attitudes. Almost invariably, the attachment to middle-class values among the leaders of British institutions (no matter what the economic and class profile of the institution's members) was related directly to the level of leadership: the higher the rank the greater the obeisance to middle-class mores. This explained the divergence that existed on race relations between MPs and local councillors, national and local trade union officials, and the editors of the national quality press and the provincial and local papers.

A central characteristic of the British middle class was its preference for gentility, moderation, pragmatism, liberalism, subtlety and intellectualism over passion, radicalism, dogmatism, forthrightness and emotionalism. In short, the middle class aspired to remain 'civilized' to the point of blandness. Against this background, it was understandable why many

MPs, senior civil servants, academics and journalists were averse to saying 'coloured immigrants', 'coloured' or 'black' instead of 'immigrants', 'Commonwealth immigrants' or simply 'newcomers'. In the early 1970s the Community Relations Commission was probably the most glaring example of this obliqueness. It kept repeating old clichés – 'host society', 'newcomers' – even producing new terms: 'ethnic groups', 'community relations', 'human relations' and so on. It used all kinds of phrases and terms, except 'colour' or 'race' – the very issues which had led to its creation in the first place.

Sometimes this evasiveness drove such moderate bodies as the Wolverhampton Association of Schoolmasters to blurt out in despair: 'Instead of talking about this problem as if it were something indecent (the kind of thing that must not be mentioned on a Department of Education and Science course where only "nice, middle class people" are present) – present it to the profession and the nation as the major challenge of the 1970s.'[29] Leaving aside the nation, the teachers in Wolverhampton could hardly have managed to get their point across to the local mayor. In mid-July 1968, after the city had witnessed three pro- and anti-Powell marches, which had been nationally reported, the mayor told the *Observer*: 'There isn't a colour problem [here] in the racial sense.'

The periodic appeals for frankness did not seem to weaken the middle-class belief that talking about a problem created one, or at least exacerbated it. Besides, in this case there was a painful realization among politicians that, unlike the death penalty or producing hydrogen bombs, there was no once-and-for-all solution to the problem; that race, like sex, was immutable; that the issue was highly inflammable; and that its implications extended beyond national boundaries. This view was also widely shared by what David Watt, the political editor of the *Financial Times*, called 'the political élite' consisting of 'political journalists, academics, and the listeners to the Third Programme [of BBC Radio]', which transcended conventional party labels.

In most situations this well-informed, vocal and articulate élite exerted a disproportionate pressure on the political leadership of the government, and more often than not had its way. This was so mainly because, as David Watt pointed out, 'the British electorate is extraordinarily passive', a conclusion based on an extensive survey conducted in the mid-1960s by David Butler and Donald Stokes, two British political scientists. Of those asked how much they felt the government paid attention to what people think, 72 per cent replied 'not much' or 'don't know'.

The passivity of British voters was blended with their almost total dependence on the government 'to drop everything into their mouths'; their feelings that 'the government is responsible for "good times" or "bad times" in general' and that 'the man in Whitehall knows best'; and a lack of confidence in their own judgement.

Under the circumstances it was not surprising that the liberal, well-educated élite made the running in such issues as licensing hours, hanging, abortion, homosexuality, divorce law, defence policies and so on. However, on coloured immigration and race it ran into popular opposition because the nature of the problem was different. The issue of capital punishment, for instance, did not directly affect an overwhelming majority of the population; nor did the fate of prospective unwed mothers, or the behaviour of homosexuals. But as residents in Britain's conurbations, hundreds of thousands of whites were already either working with or living next to blacks, or stood a chance of finding themselves in such a situation. In short, the racial issue intruded directly into the everyday experience of ordinary citizens. When this happened to a large enough segment of white British society, many voters lost their usual passivity, became restive and exposed what William Deedes, a Conservative journalist, called, 'the most damaging division ... between government and governed'.[30] And, in successive moves, they compelled the liberal political élite to retreat.

However virulent and assertive, the popular response was a reaction against the prevailing situation rather than a positive action. Though the expression of popular feelings effected changes in certain official policies, it did not alter the basic nature of British society, with its reasonably well-defined (and generally accepted) division of labour. Nor did, or could, it change the basic structure of the government, Civil Service, trade unions, the media and the universities. Because of their very nature, the day-to-day administration of these institutions remained, and would remain, in the hands of a small minority. Whatever doubts arose in the minds of this liberal minority – as a result of a spate of illiberal events in race relations and coloured immigration – soon disappeared as old, embedded values reasserted their hold.

Unsurprisingly, the periodic public protest on the interlinked issues of race and immigration was almost always accompanied by an outcry that there had been a conspiracy to exclude the voice of 'the decent, ordinary Englishman', and that there had been a 'conspiracy of silence' among politicians. There was of course no conspiracy in the formal sense of the word, but there certainly was a common inclination, shared by most of the upper- and middle-level leaders of the British institutions, towards keeping Britain 'civilized' in racial matters. In practice, it meant barring subtly, or whittling down to the absolute minimum, the airing of racist views on most of the respectable public forums; or giving them no, or as little as possible, publicity in the media. Until Enoch Powell's April 1968 speech these views and practices were dominant.

In March 1968 the author was told by a television current affairs producer in a private conversation that as a policy they used stories on race 'to the minimum' and tried to 'play them down'. That this had been the case for years was disclosed publicly by Jeremy Isaacs, once the producer of BBC Television's *Panorama* current affairs series, and later the controller of features programmes for Thames Television. 'Television current affairs deliberately underplayed the strength of racist feelings for years, out of the misguided but honourable feelings that inflammatory utterances could only do damage,' Isaacs said to the *Guardian* on 13 November 1968. 'But the way feelings erupted after Enoch Powell's speech this year was evidence to me that [racist] feeling has been under-represented on television, and other media.' Three days later, in another public speech, Powell referred to 'a tiny minority, with almost a monopoly hold upon the channels of communication, who seem not to know the facts and not to face the realities and who will resort to any device or extremity to bind both themselves and others'.

A similar situation prevailed in the press. Following a huge demonstration in London against the American involvement in Vietnam's civil war in March 1968, the *Daily Mirror*, then the country's largest-circulation newspaper, invited its readers to send in letters on *any* subject they pleased. Of the nearly 5000 letters that the paper received, more than two-thirds concerned black and Asian immigrants, and were generally critical of them. Honesty demanded that the published letters reflected this proportion. In the event only one out of ten printed letters concerned coloured immigrants.

When in the autumn of 1967 the *Observer* published an article accurately describing the feelings of black youths in London, it was criticized by its liberal readers for 'worsening race relations'. Colin McGlashan, its author, was shaken by the experience. The following July the same paper published two long, painstakingly researched articles – produced by two of its correspondents after a stay of four weeks in Wolverhampton – describing the true feelings and attitudes of the city's white and black residents. The inter-racial ill-will and animosity was laid bare. This upset the liberal lobby which urged the editor to balance these articles by covering a Midlands city with good race relations: Nottingham. This was done four months later, with the same two correspondents – John Heilpern and myself – taking up residence in the city. The claim of good race relations in Nottingham, although carefully cultivated over the years, was found to be hollow. The only difference between Wolverhampton and Nottingham was that in the latter case there was less verbal hostility towards blacks and Asians; the rest was almost identical.

Subservience to the liberal, middle-class value of 'not doing anything that might harm race relations' led to some curious situations. Though two-thirds of Britons felt that blacks and Asians drew more out of the welfare services than they contributed, very few of their elected representatives said so – and that too only at local level, not national.

This was also the case with trade unions. Though the subject continued to agitate the average trade unionist, there had been practically no expression of anxiety from national platforms. The only exception was the statement by Sir William Carron, president of the Amalgamated Engineers' Union, at the union's annual conference in 1967 that it would be 'interesting to have detailed figures of the grand total consumed in education grants, National Health Service expenses and subsistence payments to the ever-growing number of individuals who are not born in this country and who have in no way contributed towards the setting up of the fund into which they so willingly dip their fingers'.[31] The Trades Union Congress had shied away from holding a fully-fledged discussion on race and coloured immigration. That did not mean there was no concern or anxiety at the grass-roots level. There was. 'Every year the head office gets a lot of resolutions for the union's annual conference from branches all over the country which are strongly colour prejudiced,' said an (unnamed) ex-official of the Transport and General Workers Union in late April 1968. '[But] the senior officers ... see to it that none of them comes up for debate.'[32] Even though this former union official was sufficiently affected by the events that followed Enoch Powell's 20 April 1968 speech to make this revelation, he still did not wish to identify himself publicly. This was all the more striking because he was no longer on the union's payroll.

For the mass of British people, however, the situation was much simpler. Powell's speech and the tremendous popular support it received lifted, temporarily at least, the inhibition they had felt that it was morally wrong to be racially prejudiced. Indeed, more than moral inhibition was involved, as Powell's Birmingham speech showed. 'What surprised and alarmed me was the high proportion of ordinary, decent, sensible people, writing a rational and often well-educated letter, who believed that they had to omit their address because it was dangerous to have committed themselves to paper to a Member of Parliament agreeing with the views I had expressed (in Walsall in February 1968), and that they would risk either penalties or reprisals if they were known to have done so,' he said.

If, as a result of Powell's speech, white Britons lost their inhibition and fear, and spoke their mind freely, even if emotionally and inarticulately, he helped inject realism into race relations. He assisted in removing the mask of hypocrisy and revealing feelings as they actually existed. 'These prejudices must have been there before,' stated David Ennals, junior minister at the Home Office. 'He [Powell] took the lid off and we have seen what came out.'[33] To that extent he did British society a service. Knowledge of social facts 'as are' is crucially important if lasting solutions are to be conceived and applied.

'It is the popular beliefs, and they alone, which enter directly into the causal mechanism of inter-racial relations,' wrote Gunnar Myrdal, the author of *An American Dilemma*, a monumental study of race relations in America. 'The scientific facts of race and racial characteristics ... are only of secondary and indirect importance ... They are only virtual but not actual facts.'[34] Therefore the importance and discussion of popular beliefs and attitudes can scarcely be overstressed.

Powell's dramatic entry into the race relations field bewildered the liberal lobby and threw it into disarray. But its discomfiture proved temporary. It quickly recovered from the initial shock, and remained committed, as before, to creating a racially integrated society in Britain.

It wanted to see the generally sympathetic mass media assist in this direction by (a) reporting more often, and at length, racially harmonious events or non-events; and (b) by educating the 'unthinking masses'.

Before discussing (a) one must examine the general make-up of the news sections of the papers, and of newscasts on radio and television. Leaving aside the standard reporting of parliamentary proceedings, the national conferences of political parties and trade unions, the statements of prominent political and other figures, and the paraphrasing of important socio-political documents and surveys, the news sections consist of reports of natural disasters, accidents, scoops, rackets, scandals, violent or bizarre acts, dramatic political or economic changes, and present or potential human conflicts such as strikes, lock-outs, marches, demonstrations, hijackings, assassinations, ambushes and battles. This is particularly true of television. As Lord Aylesbury of the Independent Television Authority pointed out, 'Television is essentially a reporting and dramatic medium: both subjects are about the unusual.'[35] The old cliché that 'Dog bites man is not news, but man bites dog is' is even more valid for television than for newspapers. The axiom is: conflict makes news, harmony does not. Yet the liberal lobby advocates that in the case of race relations *in Britain* this general criterion be downgraded, and that such dull events as the appearance of a national politician at an elaborately arranged inter-racial nursery, for instance, be dressed up as an item of news. Its efforts have sometimes yielded results.

Some television reporters and producers went out of their way to manipulate situations to show that happily integrated communities existed in the country. Often they got away with it, but sometimes their tactics proved too crude to go unnoticed. This happened, for instance, in Southall in early 1969. 'The [BBC Television] programme – prematurely entitled *Friendly Relations* – was planned to show how the Indian community in Southall had integrated, with the white people shopping and talking in Indian shops,' reported the *Sunday Telegraph* of 2 February 1969. 'They chose a jeweller's and a confectionery shop ... When no white people appeared they went out in the street to try to persuade people to come and make out they were shopping. So few would cooperate that they were forced to call off the production.' A white official of the Southall Residents' Association commented: 'The two communities, Indian and white, do not integrate well.'

In print journalism, a distinction must be made between quality national papers and mass-circulation tabloids which, with the exception of the *Daily Mirror*, were right-wing. Like municipal councillors the tabloids reflected the racial bias of their readers, drawn overwhelmingly from the C2, D and E socio-economic groups, and were quite content to reinforce the prejudices of their readers with their reports and editorials. They had no moral or professional qualms about distorting and dramatizing stories which involved race. This was equally true of their handling of such leftist Labour leaders as Tony Benn and Ken Livingstone (nicknamed 'Red Ken'). And they had a field day when a black Labour politician, who happened to be left-wing, came into the limelight. One such public figure was Councillor Bernie Grant of north London. He was crucified for his statement that the police got 'a bloody good hiding' in the 1985 Broadwater Farm estate rioting, and nicknamed 'Barmy Bernie' (see Part I, Chapter Nine).

In the early and mid-1970s the tabloid press was in the forefront in associating mugging with young blacks, working hand in glove with Scotland Yard to foster this image. Its sympathies were openly and uncritically with the police, giving little quarter to the shunned minority.

It was a London tabloid which in 1976 sensationalized the temporary housing of a few Asian families from Malawi in a luxury hotel, and harmed race relations. Ten years later the popular press found an appetizing quarry in the decision of the Brent borough council to appoint an extra 177 teachers to rectify the situation which caused underachievement among ethnic minority pupils. It routinely described these teachers as 'race advisers' intent on 'spying' on their colleagues, and indoctrinating children with left-wing ideas. It labelled them as 'commissars' and 'thought police'. All that had really happened was that Brent, containing the highest proportion of ethnic residents in the country, had decided to improve the poor academic performance of its pupils by appointing extra teachers. The gross misrepresentation of this fact by the tabloids did disservice to harmonious race relations.

Then there was the suggestion, popular with the liberal lobby, that the media should educate the masses, and counter myths with facts and figures. An example of this would be contradicting the popular belief in the low intelligence of West Indians and Asians by highlighting the results of the Inner London Education Authority's study of Tulse Hill boys' school in 1966, involving 294 immigrant children, mostly coloured. Proportionately fewer managed the top stream (in the first year, only 21 per cent against 35 per cent for all the boys). But when only those immigrant children who had received their full education in Britain were considered, their proportion in the top stream rose to 50 per cent.[36]

But it was doubtful if presentation and re-presentation of such facts succeeded in dispelling white prejudice. 'You can go blue in the face pouring out statistics,' said a white employee of a community relations council in a West Midlands city, 'but the average white person is not convinced. I've tried. It's a waste of time.' Such a statement dovetailed with detailed studies done by academics and researchers. One such study conducted by James Halloran, a specialist on mass communications, and his colleagues in 1973 led them to conclude that television and other news media serve to reinforce already formed opinions in so far as the readers/viewers remember more readily those news items or feature articles/programmes whose content coincides with their views.[37] 'There is a tendency for the reader, listener or viewer to interpret "race related" ideas in ways that are congruent with an already existing point of view,' wrote Professor Gajendra Verma, a British academic. 'Where there is conflict, ideas that do not support existing points of view are likely to be similarly ignored or suppressed.'[38]

Given this, it was questionable that a strictly statistical approach would work even with most white teachers in multiracial schools. 'Teachers themselves may reflect some of the attitudes and beliefs found in the wide society,' noted Professor Alan Little in 1978. 'The fact is that many teachers have lower expectations of black children than white children. An interesting study was done by the National Foundation for Educational Research asking a group of teachers how they respond to certain questions about children from different backgrounds. The teachers as a group saw West Indian children as being "stupid" and "trouble makers" – very clear negative stereotypes.'[39] Earlier, an anonymous white teacher in London, writing in *New Society*, summarized the attitudes of his colleagues thus: 'The "coloured boys" are often seriously ... held responsible for the falling standards of the school. I tackled this view once in a heated

staff-room argument, but it was earnestly defended. There is a frighten-
ing *emotional* logic about race prejudice, utterly irrational, and set
inexorably deep.'[40] Here, then, was the key explanation underlying the
problem: it is emotional.

More specifically, it is visual: black or brown faces in a white society
stand out. As such, only an armchair intellectual could seriously believe
that he could contain the whites' anxiety of being taken over by the blacks
in, say, Walsall, Gravesend or Luton by telling them that nationally blacks
formed only four or five per cent of the population.

One was therefore driven to conclude that, whatever the merit of
cataloguing facts and figures in the *Guardian, Independent* or *The Times,*
Parliament or university debating halls, the tactic was not proving
effective in bringing about an emotional conversion of the white masses.
If so, then the liberal opinion-formers might as well shift their ground to
an emotional level, to the plank of Christian charity, love and compassion. Understandably, this had all along been the approach of church
leaders. But since the hold of the Church was minimal the net effect on
the bulk of the population had been negligible.

It was perhaps best, then, to discard overt sermonizing, and instead
resort to the technique of projecting simple, stark images – as is the
practice of professional advertisers for such charity organizations as
Oxfam and War on Want – to arouse sympathy and compassion among
white viewers. However, when the projected image was that of a member
of a racial 'out' group, it created a dualistic situation, engendering
sympathy among the well-off liberal minority while reinforcing the
unfavourable view that the illiberal majority held about the 'out' group.
Experiments in America and Britain had established that when exposed
to certain images, viewers remembered only those that supported their
previous convictions and beliefs.

Show a snapshot of a group of Asians playing cards in a park in
Coventry or Birmingham, and the white, liberal Briton would probably
admire the Asians for their sense of community while the illiberal would
most likely see 'wogs gambling in a park'. Show black slums in Britain or
America; and you would have the well-heeled white liberals muttering
'These poor, poor people', and the illiberals cursing the blacks for
'degrading our towns and cities'.

Besides the carefully arranged juxtaposition of pictures in the form of
television documentaries, there is a steady stream of random images
meant to convey news of events in Africa and Asia. Like all news in the
Western media, these images are centred around conflicts, tensions,
political upheavals, wars, famines and other natural disasters. Violent
anarchy in the Congo/Zaïre, the raping of white nuns by African soldiers,

civil war in Nigeria, genocide in Cambodia, brutal military repression in Burma, starvation in Ethiopia, an army coup in Pakistan, an Islamic revolution in Iran, vicious internecine conflict in Lebanon, brutal fighting between Iran and Iraq: the list is endless. And it will continue to be so for the simple statistical reason that Asia and Africa account for two-thirds of the global population.

The liberal-left minority may view these convulsions as an essential part of the social and economic development of these continents recently freed from the yoke of European imperialism. But, for the many, these images provide continuing evidence that peoples of black, brown and yellow races are indeed inherently anarchic, violent and quite incapable of self-help and self-rule. The civil wars in the Congo/Zaïre, Nigeria and Ethiopia shook the liberal beliefs of a substantial segment of the British intelligentsia, who seemed to forget that, historically, large, polyglot countries such as the Soviet Union and America have emerged as united nations only after undergoing bloody civil wars. But then, as Patrick Anderson, a British literary critic, pointed out, 'For most of us [British] the historical perspective is not acute, the sense of the past in the present even less vivid.'[41]

No wonder then that in the field of formal education – which is expected to produce citizens for a harmonious multiracial society – little attention had been paid to the innate and overt racialist bias of textbooks until the mid-1970s.

As early as 1963, this point of fundamental significance was raised by Sheila Patterson in *Dark Strangers*,[42] and again by a study group of the London Council of Social Service. 'Some readers, text-books and curricula still reflect an insular, culturally exclusive attitude, the colour–class myths of a colonial past and occasionally the nineteenth century pseudo-scientific racialism that helped to justify this past,' the group's report stated. 'Subjects of particular sensitivity in this respect are history, geography, English literature, biology and scripture.'[43]

The following examples from a history book in British schools illustrated the racist bias of many textbooks. In the chapter called 'The British in India and America' of *Histories, Book IV*, the authors write 600 words on Indian history from ancient times to AD 1600, when 'the famous' East India Company appeared on the scene. The period 1600–1763 takes up 1500 words. Of these, nearly 250 words are expended on the Black Hole of Calcutta:

> [Robert] Clive had *still more* to do *for* India. In 1756 Suraja Dowlah, the Nabob ... a *violent* youth of nineteen ... marched against Calcutta at the head of *30,000* men. The European residents with fruitless

heroism tried to defend Calcutta; but after three days they were *forced to surrender* ... A mixed company of men, women, and *children*, 146 in number, were driven into a narrow prison-cell of the fort, about 18 by 15 feet, with only two *small barred* windows to admit the air. Huddled together, and scarcely able to breathe, they had to endure the *intense heat* of a June night, from seven until six in the morning. Mad with *agony*, they *struggled* with one another ... At length the morning broke and the Nabob allowed the survivors to come forth. But there were only 23 of them, and it took some time to clear a passage through the *heaps of dead bodies* which barred the way.[44]

One might argue on a purely technical basis that it is impossible to pack 146 men, women and children into that limited space, or on historical grounds that the person responsible for whatever happened on that evening in 1756 was a *French* subaltern of the Nabob. But that is not really the point. The main question is: how important is this episode to the historical process of the founding of the British Empire in India? Not at all.

On the other hand there is no mention at all in the book of a most significant event which is widely recognized as marking the beginning of the end of the British rule in India: Brigadier-General R. E. H. Dyer's massacre in 1919 of unarmed Indians in a park in Amritsar – 379 killed and 1200 wounded. Nor is there any indication in the textbook that during the seventeenth and eighteenth centuries Britain was heavily engaged in the slave trade and slavery. The first mention of the slave trade, which occurs towards the end of the book, opens with the statement: 'Soon after the beginning of the nineteenth century the Slave Trade was abolished.'[45] This is all the more ironic because the textile industry, which marked the onset of the Industrial Revolution in Britain, was entirely dependent on the production of cotton by slave labour in the New World colonies, a point made by, among others, Karl Marx, in the nineteenth century. 'Without slavery, you have no cotton; without cotton, you have no modern industry,' he wrote in *The Poverty of Philosophy*. 'It is slavery that has given the colonies their value; it is the colonies that have created world trade; and it is the world trade that is the precondition of large scale industry.'[46]

In modern times a similar point was made by, of all politicians, Sir Winston Churchill, a Conservative who believed absolutely in the retention of the British Empire. 'The West Indies, two hundred years ago, bulked largely in the minds of all people who were making Britain and making the British Empire,' he said in an address to West Indian sugar barons just before the Second World War. 'Our possessions of the West

Indies, like that of India – the colonial plantation and development, as they were then called – gave us the strength, the support, but specially the capital, the wealth, at a time when no other European nation possessed such a reserve, which enabled us to come through the great struggle of the Napoleonic Wars, the keen competition of the commerce of the eighteenth and nineteenth centuries, and enabled us not only to acquire this world-wide appendage of possessions we have, but also to lay the foundations of that commercial and financial leadership which, when the world was young, when everything outside Europe was underdeveloped, enabled us to make our great position in the world.'[47]

Compared to those who feel that 'Britain did a lot for the "natives" ', how many feel that the 'natives' did a lot, economically, for Britain, as explained by Churchill and Marx? Very few. Yet it is vitally important that the British acknowledge the debt they owe to their former colonies and that the authors of textbooks on British history state it. Appeals for British fair-mindedness ought to be accompanied by the acknowledgement that the ancestors of present-day black and Asian immigrants played a vital role in creating the affluence that the British are enjoying today. Future generations ought to be brought up on a balanced, not grotesquely partisan, account of British history.

This began to happen on a modest scale from the late 1970s onwards, thanks largely to the earlier efforts of such organizations as the Afro-Caribbean Educational Resource Project, Teachers Against Racism and the National Association for Multi-Racial Education to correct the racist and imperialist bias in textbooks on history and social sciences.

At about the same time the political conscience of the militantly anti-racist, leftist whites had been moved sufficiently – as a result of the rise of racist, neo-fascist parties like the National Front – to goad them into forming an umbrella organization: the Anti-Nazi League. Its informal structure combined with an imaginative propaganda blitz, including sponsoring rock band performances, captured popular attention among young whites. The Grunwick strike of 1977–8 by Asian workers against a proprietor who was part-Asian helped to dilute the historical animosity of the white working class against immigrant labour. These factors, combined with Margaret Thatcher's 'swamping' statement in early 1978, helped to thwart the National Front's advance.

It was against this background that the Inner London Education Authority adopted the policy of multi-ethnic education, although with no detailed plan or timetable to implement the new policy. Yet the decision was an important landmark in the educational history of the United Kingdom. After decades of mouthing the statement 'Britain is a multiracial society', the country's largest educational authority finally got round to incorporating multiracialism into the school curriculum.

As stated earlier, it was not until 1983 that the ILEA under the leadership of Frances Morrell opted for the anti-racist version of multi-ethnic education, and pursued it with resources and adequate support. This involved: (a) supplying literature on multi-ethnic education to all the 30,000 teachers; (b) requiring every school to announce its own anti-racist statement and code of practice and publish an annual report on both subjects; (c) specifying a timetable for results; and (d) appointing monitoring officers, and providing in-service training and new teaching materials to teachers.

This policy was still in force in 1990 when the ILEA was disbanded, with each of its seventeen constituent authorities assuming responsibility for education. By then two-thirds of local authorities in the country had adopted the policy of multi-ethnic education: a welcome development. However, the implementation of the Education Reform Act 1988, which among other things prescribes a national curriculum, entailed a probable swing back to a narrow, nationalist view of history.

Unfortunately, the leaders of other national institutions had failed to take such an enlightened stance. Principal among them were the police and criminal courts.

The role of the police was crucial. It impinged on the daily life of citizens, black or white. It personified the established order, and was both the symbol and substance of the authority of the state. As such, racist attitudes and behaviour in its ranks had wide repercussions. It was a disturbing fact that the force harboured an above-average rate of racists. Aware of this, and of the multiracial composition of British cities and towns, the authorities began introducing a study of race relations into police training courses from the early 1970s. They also tried to encourage visible minority members to join the force. Some progress was made in both areas; but it was, by any measure, quite inadequate.

A 1987 survey of the employment of ethnic minority members in the various police forces compared to their proportion in the population revealed the following facts: Metropolitan area, 1.2 per cent against 14.6 per cent; West Midlands, 2.1 per cent against 11 per cent; Leicestershire, 1.7 per cent against 8.5 per cent; West Yorkshire, 0.9 per cent against 5.9 per cent; and Greater Manchester, 1 per cent against 4 per cent. Nationally, 888 ethnic police officers were only 0.8 per cent of the force – or one-sixth of the share of the ethnic minorities in the total population.[48]

This failure stemmed from the perception widely held by the ethnic minorities that police officers were racist, all too ready to harass blacks and uninterested in acting on the complaints of visible minorities. Enrolment into such a force was seen as a betrayal of one's own race, and quite incomprehensible. This view was succinctly expressed by Anthony, a twenty-year-old black, thus: 'The black man who joins the police force must be one of them guys who fall[s] from outer space still believing there's such a thing as British justice and fair play.'[49]

Lord Gifford's report on Liverpool, published in July 1989, singled out the police for 'a wholly unacceptable level of racist language and behaviour'. An insight into the inner workings of the force was provided two months later when Police Constable Surinder Singh of Notting-hamshire constabulary claimed damages for victimization by denial of promotion to the Criminal Investigation Department on racial grounds. In his evidence Singh claimed that the terms 'coon', 'nigger' and 'darkie' were used frequently by fellow police officers. Four of the forty-six black and Asian policemen gave evidence of racial discrimination.[50]

Allied to the police were criminal courts, another institution shown to be discriminatory towards blacks. Concerned about the problem, the National Association of Probation Officers began monitoring the situation in 1985. It noticed an 'unacceptable' rise in the number of black defendants remanded in custody pending trial. Drawing on a dossier of recent case histories, the Association's report stated: 'A high number of black defendants face over-harsh charges, are remanded on charges which are later dropped or changed, or are diagnosed as mentally ill.' It recommended ethnic monitoring of the entire criminal justice system and anti-racism training for the personnel involved. 'Training in racism awareness is needed for lawyers, probation officers, police, judges and magistrates, many of whom associate racism with "extreme" behaviour, and fail to understand that they, too, can discriminate,' it concluded.[51]

Coming from a body of professional people inclined to conservatism, the above recommendation deserved urgent consideration. But would it get it? Not likely.

Along with numerous other well-researched documents, the report of the National Association of Probation Officers illustrated the sweep and depth of racist feelings and attitudes among the whites exercising power. It underlined a continuing need for racism awareness, in both formal and informal terms, with a view to combating this social ill.

A cursory glance at recent British history shows that neither bland postures nor naïve beliefs had solved the inter-racial problem. The initial policy of official colour-blindness had proved a disastrous failure. The hope that 'integrated' schooling would usher in a racially harmonious society, too, proved illusory. Nevertheless, many academic researchers and professional race workers still persisted in skirting reality by devising tortuous analyses and evaluations of the racial situation.

For instance, some liberal social scientists led by Dr Mark Abrams, conducting an attitude survey for the Institute of Race Relations in 1966–7 arrived – through an ingenious and highly subjective evaluation of answers to their questionnaire – at the heartening conclusion that only 10 per cent of white Britons were racially prejudiced while 73 per cent were tolerant or tolerantly-inclined.[52] These findings, announced in July 1969, were received warmly by the media. Flattered and relieved, they splashed the conclusions in bold headlines, conveniently forgetting that only two years earlier the PEP survey had produced evidence that there was much racial discrimination against black and brown citizens. (How was one to reconcile massive racial discrimination with a society where most white citizens were free of racial prejudice?) This was one more example of brushing aside the uncomfortable reality and exaggerating the comfortable analysis.

The IRR survey also stated that the youngest of the respondents, aged 21 to 34, were the least prejudiced. (Apparently, under-21s were not interviewed.) This implied that the future was hopeful. But contemporary evidence did not support this inference. A national poll of teenagers published in November 1967 established that 30 per cent of them wanted coloured immigrants to be sent home and 68 per cent were for restoring the death penalty.[53]

Another widely-held theory, that contact between youngsters breaks down stereotypes and negative images, had yet to be proved. The contrary seemed to be the case. Taysir Kawwa's study of ethnic attitudes among British adolescents revealed that children living in an area with a high percentage of immigrants showed more negative attitudes than children living in an area with a low percentage of immigrants.[54] Peter Figueroa summarized his 1969 study of English and West Indian school-leavers in north London, thus: 'On the whole the English school-leavers were against immigrants coming to live and work in Britain. The English boys also expressed negative attitudes concerning the children of immigrants born in this country. On the whole, the English had negative stereotypes of the West Indians, while the West Indians had partly positive and partly negative stereotypes of the English.'[55]

There was as yet another notion, widely prevalent, that young children were quite unconscious of colour or ethnic differences. Scientific evidence, however, ran counter to this idea. 'Many studies have shown,' stated Professor Henri Tajfel in 1965, 'that evaluation of groups other than their own exists at a very early age.'[56] Summarizing the conclusions of various studies conducted over a quarter of a century, a report by the

Commission for Racial Equality, entitled *From Cradle to School* and published in 1990, stated: 'Research has shown that, even by the age of three, children give different values to skin colours.'[57]

Sociometric tests applied to children of different ethnic groups in three London schools (a comprehensive in 1962, a secondary in 1964 and a primary in 1964) by Taysir Kawwa revealed a significant preference for one's own group in the choice of associates.[58] Keith Rowley made a study of 1747 children, aged 7 to 15, in ten junior and five secondary modern schools in the West Midlands. In this sample 65 per cent were white, 21 per cent Asian and the rest West Indian. Children were asked three questions: whom would you prefer to sit next to in class, to play with in the playground, and to invite home to tea or a party? He found that *at all ages* they preferred their own ethnic group, some more than others – with 90 per cent of the white, 75 per cent of the Asian and 60 per cent of the West Indian children doing so.[59]

Gustav Jahoda, Thelma Veness and Ivan Pushkin studied 172 white children in three north London schools. In tests about social situations simulated through the use of dolls of different racial characteristics, 32 per cent of the children were consistently unfavourable to negro dolls. The disfavour increased with age. For three-year-olds, this figure was 22 per cent; and for six-year-olds, it was 65 per cent. In another test, 25 per cent chose very distant or distant houses for negro dolls. The choice patterns, and deliberations and spontaneous comments of many white children indicated an awareness of physical attributes and of the inferior social status of the negro.[60]

If living evidence to contradict the notion that contacts between children of different races broke down negative images was needed, one had only to turn to Liverpool, a city where blacks had settled after the First World War. The situation of extreme disadvantage to the racial minority first exposed in the late 1960s (see Chapter Five) persisted. The 1981 census of the Granby and Abercrombie wards of Toxteth – home to 70 per cent of the 30,000 black Liverpudlians – showed a 35 per cent joblessness rate, twice the city figure. When, in the aftermath of 1981 riots, the local council engaged 1400 people for landscaping, paving and house maintenance in Toxteth, only 1.8 per cent of them were black. That is, black Liverpudlians got only a quarter of the share which their numbers entitled them to.[61]

The first ever comprehensive enquiry into the city's race relations, commissioned by the town hall and led by Lord Gifford – published in July 1989 as *Loosen the Shackles* – revealed several disturbing facts. 'Nowhere in Britain are blacks so exposed to threats, taunts and abuse if they leave a certain area of the city,' concluded the report. 'Outright racial hostility to blacks exists to an extent not acceptable anywhere else in the country. Black people are denied access to jobs, even low paid ones, more systematically and comprehensively than in any other major city of black settlement.' Finally, Liverpool City Council had failed to promote lasting equal opportunities in its workforce.[62]

Liverpool's example illustrated that unless there was steady, untiring effort by public bodies and voluntary organizations to highlight the disadvantages suffered by black citizens, and attempts made to improve their lot, racial inequality would persist. There was thus no room for complacency.

Furthermore, equality between different ethnic groups needed to be defined concretely, taking into account not just race but also culture. This was all the more urgent because nearly three-quarters of the visible minority population, being of non-Caribbean South Asian origins, differed from white Britons in such vital areas of life as religion, mother-tongue, dress and cuisine.

The Rushdie affair brought to the surface the deeply-rooted prejudice of the Christian West against Islam and Muslims. This manifested itself in the usual rise in violence against racial minorities, particularly Asians, perpetrated mainly by young white working-class males, stemming from the psychological challenge presented by the cultural visibility and distinctiveness of the South Asians.[63] But this time there was an extra dimension. Many among the white liberal middle class gave free vent to their animus against Islam and Muslims.

In her essay *Sacred Cows*, Fay Weldon, an eminent novelist, compared the Bible and the Quran thus:

> The Bible, in its entirety, is at least food for thought. The Koran is food for no-thought. It is not a poem on which a society can be safely or sensibly based. It forbids change, interpretation, self-knowledge or even art, for fear of treading on Allah's creative toes ... [The Koran] gives weapons and strength to the thought police – and the thought police are easily set marching, and they frighten ... They're burning *The Satanic Verses* as once witches were burned: to keep the world safe. A bit drastic, but we see their point. Their heart is in the right place – it's just they're a bit primitive. Well, Arabs. Pakis. Muslims. All the same ... Last throes of a daft religion.[64]

While these statements were penned by someone who had, at best, superficial knowledge or understanding of the Quran or Islam, or of Islamic history or culture, the same could not be said of Conor Cruise O'Brien, a widely travelled politician-diplomat-writer. As a long-time student of Middle East politics, he was better placed to assess Islam and Muslims. 'Muslim society looks profoundly repulsive,' he wrote in the course of a book review in *The Times*. 'A Westerner who claims to admire Muslim society, while still adhering to Western values, is either a hypocrite or an ignoramus or a bit of both. At the heart of the matter is the Muslim family, an abominable institution.' He concluded the review thus: 'Arab and Muslim society is sick, and has been sick for a long time. In the last century, the Arab thinker Jamal al-Afghani wrote: "Every Muslim is sick, and his only remedy is in the Koran." Unfortunately the sickness gets worse the more the remedy is taken.'[65]

Western intellectuals such as Weldon and O'Brien were showing the symptoms of besieged medieval Christendom. And this validated the statement by Shabbir Akhtar, a Bradford Muslim leader: 'After this [Rushdie] affair, Muslims have reason to think that the Crusades are not yet over' (see Part II, Chapter Ten).

7 The Future: Assimilation or Social Pluralism?

Success comes to those who are prepared to be self-reliant.

LORD SCARMAN, addressing a meeting sponsored
by Black Rights (UK & USA).[1]

*Britain should not be allowed to become a hall of mirrors, but should be a
family of minorities constantly fashioning a common culture: open enough
to enable them to grow at their own pace and firm enough to hold all
together.*

BHIKHU PAREKH[2]

*There is no reason why cultural diversity should not be combined with
loyalty to this country.*

PRIME MINISTER EDWARD HEATH in a letter to
Bexley Community Relations Council, June 1970.[3]

Anyone contemplating the future of race relations in Britain must come
to grips with the much-reiterated themes of 'English identity' and 'the
instinct to preserve English/British identity'. In recent times no one has
articulated these better than Enoch Powell. He complemented his
nationalist views with the statement that a West Indian or an Asian, by
being born in England, did not become an Englishman.[4]

How does the substantial presence of Afro-Asian-Caribbean people
threaten English identity? And what bars for ever the descendants of
Afro-Asian-Caribbeans from becoming Englishmen and Englishwomen?
Is it their racial stock or their cultural heritage, or both?

It cannot be their racial stock if we are to take seriously the protest-
ations of Powell at being called a 'racialist' – that is, 'someone expressing
either favourable or unfavourable bias [on racial grounds]'.[5] Then
probably it is their cultural background. In that case, why did Powell
bracket West Indians and Asians together? West Indians remain culturally nearer to the British than to their West African ancestors, which is
not true of Asians. Or perhaps Powell viewed the situation in terms of the
size and concentration of the racial minorities so that, for all practical
purposes, these shielded the Afro-Asian child from absorbing British
culture? After all, his plan for repatriation was not meant to remove

blacks and Asians altogether, merely to reduce their numbers. Once that had happened, he felt, then 'the pressures towards integration which normally bear upon any small minority' would operate more effectively and lead to the 'integration' of the remaining blacks and Asians into British society; that is, help them become 'for all practical purposes indistinguishable from its other members'.

But, then, had the smallness of the black communities in such places as Liverpool and Cardiff led to their integration into the local population and made them 'indistinguishable' from the rest? The answer is: no. Yet this historical evidence was apparently ignored not only by Powell but also by such liberal sociologists as Sheila Patterson. In 1963 she concluded her study of Brixton (where a substantial number of West Indians had settled during the 1950s) with an overly optimistic prediction. 'Over the next decades in Britain the West Indian migrants and their children will follow in the steps of the Irish; they will ... gradually ... fan out of the central areas of settlement,' she wrote. '[Their] adaptation and advancement will lead to closer relationships with the local population ... and to an at least partial biological absorption ... in the local population.'[6]

Let us consider the immigrant–host relationship without regard to colour or race. It is dynamic and can be summarized thus. Initial contact and competition (for jobs and housing) are followed by accommodation and acceptance in structured situations (of work and education) whilst the immigrant is undergoing the process of acculturation. His acculturation is rewarded correspondingly by social acceptance by the host community. In time, this leads to (biological and social) amalgamation whereby the immigrant loses his previous identity and is considered a fully-fledged member of the host society – that is, he is 'absorbed' by the receiving society. Many post-war Irish immigrants graduated from initial contact to an almost complete absorption within a generation.

However, as the previous chapters have made plain, whatever their degree of anglicization or length of stay in Britain, most of the West Indian and Asian immigrants, whether in Liverpool, Brixton or Southall, have not yet been rewarded with social acceptance by the receiving society. The picture is bleak even when one is considering mere acceptance. A Policy Studies Institute poll in 1982 showed that only 16 per cent of white respondents replied 'Definitely true' when responding to the statement, 'White people have now accepted people of West Indian origin', with the figure going down to 12 per cent in the case of Asians.[7] The primary reason for this is that they are racially different from the white British, the secondary reason being cultural differences.

The evidence adduced in this book (especially in terms of the historical and contemporary attitudes of white Britons) shows why, over the past two generations, the relationship between ethnic minorities and whites has not yet graduated beyond the stage of accommodation and qualified acceptance (in formalized situations). Such a relationship is termed by sociologists as 'social, or cultural, pluralism'.

Professor Michael Banton, a British race relations specialist, defines 'social pluralism' as a system whereby 'members of different minorities enjoy equality in respect of civil rights and obligations, but keep themselves separate in marriage and mutual hospitality, while rivalling one another in other contexts – such as in political organizations'.[8] Sheila Patterson defines 'cultural pluralism' as 'a stage in which the incoming group as a whole, through its own organizations, adapts itself to permanent membership of the receiving society in certain major spheres of association, notably in economic and civic life. On its side, the receiving society accepts the group as a lasting entity, differing in certain spheres that do not directly affect the overall life of the society, such as religion, and cultural and family patterns, and sometimes even in the retention of a mother-tongue or secondary loyalties to a country of origin.'[9] Cultural pluralism has of course existed in Britain, with regard to the Jewish minority, for the last four generations. It is worth reminding ourselves that many British Jews went off to fight for Israel, the country of their historic origin, during the 1967 Middle East conflict.

Apparently Sheila Patterson had not considered the possibility of such a relationship developing in the case of West Indian immigrants even though she was aware of the cultural differences between them and white Britons, and described them at some length in *Dark Strangers*.[10] Instead of accepting these differences and predicting that they could, or would, persist, albeit in an attenuated form, she wrote: 'If accommodation and ultimately assimilation are to be achieved, the West Indian migrants must face the fact that they have to make a thorough-going and sustained effort to adapt their behaviour and values in all spheres of life.'[11]

The schoolmasterly tone of this statement was a symptom of the egocentricity from which many British sociologists, as well as politicians, suffered. They considered British society to be stable, homogeneous and unitary, and felt strongly that all newcomers who had been allowed the 'privilege' of settling here must – regardless of how shabbily they were treated by the indigenous population – rapidly adjust and conform. Patterson's statement was also highly presumptive as Neville Maxwell, a West Indian leader, pointed out. 'No West Indian, unless he was dreaming, now goes around piously seeking to be "accepted" by the native people as *Dark Strangers* all along conveyed,' he wrote. 'One must disabuse oneself of this generally accepted fallacy [among the British].'[12]

There were quite a few 'generally accepted fallacies' current even in the highest academic, political and administrative circles. One of these was that in the past all immigrants to Britain had been assimilated. This was certainly not true of the (white) Jews who began to arrive in Britain in 1875 from Russia, and settled in small numbers (120,000 in all) over a period of 40 years.

A study of the Jewish community in Edgware, north London – considered typical of the Jewish minority in the United Kingdom – conducted by Dr Ernest Krausz, and published in 1969 (nearly a century after their first arrival in Britain), revealed the following facts: 80 per cent were affiliated to synagogues; 71 per cent of the Jews with one or more children under fifteen brought up their children 'fairly strictly' or 'very strictly' (in religious terms); 35 per cent belonged to a Jewish organization or club, and another 40 per cent had belonged in the past to a similar organization; whereas only 19 per cent belonged to a non-Jewish organization or club. Nearly two-thirds felt more 'at home' in a Jewish district than elsewhere; and the same proportion considered Edgware 'a predominantly Jewish' district (although it was only 40 per cent Jewish).[13]

Despite the fact that many Jews in Krausz's sample did not work for Jewish firms and thus came in contact daily with non-Jews, and had a liberal attitude towards social mixing with non-Jews, in reality there was very little social mixing between Jews and non-Jews. 'The results show unmistakably that Jews in Edgware are on friendly terms mostly with other Jews and that their close friendships are almost exclusively from within Jewish ranks,' stated Dr Krausz. Whatever social mixing occurred, it rarely led to intermarriage as only 29 per cent of the Jews did *not* have a strong objection to intermarriage with non-Jews. The important reason for this social distance between Jews and non-Jews, noted Krausz, was 'the difference between the cultural background of the two groups'.

If this is the case with an immigrant minority which is visually indistinguishable from the majority, and which first arrived in Britain in the 1870s, what chance is there for the 'assimilationist' dream of white liberals regarding Asians and West Indians, whose cultural differences are compounded by physical distinctiveness? To be fair, outside academic and specialist circles, the word 'assimilation' is rarely used. The magic word, popularized by the media, is 'integration'.

Its present currency is derived from its extensive use in reporting events in America (beginning in the mid-1950s) concerning school segregation in the southern states. In the American context, integration was used as an antonym for *de facto* or *de jure* segregation, meaning, more specifically, discontinuation of *de jure* segregation. In Britain, however, various meanings and interpretations have been attributed to the term.

'To integrate,' states Webster's *New Collegiate Dictionary*, is 'to form into a whole; to unite or become united to form a complete or perfect whole.' Quoting Fowler's *Modern English Usage*, Lord Elton wrote in *The Times*: 'To integrate is to combine components into a single congruous whole.'[14] However, Fowler adds that the public have now borrowed the verb from psychologists with such freedom that it has become a vogue word, habitually preferred to less stylish but more suitable words such as 'merge, fuse, consolidate'.

Then we had two leading politicians at opposing poles of the political spectrum offering their definitions of integration. 'To be integrated into a population means to become for all practical purposes indistinguishable from its other members,' stated Enoch Powell. If we accept this definition then we must interpret the use of bleaching creams and hair straighteners by the Afro-Caribbeans and the discarding of turbans by Sikhs as steps towards 'integration'. Clearly he was thinking of assimilation while he was talking of integration. According to Fowler's definition, however, these two words are not far apart. At the other end was Roy Jenkins. As Labour Home Secretary, he stated in May 1966: 'I define integration not as a flattening process of assimilation but as an equal opportunity, accompanied by cultural diversity, in an atmosphere of mutual tolerance.' This was a highly subjective definition, which had no relationship with either the common understanding of the term or its dictionary meaning.

Liberal intellectuals, following their Burkeian tradition, continually attempted to dispel 'common ignorance' and dispensed 'special wisdom' to whomsoever took heed. The Race Relations Board even incorporated Jenkins's very subjective definition into one of its annual reports.[15] The Community Relations Commission never tired of it. Every liberal speaker or spokesman or publication at one point or another quoted Jenkins's definition. Yet there were few takers.

Leaving aside the 'common people' – who in this age of sociological surveys and questionnaires have not yet been polled to find out what they think 'integration' means – let us concentrate on professional and semi-professional 'race workers', those who feel dedicated to creating a racially harmonious society in Britain. A study of the active members of local community relations councils by a sociologist, in 1969, revealed that only 10 per cent thought of integration in Jenkins's terms, whereas 25 per cent defined it in assimilationist terms. Most significantly, over 50 per cent could produce no definition of integration at all.[16] But why blame them? Even the drafters of the 1965 White Paper devoted exclusively to immigration from the Commonwealth, while entitling its Part III 'Integration', left the term undefined.

However, despite the lack of a precise definition or a plethora of subjective definitions and interpretations, a strong, sentimental attachment to the ideal of integration remains. It tends to be coupled with an almost instinctive presumption that whoever so much as questions the term is an automatic advocate of 'segregation' or 'separate development'. And the dreaded, emotive word 'segregation' brings with it an agglomeration of images associated with America and South Africa. No attempt is made even by otherwise well-informed people, such as journalists, to distinguish between the 'Separate and Unequal' concept as enforced by *law* in South Africa; the 'Separate but Equal' philosophy as widely practised by *custom* in present-day America; and the 'Separate and Equal' concept as practised, through *voluntary* separation by, say, the Asians in Bradford or the Jews in Edgware. The separate lifestyle maintained by the Jewish minority, for instance, is not, and need not be, underlined by rigid belief in the philosophy of racial inferiority/superiority. This tendency for voluntary separation may be regarded as transient, if only to soothe the British liberal conscience. However, to be realistic, the transient phase must be visualized in terms of decades, not years.

A realist will find it hard to share the trepidation of British liberals at having to lower their sights from 'assimilation' to 'integration' and then to what was called 'pluralistic integration' – in fact a euphemism for 'social pluralism', but the liberals' attachment to the word 'integration' dies hard. The simple fact remains that, with the arguable exception of post-revolutionary Cuba, nowhere else in the white Western world is there as yet a just, harmoniously assimilated, inter-racial society. The case of Brazil is often cited as the ideal. However, a close examination by sociologists has revealed a flawed society.

Roger Bastide, a social scientist who carried out research for the United Nations Educational, Scientific and Cultural Organization in Brazil, concluded that it was 'a country in which prejudice is based not on race but on colour, where discrimination varies in direct proportion to the blackness of the skin'. A Brazilian professor, Florestan Fernandes, showed that the historico-social transformations that had occurred since the 1800s had benefited only the white population. 'Legally, the caste system was abolished; in practice the negro and mulatto population did not rise above the social situation they had known earlier. Instead of entering *en masse* into the social classes that were in the process of formation and differentiation, they found themselves incorporated into the "plebs".' His researches in São Paulo – Brazil's most industrially developed city – demonstrated that the traditional social systems ensured that 'white supremacy and negro inferiority would survive intact'. Summarizing these findings, Colin Legum wrote in the *Observer*: 'The cruel reality about Brazil is that it is a social pyramid in which the whitest are the pinnacle and the blackest are at the base. The process of dark people rising in this pyramid is spoken of as "whitening" themselves.'[17]

In other words, Brazilian society is indeed biased in favour of whites. And the policy of racial equality, often proclaimed by official agencies, coexists with the practice of discrimination by white citizens towards those who are not 100 per cent white. For historical reasons, there has been much inter-racial breeding – between Europeans, Africans and Amerindians – in Brazil. Yet the white bias of society has remained unaltered. This is worth noting, since many British liberals regard inter-racial breeding (which in popular parlance is called miscegenation) as a crucially important element in the creation of a racially harmonious and just society.

No doubt biological amalgamation helps to assimilate a racial minority. But one has to assess the situation in Britain, or elsewhere, quantitatively. The preponderance of men among the early West Indian migrants created amongst them a pressure to court white women. In those days the incidence of inter-racial marriage or co-habitation was substantial, probably 15 to 20 per cent, with the white partner being almost always the woman. Since then the situation has altered. As the West Indian and, later, Asian communities became more sexually balanced, and larger in size, the incentive to court white women lessened considerably. Consequently, the incidence of inter-racial marriage declined steadily. A Policy Studies Institute survey in 1982 showed that only 9 per cent of West Indian households were headed by a partner in a mixed marriage or co-habiting relationship, with 7 per cent involving a white woman. The figure for Asian households was only 4 per cent, with 3 per cent involving a white woman.[18]

Among whites, dislike of inter-racial marriage remains high. Between 70 and 90 per cent disapprove; only 7 to 13 per cent approve.[19] The author's research in this field shows that though middle-class inter-racial couples and their children experience few social or psychological problems, this is not the case with working-class families. In the majority of cases, the white spouse, female or male, has to forgo social contacts with white friends and acquaintances, and even sometimes family ties. Their children, too, experience considerable psychological problems. The two-category classification prevalent in the Anglo-Saxon world of Britian and America describes inter-racial children as 'coloured' or 'black' – not 'mulatto' or 'half-white'.

Under the circumstances, progeny of mixed marriages with a working-class background often socialize, and identify themselves, with black children. When they reach adulthood they tend either to choose black or inter-racial partners for marriage because (a) their social contacts with whites are minimal, and (b) they wish to save their children the distasteful experiences they themselves underwent during childhood and adolescence. Hence it would be unrealistic to visualize the past or present incidence of inter-racial marriage rising steadily and thus leading to the ideal of a racially amalgamated society in the not-too-distant future.

It seems therefore realistic to accept the proposition that the relationship of social pluralism – which indeed now exists – is likely to persist for the next few generations.

To be fair, after many years of myopia and fantasy-mongering, realism began to creep into sociological, administrative and political circles in the late 1960s. The change in official thinking was well captured by the difference in the tone of a report by the Committe of the Youth Service Development Council, entitled *Immigrants and the Youth Service* and published in 1967, and the one by the House of Commons Select Committee on Race Relations and Immigration, entitled *The Problems of Coloured School-Leavers* and published in 1969.

'The demand for separate provision is, then, real enough for the young immigrants,' stated the Committee of the Youth Service Development Council. 'We, as a Committee, recognize that young immigrants may genuinely feel more at home among other people with a similar background ... At the same time, we cannot lose sight of the fact that an over-emphasis on distinctiveness, rather than on shared values and attitudes, can widen, rather than narrow, the gap.'[20] In contrast, after referring to a multiracial club in Ealing, and to 'mainly coloured clubs in Wolverhampton and Huddersfield, and all-coloured clubs in Liverpool and Hackney', the House of Commons Select Committee on Race Relations and Immigration stated: 'It is pointless to dogmatize about what type of club is best. Each has to develop naturally in response to the wishes of the local population, both white and coloured. If this means that some clubs become all-white or all-coloured, no one need object as long as the club does not actively seek or bar entry to one race or another.'[21]

Here at last was a statement from a body of legislators which was at once honest and undogmatic and which, above all, recognized reality as it existed without the customary liberal guilt or moralizing, or exhortations about multiracialism and integration. It was finally realized by national and local leaders that neither sermonizing nor breast-beating would lead to the millennium of a socially integrated multiracial society in Britain.

Realism was particularly welcome in education. And it was shown by Edward Short, then Education Secretary, in early 1969. 'In my view the concept of the neighbourhood school should not be lightly abandoned,' he said. 'But to impose dispersal by legislation or by regulation in the centre regardless of local circumstances would probably create far more discord than harmony ... There would inevitably be schools with a very high proportion of immigrant children on the roll.'[22]

Indeed, by then there were already scores of schools in the country with more than 60 per cent black and Asian pupils.[23] But these schools, like the rest, needed to be judged by their scholastic and related achievements, not by their racial composition. Also, these schools needed to reflect the backgrounds and feelings of the pupils. And this deserved to be encouraged by local authorities. The first signs that this was beginning to happen came in the late 1960s. 'Members of the council feel that it would be a pity if the Indian children were to lose their own culture,' said a spokesperson of the Ealing borough council in July 1969. The council decided to arrange for the CSE (Certificate of Secondary Education) examination to be taken in Punjabi.[24]

The move towards imparting multi-ethnic education got going nationally in the late 1970s (see Chapter Six). This implied a formal acceptance of the concept of social/cultural pluralism. But was this development in tune with public opinion? The answer was provided by a poll conducted in 1982 by the Policy Studies Institute. Responding to the statement 'People of Asian and West Indian origin should try to preserve as much of their own culture as possible', 50 per cent of the whites replied 'Yes' and 40 per cent 'No'. While the white response was not as overwhelming as the Asian (with 88 per cent replying positively) or West Indian (with 80 per cent replying positively), it was nevertheless more positive than negative.[25] Such a view stemmed primarily from an attitude of 'Live and let live' which, in the case of ethnic minorities, meant leaving well alone in cultural and social matters.

A relationship whereby people of different racial stocks 'mix but do not combine' is reassuring to those white Britons who, for better or worse, do not wish to see their culture or racial stock adulterated with the Afro-Asian. This is an important factor and deserves serious consideration. Shifting the stress from integration to mere acceptance, in a neutral sense of the word, has the advantage of relieving the anxiety and fear of most white Britons. For the word 'integration' seems to imply to the average white Briton inter-racial sex and marriage. The much-detested prospect that 'Britain will soon become a coffee-coloured nation' has been an important element in engendering antipathy towards racial minorities.

Little wonder that by the early 1980s Britain was routinely described in official and unofficial statements as a multiracial, multicultural society.

This view was unchallenged until the controversy over *The Satanic Verses* in late 1988. The Muslim minority – consisting not only of settlers from South Asia and Africa but also the Middle East – felt incensed that, unlike Christianity, its faith was denied legal protection against blasphemy. 'Faced by the entrenched majority community, still overwhelmingly Christian in law and institutions if not belief, Muslims felt powerless and unprotected,' wrote Rana Kabbani, a Syrian-born, Cambridge-educated author, resident in London.[26]

The controversy illustrated a view prevalent in administrative, academic and media circles that Christianity was not only the religion of the vast majority of the British but that it was also superior to other major faiths. This perception was blatantly stated by Fay Weldon, a writer who campaigned actively on behalf of Salman Rushdie, author of the controversial book (see p. 301).

Weldon belonged to the absolutist school among British liberals who, decrying book-burning unequivocally, reiterated their belief in unfettered freedom of expression. The other school, the pragmatists, argued that nowhere in the world was freedom of expression absolute, and that among other statutes Britain's Race Relations Act of 1965 limited it by making incitement to racial hatred a criminal offence.

The moderates among the Muslim leaders demanded that the law be extended to make religious hatred a criminal offence. While agreeing with this, the traditionalists among Muslim leaders pressed their long-standing demand that the Muslim family law be incorporated into the British legal system. (In such multi-faith, secular states as India, the Muslim minority is ruled by its own religiously-based family law – a state of affairs which implies equality between the majority Hindu religion and minority Islam.) Any serious consideration of the Muslim demand by the British authorities would imply treating Islam on a par with Christianity in a Christian land, an idea far too antithetical to Western values to be entertained.

Of course, no politician would publicly offer such an argument. Instead the stock response has been and would be: there can only be one family law in Britain. Were the government to permit different family laws it would be laying the foundation of social segregation.

As it happens, whether by chance or design, the Conservative administration has already set the course of national life along these lines. A series of measures in housing and education hold the ominous prospect of rolling back the limited progress made in the fields of racially mixed housing and multi-ethnic education during the eighties. In the name of widening the choice for citizens, fresh laws have authorized them to remove their schools and housing estates out of the control of local government without laying down clear standards of social responsibility. The net result will be new institutions imbued with the values of white separatism. How serious this prospect is can be judged by the results of a 1988 survey which showed that 40 per cent of the white respondents in the Home Counties preferred all-white schools.[27]

The enforcement of the Education Reform Act 1988 in April 1990 in England and Wales will lead to drastic changes in school management and curriculum. The fixed national curriculum will mean less chance for non-European perspectives in education. As for management, each school will be allotted a specific sum according to the number of pupils on its roll, with the local school governors authorized to spend 90 per cent of the amount. Parents will be free to send their children where they wish. The pressure on head teachers (almost invariably white) to attract the maximum number of white students will most probably lead to their neglecting to cater for such ethnic children with special needs as West Indians and (bi-lingual) Asians. This will mean creeping racial segregation in schools.

Under the changed circumstances, government resistance to providing state aid to Muslim schools will crumble. And such schools will multiply.

Also, the fate of British Muslims will undergo change as the economic union of the European Community takes hold after 1992, setting the ground for political integration of the member states in the nineties. Such a development will lead to closer links between British Muslims and their 4.5 million co-religionists in the other members of the European Community.[28] At the same time, it will have much impact on British identity, which has been evolving over the past few decades.

The basic question to ask is: are we to remain prisoners of the past, insisting on a unitary image of a Briton as a person who is white, Christian, clean-shaven, wearing a suit or skirt? Or should we start conceiving a pluralistic image of being a Briton, possibly black or brown, Hindu or Muslim, wearing a turban or kanga or sari?

Notes

Full details of works referred to in abbreviated form will be found in the Select Bibliography, pp. 335–7

Preface

1. 'The case for accepting the obvious reality of voluntary separate development, and "peaceful co-existence" rather than integration as the only sensible objective of race relations policy, is clear enough, and has been cogently argued most recently by the Indian immigrant journalist Dilip Hiro in his book *Black British, White British*,' wrote Nigel Lawson. *The Times*, 27 October 1971.

2. *The Times*, 5 July 1990.

3. Cited in the BBC Television series *Mosaic* on 15 October 1989. See further pp. 257–8.

4. *Evening Standard*, 21 December 1989.

5. *Ibid*.

Introduction: A Historical View

1. *Notes of a Native Son*, p. 14.

2. Eric Williams, *Capitalism and Slavery*, André Deutsch, London, 1964, p. 7.

3. *Independent*, 29 October 1988.

4. 'Both Indian slavery and white servitude were to go down before the blackman's endurance, docility, and labour capacity,' wrote J. S. Bassett. *Slavery and Servitude in the Colony of North Carolina*, Baltimore, 1896, p. 77.

5. Liverpool's first slave-ship sailed for Africa in 1709. By 1771, one-third of *all* ships were slave-traders. By 1792, Liverpool had 42% of the total European slave trade. Williams, op. cit., p. 34.

6. A. Chater, *Race Relations in Britain*, p. 12.

7. By 1770, in London alone, there were 18,000 black slaves, forming nearly 3% of an estimated population of 650,000. (The first recorded population of London, in 1801, was 959,000.)

8. An advertisement in the *London Advertiser* in 1756 read, 'Matthew Dyer intimates to the public that he makes silver padlocks for Blacks or Dogs; collars etc.'

9. Bob Hepple, *Race, Jobs and the Law in Britain*, pp. 39–40.

10. Edward Fiddes, 'Lord Mansfield and the Somersett Case', *Law Quarterly Review* 50 (1934), pp. 499–511.

11. Michael Banton, *Race Relations*, p. 23. Slaves continued to be bought and sold after 1772 as shown by the following advertisements which appeared in a Liverpool newspaper in October 1779: 'To be sold by auction at George Dunbar's office, on Thursday next, the 21st inst., at one o'clock a black boy, aged about 14 years old, and a large Mountain Tiger Cat.' Bob Hepple points out that the courts in England 'continued far into the nineteenth century to countenance slavery', op. cit., p. 41. Lord Mansfield's judgement in 1772 gave an impetus to the anti-slavery movement and encouraged liberally inclined masters to free their slaves. But then the freed slaves found it impossible to find work and became residents of common lodging houses for destitutes in the St Giles area of London. This earned them the nickname of 'St Giles Black-birds'.

12. Andrew Halliday, *The West Indies: the Natural and Physical History of the Windward and Leeward Colonies*, London, 1837, p. 56. 'Blacks are monkeys to be trampled upon' was one of the remarks made by the dockers protesting against coloured immigrants outside Parliament in 1968. *Observer*, 28 April 1968.

13. 'The effect of the slave trade was that all Africans were considered present or potential slaves,' wrote K. L. Little, *Negroes in Britain*, p. 214.

14. Cited in Wilfred Wood and John Downing, *Vicious Circle*, p. 30.

15. Cited in Chater, op. cit., pp. 15–16.

16. *The West Indies and the Spanish Main*, Chapman and Hall, London, 1859, cited in Wood and Downing, op. cit., pp. 30–31.

17. Milton Rugoff (ed.), *The Travels of Marco Polo*, Pocket Books, New York, 1961, p. 249.

18. *Ibid.*, p. 244.

19. *The Lords of Human Kind*, Weidenfeld & Nicolson, 1969, p. 21.

20. *Ibid.*, p. 34.

21. Two generations later, Rudyard Kipling was to describe the negro as 'a big, black vain baby and a man rolled in one'. Cited in Roi Ottley, *No Green Pastures*, p. 22.

22. *The Adventures of a Younger Son*, Humphrey Milford, London, 1925, p. 57.

23. *The Competition Wallah*, Macmillan, London, Second Edition, 1866, pp. 244–5.

24. Cited in Little, op. cit., p. 211.

25. It is interesting to note that 1857 more or less marks the beginning of what Michael Banton feels might be called, by future historians, the 'century of racism' extending from 1851 to 1950. Banton, op. cit., p. 164.

26. Cited in Edward Thompson and Geoffrey T. Garratt, *Rise and Fulfilment of British Rule in India*, Macmillan, London, 1934, p. 536.

27. V. G. Kiernan, op. cit., p. 58.

28. Cited in Banton, op. cit., p. 117.

29. Cited in K. M. Panikkar, *Asia and Western Domination*, Allen and Unwin, London, 1959, p. 116.

30. *Rudyard Kipling's Verse, 1885–1926*, Macmillan, London, 1928, p. 320.

31. Cited in Little, op. cit., p. 218.

32. *Ibid.*, p. 193. D. F. Karaka, the first Indian to be elected president of the Oxford Union in the early 1930s, describes his experiences of racial discrimination in England in his book *Oh! You English*, Frederick Muller, London, 1935.

33. Little, op. cit., p. 195.

34. *Ibid.*, p. 59.

35. 'Race Prejudice: France and England', *Social Forces*, Vol. VII, 1928, p. 106.

36. Cited in Little, op. cit., p. 217.

37. Sheila Patterson, *Dark Strangers*, p. 212.

38. 'Whatever may have been the exhortations of Winston Churchill as Colonial Secretary, *Civis Britannicus sum* could never be the boast of any Indian or African,' wrote Hugh Tinker, a British historian. *New Society*, 29 February 1968.

39. Cited in Ottley, op. cit., p. 26.

40. Patterson, op. cit., p. 212.

41. Ottley, op. cit., p. 26.

42. *Ibid.*, p. 55.

Part I
1: The New Jerusalem

1. Eric Williams, *Capitalism and Slavery*, p. 33.

2. Michael Kraus estimates immigration from the West Indies to America at 30,000 a year during the period 1900–1930. *Immigration, the American Mosaic*, Van Nostrand, London, 1966, p. 97.

3. 'During the war more than 100,000 workers from the British West Indies were recruited for agricultural and industrial work in the United States.' James Wickenden, *Colour in Britain*, p. 5.

4. 'The US embassy [in Kingston, Jamaica] is the second busiest visa-issuing post in the world,' wrote Colin McGlashan in the *Observer*, 23 November 1969.

5. R. B. Davison, *West Indian Migrants*, p. 63.

6. *Ibid.*, p. 32.

7. Davison estimated that if there had been no migration, every year Jamaica would have had 47,000 more people to feed. Op. cit., p. 40.

8. *Ibid.*, p. 64.

9. Cited in Paul Foot, *Immigration and Race in British Politics*, p. 187. 'The migration [from the West Indies] rose and fell according to the demand for labour [in Britain] from year to year,' wrote Ceri Peach. 'When demand fell away, as it did between 1957 and 1959, there was a corresponding decrease in West Indian immigration.' *West Indian Migration to Britain*, p. 93.

10. R. B. Davison's study of West Indian immigrants in Britain, conducted after the 1962 Commonwealth Immigrants Act, showed that 98% of the children had been left behind. *Black British*, p. 114.

2: Children of Slavery: The Anglicized Afro-Caribbeans

1. *The Middle Passage*, p. 66.

2. 'The philosophy underlying curricula at all levels and motivating government action is that the West Indies are an appendage of Europe,' writes Neville Maxwell, *The Power of Negro Action*, p. 48. Recalling her schooldays Patricia Fullwood, a Jamaican, said: 'I knew more about Britain than about Jamaica. Knew all the kings and queens, and coal mines and copper industry and fishing industry in England more than I knew where Port Royal [the former

Jamaican capital] was, and the importance of Port Royal to Jamaica.'

3. *West Indian Gazette*, London, May 1961.

4. Nearly two generations later, a West Indian speaker at a CARD (Campaign Against Racial Discrimination) meeting suggested in all seriousness that the Queen should adopt a black baby to improve race relations in Britain.

5. Many of the words and phrases in use in the Jamaican creole (English) are not immediately intelligible to the speakers of standard English. Some of the examples are: *bangarang* (which means 'trouble'); *back, back* (meaning 'reverse'); and *rebameko* (which is a derivative of 'carry, go, come' and means 'carry it and bring it back'). As early as 1869, J. J. Thomas, a black teacher in Trinidad, published *The Theory and Practice of Creole Grammar*, a book which was reprinted in 1966.

6. When asked to complete a story about a coloured man which ran 'He finds English people discriminate against him because he is coloured and so what he does is ...' more than half of the sample of 207 West Indian youths in north London in 1969–70 said in effect: 'He comes to hate white people although he doesn't let them know it.' Though this survey was directed by two white market researchers – Dennis Stevenson and Peter Wallis – the actual interviews were conducted by trained West Indian youths.

7. At the end of their year-long survey, Stevenson and Wallis concluded that 'many coloured people, while being restrained from overt militancy by the desire to accumulate enough money to meet certain social and economic pressures emanating from home ties in the West Indies, are nonetheless extremely hostile to white people.'

8. The following incident illustrates the point. 'I recently was able to take a black American singer down the Grove [in Liverpool], the old slave market in the merchant square, and [having read a book on the subject] to give a knowledgeable account of the millions of Africans shipped into slavery via Liverpool,' wrote Stanley Reynolds, a British journalist. 'The black girl burst into tears, thinking that the odds were pretty good that her ancestors stood naked under the hammer at the Gore.' *New Statesman*, 16 January 1970.

9. In modern times 'moderate' black leaders in the US and Britain are known to be in the habit of briefing the white authorities on what they have seen or heard in the black districts, a service for which they are duly rewarded. In the old times the house-slaves used to be rewarded with the master's left-over food and clothes for similar services. 'The inherited slave complex of telling the master what was happening on the plantations dies hard with some of us,' wrote Amy Garvey, the widow of Marcus Garvey. *Garvey and Garveyism*, Collier-Macmillan, New York, 1970, p. 13.

10. *Observer*, 29 December 1969.

11. 4 November 1963.

12. Present evidence suggests that migration to Britain tends to lower the incidence of 'common law' marriage, and accelerates the emergence of patriarchal families. However, the overall situation, summed up by Valeri Knox, is that, 'With West Indians ... the dominant figure is usually the woman, who may be married to the father, co-habiting with him on a fairly settled basis or even with a number of men in succession. The mother is usually a tough disciplinarian, who will beat her child if she thinks he deserves it.' *The Times*, 22 March 1968.

3: Everywhere the Cold Shoulder

1. *Paid Servant*, Bodley Head, London, 1962, p. 100.

2. 'All the persons interviewed during the sample survey [of West Indian migrants in 1961] were asked whether they were going to Britain (a) to seek employment; (b) to join relatives; (c) to study; (d) for any other reason. They answered almost unanimously "to seek employment".' R. B. Davison, *West Indian Migrants*, p. 36.

3. This agency was set up in 1956 (with the backing of the Jamaican government) to meet the West Indian immigrants at their point of arrival, to help them adjust to the new environment, and to direct them to the national agencies or departments which could help them with jobs and social welfare. Later, in 1958, this Welfare Service was incorporated into the Migrant Services Division of the Federation of the West Indies.

4. Ruth Glass and Harold Pollins, *Newcomers*, p. 31.

5. Donald Hinds, *Journey to an Illusion*, pp. 71–2.

6. Cited in A. Chater, *Race Relations in Britain*, p. 7.

7. Hinds, op. cit., p. 59.

8. *Black British*, p. 77.

9. Willesden was a case in point. The West Indian settlement there was directly attributable to employment opportunities – at its two large hospitals, railway workshop and station and the nearby industrial estate.

10. There was no change over the next several years. The *Notting Hill Housing Survey*, published in July 1969, for instance, stated: 'Ninety-seven per cent of the less-than-£1-per-week rent and almost 80 per cent of the less-than-£2-per-week rent categories of households have UK-born heads of families. By comparison, 31 per cent of the £6–£7-per-week rent category have West Indian-born heads of households, who represent only 16 per cent of the total households in the Survey district. West Indians clearly pay, on average, a much higher rent than UK households.', pp. 38–9.

11. Pearl Jephcott, *A Troubled Area: Notes on Notting Hill*, Faber and Faber, London, 1964, p. 83.

12. *Ibid.*, p. 82.

13. London Council of Social Service, *Immigrants in London*, 1963, p. 8.

14. A West Indian in Birmingham was asked by his estate agent to pay an 'initial fee' of £65. His enquiries at a building society revealed that there was no such thing as an initial fee. Richard Hooper (ed.), *Colour in Britain*, p. 62.

15. 28 November 1961.

16. Elizabeth Burney, *Housing on Trial*, p. 214.

17. Jephcott, op. cit., p. 82.

18. 'Even in the little time I was in Grenada,' wrote Ottabah Cugoano, an educated ex-slave, in 1787, 'I saw a slave receive 24 lashes of whip for being seen in a church on a Sunday instead of going to work.' Cited in James Pope-Hennessy, *Sins of the Fathers*, Weidenfeld & Nicolson, London, 1967, p. 132.

19. Malcolm J. C. Calley, *God's People*, p. 121.

20. Clifford S. Hill, *West Indian Migrants and the London Churches*, p. 22.

21. E. J. B. Rose and Associates, *Colour and Citizenship*, p. 374.

22. *New Society*, 22 February 1968.

23. *Alta*, Winter 1967, pp. 217–18.

24. Hill, op. cit., p. 22.

25. Calley, op. cit., p. 39.

26. *Ibid.*, p. 118.

27. 'A study of churches [in Birmingham] by Robert Moore showed that ... the Seventh Day Adventist church loses white membership where blacks come in.' *Birmingham Post*, 4 October 1965.

28. Rose and Associates, op. cit., p. 372.

29. *Birmingham Planet*, 12 December 1963.

30. *Daily Herald*, 8 May 1958.

31. *Birmingham Post*, 15 April 1956.

4: Blacks Look West

1. Cited in Paul Foot, *Immigration and Race in British Politics*, p. 129.

2. Lord Gifford, Wally Brown and Ruth Bundey, *Loosen the Shackles: First Report of the Liverpool 8 Inquiry into Race Relations in Liverpool*, p. 29.

3. James Wickenden, *Colour in Britain*, p. 24.

4. *West Indian Gazette*, March 1958.

5. Many of the politically conscious West Indians tended to join such fringe British organizations as the Communist Party or the Trotskyite groups, all of which took an uncompromising stand against racism.

6. 13 October 1961.

7. Cited in Foot, op. cit., p. 44.

8. The term 'Black Power' was first used in 1959 as the title of a book on independent Ghana by Richard Wright, an Afro-American writer.

9. *Hansard*, 5 December 1968, cited in *The Report of the Race Relations Board for 1968–69*, London, p. 73.

5: White Rejection, Black Withdrawal

1. *West Indian Migration to Britain*, p. xvi.

2. *Observer*, 10 September 1967.

3. *Newcomers*, p. 60.

4. Political and Economic Planning Ltd, *Racial Discrimination*, p. 75.

5. See John Power, *Immigrants in School*, p. 13.

6. *Immigrant School Leavers and the Youth Employment Service in Birmingham*, pp. 11–12.

7. E. J. B. Rose and Associates, *Colour and Citizenship*, p. 166.

8. *Observer*, 25 September 1966.

9. *Ibid.*, 14 July 1968.

10. *The Times*, 6 December 1968.

11. *Ibid.*, 29 June 1970.

12. Between 1911 and 1961, white-collar jobs increased by 71% whereas manual jobs rose by only 2%. Bob Hepple, *Race, Jobs and the Law in Britain*, p. 62.

13. An earlier inquiry by Peter Wright in the Midlands and the North had revealed that 72% of the West Indian workers would prefer a different job from the one they had. *Ibid.*, p. 15.

14. *Race*, April 1969, p. 506.

15. *Observer*, 10 September 1967.

16. *The Problems of Coloured School-Leavers, Vol. I*, Her Majesty's Stationery Office, London, 1969, p. 56.

17. *The Middle Passage*, pp. 84–5.

6: Black Consciousness: An Afro Identity

1. Neville Maxwell, *The Power of Negro Action*, p. 66.

2. Cited in V. S. Naipaul, *The Middle Passage*, p. 66.

3. *Ibid.*, p. 67.

4. *Observer*, 10 September 1967.

5. Cited in Maxwell, op. cit., p. 50.

6. *Ibid.*, p. 50.

7. *Joffa*, March 1969, p. 8; *Race Today*, December 1969, p. 232.

8. *Observer*, 26 April 1970.

9. *Daily Telegraph Magazine*, 23 May 1969.

10 *Observer*, 10 September 1967.

11 A study by F. H. M. Raveau in France showed that whereas 75% of the French West Indians nursed memories of racial persecution only 15% of the French Africans did so. H. Renck and J. Knight (eds), *Caste and Race*, Churchill Society, London, 1966, p. 267.

7: Rise of Rastafarianism

1. 'The Jamaicans: Cultural and Social Change among Migrants in Britain', in James L. Watson (ed.), *Between Two Cultures*, p. 145.

2. Cited in Charles Husband (ed.), *'Race' in Britain*, p. 178.

3. Cited in The Runnymede Trust and The Radical Statistics Race Group, *Britain's Black Population*, p. 63.

4. *British Medical Journal*, 19 May 1979, pp. 1356–76.

5. David J. Smith, *Racial Disadvantage in Employment*, pp. 14, 35; and David J. Smith, *Racial Disadvantage in Britain*, pp. 119, 121.

6. Martin Kettle and Lucy Hodges, *Uprising! The Police, the People and the Riots in Britain's Cities*, p. 139.

7. Tavistock Institute of Human Relations, *Application of Race Relations Policy in the Civil Service*, Her Majesty's Stationery Office, London, 1980, p. 31.

8. David J. Smith, *Racial Disadvantage in Employment*, p. 104; *Racial Disadvantage in Britain*, p. 329.

9. Department of Employment, *Gazette*, 1980, vol. 88(3).

10. Commission for Racial Equality, *Looking for Work*, London, 1978.

11. *How the West Indian Child is Made Educationally Subnormal in the British School System: The Scandal of the Black Child in Schools in Britain*, pp. 5, 15.

12. Cited in Wycombe Inter-Agency Working Party, *Wycombe Is Something Else: A Report into Experiences of Black and Asian Youth in Wycombe Town Centre*, High Wycombe, 1989, p. 63.

13. 'Schools and Race', in Stuart Hall *et al.*, *Five Views of Multi-Racial Britain*, p. 64.

14. Horace Campbell, 'Rastafari: culture of resistance', in *Race & Class*, Winter 1980, vol. XXII, no. 1, p. 6.

15. Ernest Cashmore, *Rastaman: The Rastafarian Movement in England*, p. 55.

16. *Ibid.*, p. 100.

17. *Ibid.*, p. 70.

18. Muhammad Anwar, *Race and Politics: Ethnic Minorities and British Political System*, p. 101.

19. Zig Layton-Henry, *The Politics of Race in Britain*, p. 172. For specific definitions of the socio-economic categories, ranging from A to E, see note 27 on p. 327.

20. *Ibid.*, p. 171.

21. *Police Power and Black People*, pp. 11–12.

8: Urban Violence

1. Cited in Robert Reiner, 'Black and Blue', *New Society*, 17 September 1981.

2. *Independent*, 19 August 1989.

3. *The Scarman Report: The Brixton Disorders 10–12 April 1981*, p. 79.

4. *New Statesman*, 9 July 1982, p. 11.

5. *New Society*, 1 August 1986, p. 24.

6. *Daily Post*, 30 June 1982.

7. *Observer*, 26 November 1989.

8. Cited in *The Times*, 24 September 1981.

9. Michael Pratt, *Mugging as a Social Problem*, p. 151.

10. Martin Kettle and Lucy Hodges, op cit., p. 88.

11. *Ibid.*, p. 92. Lambeth was one of the four Greater London boroughs, out of thirty-three, which accounted for most of the Sus arrests in the area – the rest being Westminster (including the West End), Camden, and Kensington and Chelsea.

12. Scarman, op. cit., pp. 10, 11.

13. *Hackney Gazette*, 6 June 1980.

14. Scarman, op. cit., p. 92.

15. *Guardian*, 9 December 1981.

16. The racial breakdown was available because from the early 1970s the police forces in Britain had started using a race code on the criminal record form: IC 1 White-skinned European type; IC 2 Dark-skinned European type; IC 3 Negroid type; IC 4 Asian type; IC 5 Oriental type; and IC 6 Arabian type. Cecil Gutzmore, 'Capital, "black youth" and crime', in *Race & Class*, XXV, no. 2, 1983, pp. 18–19.

17. Home Office, *Statistical Bulletin, 13 October 1982*, Her Majesty's Stationery Office, London, 1982, pp. 1–9.

18. *Daily Telegraph*, 13 July 1981.

19. *Guardian*, 8 June 1982.

20. *New Standard*, 11 May 1981.

21. *The Times*, 13 November 1981.

22. Cited in Kettle and Hodges, op. cit., p. 201.

23. David J. Smith, 'A Survey of Londoners' in *Police and People in London, Vol. I*, Policy Studies Institute, London, 1983, p. 325.

24. Scarman, op. cit., p. 210.

25. Muhammad Anwar, *Race and Politics*, pp. 106, 109.

26. An extreme example of this was provided by Monwar Hussain, the first Asian member of the West Yorkshire County Council, who had to try for six years, from 1963 to 1969, to gain admission to the Labour Party. The party bureaucrats consistently discouraged Asian membership through vetting procedures. *New Statesman*, 30 April 1982, p. 8.

27. *Daily Telegraph*, 4 October 1983.

28. *Observer*, 11 April 1984.

29. Cited in Anwar, op. cit., p. 122.

30. A. Sivanandan, 'Blacks and Black Sections', in *Race & Class*, XXVII, no. 2, Autumn 1985, pp. 72–4.

9: Step-Citizens of Britain

1. *Independent*, 7 August 1989.

2. *Ibid.*, 18 December 1989.

3. John Benyon, *A Tale of Failure: Race and Policing*, p. 94.

4. *The Times*, 11 October 1985.

5. *Independent*, 30 September 1989.

6. *A Different Reality*, Birmingham, 1986, p. 72, cited in Daniel Lawrence, 'Racial violence in Britain: trends and a perspective', in *New Community*, vol. XIV, no. 1/2, Autumn 1987, p. 158.

7. *Morning Star*, 13 August 1986.

8. *Guardian*, 26 July 1986.

9. *Guardian*, 12 September 1986.

10. *Bristol Evening Post*, 18 May 1987.

11. *Policing London*, November–December 1986.

12. The black imprisonment rate was 775 per 100,000 versus the national figure of 98.2 per 100,000, *Independent*, 7 August 1989.

13. *New Statesman*, 9 July 1982.

14. Rozina Visram, *Ayahs, Lascars and Princes: Indians in Britain 1700–1947*, pp. 82, 92, 147.

15. The actual estimate for 1987 was 2,473,000. *The Labour Force Survey 1987: A Study of Differential Response According to Demographic and Socio-Economic Characteristics*, Her Majesty's Stationery Office, London, 1989, p. 30. The annual natural increase at 2 per cent amounted to 50,000.

16. *Independent*, 4 October 1989.

Part II
1: The Coolies of the Empire – and Britain

1. *Imperialism and Civilization*, Hogarth Press, London, 1928, pp. 37–8.

2. Although only 2% of the total Indian

population in 1920, Sikhs formed 20% of the Indian Army.

3. In 1961, the population of the Punjab was 20.3 million; that of Gujarat, 20.6 million; Sylhet, three-quarters of a million; and Mirpur, about one million.

4. This applied not only to the Indian masses but also the élite. 'They [the British] look upon us as being of inferior order,' wrote L. L. P. Garu, an Indian professor and intellectual, in 1866. 'Does not this sort of conduct … tend to demoralize us and to estrange us?' *The Social Status of the Hindus*, p. 35.

5. Cited in Eric Butterworth, *A Muslim Community in Britain*, Church Information Office, London, 1967, p. 14.

6. Cited in Paul Foot, *Immigration and Race in British Politics,*, p. 188.

2: Money Is All: The Rise of Asian Enterprise

1. Jobs on Bradford's local buses, however, remained the exclusive domain of highly educated Pakistanis and Indians. A study in Coventry, reported in the *Morning Star* (5 January 1967), showed that half of the Indian bus conductors were university graduates.

2. Breakdown of 1966 census published as Appendix X in the Report of the Race Relations Board for 1969–70, p. 58.

3. 'The majority of managers in the interview surveys found Asian workers very amenable to discipline,' wrote Peter Wright. One personnel manager commented: 'With Asiatics it [supervision] is easy enough. If you say, "Run around the car park", they will run around the car park all day.' *The Coloured Worker in British Industry*, pp. 118, 132.

4. In 1963 the estimated remittances to Pakistan from Britain amounted to nearly £26 million. E. J. B. Rose and Associates, *Colour and Citizenship*, p. 443.

5. *Observer*, 14 June 1969.

6. Rashmi Desai, *Indian Immigrants in Britain*, p. 127.

7. Referring to 'poor and illiterate' African workers who neither speak nor write French, F. H. M. Raveau stated, 'They have regrouped themselves in Paris and France and have achieved *homoestasis* which shelters them from the psychocultural trauma of displacement.' *Caste and Race*, p. 267.

8. 'Those who have the most clear-cut and distinct culture of their own are the least likely to become involved in friction; they do not wish to enter or to become integrated in the British system,' wrote James Wickenden. 'They are not hurt by rejection of a society they have no wish to enter; the chances of social misunderstanding are thus less.' *Colour in Britain*, pp. 18–19.

9. *Morning Star*, 8 September 1967.

10. Fifteen of the Indian bus conductors in Coventry were qualified teachers. *Ibid.*, 5 January 1967.

11. Referring to the July 1962–October 1965 period, John Power, a British educationist, doubted 'whether even 10% of them [those Commonwealth teachers with B vouchers] have found employment in English schools'. *Immigrants in School*, p. 25.

12. *Confessions of a Native-Alien*, Routledge and Kegan Paul, London, 1965, p. 158.

13. A survey of Indians in Coventry in 1965 showed that only 4% cent were self-employed. In comparison 70% were in unskilled and semi-skilled jobs, and 18% in skilled factory work. Dewitt John, *Indian Workers' Associations in Britain*, Oxford University Press, Oxford, 1969, p. 29.

14. 'Though there are four major linguistic, ethnic, religious and social differences between them [the West Indians] and the Pakistanis and Indians,' wrote Ceri Peach, 'from the point of view of the host society, they were all in the same economic and social position, occupied largely the same type of locality and their distributions were explicable only when they were considered together.' *West Indian Migration to Britain*, p. xvii.

15. E. J. B. Rose and Associates, op. cit., p. 443. During this period the number of Pakistani cafés in Bradford rose from three to sixteen.

16. Eric Butterworth, *A Muslim Community in Britain*, p. 18.

17. Rose, op. cit., p. 455.

18. Derek Humphrey and Michael Ward, *Passports and Politics*, p. 151.

19. Out of the 187 Pakistanis interviewed during a survey in Bradford only thirty could speak no English at all, that is, one out of every six. E. J. B. Rose and Associates, op. cit., p. 321.

20. Only 80,000 people in Scotland speak Gaelic. *Race Today*, September 1969, p. 154.

Of the 2.5 million people in Wales, only half a million speak Welsh.

3: No Faces Like Sikh Faces

1. This occasion led to the formation of the Central Committee of Gurdwaras (Great Britain).

2. In the late 1960s the Shromani Akali Dal claimed a membership of nearly 30,000 out of an estimated Sikh population in Britain of some 300,000.

3. *Guardian*, 8 April 1969.

4. During his subsequent visit to Britain, Jathedar Santokh Singh, one of the leaders of the Sikh demonstrators in Delhi, told his audiences at various meetings, 'The death of Jolly could have had serious repercussions on British interests in India ... it would have definitely put the lives of British nationals [there] in danger.' *Race Today*, October 1969, p. 188.

5. *The Times*, 10 April 1969.

4: Equal Before Allah

1. *The Pakistani Family in Britain*, p. 7.

2. *A Letter to Christendom*, p. 9.

3. The Grand Mosque in Mecca, Saudi Arabia, the birthplace of the Prophet Muhammad, is the holiest shrine of Islam followed by the mosque in Medina, Saudi Arabia, where the Prophet Muhammad is buried.

4. October 1969, p. vii.

5: Communal Leadership

1. Brigadier-General R. E. H. Dyer had died a natural death in 1927.

2. Paul Foot, *Immigration and Race in British Politics*, p. 43.

3. *Ibid.*, p. 73.

4. *Ibid.*, p. 46.

5. During the period of Pakistan's withdrawal from the Commonwealth (1972–89), the two High Commissions became embassies.

6: Culture of the Indian Subcontinent

1. Michael Kraus, *Immigration, the American Mosaic*, p. 69.

2. Cited in E. J. B. Rose and Associates, *Colour and Citizenship*, p. 459.

3. *South-East Asia: Race, Culture and Nation*, Oxford University Press, Oxford, 1966, p. 57.

4. Though nominally Christian, modern British society has, for all practical purposes, lost interest in religion whereas the Muslim or Sikh immigrant comes from a rural environment where religion is part of the general milieu. But even if the Western country to which the Sikh or Muslim migrated were religious, that is Christian, it would still mean a secular environment for him.

5. *New Society*, 22 February 1968.

7: Asian Youth: Conflict and Synthesis

1. Cited in Charles Husband (ed.), *'Race' in Britain*, p. 183.

2. *Observer Magazine*, 19 November 1989, p. 46.

3. *Ibid.*, p. 48.

4. Arthur J. Arberry, *The Koran Interpreted*, Oxford University Press, Oxford, 1964, ch. XXIV, v. 31.

5. J. H. Taylor, *The Half-Way Generation: A Study of Asian Youths in Newcastle upon Tyne*, pp. 85–6.

6. E. J. B. Rose and Associates, *Colour and Citizenship*, p. 465.

7. *New Society*, 1 June 1967.

8. David Beetham, *Immigrant School Leavers and the Youth Employment Service in Birmingham*, p. 15.

9. *Independent Magazine*, 23 September 1989, p. 34.

10. *New Society*, 1 June 1967.

11. Just under a quarter of the Pakistani Students' Federation members in London had suffered racial attacks in 1969. The areas included Notting Hill Gate, Shepherd's Bush, the Chelsea–Fulham district and King's Cross. *The Times*, 16 April 1970. That the situation had not improved over the next two decades became apparent when a survey of 100 overseas students of Leicester University revealed 50% claiming racial harassment. *Guardian*, 23 October 1989.

12. Beetham, op. cit., pp. 14–15.

13. *Ibid.*, pp. 17, 32.

14. Cited in E. J. B. Rose and Associates, op. cit., p. 321.

15. *Race*, April 1970, pp. 397–413.

8: Asians in Transition

1. *The Experience of Black Minorities in Britain*, The Open University Press, Milton Keynes, 1981, p. 19.

2. 'Some introductory remarks on race and politics in Britain', in Robert Miles and Annie Phizacklea (eds), *Racism and Political Action in Britain*, p. 15.

3. In BBC Radio 4's 'File on 4', 25 February 1981. Cited in Charles Husband (ed.), *'Race' in Britain*, p. 150.

4. It was this drive which explained why, in his study of Asian youngsters in Newcastle upon Tyne, Taylor discovered that 21% had gained admission to university or polytechnic. *The Half-Way Generation*, p. 243.

5. John Rex, 'West Indian and Asian Youth', in Ernest Cashmore and Barry Troyna (eds), *Black Youth in Crisis*, pp. 61–2.

6. Cited in Zig Layton-Henry, *The Politics of Race in Britain*, p. 172.

7. BBC Radio 4's 'File on 4', 25 February 1981. Cited in Husband (ed.), op. cit., p. 190.

8. The other murders (by arson) which stirred the Asian community into action were those of Parveen Khan and her three children in Walthamstow in July 1981.

9. These figures are from the two studies on electoral politics by Muhammad Anwar of Community Relations Commission/ Commission for Racial Equality, cited in Zig Layton-Henry, op. cit., p. 171.

10. *Daily Telegraph*, 24 April 1979.

9: Political Integration, Cultural Co-existence

1. 'West Indian and Asian Youth', in Ernest Cashmore and Barry Troyna, *Black Youth in Crisis*, p. 64.

2. *Observer Magazine*, 19 November 1989, p. 48.

3. David J. Smith, *Racial Disadvantage in Britain*, p. 92.

4. Colin Brown, *Black and White Britain*, pp. 93–4.

5. Cited in *Annual Report of the Commission for Racial Equality: January to December 1987*, London, 1988, p. 50; and *Independent*, 13 December 1989.

6. Cited in *Guardian*, 7 September 1989.

7. Metropolitan Police 2 Area (East), 'Racial Incidents 1987', a paper submitted at the Racial Incident Seminar at Toynbee Hall, London, in January 1988.

8. *Ibid.*

9. Cited in *Guardian*, 7 September 1989; and *Annual Report of the Commission for Racial*

Equality: January to December 1987, London, 1988, p. 5.

10. Brown, op. cit., p. 32.

11. *Sunday Times*, 30 July 1989.

12. *Independent*, 30 October 1987.

13. Brown, op. cit., p. 24.

10: The Rushdie Affair: Dialogue of the Deaf

1. Cited in *Sunday Times Magazine*, 28 May 1989, p. 29.

2. *A Letter to Christendom*, p. 9.

3. *Sunday Times Magazine*, 28 May 1989, p. 22.

4. Tehran Radio, 14 February 1989.

5. *Guardian*, 20 February 1989.

6. *Ibid.*, 25 February 1989.

7. The other pertinent Quranic verse is:
Those who molest God and His
    Messenger –
them God has cursed in the present world
    and
the world to come, and has prepared for
    them
a humbling punishment.   (33:57)
The fact that Kaab ibn al Ashraf, one of the persons executed in Mecca for mocking the Quran or the Prophet Muhammad, was not a Muslim means that attacking the sanctity of the Prophet or the Quran was as much of a capital offence for non-Muslims as it was for Muslims. This explains why Khomeini included the publishers of *The Satanic Verses* in his religious decree. See further, *Judgement of Ulama. Traditionalists and Other Authorities concerning Punishment for the Slander of the Prophet*, Muslim Students' Association (Persian Speaking Group), Berkeley, CA, 1989.

8. *Independent*, 21 and 22 February 1989.

9. *Ibid.*, 16 December 1989.

10. The Harris poll, conducted in September 1989, consisted of 674 Muslims. BBC Television's *Public Eye* series, 20 October 1989. By then four bookshops in London and York selling *The Satanic Verses* had been damaged by bomb explosions.

11. *New Statesman and Society*, 5 May 1989, p. 11.

12. *Guardian*, 2 August 1989.

13. Cited in Iqbal Wahhab, *Muslims in Britain*, p. 16.

14. *Independent*, 22 July 1989.

15. *Sunday Times Magazine*, 28 May 1989, p. 26.

16. The breakdown was: Muslims with origins in the Indian subcontinent – 762,000; Muslims from other parts of the Commonwealth, mainly East Africa, West Africa, Cyprus and Malaysia – 98,000; Muslims from North Africa, the Middle East and Iran – 130,000; and white and Afro-Caribbean converts – 30,000. Iqbal Wahhab, *Muslims in Britain: Profile of a Community*, p. 8. Excluding the converts in Britain, Ceri Peach of Oxford University's School of Geography put the estimate of Muslims in Britain at 871,000. *Independent*, 17 January 1990.

17. 9 July 1989.

18. *Public Eye*, 20 October 1989.

19. *Guardian*, 17 July 1989.

20. *Independent*, 29 July 1989.

21. *Public Eye*, 20 October 1989.

22. When the resolution, which included endorsement of the death sentence for Salman Rushdie, was put to vote in the mosques – including the ones in Walthamstow, London, and Sparkhill, Birmingham – it received almost unanimous backing. *Guardian* and *Independent*, 16 December 1989.

23. BBC Television, *Public Eye*, 20 October 1989.

Part III
1: The 'Open Door' Closes

1. Cited in Paul Foot, *Immigration and Race in British Politics*, p. 130.

2. *Listener*, 20 March 1969.

3. *Race Today*, July 1969, p. 79.

4. 'The Commonwealth is a multi-racial society and it is in this that its unique opportunity of serving the world and the greatest single peril to its survival both consist,' wrote the authors of *Wind of Change – The Challenge of the Commonwealth*, Conservative Political Centre, London, 1960, p. 29.

5. Cited in Foot, op. cit., p. 131.

6. E. J. B. Rose and Associates, *Colour and Citizenship*, pp. 211–12.

7. Cited in Foot, op. cit., pp. 130, 190.

8. Cited in Rose, op. cit., pp. 214–15.

9. Foot, op. cit., p. 135.

10. *Ibid.*, p. 191.

11. *Ibid.*, p. 178.

12. Sheila Patterson, *Immigration and Race Relations in Britain, 1960–67*, p. 410.

13. 12 October 1965.

14. *Race Without Rancour*, Conservative Political Centre, London, 1968, p. 10.

2: Coloured Immigration and Race Relations: A Composite Policy

1. Colin Brown and Pat Gay, *Racial Discrimination: 17 Years After the Act*, p. 32.

2. Cited in Bob Hepple, *Race, Jobs and the Law in Britain*, p. 129.

3. *Ibid.*, p. 130.

4. Cited in E. J. B. Rose and Associates, *Colour and Citizenship*, p. 200.

5. Hepple, op. cit., p. 130.

6. Enoch Powell then went on to prophesy that 'There will be subsequent phases, when the problem will resume its place in public concern and in a more intractable form, when it can no longer be dealt with simply by turning the inlet tap down or off.' *Daily Telegraph*, 16 February 1967.

7. *Guardian*, 4 February 1967.

8. *Ibid.*

9. Cited in *Immigration and Race*, Conservative Political Centre, London, 1968, p. 5.

10. *Sun*, 19 October 1967.

11. In May 1971 this quota was raised to 3000 vouchers a year.

12. *Guardian*, 23 February 1968.

13. *Ibid*, 12 June 1968; and The Runnymede Trust and The Radical Statistics Race Group, *Britain's Black Population*, p. 34. However, the Commission of the European Convention on Human Rights failed to bring about a friendly settlement between the parties through conciliation. It sent a confidential report to the Committee of Ministers of the Council of Europe. This Committee neither acted on the report nor forwarded it to the Court of Human Rights.

14. Cited in David McKie and Chris Cook, *Election '70*, Panther Books, London, 1970, pp. 100–101.

15. *Sunday Times*, 7 May 1967.

16. *The Report of the Race Relations Board for 1966–67*, London, 1967, p. 16.

17. *The Times*, 7 October 1967.

18. *Guardian*, 9 April 1968.

19. *Daily Telegraph*, 10 April 1968.

20. *The Times*, 11 April 1968.

21. *Ibid.*, 9 August 1968.

22. 'For the purpose of this Act a person discriminates against another if on the ground of colour, race or ethnic or national origins he treats that other ... less favourably than he treats or would treat other persons ...' *Race Relations Act 1968*, p. 1.

23. *Birmingham Post*, 4 March 1970.

24. *The Report of the Race Relations Board for 1968–69*, pp. 22, 13, 12.

25. In December 1971, General Amin had accused Asians of social exclusiveness and such evils as robbing the country of its valuable foreign exchange, overcharging and undercutting African traders, smuggling, and corrupting African officers. The Asians responded by rebutting each of the charges and left the onus for improving relations with the Amin administration. Yash Tandon, *Problems of a Displaced Minority: The New Position of East Africa's Asians*, Minority Rights Group, London, 1973, p. 21.

26. Of the rest, 10,000 went to India; 6,000 to Canada; 1,000 to America; and 4,000 to United Nations camps in Italy, Austria and Switzerland.

27. *Guardian*, 17 August 1972.

28. *Passports and Politics*, p. 177.

29. *The Times*, 17 October 1972.

30. David J. Smith, *Racial Disadvantage in Britain*, pp. 230–33. Also see David J. Smith, *The Facts of Racial Disadvantage*, tables B 84 and B 89.

31. *Racial Discrimination*, Cmnd 6234, Her Majesty's Stationery Office, London, 1975.

32. Cited in Ernest Ellis Cashmore and Barry Troyna, *Introduction to Race Relations*, p. 62.

33. *House of Commons First Report from the Home Affairs Committee, Session 1981–82: Commission for Racial Equality*, vol. I, Her Majesty's Stationery Office, London, November 1981, pp. xi and xii.

34. *Independent*, 19 May 1989.

35. *Annual Report of the Commission for Racial Equality: January to December 1986*, CRE, London, 1987, p. 7.

36. *Annual Report of the Commission for Racial*

Equality: January to December 1987, CRE, London, 1988, pp. 13 and 17. Of the 78 and 146 individual employment complaints settled in 1986 and 1987, about two-thirds were successful before or after hearing by an industrial tribunal.

37. Brown and Gay, op. cit., p. 32.

38. *Ibid.*, p. 6.

3: Inter-racial Harmony and Integration

1. Peter Wright, *The Coloured Worker in British Industry*, p. 185. In this book all firms were given fictitious names.

2. Cited in E. J. B. Rose and Associates, *Colour and Citizenship*, p. 383.

3. Paul Foot, *Immigration and Race in British Politics*, p. 224.

4. Cmnd 2739, pp. 15–16.

5. *Ibid.*, pp. 16 and 17.

6. Rose, op. cit., p. 385.

7. *Observer*, 28 April 1968.

8. Wright, op. cit., pp. 167–70.

9. *Ibid.*, p. 180.

10. *Ibid.*, pp. 184–5. Since then Australia and New Zealand have discontinued their 'Whites only' immigration policies, and now have a substantial body of Asian and black immigrants.

11. *Second Report of the Commonwealth Immigrants Advisory Council*, Cmnd 2266, February 1964, p. 26.

12. Cmnd 2226, para. 26.

13. Cited in Rose, op. cit., p. 268.

14. Cmnd 2739, p. 11.

15. p. 40.

16. *The Times*, 4 November 1963.

17. 'Neighbourhood School' in *New Society*, 23 June 1966.

18. National Association of Schoolmasters, *Education and the Immigrants*, 1969, p. 43.

19. In 1987, of the ninety-six functioning CRCs, eighty-seven received £2.2 million from the CRE and £2.4 million from the local authorities. *Annual Report of the Commission for Racial Equality: January to December 1987*, London, 1988, pp. 99–103.

20. The proportion of West Indian women aware of the CRE and CRCs was the same as men; but Asian women aware of these

organizations were about half as numerous as men. Colin Brown, *Black and White Britain: The Third PSI Survey*, p. 292.

21. Brian D. Jacobs, *Black Politics and Urban Crisis in Britain*, p. 101.

22. *Ibid.*, p. 101. By the late 1980s this figure had risen marginally to £100 million. *Guardian*, 4 July 1989.

23. Brian D. Jacobs, *Racism in Britain*, p. 157.

24. In the 1974 survey the figures were almost reversed, with more than half of the West Indians and a third of the Asians replying 'better'. Brown, op. cit., p. 277.

4: White Powell, White Power

1. Cited in Kenneth Leech, *Struggle in Babylon*, p. 78.

2. In reality the population with New Commonwealth origins in 1982 increased only to approximately 2.2 million, of whom about 80% were black or brown, the rest being white British born in the former (coloured) colonies. Colin Brown, *Black and White Britain*, p. 2.

3. *Observer*, 28 April 1968.

4. In March 1973 the authorities specified that the intending repatriate could own £500 and still be eligible for a grant to cover his family's travel expenses. In the previous year about 200 immigrants had returned home, half of them under the 1971 Act provisions and the other half under the older scheme run by the Supplementary Benefits Commission (SBC). Given the SBC scheme, there was no reason to include repatriation in the 1971 Act, except as a sop to racists.

5. Paul Gordon, *White Law: Racism in the Police, Courts and Prisons*, pp. 35–6.

6. *Guardian*, 1 June 1969, reporting the BBC's *Panorama* programme.

7. p. 490.

8. Cited in Wilfred Wood and John Downing, *Vicious Circle*, p. 24.

9. pp. 488–9.

10. *New Society*, 21 September 1967.

11. Cited in *Standard Recorder*, December 1972.

12. *Sunday Times*, 19 April 1981.

13. The defection of the British National Party members from the National Front in 1975 had only a marginal effect on the organization.

14. *Hansard*, 4 March 1976, col. 1548.

15. Zig Layton-Henry, *The Politics of Race in Britain*, p. 150.

16. *Independent*, 3 December 1987.

17. Cited in Charles Husband (ed.), *'Race' in Britain*, p. 191.

18. *Hansard*, 28 January 1981, cols 941–50.

19. According to the 1966 census, in Greater London alone there were 287,610 Irish-born people, nearly 3.5% of the total population. *New Society*, 14 March 1968.

5: Room at the Bottom

1. Peter Wright, *The Coloured Worker in British Industry*, p. 42.

2. Political and Economic Planning Ltd, *Racial Discrimination*, p. 72.

3. *New Statesman and Society*, 9 August 1988, p. 38.

4. Wright, op. cit., p. 42.

5. *Ibid.*, pp. 42, 44, 62. The reason that no coloured bus crews were to be seen in many parts of the country until well into the late 1960s, according to bus companies and local authorities, was that enough white labour was available. E. J. B. Rose and Associates, *Colour and Citizenship*, pp. 309–10.

6. *Guardian*, 21 September 1962, 7 January 1965; *The Times*, 14 June 1962.

7. Wright, op. cit., pp. 81, 46–7.

8. *The Times*, 27 January 1965.

9. *Telegraph & Argus*, 27 July 1961.

10. Wright, op. cit., p. 74.

11. *Guardian*, 18 August 1966.

12. *Lancashire Evening Telegraph*, 25 and 26 June 1965.

13. *How Colour Prejudiced is Britain?*, p. 137.

14. W. W. Daniel, *Racial Discrimination in England*, p. 108.

15. Oscar Gish in *Newsletter*, November/December 1968, p. 455.

16. Rose, op. cit., p. 307.

17. *News Chronicle*, 1 March 1954.

18. *Daily Herald*, 10 October 1963, 11 April 1961; *The Times*, 27 January 1965.

19. Rose, op. cit., p. 317.

20. *Observer*, 26 February 1967.

21. 18 August 1966.

22. *The Times*, 26 October 1967.

23. Political and Economic Planning Ltd, *Racial Discrimination*, p. 71.

24. *Ibid.*, pp. 71–2.

25. *Ibid.*, p. 78.

26. Cmnd 2739, p. 10.

27. Elizabeth Burney, *Housing on Trial*, p. 188. By 1966, some 15 years after the first black and Asian families arrived in Wolverhampton, the Labour-controlled council had accommodated only 122 'non-European' families in public housing. They formed 0.3% of the 38,400 tenants of the council, which owned nearly 40% of the city's total housing stock. The black and Asian population of Wolverhampton was then about 6%. *Ibid.*, pp. 185, 190, 194.

28. Rose, op. cit., p. 240.

29. Political and Economic Planning Ltd, op. cit., p. 86.

30. *The Times*, 26 October 1967.

31. Burney, op. cit., p. 73.

32. Political and Economic Planning Ltd, op. cit., p. 93.

33. *Ibid.*

34. *Birmingham Evening Mail*, 13 February 1966.

35. Political and Economic Planning Ltd, op. cit., p. 91.

36. *The Times*, 31 December 1969.

37. Daniel Lawrence's letter of 3 December 1968 to the author.

38. David J. Smith, *Racial Disadvantage in Britain*, p. 289.

39. *Ibid.*, pp. 236–7.

40. *Ibid.*, p. 235.

41. Cited in The Runnymede Trust and the Radical Statistics Race Group, *Britain's Black Population*, p. 76.

42. Colin Brown, *Black and White Britain*, p. 124.

43. p. 41.

44. *Independent*, 19 September 1989.

45. *Annual Report of the Commission for Racial Equality: January to December 1987*, p. 6.

46. Colin Brown and Pat Gay, *Racial Discrimination*, p. 31.

47. Cited in *Independent*, 29 October 1989.

48. *Observer*, 21 May 1988.

49. Chris Ranger, *Ethnic Minority School Teachers: A Survey in Eight Local Education Authorities*, Commission for Racial Equality, London, 1988, pp. 65–6.

50. Muhammad Anwar and Ameer Ali, *Overseas Doctors: Experience and Expectations*, Commission for Racial Equality, London, 1987, p. 73.

51. *Ibid.*, pp. 72–6.

52. John Brennan and Philip McGeevor, *Employment of Graduates from Ethnic Minorities*, Commission for Racial Equality, London, 1987, p. 71.

53. Of the 618 ethnic lawyers, 72% were South Asian, 14% Chinese, 11% Afro-Caribbean, and the rest African. *New Community*, vol. 16, no. 1, 1989, p. 119.

6: Contemporary White Attitudes and Practices

1. Cited in Richard Hooper (ed.), *Colour in Britain*, p. 134.

2. *Independent*, 19 August 1989.

3. *Ibid.*, 29 October 1989.

4. Clifford S. Hill, *How Colour Prejudiced Is Britain?*, p. 56.

5. Even by the very mild standards of judgement used by five social scientists, conducting a survey of whites' racial attitudes for the Institute of Race Relations in 1966–7, some 27% were considered 'prejudiced or prejudice-inclined'. E. J. B. Rose and Associates, *Colour and Citizenship*, p. 553.

6. *Ibid.*, p. 571.

7. 'Immigrants and the Social Services', in *The National Institute of Economic and Social Research Economic Review*, August 1967, pp. 28–40.

8. Rose, op. cit., p. 571.

9. According to the 1966 census, only 11% of the coloured immigrants were 45-plus years old compared to 38% of the total population. Cited in Rose, op. cit., p. 111.

10. *Ibid.*, p. 121.

11. *Observer*, 14 July 1968.

12. Two-thirds of the white respondents estimated the coloured population to be either 2–5 million, or more than 5 million. Rose, op. cit., p. 570. The 1966 census provided the following breakdown of people born outside the UK: from New (i.e. coloured) Commonwealth, 730,000 (excluding an estimated 100,000 whites recorded as born in the Indian subcontinent and a substantial number born in Africa); from the Irish Republic, 675,000; from foreign countries

(mainly Europe and America), 840,000; and from the Old (i.e. white) Commonwealth, 113,000. In racial terms, therefore, the figures were: black or brown immigrants, 730,000; white immigrants, 1,628,000.

13. Cmnd 2739, August 1965, p. 5.

14. *Observer*, 14 July 1968.

15. Peter Wright, *The Coloured Worker in British Industry*, pp. 193–4.

16. Rose, op. cit., p. 569.

17. *Observer*, 14 July 1968.

18. Cited in Paul Foot, *Immigration and Race in British Politics*, p. 128.

19. Wright, op. cit., p. 108.

20. Rose, op. cit., p. 569.

21. White also compared the measurements of anatomical features of over fifty negroes with those of whites, and concluded that the negro was nearer to the ape 'in bodily structure and economy' than was the European. Cited in Michael Banton, *Race Relations*, p. 20.

22. *Ibid.*, p. 157.

23. *Observer*, 14 July 1968.

24. Hill, op. cit., p. 89.

25. Cited in *Joffa*, March 1969, p. 8.

26. *Race Today*, May 1969, p. 13.

27. Market and social researchers divide British society into six socio-economic groups: A (professionals), B (managers), C1 (white collar), C2 (skilled manual workers), D (semi- or unskilled manual workers), and E (without earned income). Categories C2, D and E comprise the 'working class'. In 1990 the breakdown of the household heads was: A, 3%; B, 15%; C1, 23%; C2, 28%; D, 18%; and E, 14%. *Guardian*, 23 April 1990.

28. *The Times*, 20 June 1970.

29. National Association of Schoolmasters, *Education and the Immigrants*, p. 44.

30. *Race Without Rancour*, p. 32.

31. *Guardian*, 25 April 1967. When the inevitable protest from the liberal lobby followed, Sir William Carron cleverly pointed out that he had never used the word 'immigrant'. By carrying the art of subtlety further than his critics had done he successfully outwitted them.

32. *Observer*, 28 April 1968.

33. *The Times*, 27 April 1968.

34. *An American Dilemma*, Harper and Row, New York, 1944, p. 110.

35. *The Times*, 3 December 1969.

36. *Sunday Times*, 28 April 1968. A study by the Policy Studies Institute's David Smith and Sally Tomlinson of 3,000 pupils in 20 comprehensive schools in four urban areas between 1981 and 1986 – entitled *The School Effect: A Study of Multi-Racial Comprehensives* – concluded that differences in educational achievements between ethnic minority and white school-leavers are small and narrowing. 'The differences in exam results attributable to ethnic group are much smaller than those attributable to the school,' stated Smith and Tomlinson. 'In other words what school a child goes to makes far more difference (in terms of exam results) than what ethnic group he or she belongs to.' *Guardian*, 28 June 1989. See also Appendix IV.

37. James Halloran, Paul Hartmann and Charles Husband, 'Mass Media and Social Attitudes', *Social Science Research Council Newsletter*, June 1974, pp. 17–32.

38. 'Attitudes, Race Relations and Television', in John Twitchin (ed.), *The Black and White Media Show*, p. 128.

39. 'Schools and Race', in Stuart Hall *et al.*, *Five Views of Multi-Racial Britain*, pp. 64–5.

40. 23 June 1966.

41. *Sunday Telegraph*, 12 November 1967.

42. pp. 210–11.

43. Cited in Sheila Patterson (ed.), *Immigrants in London*, p. 39.

44. Sir Henry Marten and E. H. Carter, rev. edn, 1953, pp. 37–8. (Author's italics.)

45. *Ibid.*, p. 287.

46. Cited in A. Chater, *Race Relations in Britain*, p. 14. The large-scale textile industry in Britain and the world trade played havoc with the hand-spinning and hand-weaving industry of British India. 'The [resulting] misery hardly finds a parallel in the history of commerce,' wrote the Governor-General of India in his annual report of 1834–5. 'The bones of the cotton weavers are bleaching the plains of India.' The population of Dacca (now Dhaka), a leading centre of hand-weaving, for instance, fell from 150,000 in 1818 to 20,000 in 1836. *Ibid.*, p. 15.

47. Cited in Neville Maxwell, *The Power of Negro Action*, pp. 7–8.

48. Robin Oakley, *Employment in Police*

Forces: A Survey of Equal Opportunities, Commission for Racial Equality, London, 1988, p. 11.

49. Cited in Derek Humphrey, *Police Power and Black People*, p. 226.

50. *Guardian*, 19 July 1989; *Independent*, 20 September 1989.

51. *Independent*, 18 December 1989.

52. Rose, op. cit., p. 553. This astonishing conclusion was drawn on the basis of four main questions put to the respondents. Three of these concerned housing. In the face of strong criticism from academic and other sources, Nicholas Deakin, one of the authors of *Colour and Citizenship*, which first included Abrams's survey result, modified the interpretation of the results in his abridgement of that book, *Colour, Citizenship and British Society*. The two interpretations were:

Abrams's terms		Deakin's terms
Tolerant	35 per cent	Tolerant
Tolerant-inclined	38 per cent	Mildly prejudiced
Prejudice-inclined	17 per cent	Prejudiced
Prejudiced	10 per cent	Intensely prejudiced.

So, according to Abrams, 73 per cent of whites were tolerant or tolerantly-inclined; whereas, according to Deakin, 65 per cent were mildly prejudiced, prejudiced or intensely prejudiced. *Colour and Citizenship*, p. 553, and *Colour, Citizenship and British Society*, pp. 318–19.

53. Cited in *New Society*, 3 July 1969.

54. Cited in *Race Relations Abstract*, Spring 1969, p. 31.

55. *Race*, April 1969, p. 507.

56. Richard Hooper (ed.), *Colour in Britain*, p. 136.

57. *Independent*, 19 February 1990.

58. Cited in *Race Relations Abstract*, Spring 1969, p. 31.

59. *New Society*, 2 May 1968.

60. Cited in Michael Banton, *Race Relations*, pp. 60–1.

61. *New Statesman*, 9 July 1982.

62. *Guardian*, 19 July 1989; *Independent*, 19 August 1989.

63. In Metropolitan London the number of serious racially-motivated assaults during the first half of 1989 rose by 60% – from 120 to 190. The increase was noticed in six of the eight police areas. *Guardian*, 14 August 1989; *The Times*, 19 August 1989.

64. *Sacred Cows*, pp. 6–7, 9.

65. *The Times*, 11 May 1989. Jamal al-Afghani was an Afghani (as his name signified), not an Arab.

7: The Future: Assimilation or Social Pluralism?

1. *The Times*, 21 January 1982.

2. *Independent*, 29 October 1988.

3. Cited in *Race Relations Bulletin*, July 1970, p. 1.

4. This runs contrary to the definition of an Englishman in the *Pocket Oxford Dictionary*: 'someone English by birth, descent or naturalization'.

5. Webster's *New Collegiate Dictionary*, 1961, p. 696.

6. Sheila Patterson, *Dark Strangers*, p. 343.

7. Colin Brown, *Black and White Britain*, p. 290.

8. *New Society*, 9 November 1967.

9. Patterson, op. cit., pp. 21–2.

10. *Ibid.*, pp. 200–206.

11. *Ibid.*, p. 352.

12. *The Power of Negro Action*, p. 12.

13. Ernest Krausz, 'Jews in Britain: Integrated or Apart?', a paper presented to the Fourth Annual Conference of the Institute of Race Relations, London, 1969.

14. 20 March 1969.

15. *Report of The Race Relations Board for 1966–67*, para. 44, pp. 16–17. This paragraph also stated that 'They [West Indians and Asians] are identifiable and will remain identifiable, unless they are wholly assimilated into the native population. But assimilation … is not the policy of Her Majesty's Government.' It must be noted that assimilation could not possibly be the official policy. Because to be 'wholly assimilated' into the native population, black or brown citizens would either have to get their skins bleached or be married on a massive scale to whites.

16. As described by the researcher, Daniel Lawrence, to the author in September 1969.

17. 10 March 1968.

18. Brown, op. cit., p. 33.

19. Figures vary with the wording of the question. The Gallup poll in 1961, for instance, asked: 'Do you think that marriage between a white person and a coloured person

is, or is not, advisable?' In contrast, a few years later Clifford S. Hill asked: 'Would you approve of your sister, or your daughter, marrying a coloured person?' *How Colour Prejudiced is Britain?*, p. 39. Characteristically enough, no national poll of blacks and Asians has yet been taken on the subject.

20. Department of Education and Science, London, 1967, p. 13.

21. *House of Commons Report from the Select Committee on Race Relations and Immigration: The Problems of Coloured School-Leavers*, vol. I, July 1969, p. 56.

22. Cited in National Association of

Schoolmasters, *Education and the Immigrants*, p. 22.

23. In 1969, in Birmingham alone, sixteen schools had more than 60% black and Asian children. *Race Today*, May 1969, p. 25.

24. *Evening Standard*, 1 July 1969.

25. Brown, op. cit., pp. 283, 289.

26. *A Letter to Christendom*, p. 8.

27. *Guardian*, 7 September 1988.

28. In 1989 France alone had nearly 3 million Muslims and West Germany more than a million.

Appendix I

General Election Results, and Race and Immigration Laws, since 1945*

Year	Conservative	Labour	Liberal	Others	Total	Governing Party	Legislation Passed
1945	197	393	12	38	640	Labour	British Nationality Act 1948
1950	298	315	9	3	625	Labour	
1951	311	295	6	13	625	Conservative	
1955	345	277	6	2	630	Conservative	
1959	365	258	6	1	630	Conservative	Commonwealth Immigrants Act
1964	304	317	9	—	630	Labour	British Nationality Act 1964
							British Nationality (No. 2) Act 1964
							Race Relations Act 1965
1966	253	364	12	1	630	Labour	Commonwealth Immigrants Act 1968
							Race Relations Act 1968
							Immigration Appeals Act 1969
1970	330	288	6	6	630	Conservative	Immigration Act 1971
1974 February	297	301	14	23	635	Labour	
1974 October	277	319	13	26	635	Labour	Race Relations Act 1976
1979	339	269	11	16	635	Conservative	British Nationality Act 1981
1983	397	209	17	27	650	Conservative	
1987	376	229	17	28	650	Conservative	Immigration Act 1988

* Sources: F. W. S. Craig (ed.), *British Electoral Facts*, Parliamentary Research Services Department, Gower Publishing Co., Aldershot, Fifth Edition, 1989; and Paul Gordon, *Race in Britain: A Research and Information Guide*, The Runnymede Trust, London, 1988.

Appendix II: Figures of Immigration from Colonies and New Commonwealth 1948–88

Table 1 Net Immigration from Colonies and New Commonwealth: 1 January 1948 to 30 June 1962*

Period	West Indies	India	Pakistan	Others	Total
1948 to 1953	14,000	2,500	1,500	10,000	28,000†
1954	11,000	800	500	6,000	18,300†
1955	27,550	5,800	1,850	7,500	42,700
1956	29,800	5,600	2,050	9,400	46,850
1957	23,000	6,600	5,200	7,600	42,400
1958	15,000	6,200	4,700	3,950	29,850
1959	16,400	2,950	850	1,400	21,600
1960	49,650	5,900	2,500	−350	57,700
1961	66,300	23,750	25,100	21,250	136,400
30 June 1962	27,037	19,245	23,837	13,652	83,771

* Sources: *Home Office: Control of Immigration Statistics: 1 July 1962 to 31 December 1962*, Cmnd 2379, HMSO, London, 1964; *Hansard*, 18 March 1965; and *White Paper on Immigration*, Cmnd 2739, HMSO, London, 1965.
† Author's estimate

Table 2 Number of Citizens of Colonies and New Commonwealth Allowed to Settle in Britain: 1 July 1962* to 31 December 1972**

Period	West Indies	India	Pakistan	UK Passport Holders from East Africa	Others	Total
1 July to 31 December 1962	7,004	2,855	1,106	—	7,849	18,814
1963	7,928	17,498	16,336	—	15,287	57,049
1964	14,848	15,513	10,980	—	20,776	62,117
1965	14,828	17,086	9,401	—	12,336	53,651
1966	10,928	16,708	10,245	—	8,721	46,602
1967	12,424	19,067	18,644	—	7,513	57,648
1968	7,013	23,147	13,426	—	12,617	56,203
1969	4,531	10,958	12,658	6,249	5,795	40,191
1970	3,934	7,158	9,863	6,839	5,707	33,501
1971	2,774	6,874	6,957	11,564	5,006	33,175
1972	2,453	7,589	5,399	34,825†	9,584	59,850

* On this date the Commonwealth Immigrants Act 1962 became law.
** Sources: *Home Office: Control of Immigration Statistics: 1963*, Cmnd 2658, HMSO, London, 1964; *White Paper on Immigration*, Cmnd 2739, HMSO, London, 1965; and *Home Office: Control of Immigration Statistics: 1964* to *Home Office: Control of Immigration Statistics: 1972*, Cmnds 2979, 3258, 3594, 4028, 4327, 4620, 4951, 5285, 5603, HMSO, London, 1965 to 1973.
† This figure includes about 27,000 Uganda Asians.

Table 3   Number of Citizens of Colonies and New Commonwealth Allowed to Settle in Britain: 1 July 1973* to 31 December 1988**

Period	West Indies	India	Pakistan	Bangladesh†	UK Passport Holders from East Africa	Others	Total
1973	2,685	6,240	3,638	1,753	10,443	7,488	32,247
1974	3,198	6,654	4,401	1,022	13,436	13,820	42,531
1975	3,698	10,195	7,724	3,276	13,792	14,580	53,265
1976	2,697	11,021	11,699	3,975	11,655	13,966	55,013
1977	2,237	7,339	13,331	3,306	6,401	11,541	44,155
1978	1,753	9,886	12,425	4,385	5,350	9,140	42,939
1979	1,282	9,268	10,945	3,915	4,038	7,599	37,047
1980	1,080	7,930	9,080	5,210	3,030††	7,290	33,620
1981	980	6,590	8,970	5,810	2,780	6,240	31,370
1982	770	5,410	7,750	7,020	2,720	6,710	30,380
1983	750	5,380	6,440	4,870	3,280	6,830	27,550
1984	680	5,140	5,510	4,180	2,690	6,600	24,800
1985	770	5,500	6,680	5,330	2,180	6,590	27,050
1986	830	4,210	5,580	4,760	1,680	5,600	22,660
1987	890	4,610	3,930	3,080	1,860	6,460	20,830
1988	1,030	5,020	4,280	2,890	1,910	7,670	22,800

* On this date the Immigration Act 1971 became law.

** Sources: *Home Office: Control of Immigration Statistics: 1979*, Cmnd 7875, HMSO, London, 1980; and *Home Office: Control of Immigration Statistics: 1988*, Cmnd 726, HMSO, London, 1989.

† Bangladesh was established in December 1971.

†† The classification was changed from 'UK Passport Holders from East Africa' to 'British Overseas Citizens'.

Appendix III: Estimated Ethnic Minority Populations of Great Britain*

Ethnic Group	Estimated Population (thousands) 1981	1988	% of Total Ethnic Minority Population (1988)	% Change during 1981–88 Thousands	%
West Indian	528	468	17.4	− 60	− 11.4
African	80	122	4.5	+ 42	+ 52.6
Indian	727	814	30.2	+ 87	+ 9.4
Pakistani	284	479	17.8	+ 195	+ 68.7
Bangladeshi	52	91	3.4	+ 39	+ 75.0
Chinese	92	136	5.1	+ 44	+ 47.8
Arab	53	66	2.5	+ 13	+ 24.5
Mixed	217	328	12.2	+ 111	+ 51.2
Other**	60	184	6.9	+ 124	+ 206.7
All Ethnic Minority Groups	2,092	2,687†	100.0	+ 595††	+ 28.4
White	51,000	51,632	–	+ 632	+ 1.2
Not Stated	608	343	–	− 265	− 43.6
Grand Total	53,700	54,662	–	+ 962	+ 1.8

* Source: *Population Trends No. 60, Summer 1990,* Office of Population Censuses
& Surveys, HMSO, London, 1990, pp. 35–8.

** 'Other' includes settlers from the rest of the New Commonwealth and such Third
World countries as Iran.

† Almost half were born in Great Britain.

†† This gives an average annual increase of 74,400 in the total ethnic minority
population.

Appendix IV: Correlation between Ethnicity and Educational Performance*

Results of the ILEA Survey on the 1987 marks for 16-year-olds sitting the final year of the old CSE and GCE O-level examination

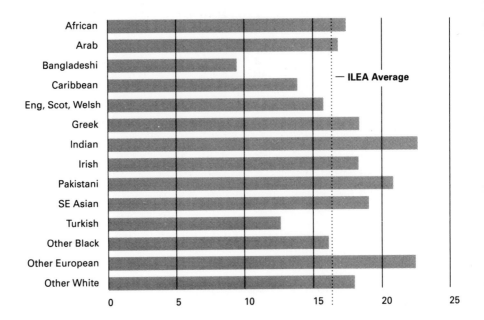

Bars represent average score of children in each ethnic group

* Source: The Research & Statistics Unit of the Inner London
Education Authority (ILEA), London, published in the *Independent*,
9 March 1990.

Select Bibliography

Anwar, Muhammad, *The Myth of Return: Pakistanis in Britain*, Heinemann Educational Books, London, 1979.
— *Race and Politics: Ethnic Minorities and British Political System*, Tavistock Publications, London, 1986.

Appignanesi, Lisa, and Maitland, Sara (eds), *The Rushdie File*, Fourth Estate, London, 1989.

Banton, Michael, *Race Relations*, Tavistock Publications, London, 1967.

Beetham, David, *Immigrant School Leavers and the Youth Employment Service in Birmingham*, Institute of Race Relations, London, 1968.

Benyon, John, *A Tale of Failure: Race and Policing*, Centre for Research in Ethnic Relations, University of Warwick, Coventry, 1986.

Brown, Colin, *Black and White Britain: The Third PSI Survey*, Heinemann Educational Books, London, 1984.

Brown, Colin, and Gay, Pat, *Racial Discrimination: 17 Years After the Act*, Policy Studies Institute, London, 1985.

Burney, Elizabeth, *Housing on Trial*, Oxford University Press, Oxford, 1967.

Calley, Malcolm J. C., *God's People: West Indian Pentecostal Sects in England*, Oxford University Press, Oxford, 1965.

Cashmore, Ernest, *Rastaman: The Rastafarian Movement in England*, Allen & Unwin, London, 1979.

Cashmore, Ernest, and Troyna, Barry (eds), *Black Youth in Crisis*, Allen & Unwin, London, 1982.
— *Introduction to Race Relations*, Routledge & Kegan Paul, London, 1983.

Chater, A., *Race Relations in Britain*, Lawrence & Wishart, London, 1966.

Coard, Bernard, *How the West Indian Child is Made Educationally Subnormal in the British School System: The Scandal of the Black Child in Schools in Britain*, New Beacon Books, London, 1971.

Cox, Oliver Cromwell, *Caste, Class and Race*, Monthly Review Press, New York, 1959.

Daniel, W. W., *Racial Discrimination in England*, Penguin Books, Harmondsworth, 1968.

Davison, R. B., *West Indian Migrants: Social and Economic Facts of Emigration from the West Indies*, Oxford University Press, Oxford, 1962.
— *Black British*, Oxford University Press, Oxford, 1966.

Deakin, Nicholas, *Colour, Citizenship and British Society*, Panther Books, London, 1970.

Desai, Rashmi, *Indian Immigrants in Britain*, Oxford University Press, Oxford, 1963.

Dummett, Ann, *A Portrait of Racism*, Penguin Books, Harmondsworth, 1973.

Foot, Paul, *Immigration and Race in British Politics*, Penguin Books, Harmondsworth, 1965.

Fryer, Peter, *Staying Power: The History of Black People in Britain*, Pluto Press, London, 1984.

Gaffney, John, *Interpretation of Violence: The Handsworth Riots of 1985*, Centre for Research in Ethnic Relations, University of Warwick, Coventry, 1987.

Gifford, Lord, Brown, Wally, and Bundey, Ruth, *Loosen the Shackles: First Report of the Liverpool 8 Inquiry into Race Relations in Liverpool*, Karia Press, London, 1989.

Glass, Ruth, and Pollins, Harold, *Newcomers*, Allen & Unwin, London, 1960.

Gordon, Paul, *White Law: Racism in the Police, Courts and Prisons*, Pluto Press, London, 1983.

Hall, Stuart, *et al.*, *Five Views of Multi-Racial Britain: Talks on Race Relations Broadcast by BBC TV*, Commission for Racial Equality, London, 1978.

Hashmi, Farrukh, *The Pakistani Family in Britain*, Community Relations Commission, London, 1969.

Helweg, A., *Sikhs in England*, Oxford University Press, Oxford, 1979.

Hepple, Bob, *Race, Jobs and the Law in Britain*, Allen Lane, The Penguin Press, London, 1968.

Hill, Clifford S., *West Indian Migrants and the London Churches*, Oxford University Press, Oxford, 1963.
— *How Colour Prejudiced Is Britain?*, Panther Books, London, 1967.

Hinds, Donald, *Journey to an Illusion*, Heinemann, London, 1966.

Hiro, Dilip, *The Indian Family in Britain*, Community Relations Commission, London, 1969.

Hooper, Richard (ed.), *Colour in Britain*, British Broadcasting Corporation, London, 1965.

Humphrey, Derek, *Police Power and Black People*, Panther Books, London, 1972.

Humphrey, Derek, and Ward, Michael, *Passports and Politics*, Penguin Books, Harmondsworth, 1974.

Husband, Charles (ed.), *White Media and Black Britain*, Arrow Books, London, 1975.

— *'Race' in Britain: Continuity and Change*, Hutchinson, London, 1982.

Jacobs, Brian D., *Black Politics and Urban Crisis in Britain*, Cambridge University Press, Cambridge, 1986.

— *Racism in Britain*, Christopher Helm, Bromley, 1988.

Kabbani, Rana, *A Letter to Christendom*, Virago Press, London, 1989.

Kettle, Martin, and Hodges, Lucy, *Uprising! The Police, the People and the Riots in Britain's Cities*, Pan Books, London, 1982.

Kiernan, V. G., *The Lords of Human Kind*, Weidenfeld & Nicolson, London, 1969.

Layton-Henry, Zig, *The Politics of Race in Britain*, Allen & Unwin, London, 1984.

Layton-Henry, Zig, and Rich, Paul B. (eds), *Race, Government and Politics in Britain*, Macmillan, London, 1986.

Leech, Kenneth, *Struggle in Babylon: Racism in the Cities and Churches in Britain*, Sheldon Press, London, 1988.

Little, K. L., *Negroes in Britain*, Kegan Paul, London, 1947.

Maxwell, Neville, *The Power of Negro Action*, The Author, London, 1965.

Miles, Robert, and Phizacklea, Annie, *Racism and Political Action in Britain*, Routledge & Kegan Paul, London, 1979.

Naipaul, V. S., *The Middle Passage*, André Deutsch, London, 1962.

Ottley, Roi, *No Green Pastures*, John Murray, London, 1952.

Parekh, Bhikhu (ed.), *Colour, Culture and Consciousness*, Allen & Unwin, London, 1974.

Patterson, Sheila, *Dark Strangers*, Penguin Books, Harmondsworth, 1965.

— *Immigration and Race Relations in Britain, 1960–1967*, Oxford University Press, Oxford, 1969.

Peach, Ceri, *West Indian Migration to Britain: A Social Geography*, Oxford University Press, Oxford, 1968.

Political and Economic Planning Ltd, *Racial Discrimination*, PEP, London, 1967.

Power, John, *Immigrants in School*, Councils and Education Press, London, 1967.

Pratt, Michael, *Mugging as a Social Problem*, Routledge & Kegan Paul, London, 1980.

Ramdin, Ron, *The Making of the Black British Working Class in Britain*, Wildwood House, Aldershot, 1987.

Ratcliffe, P., *Racism and Reaction*, Routledge & Kegan Paul, London, 1981.

Rex, John, and Moore, Robert, *Race, Community and Conflict: A Study of Sparkbrook*, Oxford University Press, Oxford, 1967.

Rose, E. J. B., and Associates, *Colour and Citizenship*, Oxford University Press, Oxford, 1969.

The Runnymede Trust and The Radical Statistics Race Group, *Britain's Black Population*, Heinemann Educational Books, London, 1980.

Scarman, Lord, *The Brixton Disorders 10–12 April 1981*, Pelican Books, Harmondsworth, 1982.

Sivanandan, A. V., *A Different Kind of Hunger*, Pluto Press, London, 1982.

Smith, David J., *Racial Disadvantage in Employment*, Political and Economic Planning Ltd, London, 1974.

— *The Facts of Racial Disadvantage*, Political and Economic Planning Ltd, London, 1976.

— *Racial Disadvantage in Britain: The PEP Report*, Penguin Books, Harmondsworth, 1977.

Taylor, J. H., *The Half-Way Generation: A Study of Asian youths in Newcastle upon Tyne*, NFER Publishing Company, Windsor, 1976.

Twitchin, John (ed.), *The Black and White Media Book: Handbook for the Study of Racism and Television*, Trentham Books, Stoke-on-Trent, 1988.

Visram, Rozina, *Ayahs, Lascars and Princes: Indians in Britain 1700–1947*, Pluto Press, London, 1984.

Wahhab, Iqbal, *Muslims in Britain: Profile of a Community*, The Runnymede Trust, London, 1989.

Walker, Martin, *The National Front*, Fontana Books, London, 1977.

Watson, James L. (ed.), *Between Two Cultures: Migrants and Minorities in Britain*, Basil Blackwell, Oxford, 1977.

Webster, Richard, *A Brief History of Blasphemy: Liberalism, Censorship And The Satanic Verses*, The Orwell Press, Southwold, 1990.

Weldon, Fay, *Sacred Cows*, Chatto & Windus, London, 1989.

Wickenden, James, *Colour in Britain*, Oxford University Press, Oxford, 1958.

Wood, Wilfred, and Downing, John, *Vicious Circle*, Society for the Propagation of Christian Knowledge, London, 1968.

Wright, Peter, *The Coloured Worker in British Industry*, Oxford University Press, Oxford, 1968.

Photo Credits

West Indian immigrants
HULTON PICTURE COMPANY
SS Empire Windrush
CAMERA PRESS
'No Coloureds' sign
REX FEATURES
Arrival of Kenyan Asians
HULTON PICTURE COMPANY
Pro-Powell march
HULTON PICTURE COMPANY
Enoch Powell
HULTON PICTURE COMPANY
Anti-Nazi League demonstration
FRANK SPOONER PICTURES
Bob Marley
REX FEATURES
Grunwick strike
HULTON PICTURE COMPANY
Demonstration against arrival of
Ugandan Asians
REX FEATURES
National Front press conference
HULTON PICTURE COMPANY

Diane Abbott
LABOUR PARTY
Paul Boateng
LABOUR PARTY
Keith Vaz
POPPERFOTO
Bernie Grant
LABOUR PARTY/PRESS ASSOCIATION
David Pitt
PRESS ASSOCIATION
Aftermath of the Brixton riot
REX FEATURES
Aerial view of riot-torn Handsworth
PRESS ASSOCIATION
Funeral procession in Walthamstow
CHRIS STEELE-PERKINS/MAGNUM PHOTO'S
British Movement demonstration
CHRIS STEELE-PERKINS/MAGNUM PHOTO'S
Salman Rushdie demonstration
AUTHOR'S COLLECTION

Index

A Different Reality, 100
A Spur to Racialism, 207
Abbot, Diane, 102, 103
Abercrombie, Ralph, 20
Abrams, Mark, 299
Abyssinia, *see* Ethiopia
Acculturation, 126, 149–50, 151–2, 158–9, 304
Action Committee Against Racial Attacks (ACARA), 170
Adams, Gabriel, 72
Adams, Leonard, 87
Afghanistan, 182, 183
Africa and Africans, 3, 13, 18, 19, 25, 31, 48, 61–2, 63, 65, 72, 73, 144, 229, 284, 293
Afro-Americans, viii, 24, 25, 43, 48
Afro-Caribbeans, *see* West Indians
Afro-Caribbean Club, 100
Afro-Caribbean Educational Resource Project, 71, 229, 296
Air Pak, 123
Akhtar, Shabbir, 182, 302
Akram, Muhammad, 155
al-Afghani, Jamal, 302
Al Aqsa mosque, 134
al Ashraf, Kaab ibn, 185
Al Mujahid, 188
Ali, Altab, 170
Ali, Haji Tasleem, 134
Ali, Taeeb, 118
Ali, Tariq Mahmood, 175
Ali, Tosir, 161
Aliens, Restrictions Act 1914, 251
All India Radio, 123
Alvi, Hamza, 46
Amalgamated Engineers' Union, 289
Ambrosius, Geraldine, 101
America and Americans, 144, 182, 269, 294, 306, 308
    Black Power movement in, 48, 49, 62, 63
    Christian churches in, 31, 33, 62
    civil rights movement in, viii, 43, 48, 140
    desegregation in, 306–7
    history of, 5, 6
    immigration into, 14, 15, 199
    Ku Klux Klan in, 45
    race relations in, 10, 218
    race riots in (1967), 218
    in Vietnam, 47, 82
    and West Indians, 14, 15
American Indians, 1, 33, 47, 309
Amerindians, *see* American Indians
Amin, Idi, 223, 224
Amory, Merle, 94
Amritsar, 139, 180
An American Dilemma, 290
Anglican church, 32, 33, 192
Anglo-Asian Society, 180
Anglo-Fanti, The, 7
Anglo-West Indian Society, 180
Anguilla, 30
Annual Report of the Commission for Racial Equality 1986, 275
Anti-Nazi League (ANL), 91, 170, 171, 172, 173, 296
Anti-Racist Committee of Asians in East London (ARC–AEL), 169, 170
Antigua, 19
Anwar, Muhammad, 94
Arab–Israeli War (1973), 182
Arabian Peninsula, 110
Arabic language, 134, 143, 154
Arbitration, Conciliation and Advisory Service (ACAS), 167–8
Aryan tribes, 110
Ashcroft, Peggy, 9
Asia, 134
Asia and Asians, *see* Part II *passim*; viii, 256, 293, 294, 303–4, 308, 312
    and British Broadcasting Corporation, 125–6
    in British Empire, 108
    in business, 120–3, 124, 125, 137, 141, 164, 177–8, 282
    characteristics of, 149
    and Christianity, 154, 155
    cinema, 118, 124, 140, 156
    class composition of, 178, 179
    and Community Relations Councils, 236, 242, 243
    culture of, 113, 118, 119, 136–7, 143–4, 145–8, 150–1, 158, 254–6, 311
    and Conservative Party, 140, 167, 168, 179–80
    from East Africa, 77, 108, 123, 124–5, 142, 161, 164, 166–8, 178, 212–16, 223–5

Asia and Asians *cont.*
  education and educational performance of,
    53, 126, 148, 162, 272, 292, 311, 313
  employment pattern of, 67, 68, 111–12,
    117, 149, 178, 262–5
  and English language, 125, 126, 148,
    155–6, 157, 231
  family life of, 146, 150, 156–7, 164–5
  house ownership among, 274, 275
  as indentured labour in British Empire, 108
  and Indian languages, 143–4, 155, 177
  from Kenya, 77, 142, 212–16
  and Labour Party, 77, 78, 79, 93–6, 102,
    140, 177, 190
  leadership of, 116, 137, 138, 139–41, 172
  and local government, 93–4, 96, 177
  from Malawi, 256, 291
  migration to Britain, 110–15
  marriage customs of, 146–7, 158, 159
  and the National Front, 169, 175, 254–5
  and the National Health Service, 280
  and police, 172–3, 174–5, 179
  and Enoch Powell's April 1968 speech, 142,
    161, 162, 171
  press, 123
  and race riots, *see under* Race Riots,
    individual cities and metropolitan areas,
    particularly Southall
  racial discrimination in employment, 67–9,
    119–20, 131, 160, 162–3, 217–18, 225,
    231–2, 238, 262–5, 266–7, 276–8
  racial discrimination in housing, 120, 218,
    225, 267–75
  racial harassment and violence against, 161,
    164, 169–70, 174–5, 178–9, 248, 249,
    259
  religious composition of, 181
  school children's dispersal, 239, 310–11
  settlement pattern of, 117, 120, 122–3, 178,
    179
  size of the community, ix
  and trade unions, 139–40, 166–8, 231,
    264–6
  from Uganda, 77, 125, 223–5
  voting pattern of, 78, 96, 168, 172
  white attitudes towards, 304–5, 311
  whites, perception of, 150–1, 157–8, 165–6,
    187–8
  and women, 147, 150, 153–4, 156, 158–9
  youths and youth clubs, 150, 151–2, 156,
    159–61, 164–5, 169, 171–6, 228, 231,
    266–7, 271, 277
Asian Labour Party Alliance (ALPA), 94
Asian Youth Movement, 172, 175
Aslam, Mehtab, 157
Association of Professional, Executive and
    Computer Staff (APEX), 167

Association of Scientific, Technical and
    Managerial Staff (ASTMS), 248
Association of Sunni Muslims, 186, 192
Atkinson, Norman, 102
Attlee, Clement, 9
Australia and Australians, viii, 110, 163, 198,
    239
Aylesbury, Lord, 290

Babylon, 72
Bailey, Michael, 87
Baldwin, James, 1
Bangladesh and Bangladeshis, viii, 117, 118,
    122, 132, 141, 150, 151, 172, 185, 225,
    277
Bangladeshi Welfare Association, 172
Bangladeshi Youth League, 172
Banton, Michael, 3, 279, 305
Baptist church, 31, 32
Barbados, viii, 2, 19, 197
  anglicization of, 19
  Christianity in, 32
  economy of, 16–17
  see also West Indians in Britain
Barry, Ralph, 32
Basi, Umerao Singh, 112
Basra, Gurmail Singh, 180
Basra, Manmohan Singh, 138
Basti, Muhammad Akhundzadeh, 186
Bastide, Roger, 308
Basutoland, 9
Battersea, 103
Beetham, David, 52, 53, 156, 162
Bell, Ronald, 220–1
Bengali Housing Action Group (BHAG), 169,
    172
Bengali language, viii, 124, 155
Benn, Tony, 291
Bentley, Stuart, 134
Bethnal Green and Stepney Trades Council,
    171
Bhandari, G. S., 114
Bhindranwale, Sant Jarnail Singh, 180
Bhopal, 133
Bhownaggree, Mancherjee, 78, 102–3
Bible, 75, 136, 301
Bidwell, Sydney, 94
Bird, Vere, C., 62
Birmingham, 34, 241, 248
  Asians in, 93
  city council, 100, 200, 271, 272
  Co-ordinating Committee Against Racial
    Discrimination formed in, 42
  ethnic councillors in, 93
  Indians in, 138
  labour shortage in, 36
  Ladywood by-election (1977), 78

Muslims in, 135
Pakistanis in, 133
Pentecostal churches in, 34
prostitution in, 36
race riots in Handsworth (1985), 97–8,
   99–100, 177
racial discrimination in, 29, 276
racial violence in, 161
West Indians in, 28, 29–30
Birmingham Evening Mail, 202
Birmingham Immigration Control Association,
   202, 204
Birmingham Post, 29
Black, definition of, viii
Black and Asian Advisory Committee, 96, 103
Black and Asian Socialist Society, 104
Black and White Café, Bristol, 85
Black Freedom march, 176
Black Hole of Calcutta, 284, 294–5
Black Panthers
   in Britain, 63
   in Trinidad, 63
Black People's Alliance, 64, 95, 142–3
Black People's Manifesto, 78
Black Power movement, 46–9, 62, 63, 72, 76
Black Sections (Labour Party), 95–6, 102,
   103–4
Black Studies, 70, 229, 230; *see also* Education,
   multi-ethnic
Black Unity and Freedom Party, 76
Blackburn, 256
Blackman, 71
Blackshirt, 254
Blakelock, Keith, 99
Blasphemy, 184, 191, 192
Bleher, Sahib Mustaqim, 191
Bloom, Leonard, 253
Blumenbach, J. F., 283
Boateng, Paul, 94, 102
Bogle, Paul, 20, 69
Bombay, 149, 185
Boxer Rebellion, 110
Bradford, 119, 176, 267
   Asian businesses in, 121
   Asians in, 93, 172
   Indians in, 114
   Muslims in, 134, 135, 184
   Pakistanis in, 114, 117, 118, 123, 134
   and Rushdie affair, 184
   West Indians in, 175
   Young Asians in, 172, 175
Bradford Black Collective, 76
Bradford Twelve, 175
Braithwaite, E. R., 27
Brazil, 308–9
Brent, 94, 102, 217, 272, 277, 291–2
Brent Trades Council, 167

Bristol, 43
   police raids in, 85, 100, 101
   race riots in (1981), 85–6, 92
   racial harassment in, 178–9
   West Indians in, 85
Britain and British, 52–3, 100, 101, 144, 295
   and Asians, 107–15, 149
   characteristics of, 149, 284–6, 289
   and churches, 34
   and economy, 69, 175–6
   and Islam, 1, 181, 182
   labour shortage in, 17, 36, 199, 261–3
   middle class values, dominance of, 284–6,
      287
   and the Middle East, 181, 182
   and racial discrimination, *see* racial
      discrimination
   unemployment in, 275–6
   and West Indians, 15–18, 36
British Black Power Party, 64
British Broadcasting Corporation (BBC), 125,
   187, 189, 192, 233, 259, 286, 291
British Caribbean Welfare Service, 26, 41
British Guiana, 108
British Movement (BM), 168, 169, 258, 259
British Muslim Action Front, 187
British National Party (BNP), 246, 247, 256,
   257, 258
British Nationality Act
   1948, 198, 259
   1981, 259–60
British Union of Fascists, 254
British West Indies, *see* West Indies
Brixton, 119, 240, 255
   black unemployment in, 54, 84
   Pentecostal church in, 34
   police in, 84, 85, 87
   race riots in (1981), 84, 85, 87–8, 90, 92,
      98
   West Indians in, 27, 28, 119, 255
Broadwater Farm estate, 98, 100, 101, 177
Broadwater Farm Youth Association, 98, 101
Brockway, Lord, 207, 209, 210, 232
Brown, Colin, 178, 209
Brown, Roosevelt, 63
Brown, Wally, 81
Bryan, Stanley, 27
Burma, 9, 108, 294
Burney, Elizabeth, 267, 269, 270, 272
Burt, Robert A., 233
Butler, David, 186
Butler, Lord, 202

Cabot, John, 197
Calcutta, 112, 149, 294–5
Callaghan, James, 199, 209, 216, 250, 258
Cambodia, 294

Campaign Against Racial Discrimination
(CARD), 44–5, 46, 119, 125, 141, 207,
218, 266
Canada, viii, 110, 112, 147, 198
Cardiff, 304
race riot in (1919), 8, 37–8
racial discrimination in, 253
Carib Club, 79
Caribbean Quarterly, 59
Caribbeans, *see* West Indians in Britain
Carmichael, Stokely, 47–8, 218
Carron, Sir William, 289
Cashmore, Ernest, 74, 75
Caucasoids, viii
Central Intelligence Agency, 47
Central Race Equality Unit, Haringey, 244
Ceylon, *see* Sri Lanka
Chaggar, Gurdip Singh, 169, 172
Charles II, King, 13
Chase, Clifford, 13
Chesham, Lord, 210
Chesterton, A. K., 254
China and Chinese, viii, 109, 148
Chisiza, Dunduzu, 61
Christ, Jesus, 31, 155, 184
Christianity and Christians, 32, 33, 136, 152,
184, 185–6, 188, 189, 192, 193, 293,
312, 313
Church of England schools, 188
Churchill, Sir Winston, 209, 295–6
Clarke, Jonathan, 26
Clive, Robert, 294
Coard, Bernard, 69
Code of Practice for Employers, 231
Colman, Andrew, 83
Columbus, Christopher, 5, 20, 197
Colour and Citizenship, 33, 237, 252, 253, 266
Colour bar, *see* Racial discrimination
Coloured, definition of, vii–viii
Committee of Afro-Asian-Caribbean
Organizations (CAACO), 42
Committee of the Youth Service Development
Council, 310
Commonwealth, British, 193, 197–8
New, viii, 198, 200, 203, 206, 235, 264,
277
Old, viii, 206
Commonwealth Citizens Consultative
Committees, 234
Commonwealth Immigrants Act 1962, vii,
114, 143, 203, 204–5, 210, 212, 251
Commonwealth Immigrants Act 1968, 142,
143, 161, 209, 214–15, 249, 251
Commonwealth Immigrants Advisory
Committee, 234, 240
Commonwealth immigration control, *see*
Immigration control

Commonwealth of Nations, British, *see* British
Commonwealth
Commonwealth Prime Ministers' Conference
1969, 63, 143
Commission for Racial Equality (CRE), 69,
71, 175, 178, 179, 226–32, 241–4, 260,
275, 276, 277, 278, 299–300
Commission of the European Convention on
Human Rights, 215
Communist Party, 78, 79, 103, 168, 177
Community Relations Commission, 226, 235,
241, 286, 307
Community Relations Councils (CRCs), 171,
187, 235–7, 241–3, 244, 303, 307
Confederation of British Industry, 219, 266
Congo, *see* Zaïre
Conservative Party, 45, 99, 102–3, 312–13
and Asians, 140, 167, 168, 179–80
and Commonwealth immigration, 41–2,
199, 202, 206, 207, 211–12, 214, 223,
246–7, 249–50
and Grunwick strike, 251, 257
and Muslims, 192
and National Front, 257, 258
and parliamentary elections
(1959), 202
(1964), 44
(1970), 222
(1979), 78, 168, 275
(1983), 93, 94, 97
(1987), 102
and race relations laws, 209–11, 220–1, 227,
247, 257, 258
and the Uganda Asians crisis, 223–5, 254
and West Indians, 78, 168, 180
Co-ordinating Committee Against Racial
Discrimination (CCARD), 42, 43, 45,
140
Costa Rica, 14
Councils of Social Service, 233, 235
Coventry, 138, 161, 248
Coxsone, Lloyd, 90
Creole language, 21, 61, 75
Criminal Attempts Act 1981, 92
Cromwell, Oliver, 2
Cross, Malcolm, 228
Crossman, Richard, 206
Crusades, 1, 182, 302
Cuba, 14, 308
Cyprus and Cypriots, 22, 116, 145, 163,
217–18, 220

Daily Gleaner, 42
Daily Mirror, 214, 291
Daily Telegraph, 173, 220
Dam Dam Taskal, 180
Dark Strangers, 294, 305

Darling, Alastair, 191
Darragh, John, 27, 282–3
Darwin, Charles, 7
Das, Guru Darshan, 180
Davis, Jefferson, 6–7
Davison, R. B., 27
Deedes, William, 207, 287
Delhi, 185
Desai, Jayaben, 167
Desai, Rashmi, 118
Desai, Sunil, 167
Desdemona, 9
Detroit, 218
Dewsbury, 189, 190
Dhami, Trilok Singh, 128
Discrimination, *see* Racial discrimination
District Support Units, Police, 86
Divali, 145
Dormey, Jack, 167
Douglas-Home, Sir Alec, 200–1, 206, 211
Dowlah, Suraja, 294
Driberg, Tom, 209, 232
Dunkley, Lance, 59
Dutch, *see* Holland
Dyer, Brigadier-General R. E. H., 139, 295

Ealing, 57, 94, 177, 310, 311
East Africa, viii, 108, 110, 168, 225
East India Company, 108, 197–8, 294
East Pakistan, 111, 141, 250
Economist, 8, 201, 207, 260
Edgware, 306
Education, 294, 310
    and Asians, 53, 126, 148, 162, 277, 292,
        311, 313
    institutional racism in, 229–30
    integration in, 239
    multi-ethnic, 70, 71, 228–30, 296–7, 311,
        312–13
    and Muslims, 135, 188–90, 192, 313
    racial discrimination in, 70, 71, 226,
        229–30, 231, 277, 294–6, 313
    schools and schoolchildren's dispersal, 49,
        51–2, 239, 310–11
    textbooks in, biased, 294–5
    university, 7, 278
    and West Indians, 49, 52–3, 69, 229, 277,
        292, 311, 313
Education Act 1944, 188
Education for All, 230
Education Reform Act 1988, 190, 313
Educational Forum for the People, St Vincent,
    63
Edwardes, Herbert, 6
Eid al Adha, 188, 199
Eid al Fitr, 188
Ellesmore, Lord Chief Justice, 197

Ellesworth Port, 90
Elton, Lord, 307
Empire Windrush, 15, 27, 30, 199
Engineering Employers' Federation, 266
Ennals, David, 290
Ershad, Hussein Muhammad, 185
Ethiopia, 67, 71, 294
Ethiopian World Federation Incorporated,
    72–3
European Common Market, *see* European
    Community
European Community, ix, 186, 253, 260, 313
European Convention on Human Rights, 215,
    259
European Human Rights Declaration, 216
European Voluntary Workers Scheme, 199

Fabians, 103
Fahd, King, 186, 187
Faisal ibn Abdul Aziz, King, 134
Fantis, 65
Farmer, Peter, 273
Faruq, Muhammad, 116
Federation of Bangladesh Youth
    Organizations, 231
Fernandes, Florestan, 308
Fernyhough, Ernest, 130, 131
Fiqueroa, Peter, 55, 299
Fiji, 109, 110, 112
First World War, 110, 198, 300
Foner, Nancy, 67
Foot, Paul, 204
Fox, Immanuel, 72
France and the French, 107, 108, 144, 295
Francis, Dai, 247
Franks, Lord, 256, 258
Free University for African, Asian and West
    Indian Studies, 64
Friendly Relations, 291
From Cradle to School, 300
Fullwood, Patricia, 19, 60

Gaelic language, 126
Gaitskell, Hugh, 17, 204
Gaitskell, Julia, 163
da Gama, Vasco, 5
Gandhi, Indira, 180
Gandhi, Rajiv, 180
Garvey, Marcus and Garveyism, 20, 48, 61, 69,
    71, 284
Gata-Aura, Tarlochan, 175
Gay, Pat, 209
Gay News, 184
Ghose, Zulfikar, 119–20
Ghulam, 155
Gifford, Lord, 99, 298, 300
Giles, Raymond, 229

Gill, Gurbachan Singh, 112, 122, 127, 137
Gill, Harpal Singh, 175
Glasgow, 37
Glass, Ruth, 26, 50
Glorious Revolution of 1688, 284
Goebbels, Josef, 247
Gordon-Walker, Patrick, 44, 205
Gough, Ronald, 130–1
Grant, Bernie , 95, 99, 101, 102, 103
Grant, Charles, 5
Greater Britain Movement, 254
Greater London, 51, 54, 176, 244
  Asian councillors in, 93, 96
  Asians in, 117, 139
  black councillors in, 93, 96
  Black Sections (Labour Party) in, 95
  employment needs of, 54
  Muslims in 133, 135, 184, 187
  and National Front, 255, 256, 257, 258
  Pentecostal churches in, 34
  police and police complaints in, 82–3, 84–5,
    87, 98–100, 101, 172–3, 251–2, 297
  race relations research in, 299–300
  race riots, *see under* Race Riots, Brixton,
    Camden, Deptford, Notting Hill, Southall
    and Tottenham
  racial discrimination in employment, 262,
    276
  racial discrimination in housing, 275, 279
  racial harassment and violence in, 161,
    178–9
  Special Patrol Group (SPG), 84, 85, 172–3
  West Indians in, 28, 117
  youth clubs in, 57
Greater London Council (GLC), 77, 102,
  169–70, 175, 230, 257
Greek immigrants, 253
Grenada, 62
Griffiths, Peter, 140, 206, 211
Groce, Cherry, 98
Groce, Michael, 98
Grunwick Processing Laboratories strike, 166,
  167–8, 251, 257, 296
Guardian, 91, 92, 267, 293
Gujarat and Gujaratis, 109–10, 112, 144,
  166–7
Gujarati language, viii, 124, 155
Guyana, 108

Hackney, 57, 96, 168, 171, 178, 240, 244,
  310
Hadiths, 183
Haile Selassie, 67
Halifax, 90
Hall, George, 282, 284
Halloran, James, 292
Ham, 3

Hamilton, Robert, 35
Handsworth, 51, 120, 156
  (1985) race riots in, 97–8, 99–100, 177
  see also Birmingham
Harambee Associations, 231
Haringey, 102, 244
Harris, Sydney, 55–6
Harrison, Bob, 222
Harte, Bill, 57
Hashemi, Mahmood, 123
Hashmi, Farrukh, 133
Hasnie, Nasim, 187
Hattersley, Roy, 190, 259–60
Hausas, 65
Hawkins, Sir John, 1, 31
Healey, Denis, 204
Heath, Edward, 223, 224, 225, 247, 248, 249,
  250, 251, 253, 303
Heilpern, John, 288
Heseltine, Michael, 91
High Wycombe, 27, 30, 49, 265
Hill, Clifford S., 33, 264, 284
Hindi language, 124, 140
Hinds, Donald, 27
Hinduism and Hindus, 108, 110, 111, 126,
  131–2, 145–6, 148, 154, 312, 313
  caste system in, 131–2
  and Christianity, 154, 155
  and Islam, 154, 312;
  marriage customs in, 147
  taboos in, 132, 146, 150, 155
Histories, Book IV, 294
Hitler, Adolf, 224
Hizb-e Tahrir, 188
Holi, 145
Holland, 107, 144
Home, Lord, *see* Douglas-Home, Sir Alec
Honduras, 14
Hong Kong, viii, x, 110, 212
Hood, 20
Hoshiarpur, 112
House of Commons, 199
House of Commons Employment Committee,
  231
House of Commons Home Affairs Committee,
  228, 242–3
House of Commons Select Committee on Race
  Relations and Immigration, 57, 216, 257,
  310
House of Lords, 167, 250
Housing on Trial, 267
Howarth, David, 237
Howe, Sir Geoffrey, 185
Huddersfield, 34, 57, 310
Hughes, Robert, 33
Hull, 37, 90
Hume, David, 3–4

Humphrey, Derek, 79–80, 223–4
Hungarian immigrants, 262, 268
Hunter, Guy, 148
Hurd, Douglas, 184, 192

Iberians, 109
Ibos, 65
Illegal Immigration Intelligence Unit, 251–2
Immigrants and the Youth Service, 310
Immigrants in London, 241
Immigration Act 1971, 223, 251, 255
Immigration Appeals Act 1969, 250, 251
Immigration control, 200–3, 250, 257–8
Immigration from the Commonwealth (1965),
    269
    see also White Paper on Commonwealth
    Immigration 1965
Imperial Fascist League, 254
Imperial War Conference 1917, 198
Indentured labour, 18, 108–9
India and Indians, viii, 9, 18, 107–15, 116,
    122, 132, 136, 137, 144, 148, 150,
    197–9, 256, 312
    see also Asia and Asians
India League, 124, 138
India Weekly, 124
Indian Associations, 132, 138
Indian Mutiny, 6
Indian subcontinent, viii, 257
Indian Workers' Association–Great Britain
    (IWA–GB), 44, 45, 139, 142, 143, 176
Indian Workers' Associations, 86, 132, 138,
    139–41, 167, 172, 173
    and trade unions, 139–40
Independent, 190, 293
Independent Television Authority, 290
Inner London Education Authority (ILEA),
    71, 229, 292, 296–7
Instant Support Units, Police, 86
Institute of Race Relations, 80, 280, 281, 283,
    299
Integration, 193, 233, 236–7, 298–9, 304,
    306
    definitions of, 240, 307–8
    economic, 237–8
    educational, 49, 51–2, 239–41, 298–9,
        310, 311, 313
    as official policy, 46
    pluralistic, 308
    social, 56–7, 238–9, 240–1
International Commission of Jurists, 215
International Congress of Dialectics of
    Liberation, 47
International Friendship Councils, 234
International Sikh Youth Federation, 180
Inter-racial co-habitation/marriage and
    children, 309–10

Iran, 110, 181, 182, 183, 184, 186, 187, 192,
    294
Iraq, 183, 294
Irish and Irish Republic, 33, 42, 52, 204, 206,
    260, 261, 281, 304
Isaacs, Jeremy, 288
Islam, Yusuf, 191
Islam and Muslims, 1, 108, 110, 126, 132,
    133–7, 181, 182–93
    and blasphemy law, 184, 191
    in Britain, 133–7, 153–5, 183–93
    and Christianity, 154, 188, 189
    and Conservative Party, 192
    cultural identity of, 136, 187
    edicts of, 133
    and education in Britain, 135, 188–90, 192,
        313
    in European Community, 313
    family law in, 192, 312
    and Hindus, 154, 312
    and Iran, 182–3, 185, 186–7, 192
    and Islamic law, 182, 183, 185, 192
    Ismaili sect in, 110
    and Labour Party, 190, 191–2
    marriage customs in, 147
    and religious hatred, 312
    and Rushdie affair, 181, 182–93, 301–2
    and Saudi Arabia, 135, 184, 186, 187
    Shia sect in, 183, 186
    social values of, 187, 189
    Sunni sect in, 183, 186
    taboos in, 136, 150, 155, 188
    white attitudes towards, 181–2, 188, 190,
        191, 192–3, 301–2
    and whites, perception of, 187–8
    and women, 147, 150, 153–4
    young Muslims, 187, 188, 192–3
Islamabad, 184
Islamic Conference Organization, Jiddah, 184,
    186
Islamic Cultural Centres, 135, 187
Islamic Foundation, 187
Islamic Party of Britain, 191
Islington, 217, 271
Israel, 305
Italy and Italians, 71, 72, 145, 146, 253, 261

Jah, 72
Jahoda, Gustav, 300
Jamaica and Jamaicans, viii, 15, 62, 67
    anglicization of, 19, 20
    and Black Power Movement, 62, 63
    and Christianity, 31, 32
    and creole language, 21, 61, 75
    economy of, 13–14, 16, 17
    and education, 19, 20–1
    history of, 2, 13, 60

Jamaica and Jamaicans *cont.*
 indentured labour in, 108
 Rastafarianism in, 71–3
 self-identity of, 61
 and slavery, 23
 see also West Indians in Britain
Jamestown, 197
Jang, 191
Jarret, Cynthia, 98
Jarret, Floyd, 98
Jenkins, Roy, 82, 218, 227, 255, 256, 307
Jephcott, Pearl, 28
Jerusalem, 1, 134
Jesus, 31
Jews and Judaism, 72, 136, 224
 in Britain, 126, 136, 188, 305, 306, 308
 and schools, 188, 190
 and women, 190
Jillani, R. B., 111
Joint Council for the Welfare of Immigrants,
 260
Jolly, Sohan Singh, 130–1, 155
Jones, Claudia, 40
Jones, K., 280
Jordan, Colin, 247, 254
Joshi, Jagmohan, 142
Jowell, Roger, 163
Jullundur, 112
Junior Chamber of Commerce, Keighley,
 266–7

Kabbani, Rana, 133, 182, 312
Kareem, Abdul, 121–2
Kareemi Fashions, 121
Kashmir, 111
Kaur, Manjit, 159
Kawwa, Taysir, 299, 300
Kazi, Abdul, 147
Keighley, 217, 263, 266, 273
Kenya and Kenyanization, 212, 213, 214
Kerr, Seton, 6
Khalistan movement, 180–1
Khama, Sereste, 9
Khamanei, Ali, 185, 192
Khan, Akbar Ali, 138
Khan, Haider, 145
Khatra, Jasbir Singh, 160
Khomeini, Ayatollah Rahollah, 183, 192
 on *The Satanic Verses*, 184–5, 186
Kiernan, V. G., 5, 6
King, Martin Luther, 43, 44, 46, 142
Kingston, 61, 73
Kinnock, Neil, 95, 96
Kipling, Rudyard, 7, 20
Kirby, Henry, 248
Kitchener, Lord, 7
Koran, *see* Quran

Kraus, Michael, 146
Krausz, Ernest, 306
Krishna, Lord, 150
Ku Klux Klan, 45

Labour Lawyers, 103
Labour Party, x, 45, 77, 99, 102, 103–4, 198
 and Asians, 93–6, 140, 212–16, 225
 and blacks, 77–9, 93–6
 and Black Sections, 95–6, 102, 103–4
 and Commonwealth immigration, 42–3,
  197, 200, 202, 203–4, 211–17, 250–1,
  255–6
 and the Liberal Party, 258
 and Muslims, 190, 191–2
 and the National Front, 256–7
 and parliamentary elections
  (1964), 44, 205, 210
  (1966), 46, 211
  (February 1974), 225
  (October 1974), 225
 and race relations laws, 77, 209–11, 216,
  217, 218, 225, 226–7
 and Uganda Asians crisis, 224
 and West Indians, *see* blacks *above*
Labour Zionist Society, 104
Lambert, Angela, 1, 280
Lambeth Council for Community Relations,
 86–7, 92
Lapière, R. T., 8–9
Lateef, Abdul, 116
Law Society, 278
Lawrence, Danny, 273
Lawson, Nigel, vii
Layton-Henry, Zig, 257
League of Empire Loyalists, 254
Leamington Spa, 142
Lebanon, 294
Lebor, John, 94
Leeds, 30, 46, 64, 90, 93, 178–9
Legum, Colin, 309
Leicester, 93, 102, 177, 178
Lestor, Anthony, 218–19
Lewis, Gordon, 199
Lewisham, 178
Liberal Party, 78, 93, 94, 102, 170, 216, 221,
 258
Lincoln, Abraham, 70
Lindsay, Sir Martin, 201
Lipton, Rose, 33
Little, Alan, 70, 292
Little, Kenneth L., 7, 209
Litton Industries, 166–7
Liverpool, 33, 252, 300–1, 304
 Asians in, 38
 blacks in, 300–1
 Methodist church in, 33

police and police complaints in, 82, 88–9, 298

race riots in
  (1919), 37
  (1948), 38
  (1981), 88–9, 90
racial discrimination in, 88–9, 252, 300–1
youths in, 57, 252, 310
Liverpool 8 Defence Committee, 92
Living in Terror, 178
Livingstone, Ken, 230, 291
Lloyd-George, Gwilym, 209–10
Local elections,
  (1974), 77
  (1977 GLC), 169–70
  (1978), 258
  (1981 GLC), 230, 257
  (1982), 93
  (1986), 93, 96, 177
Local government, 93, 177, 226, 233–6, 243, 244, 269–73, 300–1
Local Government Act 1966, 243, 277
Locke, John, 1
London, *see* Greater London
London Council of Social Service (LCSS), 240, 241, 294
Long, Edward, 4
Loosen the Shackles, 300
Lumumba, Patrice, 58
Luthra, Mohan, 178
Luton, 34, 161, 293
Lyon, Alex, 256

MacColl, Donald, 212
McCarran–Walter Act 1952, 15, 114, 199
McCrindle, Robert, 254
McCrystal, Cal, 182
McGlashan, Colin, 24, 50, 288
McNish, Kate, 65
Madden, Max, 188, 190
Mahound, 183
Malabar, 5
Malawi, 256, 291
Malaya, 108
Malaysia, viii, 110
Malcolm X, 45, 46
Manchester, 46
police in, 89–90
race riots in
  (1919), 37
  (1981), 89–90, 92
racial discrimination in, 46, 276
Mangrove Restaurant, 79
Mani, Sinna, 95
Manley, Norman, 41, 62
Manpower Services Commission, 176, 231
Mansfield, Lord, 2–3

Mansfield Hosiery Mills, 166
Marley, Bob, 73, 74, 75
Markazi Kameet Tabligh-e Islam, 134
Marx, Karl and Marxism, 176, 183, 295, 296
Mashriq, 124, 134, 143
Massacre Action Committee, 87
Mauritius, 108, 109
Maxwell, Neville, 59, 62, 305
Mecca, 113–14, 135, 183, 185, 186
Media, 287–8, 289–92
Medina, 186
Meena, 153
Melvin, Graham, 99
Methodist church, 32, 33
Metro Club, 79
Metropolitan Police, *see* Greater London, police and police complaints in
Metropolitan Police Act 1939, 92
Meyer, A., 147
Middle East, 181, 182, 312
Migrant Services Division, 41
Miles, Robert, 164
Milner-Holland Report, 268
Ministry of Repatriation, 250
Mirpur, 112, 134
Mods, 67
Moguls, 110
Moledina, Amin Ali, 98
Moledina Qassim Ali, 98
Mongoloids, viii
Morgan, Henry, 20
Morovian missionaries, 31
Morrell, Frances, 230
Moses, 31
Moss Side, *see* Manchester
Moss Side Defence Committee, 92
Mugging, 83
Muhammad, Prophet, 136, 147, 183, 184, 185
Mullard, Chris, 230
Multi-ethnic education, *see* Education, multi-ethnic
Muslim Charter, 191
Muslim College, 187
Muslim Educational Services, 135, 188
Muslim Educational Societies, 183
Muslim Institute, 192
Muslim World League, 135, 186, 187
Muslims, *see* Islam and Muslims
Myanmar, *see* Burma
Myrdal, Gunnar, 290

Naipaul, V. S., 19, 58
Nanak, Guru, 128, 132, 150
Naoroji, Dadabhai, 102
Napoleonic Wars, 296
National Assistance Board, 280
National Association for Freedom, 167

National Association for Multi-Racial Education, 70, 229, 296
National Association of Asian Youth, 169
National Association of Probation Officers, 97, 298
National Committee for Commonwealth Immigrants (NCCI), 46, 217, 234–5, 266
National Council for Civil Liberties (NCCL), 207
National Dwelling and Housing Survey 1977, 274
National Federation of Pakistani Associations (NFPA), 44, 45, 46, 141
National Foundation for Educational Research, 70, 292
National Front (NF), 77, 91, 168–71, 175, 253–8, 296
National Health Service (NHS), 67, 138, 264, 277–8, 280
National Insurance, 138
National Muslim Educational Council, 135, 183
National Socialist Party, 254
National Union of Railwaymen, 248
Nebuchadnezzar, 72
Negritude, 72
Negroes and negroid, vii, viii, 3, 23, 58, 65, 283, 300, 309
Negroes in Britain, 209
Nehra, Jaswant Singh, 112
Nehru, Jawaharlal, 139
Nelson, Lord, 19
New National Front, 169
New Society, 150, 241, 292
New Standard, 91
New Zealand, viii, 198, 239
Newark, 218
Newham, 179, 277
Newman, Sir Kenneth, 99
Nigeria and Nigerians, 63, 294
Nijjar, Dilawar Singh, 150–1
Noah, 3
Nolan, Justice, 191
Northern Ireland, 253
Notting Hill, 240
  Asians in, 139
  race riots (1958), 37, 38, 39–40, 200
  West Indians in, 28, 30
Nottingham, 233, 248, 273
  Commonwealth Citizens Consultative Committee for the Welfare of Coloured People in, 233
  Council of Social Service in, 233
  police in, 39
  race relations in, 288–9
  race riots (1958), 38–9, 233
  West Indians and West Africans in, 27–8, 38

O'Brien, Conor Cruise, 301–2
Observer, 202, 237, 286, 309
O'Dwyer, Sir Michael, 138–9
Old Testament, 75, 136
Olympic Games 1972, 224
One Nation Group, 180
Operation Condor, 100
Operation Delivery, 100, 101
Operation Swamp, 81, 87
Origin of Species, 7
Osborne, Sir Cyril, 37, 197, 199, 201, 202, 206, 209, 214
Othello, 9
Ottley, Roi, 9
Overseas Volunteers Scheme, 199
Oxfam, 293
Oxford, Kenneth, 89

Paddington, 240
Pakistan and Pakistanis, viii, 112, 113–14, 116, 122, 132, 133–4, 135, 136, 137, 140–2, 144, 147, 150, 151, 182–3, 198–9, 225, 263, 267, 273, 277, 294
  see also Asia and Asians
Pakistani Welfare Associations, 132, 172
Panama Canal, 14
Parekh, Bhikhu, 82, 164, 261, 303
Parliament, 57, 167, 216, 228, 231, 242–3, 250, 257
  elections to
    (1959), 202
    (1964), 44, 205, 210
    (1966), 46, 140, 211
    (1970), 223
    (February 1974), 225, 253
    (October 1974), 168–9, 225
    (1979), 78, 168, 172, 258, 275
    (1983), 93, 94, 97
    (1987), 102, 103, 177
  ethnic minority members of, 78, 94, 95, 102, 103
  social background of MPs, 285
Patel, Manibhai, 94
Patten, John, 192
Patterson, Sheila, 9, 294, 304, 305
Peach, Blair, 173
Peach, Ceri, 50
Pearson, Dorothy, 60
Pentecostal church, 31–2, 33–4, 62
Perrot, Roy, 237
Phizacklea, Annie, 164
Pitt, David, *see* Pitt, Lord
Pitt, Lord, 44, 46, 77–8, 102, 103
Pluralism, cultural, 305
  social, vii, 303, 305
Poale Zion, 96, 104
Police, 97, 297

Police *cont.*
  and Asians, 86, 172–3, 174–5, 179, 242
  community policing by, 81–2, 93, 98
  and Community Relations Councils, 86–7,
    92, 236, 242
  District Support Units of, 86
  ethnic composition of, 297
  history of, 81–2
  and illegal immigrants, 251–2
  Instant Support Units of, 86
  and mugging, 83
  and race relations, 297–8
  and race riots in
    Bristol, 85, 100, 101
    Brixton, 84, 85, 87
    Handsworth, 97–8, 99–100
    Liverpool, 82, 88–9, 298
    Manchester, 89–90
    Nottingham, 39
    Tottenham, 98–100
  racial discrimination in, 97, 297, 298
  Special Patrol Group of, 84, 85, 172–3
  and Sus law, 84, 92
  and West Indians, 63, 79, 80, 81, 83, 84,
    85–6, 92, 93, 98, 99, 100, 101, 228, 231,
    242, 266–7, 276, 277, 298, 299
Police Act 1976, 82
Police Against Black People, 80
Police Complaints Board, 82–3
Police Federation, 83
Policy Studies Institute, 92, 178
  surveys by
    (1982), 178, 243, 244, 274, 304, 309, 311
    (1984–5), 232, 276
Polish Resettlement Act, 199
Political and Economic Planning Ltd (PEP),
  46, 47, 50–1, 67, 217, 299
  surveys by
    (1967), 46, 47, 50–1, 217–18, 262,
      267–74, 299
    (1973–5), 67–8, 118, 178, 222, 225,
      273, 274, 276
Polo, Marco, 5
Pope-Hennessy, James, 284
Portuguese, 5
Poverty of Philosophy, The, 295
Powell, Enoch, 246, 252, 253
  on English identity, 303
  on immigration and race, 57–8, 59, 60, 64,
    142, 161, 162, 246–9, 255–6
  on integration, 303–4, 307
  on Kenya Asians, 212, 213, 214
  on media, 288, 289–90
  on Race Relations Bill 1968, 220, 247
  on repatriation, 246–7, 249–50
  on Uganda Asians, 223–4
Pratt, Michael, 83

Prejudice or Principle, 207
Prescott-Clarke, Patricia, 163
Preston, 90, 248
Prison Reform Trust, 97, 101
Problems of Coloured School-Leavers, The, 310
Progressive Labour Party, Bermuda, 63
Public Order Act 1963, 210, 227
Punjab and Punjabis, 110, 111, 112, 167
Punjabi language, viii, 140, 143, 155
Punks, 67
Pushkin, Ivan, 300

Quran, 136, 147, 154, 183, 184, 301, 302
  on blasphemy, 185
  on polygamy, 147
  on women's dress, 153–4
Qureshi, Muhammad Ismail, 185

Race: A Christian Symposium, 34
Race Action Group, 77, 95
Race Relations Acts
  (1965), vii, 143, 210–11, 217, 312
  (1968), 143, 163, 209, 217, 219–22, 225,
    232, 247, 249
  (1976), 79, 222, 226–7, 232, 241, 255, 258
Race Relations Board, 217, 218, 221–3, 226,
  307
Race Relations Unit, Hackney, 244
Race Riots, 8
  analysis of
    (1981), 91, 92
    (1985), 99–100
  Bristol (1981), 85–6, 92
  Brixton (1981), 84, 85, 87–8, 90, 92, 98
  Camden (1954), 38
  Cardiff (1919), 37
  Deptford (1949), 38
  Glasgow (1919), 37
  Handsworth (1985), 97–8, 99–100, 177
  Hull (1919), 37
  Liverpool (1919), 37; (1948), 38; (1981),
    88–9, 90
  London (1919), 37; *see also* Greater London
    race riots
  Manchester (1919), 37; (1981), 89–90, 92
  Notting Hill (1958), 37, 38, 39–40, 200
  Nottingham (1958), 38–9, 233
  Southall (1981), 90, 94, 174–5
  Tottenham (1985), 98–9, 102
  Race Today, 134
Race Today Collective, 76
Racial Adjustment Action Society (RAAS), 45
Racial discrimination, 7, 8–9, 14, 41, 43,
  44–5, 50, 76, 118, 160–1, 234, 279–80,
  281–2
  in churches, 30–1, 32–3, 46
  in courts, 97, 298

Racial discrimination *cont.*
  in education, 70, 71, 226, 229–30, 231,
    277, 294–6, 313
  in employment, 26, 27, 53–6, 67–9, 84, 88,
    89, 93, 97, 101, 119–20, 131, 160,
    162–3, 166–8, 217–18, 222, 225, 227,
    231–2, 238, 262–7, 275–8, 300–1
  in housing, 27–9, 46, 50–1, 120, 218, 222,
    225, 262, 267–75
  in immigration, 215, 223, 251
  indirect, 226, 227
  laws against, vii, 79, 143, 163, 209, 217,
    218, 219–23, 225, 226–7, 232, 241, 247,
    249, 255, 258, 307
  in National Health Service, 67, 264, 277–8
  in personal services, 30–1, 34–5, 46, 222
  in police, 97, 297, 298
  in public places, 30–1, 34–5, 46, 222
Racial harassment and violence, 36, 43, 55–6,
  161, 178–9, 183, 210, 227–8, 241, 247,
  259
Racial inferiority/superiority, 1, 3–4, 5, 6, 7, 9,
  259, 281–3, 284
Racial prejudice, *see* Racial discrimination
Railton Road Youth and Community Centre,
  84
Raison, Timothy, 86
Raleigh, Walter, 20
Ram, Gurdas, 116
Ramadan, 135–6, 154
Randhwa, Ranjit, 161–2
Ranger, Chris, 277
Ras Makonnen, 71
Ras Tafari, 71, 72
Rastafarianism and Rastafarians, 70, 80
  doctrine of, 72–4
  history of, 71–2
  and Jamaica, 71–3
  and marijuana, 76, 79
  and police, 79
  and reggae music, 73–4
  social background of, 75, 80
  and young West Indians, 75–6
Rasul, 155
Read, John Kingsley, 169, 246
Reading, 90
Reggae music, 73–4
Repatriation, 250
  see also Enoch Powell, on repatriation
Rex, John, 164–5, 175, 271, 284
Richardson, Jo, 95
Robeson, Paul, 9
Rock Against Racism, 170
Rock music, 73
Rockers, 67
Rodney, Walter, 63
Rogers, George, 200

Roman Catholic church and schools, 32, 33,
  188, 190
Rowley, Keith, 300
Royal Commission on Criminal Procedure, 80
Runcie, Robert, 186
Rushdie, Salman, 181, 183, 185, 186, 312; *see*
  also Satanic Verses, The
Rushdie affair, 181, 182–93, 301–2
Sacred Cows, 301
Sahgal, Preetam, 160
St Kitts, 14, 30
St Lucia, 32
St Vincent, 30, 32
Saklatvala, Shapurji, 103, 177
Salmon, Judge, 40
Sanai, Hojatalislam Hassan, 185
Sandhu, Tarsem Singh, 129–30
Sandhu, Balbir Singh, 137
Sandys, Duncan, 214, 220, 232
São Paulo, 308
Satanic Verses, The, 181, 183–4, 186, 188,
  190–1, 193, 301, 311–12
Saudia Arabia, 135, 184, 186, 187
Scarman, Lord, 81, 84, 87, 88, 92, 93, 303
Second World War, 14, 20, 129, 198, 260,
  261
Sekyi, Kobina, 7
Selassie, Haile, *see* Haile Selassie
Separate development, vii, 308
Seventh Day Adventist church, 34
Severus, Septimius, 1
Shah of Iran, 182
Sharia, *see* Islam and Muslims, Islamic law
Sharma, Arvind, 154, 174
Shaw, Stephen, 97
Shearer, Hugh, 62
Sheffield, 35, 90, 217, 248
Shia Muslims, 183, 186
Short, Edward, 310
Shromani Akali Dal (SAD), 130
Sicily, 116, 145
Sikhism and Sikhs, 110–11, 126, 127, 149,
  162
  in Britain, 110–11, 112, 127–32
  in Canada, 110, 112, 147
  castes in, 145
  in Fiji, 112
  and Khalistan movement, 180–1
  marriage customs in, 147
  and Second World War, 129
  taboos in, 146, 155
  turban agitation by, 130–1, 155, 237, 307
Silverman, Julius, 100
Simey, Lord, 252
Singapore, vii, 100
Singh, Ajit, 149
Singh, Gurnam, 117, 127

Singh, Guru Gobind, 128, 129
Singh, Harnam, 158
Singh, Jaswant, 153
Singh, Sant Fateh, 129
Singh, Surinder, 298
Singh, Udham, 138–9
Singh, Ujjager, 138
Sins of the Fathers, 284
Skinheads, 67, 161, 174, 259
Slave trade and slavery, 1–2, 4, 6–7, 13–14,
    18, 19–20, 21–3, 24–5, 31–2, 36, 48, 53,
    60, 70, 107–8, 113, 283–4
Slough, 30, 51, 158, 217
Smethwick, 44, 128, 140, 205
Smith, David J., 68
Social Democrats, 93, 102
Socialist Health Associations, 103
Somersett, James, 2
Sommerfield, Paul, 81
Soskice, Sir Frank, 197, 211
Sondhi, Amrit Kaur, 151
South Africa, 1, 10, 108, 237, 308
South Asians, *see* Asia and Asians
South London Islamic Centre, 188
South Shields, 133
Southall, 169, 172, 174, 239, 248
    Asians in, 121, 122, 158
    Indian Workers' Association in, 140–1
    race riots in (1981), 90, 94, 174–5
    racial discrimination in, 46, 119
    Sikhs in, 137
    young Asians in, 169, 172, 173, 174–5,
        176, 231
Southall Youth Movement (SYM), 169, 172,
    173, 174–5, 176, 231
Soviet Union, 294
Spain, 2, 107
Spectator, 8, 9
Special Patrol Group (SPG), Police, 84, 85,
    172–3
Springer, Hugh, 59
Sri Lanka, 5, 9, 108
Standing Conference of Afro-Caribbean and
    Asian Councillors, 78
Standing Conference of Pakistani
    Organizations, 86
Statute of Westminster, 1931, 198
Stephenson, Paul, 37, 43, 52
Stevens, Cat, *see* Islam, Yusuf
Stevens, Philip, 83
Stokes, Donald, 286
Strangers Within, 207
Straw, Jack, 190
Sun, 213
Sunday Telegraph, 291
Sunday Times, 179, 189, 214, 271
Sunni Muslims, 183, 186

Sus law, 84, 92
Swann Committee, 230
Sylhet, 112

Tajfel, Henri, 299
Tamlin, Patrick, 180
Tarzan, 64
Taylor, J. H., 155
Teachers Against Racism, 70, 229, 296
Tebbit, Norman, x
Teddy boys, 36, 39, 67
Terrelonge, Roy, 14–15
Thackeray, William Makepeace, 5–6
Thakroodin, James, 95
Thatcher, Margaret, ix–x, 91, 99, 177, 183,
    228, 244, 257, 258, 275, 296
Times, The, vii, 44, 56, 92, 221, 293, 302, 307
Tipton, 117
Tomney, Frank, 201
Toor, Tarsem Singh, 180
Tooting, 117
Tosh, Peter, 73
Tottenham, police in, 98–100
    race riot in (1985), 98–9, 102
Tower Hamlets, 168, 171, 179, 275
Toxteth, *see* Liverpool
Trade Unions, 139–40, 166–8, 207, 231, 248,
    262, 263, 264–6, 285, 289
Trades Union Congress (TUC), 167, 219,
    256–7, 265
Transport and General Workers Union
    (T&GWU), 166, 207, 265, 266, 289
Trelawney, Edward J., 6
Trevelyan, George O., 6
Triangular Trade, 2
Trinidad, 15, 58, 62
    and Black Power movement, 62–3
    and Christianity, 32, 33
    calypso in, 62
    economy of, 16
    education in, 19, 20
    history of, 14, 15, 32
    indentured labour in, 108
    see also West Indians in Britain
Trollope, Anthony, 4, 159
Twelve Tribes of Israel, 73
Tyler, Andrew, 178
Tyndall, John, 254

Uganda, 77, 125
    expulsion of Asians from, 223–5
Uganda Resettlement Board, 125, 224, 225
Union of Muslim Organizations in the United
    Kingdom and Eire (UMO), 34–5, 183,
    187, 192
United Afro-West Indian Brotherhood, 72
United Black Youth League, 175

United Nations, 183
United Nations Educational, Scientific and
 Cultural Organization, 308
Universal Coloured People's Association
 (UCPA), 47, 48, 63, 72, 76
Urban Programme, 243–4
Urdu language, viii, 124, 143, 155
Utrecht, Treaty of (1713), 2

Vagrancy Act 1824, 84
Vancouver, 110
Vaz, Keith, 102, 177, 190
Veness, Thelma, 300
Venezuela, 14
Verma, Gajendra, 292
Victoria, Queen, 20, 198
Viking Penguin, 183, 191

War on Want, 293
Ward, George, 167
Ward, Michael, 223–4
Watt, David, 286
Webb, David, 98
Weldon, Fay, 301, 312
Welsh language, 126
West Africa and West Africans, ix, 1, 2, 15, 38,
 64–6, 109, 303–4
West Bromwich, 217, 248, 254, 255, 262
West Indian Development Council, Bristol,
 43
West Indian Gazette, 40
West Indian Standing Conference (WISC), 41,
 44, 45, 46, 76, 92, 141, 142, 143, 264
West Indian Student Centre, 63–4
West Indians in Britain, *see* Part I *passim*; viii,
 ix, 10, 14, 16, 30, 33, 40, 107, 109, 110,
 120, 199, 201, 261–2, 295–6, 304
 and Africa, 3, 13, 18, 19, 25, 31, 48, 61–2,
 63, 65, 72, 73
 and America, 14, 15, 114, 199
 anglicization of, 19–20
 and Black Power Movement, 47–8, 62, 63,
 72, 76
 in business, 22
 characteristics of, 30, 52–3
 and Christianity, 30–4, 46, 62, 75, 136
 class composition of, 68
 and Communist Party, 78, 79, 168
 and Community Relations Councils, 236,
 242, 243
 and Conservative Party, 78, 168, 180
 and creole language, 21, 61, 75
 education and educational performance of,
 19, 20, 21, 49, 52–3, 69, 70, 71, 228–30,
 277, 292, 311, 313
 employment pattern of, 53–6, 67–9, 262–5
 and Ethiopia, 67, 71
 family life of, 22, 24–5, 30, 53, 113
 house ownership among, 275
 indentured labour in, 108
 and Labour Party, 77–9, 93–6, 102, 103–4
 and local government, 93, 96, 177
 migration to Britain, 15–18, 114–15,
 199–200
 and National Health Service, 280
 and Pentecostal church, 33–4
 and police, 63, 79, 80, 81, 83, 84, 85–6, 92,
 93, 98, 99, 100, 101, 228, 231, 242,
 266–7, 276, 277, 298, 299
 and Enoch Powell's April 1968 speech,
 57–8, 59, 60, 64
 and race riots, *see under* Race riots,
 individual cities and metropolitan areas,
 except Southall
 and racial discrimination in
 employment, 26, 27, 53–6, 67–9, 84,
 88, 89, 93, 97, 101, 163, 217–18, 225,
 231, 262–7, 276–8, 300–1
 housing, 27–9, 46, 50–1, 218, 225, 262,
 267–75
 personal services, 30–1, 34–5, 46, 222
 racial harassment and violence against, 36,
 43, 55–6, 178–9, 259
 and Rastafarianism, 75–6
 and reggae music, 73–4
 and Second World War, 14, 20
 self-identify of, 57, 59–66, 69–71, 75–6,
 229
 settlement pattern of, 117
 size of the community, ix
 and trade unions, 231, 264–6
 voting pattern of, 78, 79, 96
 and West Africans, 64–5
 white attitudes towards, 304–5, 307, 311
 whites, perception of, 284
West Indies, 15, 16
 economy of, 14, 26, 35–6
 history of, 19–20
 Indians in, 108, 126
West Indies Federation, 41
West Midlands Caribbean Association, 41
West Midlands County Council, 100
What Next?, 259
White, Charles, 283
White attitudes to
 acceptance of Asians, 304–5
 all-white schools, 313
 black images, 293
 black sexuality, 283
 retention of ethnic cultures, 311
 government, 286
 intelligence of non-whites, 282–3, 292
 inter-racial marriage and children, 309–10,
 311

Islam and Muslims, 181–2, 188, 190, 191, 192–3, 301–2
Enoch Powell's April 1968 speech, 247–9, 289–90
race relations, 284–7
skin colour, 281–2, 299–300
slaves and slavery, 283–4
Third World events, 293–4
acceptance of West Indians, 304–5, 307
White Paper on Commonwealth immigration 1965, 45, 206, 211, 217, 234, 240, 269, 307–8
White youths, 258–9, 277, 299
involvement in race riots 86, 89, 90, 175
see also Mods, Rockers, Skinheads and Teddy boys
Whitelaw, William, 86, 90, 259, 260
Whitty, Larry, 103
Wilberforce, William, 19–20, 70
Willesden West Indian Association, 63
Williams, Eric, 162–3
Williams, Francis, 4
Willis, Carole F., 83
Wilson, Sir Harold, 205, 207, 225, 250
Woking, 133
Wolmar, Christian, 276
Wolverhampton, 49, 90, 248, 273, 277
Asians in, 49, 138, 249, 265
ethnic employment in, 54
Pentecostal churches in, 33–4

race relations in, 288–9
Sikhs in, 129–31, 155
West Indians in, 28, 30, 49, 249
youth clubs in, 57, 310
Wolverhampton Association of Schoolmasters, 241, 245, 286
Woolcombers Association, Bradford, 267
Woolf, Leonard, 108
Working Party of Liverpool Youth Organizations, 252
World Association of Muslim Jurists, 185
Wright, Peter, 238, 262, 263

Yearbook of Social Policy, 1981, 228
Yorubas, 65
Young Fabians, 207
Young Muslim Organization, 188
Young National Front, 256
Young Power, Trinidad, 63
Young Socialists, 95
Youth clubs, 57
Youth Training Scheme, 231

Zaïre, 58, 59, 293
Zakaria Muslim Girls' High School, 189, 193
Zia al Haq, General Muhammad, 182
Zion, 72
Zong, 2
Zulu War, 284